ELVIS PF
GOSPEL SINGER

AN INSPIRATIONAL LIFE

by

Madeleine Wilson

Shalom Publishing

Contents

Dedication

To all Elvis fans worldwide, with special thanks to those who prayed for Elvis through his most trying times.

Acknowledgements

My grateful thanks go to the many people who have contributed to the writing of this book, through personal contact and encouragement and/or their own writings, including all those mentioned in the bibliography. I would particularly like to thank:

Alyson Adams, Patsy Andersen, Sherman Andrus, Joseph Atkins, Rev. Fred Bennett, James Blackwood, Terry Blackwood, Bill Burk, Marina Buswell, Marion and Joanne Carson, Rev. Wally Cason, Pam Caviness, Nick Dadd, Rev. Christine Darg, David and Jean Dyson, Mary Dyson, Rev. Rex and Caroline Dyson, Dixie Locke Emmons, Ed Enoch, Martin Fox, Larry Geller, Pål Granlund, Peter Guralnick, Glen Hardin, Ron and Denise Harper, Sue Harris, Ted Harrison, Andrew Hearn, June Juanico, Michael King, Becky Martin, Julie Anne McBride, Janelle Mc Comb, Arne Metzner, Joe Moscheo, Jim Murray, Billy Nashad, Shaun Neilson, Anne E Nixon, Rev. Fred Omvlee, Kim Ong, Sylvia Oudhoff, Danny Owen, Nigel Patterson, Judy Peiser, Annie Presley, Donna Presley, Karen Sue Presley, Nicola Prentis, Jim Reid, Don Richmond, Rev. Bruce Sheasby, Trevor Simpson, Frank Skinner, Kirsten Skjaerpe, Todd Slaughter, Jack Soden, Lyn Sperling, David Stanley, Gordon Stoker, Dr. Tony Stone, Bud and Mary Stonebreaker, Larry Strickland, Donnie Sumner, Lynn Royce Taylor, David Wade.

I am also extremely grateful for the loving support of my husband Peter (J Peter Wilson), and all our faithful prayer partners, including Mother Dolores Hart and her community in Bethlehem, Connecticut, USA.

Finally, I wish to express my undying gratitude to my Lord, Jesus Christ, without whom none of this would have been possible.

About the Author

Madeleine Wilson was born in 1944 in the village of Cottingham in East Yorkshire, England.

Being an only child, she had quite a sheltered upbringing, but not so sheltered that she did not listen to Elvis' records as a teenager, though she was not a fan at the time. Being of a curious mindset, she was very interested in science and obtained a Bachelor of Science degree in Chemistry from Hull University. She then went on to engage in research at ICI Ltd in Harrogate, followed by training to become a teacher, after which she taught Chemistry and Maths in the local college and schools.

Whilst in Harrogate she met and married James Peter Wilson, a textile technologist. They produced three children: Marina, Hannah, and Aaron, and now have five grandchildren.

Madeleine became a fan of Elvis Presley when she watched some of the TV programmes in January 1995 which were aired to celebrate his 60th birthday. After watching the programmes, she wept for a week. It was such a strong experience, that she prayed and asked the Lord what it was all about, and felt led to start researching into Elvis' life, discovering that not only was he brought up as a Christian, but that he was called to be an evangelist.

During her research, she has been privileged to meet members of Elvis' family and friends and musicians who understood his spiritual yearnings, and she began to understand this simple yet complex man whom she never met. She also began to understand his calling, something which is a continuing story. It is a story of dreams, hopes, passion, disappointment, and ultimate victory.

When asked about Elvis' religion Madeleine says, "Elvis' idea of religion was not necessarily attending church, but rather one's personal relationship with God and how one lives one's life."

About the charges that Elvis' lifestyle was out of keeping with a faith commitment, she says, "It depends which part of his lifestyle you are referring to. If you mean his dependence on prescription drugs, his immoral sexual activity, unhealthy eating habits and his occasional temper tantrums, then yes, I will say his lifestyle was out of step with his faith commitment.

"If, however, you mean his generosity with his money, spending hours counselling and encouraging relatives and friends and fans from the Word of God, successfully praying for people to be healed, honouring his parents by buying them their dream home and living with them as an extended family at Graceland, being sweet-natured, not harbouring bitterness, having a sense of fun and joy for life, and crying out to God in anguish for forgiveness and direction, then I would say his lifestyle was fully in step with his commitment to God."

To share her stories of Elvis with others having the same interest, she started the Elvis Gospel Fan Club in 1998, with her husband, organising several Elvis Gospel events both in the UK and the USA. She also produced a booklet, "Prayers of Elvis," in 2002.

Madeleine is now retired, still happily married to Peter, and enjoying life by the sea in Bridlington, in East Yorkshire, England.

She is hoping that her 25 years of research has produced a book that will interest, delight and challenge those who read it.

Introduction

It has been said that the formula of a great tragedy is that a fatal flaw prevents tremendous potential from being realised, and the ending is one of ruin not of joy.

In many ways, the life story of Elvis Presley can be seen as one of tragedy, but I would maintain that it is a story of triumph. It is certainly one of triumph over adversity in the material sense as Elvis, who was born in a two-room cabin in Mississippi, USA, lived in relative poverty until he shook, rattled, and rolled his way into fame and fortune in the mid-nineteen fifties. He lived to see his childhood dream of buying a big house and cars for his parents come true.

The news of his demise, in 1977, at the age of 42 sent shock waves around the world, though many who were close to him, on reflection, commented that they had begun to notice that he was not well. Tragic was a word accurately used to describe the lead up to, and the circumstances, of his death.

Elvis was brought up in the Bible Belt of the USA, where praying, praising God and discussing spiritual matters was not only for church meetings but was also part of many people's everyday lives. That was certainly the case with the Presley family and their friends. Consequently, Elvis knew his Bible well and was taught at an early age to pray and trust in God. There is no doubt that his first flush of fame took him off the narrow path. He however, always acknowledged that his voice was a gift from God. In later years as he matured and began to reflect on his purpose in life, he became convinced that he was to use his voice to sing of God's love and goodness and mercy. He had many times in his later years expressed his desire to perform a full gospel concert, and I understand that at the time of his death, plans were in hand for this to happen.

In this book, distilled from over 25 years of research since I became an Elvis fan in 1995, I explore Elvis' love of gospel, both the music and the message, his spiritual journey, and the continuing worldwide inspiration that he and the songs he sang have had, and still have, on the lives of people today. I also suggest the source of this inspiration.

As you join me in journeying through Elvis' life, you will see the influence and impact he had, not only on his family, friends and entourage, his fellow musicians, management, and fans, but also complete strangers.

Elvis was alive in a specific historical time, and I have endeavoured to give some insight into the world in which he lived, and some of the people who influenced him. Where I have quoted from someone's spoken or written word, I have used their spelling and grammar and not "corrected" it, as I believe that is more authentic.

So, I hope that you enjoy travelling with Elvis through his life and even feel that you get to know him a little better.

God bless you, Madeleine Wilson.

Chapter 1

Tupelo Honey[1] – Sweet Beginnings

He nourished them with honey from the rock. (Deuteronomy 32:1)

Elvis, about 3 years old
with his parents.

Many people have described Elvis as "sweet." What was the source of this "sweetness"? Perhaps it was the Holy Spirit, that *Sweet, Sweet Spirit* whom he so loved to sing about. As we shall discover, Elvis' roots were indeed sweet, though tinged with hardship.

Elvis Aaron Presley was born in a two-room wooden cabin in Tupelo, Mississippi on 8th January 1935, 35 minutes after his twin brother Jesse Garon who was stillborn. Although on 7th February 1934, Tupelo became the first city to receive power from the Tennessee Valley Authority, thus giving it the nickname "the First TVA City," the Presley home had no electricity nor indoor water supply.

The birth was not an easy one for Gladys – she started labour in the middle of the night and so Vernon immediately went to fetch his mother and father, Jessie and Minnie Mae, who lived next door on Old Saltillo Road. If all had been well, Minnie Mae would have helped deliver the baby, but she could tell that all was not well, so they called for Dr Hunt who was 68 years old and had already delivered 918 babies. Dr Hunt had also established a reputation as the "poor man's doctor" and, although his fees were very low, the Presleys could not pay, so he was paid later by welfare. Because even the poor man's doctor's fees were too high, Dr Hunt had not seen very much of the family as they were rarely ill enough to warrant a doctor's attention. Consequently, Dr Hunt did not know that Gladys was carrying twins. Jesse Garon was stillborn at 4am,

---

[1] ***Tupelo Honey*** is not only the title of a song by Van Morrison but is also a type of honey produced in the Southern states of the USA, where the Tupelo Gum trees thrive in the swampy conditions. The honey produced by bees which forage on the nectar of those flowers is the only honey that never granulates but remains a delicious, flowing, golden liquid.

followed by Elvis at 4.35am. Elvis' birth record shows his name as Evis Aaron, most probably because this was the way Vernon pronounced the name Elvis (which was Vernon's own middle name), barely pronouncing the "l". The birth record also shows that Vernon was a labourer, aged 18, and Gladys a housewife, aged 21.

This only child was named Elvis after his father and Aaron in honour of Aaron Kennedy, the song leader at church, a friend of the family who Vernon greatly admired. It was Aaron Kennedy who later on would encourage Elvis to learn to read well so that he could appreciate his Bible.

Right from the beginning of his life, Elvis knew that he was loved, that he was special and that one day he would do great things. During her labour pains, Gladys is reported as saying, "I know it will be a boy – a boy who will be a joy to the world. I will live so my boy can live. He has a wonderful life ahead of him."

Elvis remained the only child of Vernon Elvis and Gladys Love Presley, though Gladys did have a miscarriage when Elvis was about seven years old. The USA had entered the Second World War in 1942. Vernon was not drafted but went to help build a camp for German prisoners of war in Como, Mississippi over 170 miles away. While Vernon was away, Gladys miscarried and was taken to hospital, accompanied by Elvis. However, she refused to be admitted until Elvis' Uncle Noah came to get Elvis and look after him. Again, welfare paid the hospital fees.

In an interview with Good Housekeeping magazine in 1978, Vernon said:

"Gladys and I were so proud of Elvis and enjoyed him so much that we immediately wanted more children. But, for reasons no doctor could understand, we had none. While Elvis grew from infant to toddler to lively little boy, we consulted doctors about our failure to have another child. We prayed about it, too.

"When Elvis was about 10 years old, the reason was revealed very clearly to me in a way that I can't explain – I can only say that God spoke to my heart and told me that Elvis was the only child we'd ever have and the only child we'd ever need. Elvis was a special gift who would fill our lives completely. Without little Jesse, who was born dead, without the other children we'd hoped to have, we understood that we were an extraordinarily complete family circle. As soon as I realized that Elvis was meant to be an only child, I felt as though a burden was lifted. I never again wondered why we didn't have additional sons and daughters. It's hard to describe the feelings Elvis, his mother and I had for each other. Though we had friends and relatives, including my parents, the three of us formed our own private world. Elvis was a good child who seldom gave us trouble. I did spank him a few times, but now that I think back, I believe it was for nothing."

The Bible says that the tongue is an instrument of life or death and that we can choose how to use it. Elvis' parents and family always spoke well of him and, in a sense, prophesied his success. Mrs Oleta Grimes, Elvis' fifth-grade teacher at Lawhon School in Tupelo, said that he was just a sweet child and that people who knew him well just loved him. She never heard anyone say anything bad about him.

Elvis' Singing Voice is Already Noticed

Every morning at Lawhon School began with a chapel service. Elvis would often take part by singing a solo, such as *Old Shep* or *God Bless My Daddy,* or by saying a prayer. Mrs Grimes, who taught her pupils the song *Old Shep*, said that Elvis was best in chapel time because he liked to sing, and he did it so well. "We sang out of this book, like a church book, and each child had a turn and we just let them sing what they wanted. This was every morning. He came back to my school in later years. It was right after his mother died, and we talked about her. He went into my classroom and told the boys and girls that I had one time been his teacher." Mrs Grimes said of Elvis he was "a real good little boy who liked people and knew God. There is something nice about everyone. There is everything nice about Elvis."

Mrs Grimes was instrumental in encouraging Elvis to sing in public as she had noticed that Elvis had a good, sweet voice and it was she who arranged for him to enter the Children's Talent Contest at the Mississippi Alabama fair in 1945.

The Presleys were part of an extended family and had many relatives in the area that helped each other through the economic depression of the 1930s.

They were descended from David Presley, who arrived in North Carolina in 1845 from Ireland. His family were originally from Scotland but had moved to Ireland and then, because of hardship caused by the potato blight, sailed to the USA to seek a new and, hopefully, more prosperous life. Some researchers believe that the Presley family originated in Wales and cite the fact that there is a St Elvis farm near Solva, in Pembroke, and that Saint David, patron saint of Wales, was baptised by a Bishop Elvis around AD 500. Wales has a mountain range called the Preseli Mountains, and, of course, Welsh men are renowned for their wonderful singing!

The Bible Belt

Belonging to a church community was an integral part of the Presley's lives in the 1930s, as was the teaching of the gospel in schools. No wonder that this part of America is known as the Bible Belt.

The 1828 edition of Webster's American Dictionary of the English Language defines the Bible as "The Book by way of eminence; the sacred volume, in which are contained the revelations of God, the principles of Christian faith and the rules of practice. It consists of two parts, called the Old and New testaments. The Bible should be the standard of language as well of faith."

Elvis was brought up to believe that "The fear of the Lord is pure. The ordinances of the Lord are sure and altogether righteous. They are more precious than gold, than much pure gold, they are sweeter than honey from the comb. By them is your servant warned, in keeping them is great reward." (Psalm 19:9-11)

Raising Patriots

According to Becky Martin, an elementary school friend of Elvis, whom we visited in her home in Lake Street just opposite the Lawhon School, lessons at Lawhon included learning the names of the presidents and the names of the state capitals, the Gettysburg Address and a poem called "Crossing the Bar." The Gettysburg Address was President Lincoln's speech made in 1862, honouring those who were killed in the two-day battle. The address ends: "That we here highly resolve that these dead shall not have died in vain – that this nation under God shall have a new birth of freedom – and that government of the people, by the people, for the people shall not perish from the earth." These young children in Tupelo were taught to be proud of their country, to be patriotic. The following is some of the history which Elvis would have learned:

On 9th November 1620, the ship the Mayflower, carrying a group of Puritans, landed at Cape Cod in America. Their pilgrimage began in 1604, which saw the start of the persecution of the Puritans in Britain. They were persecuted because of their belief that conversion was central to the Christian faith. They believed that "when a man's sin comes upon him like an armed man, and the tide of his thoughts is turned" that is "the moment when God's grace entered the soul and began the work of redemption." They were spied upon and imprisoned, and life became very difficult for them. In 1608, many of them moved to Holland where they could practise their faith without harassment, but they were still looking for somewhere new where they could put down their roots.

At the time, the East Coast of America was being colonised, and a group of Puritans decided that that was the place for a new beginning. So, they returned to England and made preparation to set off from Plymouth on the Mayflower on 16th September 1620. They arrived at Cape Cod on 19th November and, after some reconnaissance for a more suitable place to settle, they sailed into Plymouth harbour on 16th December. On 25th December, they started to build their first house. It was a hard winter. This is how a historian of the time, William Bradford described it:

"And for the season it was winter, and they that know the winters of that country know them to be sharp and violent, and subject to cruel and fierce storms, dangerous to travel to known places, much more to search an unknown coast. Besides, what could they see but a hideous and desolate wasteland, full of wild beasts and wild men – and what multitudes there might be of them they knew not … What could now sustain them but the Spirit of God and His grace?

"May not and ought not the children of these fathers rightly say: 'Our fathers were Englishmen, which came over this great ocean, and were ready to perish in this wilderness; but they cried unto the Lord, and He heard their voice and looked on their adversity. Let them forever praise the Lord because He is good: and His mercies endure forever.'"

Despite their difficulties, the Puritans settled and planted crops and, the next year in 1621, they gathered in their first harvest and gave grateful thanks to God. This was the first Thanksgiving Day, which is still celebrated by Americans all over the world.

The first president of the United States, George Washington, appreciated the foundation on which the fledgling country was laid and saw America as "a city set upon a hill – a beacon to all nations of the world declaring the blessings of a nation who God is the Lord." In his inaugural address in 1789, he said:

"No people can be bound to acknowledge and adore the invisible hand which conducts the affairs of men, more than the people of the United States. Every step, by which they have advanced to the character of an independent nation, seems to have been distinguished by some token of providential agency …" Washington saw America as having a mission to the nations and that, through her example, others would find the truth of the Christian Gospel.

On 6th March 1799, the second president, John Adams, seeing that America was straying from its Godly beginnings, proclaimed a national fast day and called the nation to "implore His pardoning mercy, through the great Mediator and Redeemer, for our past transgressions, and that, through the grace of His Holy Spirit, we may be disposed and enabled to yield a more suitable obedience."

Abraham Lincoln also recognised the needs of America to deal with its sins against God and against one another and, on Thursday 30th April 1863, he called a Day of National Humiliation. He instructed the nation, "We have been the recipients of the choicest bounties of heaven; we have preserved these many years in peace and prosperity; we have grown in number and in wealth and power as no other nation has ever grown, but we have forgotten God. We have forgotten the gracious hand that preserved us in peace and multiplied and enriched and strengthened us and we have vainly imagined in the deceitfulness of our hearts that all these blessings were produced by some superior wisdom and virtues of our own. Intoxicated with unbroken success we have become too self-sufficient to feel the necessity of redeeming and preserving grace, too proud to pray to the God who made us. It behooves us then to humble ourselves before the offended Power, to confess our national sins and to pray for clemency and forgiveness."

This diet of awareness of God and the place of America in history greatly influenced Elvis' outlook on life and stayed with him for the rest of his life. He was a great patriot as signified by the use of the jewelled American eagle emblazoned across the front and back of the suit that he wore for the TV show "Aloha from Hawaii" which was transmitted worldwide via satellite in January 1973. Elvis had asked his costume designer to produce a costume that would say "America" to the whole world.

Elvis regularly attended the AoG (Assembly of God) church in Adams Street, East Tupelo, with his parents. Gladys' uncle, Gains Mansell, became the preacher of the church in 1937. He had built the small two-roomed, wood-framed building with his own hands. Over its door was a sign saying, "You are Welcome." It was here that one Sunday morning, the shy two-year-old Elvis, slipped from his mother's lap, ran down the aisle and scrambled onto the platform to join the choir. He was too young to memorise all the words, but he held the tunes with his sweet young voice. (The church building has now been moved to Elvis' birthplace.)

Terrifying Devastation

On 5th April 1936, an F5 tornado with winds of more than 260 mph ripped through Tupelo. These were the days when there was no early warning system, so it came like a bolt out of the blue with not one of the approximately 7,000 residents being at all prepared for the devastation of that day. One-third of the city's houses were piled up in the streets. Most of the business district escaped damage. Those churches, hotels and schools still standing were converted into hospitals. Although the Tupelo-Gainsville tornado is often called "The Forgotten Outbreak," it is, to date, still one of the deadliest outbreaks in the history of the United States. The Gum Pond area of Tupelo was the worst hit during the tornado. Homes along the pond were swept into the water with their victims. Most of the bodies of the people reported killed in Tupelo were found in Gum Pond, the area which is now Gumtree Park.

The final Tupelo death toll of 250 with 700 injured was much higher than the official records show because the racial inequality of the time meant that the names of the African Americans who died – their communities were decimated – were not listed in the Official Roll of the dead. Tragically, the total death toll still remains unknown.

Despite all this, there were some amazing escapes as reported by the Greenwood Commonwealth newspaper. On 7th April, they wrote, "hundreds of miraculous escapes were reported today." Among them:

Carl E Smith, auto dealer and his family, saying their bedtime prayers remained kneeling. The storm snatched the roof off their house and drove an oak tree through the front porch into the bedroom. No one was hurt.

H D McCarter crawled in bed with his wife and three children and covered them all with a feather mattress. The house was carried ten feet. Timbers were driven through the wall above the bed. The roof of the house went away. No one was injured.

Jim Davenport, a farmer, living three miles east of Tupelo saved his family of four by throwing them to the ground and falling over them while the tornado tore down his house.

The house of Dr Charles Nash, a dentist, was the last house on the southern edge of the storm's path. He found himself in a wardrobe after the storm, uninjured, but unable to explain how he got there.

So where was the one-year-old Elvis and his family at this time? Not surprisingly, as it was Palm Sunday, they were at the evening service in church. According to Elaine Dundy in her book, "Elvis and Gladys," suddenly Vernon's father, J D, appeared at the back of the church to signal them to come out as there were storm warnings. They hurried into the school bus and Noah Presley drove them to his house which was larger and stronger so they could all be accommodated. The menfolk lined up against the south wall of the house to brace the planks against the worst that was to come. When the storm twisted through East Tupelo, the house remained intact.

When it was all over, they went outside and could see the devastation of Tupelo before them. Noah and the other men drove down to the main town to offer any help they could. Next day, when Vernon, Gladys and Elvis arrived at their own home, the first thing they saw was that St Mark's Methodist church directly opposite their home had been totally razed to the ground by the tornado. Their own home was untouched. The Presleys were forever grateful for what they considered a miracle that had saved their home and their lives.

"Despite the swiftness of the blow, the frightful loss of life, the staggering destruction of property, the people of that city have lifted their heads from grief to face the future in an unconquerable determination to rebuild a better, greater, and fairer city. Such an unquenchable spirit makes them neighbors to the rest of the world."

These words were penned by William Clifford Morse, PhD, Mississippi State Geologist in his bulletin about the devastating Tupelo tornado of 5th April 1936.

A Prison Sentence

On 25th May 1938, Elvis' father, Vernon, along with two others, was sentenced to three years in the Mississippi State Penitentiary at Parchman Farm for forging a cheque. Vernon had sold a hog to Orville Bean and had received a cheque for $4. He thought that he "had been sold short," so, encouraged by two friends, he altered the cheque closer to the amount he believed he deserved. It is thought that they changed the cheque to $14. The community of East Tupelo, including Gladys herself, rallied support from the church and the

Mayor of East Tupelo, Noah Presley, and others of influence to put pressure on Orville Bean to be lenient and not to press charges. However, for whatever reason, this was lost on Orville, who was very angry that an employee should try to cheat him.

Thankfully, Vernon served only nine months of the prison sentence as the local community had got together a petition citing hardship and the fact that the Presley family were a good influence in the town, and surely Gladys would have been praying for her husband's early release. The first and third Sunday of every month were visiting days at Parchman and, as soon as Vernon had visiting privileges, Gladys and Elvis would visit him whenever she could find a friend or relative to drive the 4–5 hours to Parchman and back. Although Parchman was notorious for brutal hard labour, the visits did have conjugal rights. So at some stage during the visit, Vernon and Gladys would leave Elvis with whoever had brought him and disappear for a while.

During this time, Gladys did not want to stay with just the two of them in their home, so she moved in with relatives in South Tupelo, never to go back to the house where Elvis was born. While Vernon was away and not earning, Gladys, when she felt confident enough to leave three-year-old Elvis with her relatives, went to work at Mid-South Laundry in Tupelo. Previously, before she had Elvis, she had worked at the Tupelo Garment Company as a machinist.

The Move South

The search for better-paid work led Vernon, Gladys, and Elvis, along with Vernon's cousin, Sales Presley, his wife Annie, and their children, to move to Pascagoula, a port near Biloxi on the Gulf of Mexico. The men undertook unskilled work in the shipyards, whose workload had expanded because of US involvement in the Second World War. They were there in 1940 for only eight months as the work was very hard and took place in oppressive heat. It was during this time that Annie and Gladys cemented their already close relationship as they were strangers in town, so relied solely on each other for company.

Singing, Robust Preaching and Expectations in Church Services

It was popular for churches to have "singings" where church members would perform their favourite hymns for the rest of the congregation. As Elvis grew older, he would sing as a trio with his parents in other churches in the neighbourhood. The Presleys gained a reputation for being good singers. For example, when attending a service at the Free Will Baptist Church, Vernon and Gladys were called up to sing. They sang *If We Never Meet Again This Side of Heaven*, with Vernon singing tenor and Gladys alto. Also, in another church, they sang *Amazing Grace, Old Rugged Cross* and *Working on a Building* to a congregation of about 300.

Full immersion water baptism was preached at church, as they believed that to be authentic a person had to make a personal decision to follow Jesus, which babies cannot do. Until the AoG Church built its baptistry, people were baptised in the local town creek. When they had built the baptistry, the fire truck would come to fill it for them. Several sources mention that Elvis was baptised in 1944, some say baptised in the Holy Spirit. Frank Smith is adamant that he did not baptise Elvis.

In 1944, the 19-year-old Frank Smith became co-pastor with Gains Mansell at the AoG church. His father had been a drunkard and Frank had been saved by his mother's nightly prayer for the salvation of her sons. He married one of the Presley's neighbours, Corene Randall and they became good friends of the Presleys.

Frank's method of preaching was to intersperse his sermons with hymns, accompanying himself on a guitar. He would encourage people to be "real" before God. In one sermon he preached:

"There's nothing wrong with weeping. It's a way of emptying your heart. If you break down and cry, you empty your heart of grief. Strong men weep. Hear me, I said strong men weep in the presence of God. A superintendent of Sunday School, a strong man, an automobile mechanic, and a good one wept and said, 'I'm crying, but don't pity me I'm crying because I am in the presence of God.' By crying, you empty your heart of all that emotion." During the service, people came down to the front to receive prayer for healing. Frank prayed "Lord, melt my heart, melt my heart."

Another time he said:

"What's wrong with Christianity today? We're still of this world not separated from it as we should be. Separate yourself from the world. We've got to separate ourselves from the world before we have revival in our hearts. Get to where nothing matters but God."

Although Elvis could not have heard that sermon, he would be aware of its advice and, later, in the difficult times, would remove himself from the world and retreat to the sanctuary of his beloved home, Graceland in Memphis.

House Moves

In 1946, the Presley's moved from East Tupelo to Mulberry Alley, near to Shake Rag, a very poor part of Tupelo where the coloured people lived. There the 11-year-old Elvis would slip out of his mother's sight and go over to Shake Rag with friends and listen to a different kind of music, which expressed the pain and hurt of generations that still had a strong vein of hope. Elvis would have noticed that the singing in the churches of the coloured people was somehow more exuberant and expressive than the music he heard in his own church. A few months later, they moved to North Green Street to a Whites-only designated area in a "respectable" coloured neighbourhood.

Peter Guralnick, in his book "Last Train to Memphis," says of the regular church revivals held in North Green Street, "People would come from all over, dressed up in their finest regalia, the women in pink and yellow and hot fuchsia, wearing fantastic, feathered boa hats and carrying their weight without apology, the preachers preaching without anything to hold them back. getting lost in their Bible, chanting breathing, snorting rhythmically, gutturally, breathlessly, until their voices soared off into song. You didn't have to go inside to get the feeling – the sound, the sense, the allure, were all around you. You only had to walk up the street and the street was *rocking.* There was really nothing like it, you had to hand it to the coloured people, they really knew how to live. If you lived on North Green Street, you breathed it in as natural as air – after a while, you got used to it, it became yours too, *it was almost like being in church."*

Perhaps that is why, later, when they moved to Memphis, Elvis would still like to visit the Black churches to hear the lively, powerful singing and ecstatic preaching.

Elvis Goes Public

Singing wasn't just for Church. The family would often sing at home and, around 1943, eight-year-old Elvis would attend Saturday afternoon Jamborees in downtown Tupelo. These were organised by the local radio station WELO and were an amateur talent hour that was broadcast from the Courthouse. It had live audiences of about 150 and anyone wanting to sing on-air would just walk up and say, "I want to go on." Elvis did this quite often, mostly singing *Old Shep,* but also gospel and popular ballads. WELO is where Elvis first heard Mississippi Slim, aka Carvel Lee Ausborn, a country singer from East Tupelo, whom Elvis greatly admired and made sure he got to know. Although Elvis was painfully shy, especially with strangers and older people, he had a quiet determination. Even at that early age, Mississippi Slim remembers Elvis insisting that he accompany him on his guitar at one of the Saturday afternoon Jamborees. Slim confided in a fellow musician, "Hell, I got to play for him. His timing's all off, but he's doing a good job for an eight-year-old." Elvis told Mississippi Slim that he wished he could sing as well as him, and Slim replied, "You're good to be as young as you are – you just keep on working."

Elvis did keep on working, and this was rewarded on 3rd October 1945 when, aged 10, he came fifth in the Mississippi–Alabama Fair and Dairy Show talent contest in Tupelo. Standing on a chair to reach the microphone, without musical accompaniment, he sang *Old Shep.* The prizes were awarded according to the volume of audience applause. Elvis didn't win a prize, however, coming fifth was an encouragement, and being appreciated by a crowd of over 1,000 people no doubt fanned into flame his desire to become a performer.

Elvis' First Guitar

After Elvis got his guitar for his 11th birthday, he would go with school friend James Ausborn, (Slim's younger brother) and sit quietly in the studio during the broadcasting of the radio show. Slim would help him, teaching him new chords and timing. In fact, Elvis became good enough to appear on Slim's radio show, though his first scheduled appearance when he was 12 showed how shy Elvis really was. The week before, Slim had announced that a young lad, Elvis Presley, would be on the next week. However, Elvis had such an attack of nerves that he could not do it. He did, though, appear the following week and several times after that.

There are various versions of the story of the purchase of Elvis' first guitar on his 11th birthday 8th January 1946, however, the most reliable is contained in the following letter written by Forrest Bobo, who was the person who made the sale.

The letter, which was written on 2nd October 1979, on Tupelo Hardware Company letterhead says:

GOOD MORNING –

My name is Forrest L. Bobo from Tupelo, Mississippi. I am 78 years young today, but I can well remember the afternoon when Elvis Presley and his mother came into Tupelo Hardware, where I worked for twenty years. He wanted a 22-cal. rifle and his mother wanted him to buy a guitar. I showed him the rifle first and then I got the guitar for him to look at. I put a wood box behind the showcase and let him play with the guitar for some time. Then he said that he did not have that much money, which was only $7.75 plus 2% sales tax.

His mother told him that if he would buy the guitar instead of the rifle, she would pay the difference for him. The papers have said that the guitar cost $12.50 but at that time you could have bought a real nice one for that amount. The small amount of money that he had to spend had been earned by running errands and doing small jobs for people.

I am proud to have been a little part in Elvis' life. I had supper with Elvis the night he left for his first audition. We all wished him a great success, and he sure made a great life for himself and the rest of the world.

Thank you for your time, Forrest L. Bobo

Elvis later recalled that the day before they went to the shop, he had discussed his desire for a guitar while they were in the storm cellar hiding from a tornado. Most probably, Gladys engaged Elvis in a conversation about his birthday to take his mind off the scary, shrieking, crashing sounds of the tornado above. (There was a tornado in Tupelo at 5am on 7th January 1946, though nowhere near the scale of the one in 1936.)

Several other people were involved with teaching Elvis to play the instrument, including Frank Smith and Elvis' uncles, Johnny and Vester.

It was around this time that Elvis started to play the piano. The family of course would not have been able to afford one at home, but he had plenty of opportunity at school and church to learn to play. He was self-taught. Once when asked who taught Elvis to play the piano Glen Hardin, one of Elvis' pianists in the seventies said, "No-one, he was a terrible piano player!" Of course, by Glen's professional standard he was, but Elvis preferred the piano to the guitar and played well enough to enjoy himself and even accompanied himself on the piano in concerts in his later years.

Discipline and Prayer

The discipline imposed by his parents was rigorous by today's standards, but it worked. One admonishment that Elvis remembered was the first time he stole something. He took two empty cola bottles from a neighbour's porch. (In those days, people saved their empty glass bottles to return to the shop and receive the deposit which had been included in the purchase price.) His mother questioned him about the bottles, and he admitted his wrongdoing. Gladys took him by the hand to return the bottles. That was embarrassment enough, but his mother then informed him that he was to confess his sin to the church next Sunday morning. The fateful morning arrived, and a tearful Elvis whispered his wrongdoing to the entire AoG congregation and ran out of the church. He never again took anything without permission.

At an early age, he learned to pray, both in church and at home. He would have heard his parents praying. Vernon, in an interview with Good Housekeeping, said, "He had developed acute tonsillitis with such a high fever, he was on the verge of convulsions. Gladys and I were afraid that we were going to lose him." Even the doctor had given up on him and suggested they call in another. They did not do that, but instead, "My wife and I turned in prayer to the greatest healer of all, God. I do believe in miracles so that day I prayed to God that he would miraculously heal our child. My wife and I prayed together and separately, and, by night, I could see that Elvis was better."

Elvis' Aunt Nash, Vernon's sister who was nine years old when Elvis was born and spent many hours with the family, said, "Prayer was and always has been an important part of life for the Presley family. I can remember Vernon on his knees in church praying. I heard him so many times in his bedroom praying. When Elvis was small, he would lay his hands on Vernon and Gladys when they were sick and pray for them. He would tell them 'Jesus will make it all better.'"

***

Elvis was a dreamer. On the porch, he and his Aunt Nash would talk about what they would like to do when they grew up. Elvis said he wanted to be a truck driver and a singer and Nash said she would like to be a nurse and a gospel singer. Nash says, "One of those people became a pretty popular singer and it wasn't me!" Aunt Nash did fulfil her dream, though in a slightly different way. She became a preacher and was ordained as a minister in the AoG in 1978, pastoring a church in Walls, Mississippi. Elvis also told her that he was going to buy his mom and dad a big house and many cars. As we all know, that came true and more. The Bible says that the Lord can do more than we can ever imagine or dream of.

Elvis' Aunt - Annie Presley

The role the church played in the lives of the Presleys can be exemplified by the recollections of Annie Presley whom I visited in her home in Tupelo. Annie was married to Sales Presley, the brother of Vernon Presley. Twice a week Vernon and Gladys, and Sales and Annie would visit, sit on their porches, and sing hymns. Annie said, "That's all there was to do in those days. Vernon and Gladys both had fine voices. Gladys sang alto."

Annie told me that, at church each child was given a pocket New Testament, and later, a full Bible, which they would bring to church. Apart from the Sunday services they had prayer meetings and Bible studies during the week. The church members would vote on such matters as the purchase of a piano. The dress and behaviour codes were very strict. She told us that a gospel group, "The Sunflower Sisters," from Memphis visited their church and were disapproved of for their permed hair and "fancy" dress. Also, people were turned out of the church for immorality.

The AoG Church in East Tupelo was built around 1938 and they had long and lively services. Annie said, "If you got home by midnight, you were doing good." The services started at about 7pm. They would sing several songs and then the preacher would preach for an hour or two. After that, they would have the altar call (calling people up to the front who wanted to give their lives to Jesus). The service would last for another two or three hours with people shouting and singing, jumping up and praising God in English with phrases such as "Praise the Lord," "Thank you, Jesus," "Hallelujah," "Glory," "I love you, Lord," and praying in tongues.

Annie recalled that the people believed in healing prayer, which was a regular occurrence. Annie's husband, Sales, became very ill and the church prayed for him, but there was no sign of healing. The Elders said that Sales and Annie must have done something wrong for this illness not to be healed and told them to examine their own lives for any sin which would prevent healing. Annie said they "tore themselves apart" to discover anything that was preventing the healing. They were very distressed. Finally, one of the Elders decided to fast and pray for five days and nights and said God told him that it was Sales' time to die. Although in one way it was not good news, it was a great relief to them and freed them from guilt. The Elders apologised for their wrong attitude to the couple. Sales died at the age of thirty-three with Annie by his bedside in hospital. His final prayer was: "God I can't stand the pain. I surrender my life to you. Please take care of my wife and children." He fell unconscious and died a few hours later.

Annie then went on to tell of the goodness of God in looking after her and her children. One day, the eve of Thanksgiving, Annie made some biscuits and gravy, using up the last food they had in the house. She told her children to eat everything up, and, as they had no more food they must now trust in God for their next meals. They went to bed and slept late. Meanwhile, at the Thanksgiving service the next day, the Pastor asked the congregation to pray and ask God to lay on their hearts anyone who was in need that day. One of Annie's relatives, whom they had not seen for some time, thought of them and took round some food. One of the children, much to Annie's embarrassment, looked through the food parcel and said, "Mom, if there was some shortening, we could make some biscuits." The relative then realised that there was no food in the house and came back with more groceries. Families would always help each other out if they knew of the need, and sometimes it was God himself who gave them that information directly.

At this point in the conversation, Becky Martin, a school friend of Elvis, who had taken me to see Annie, related a story of a young man who had knocked at her door and wanted to borrow $5. Although she could not really afford it, she gave him all that she had at the time, which was $4.95. She also offered him a drink. That very same day in the post she unexpectedly received a letter from the bank, including a cheque for $25. Becky saw this as God's provision and believes that we should never be afraid to give to someone in need, even if we feel we can't afford it because God is faithful and will repay us many times over.

Nine years after Sales' death, Annie married another Presley, Sale's cousin, John Delton and had a daughter by him. According to Annie, the Presleys were attending the Second Baptist church when they left Tupelo in 1948. Annie visited Gladys several times in Memphis after Elvis had started earning a lot of money and had bought Graceland for himself and his parents. Gladys confided in Annie that she would give anything to have to trust in God again for their physical needs. "Money don't mean anything," Gladys observed, adding that all she could do now was to sit and look out of the window.

I had a good time with Annie and noticed a plaque on her front door saying, "Welcome to the Presleys" and the scripture "As for me and my house, we will serve the Lord." (Our home has that scripture on the wall near our front door.)

Annie's grief over her husband's illness and death had not turned her against God, but she was disappointed in the initial harshness of the church's attitude to Sales' illness, and she eventually left the AoG for a Baptist church. Perhaps it is this lack of graciousness displayed by some of the churches that discouraged Elvis from becoming more involved in church as an adult. He disliked the cold, hard religiosity and judgementalism, which often pointed the finger of condemnation. As we shall see later, Elvis was much affected by this attitude.

After he became famous, Elvis would drop by Annie's house to visit. One time he visited, he tried to slip into Tupelo, unnoticed, to attend a Gospel Singing night at Lawhon School which he had attended. He had parked his pink Cadillac near Annie's in what he thought was a safe place. But, on returning to the car, he found a bunch of boys, all of whom he knew, doing something to his car. The damage caused cost nearly a thousand dollars, but Elvis refused to prosecute them because he knew what hard times they were having and that they were jealous of his success. After that, every time he went back to Tupelo, he parked his car at the Police Station.

First Girlfriend?

One of Elvis' girlfriends (he was about twelve at the time) was Magdalene Morgan. She played the piano at the AoG church they attended with their families. Magdalene had had her eyes on Elvis, and she knew – just knew – that one day, sooner or later, they would become "an item."

For his book, "Early Elvis, The Tupelo Years," Bill E Burk interviewed Magdalene in the early 1990s.

Magdalene told Bill, "I guess my infatuation with Elvis started in that little church up in East Tupelo. He sang and picked the guitar, I sang and played piano." Sometimes she would accompany Elvis as he sang from behind the pulpit – gospel songs like *Amazing Grace, The Old Rugged Cross* and some of the older hymns. They were always in the Christmas plays together. One time, she was especially thrilled as she played Mary and Elvis played Joseph.

"He was just my ideal guy. He was very pleasant, very polite. He didn't talk a whole lot. Elvis was kind of embarrassed a lot. He did not like crowds. He would talk to me a lot if we were by ourselves, like when my mother and I would visit the Presley home, which we did often because Gladys was my mom's best friend. He and I would sing. We would hold hands and talk. We would go for walks in the woods out behind his house and he would talk about school, church and singing and what he wanted to be when he grew up. He always talked about wanting to be a singer and he would marry someone who would have to be a lot like his mama. He was just my little guy, you know.

"At that time, I was very young. I didn't expect my life to end or go anywhere without Elvis because he was my man. I was right there with him when he sang his very first song on WELO Radio. I was so proud of him!"

Magdalene attended some of Elvis' birthday parties. She said that although they were very poor, they managed to have beans, potatoes, and meat. Gladys made a birthday cake with frosting, and sometimes ice cream in an old-time ice cream freezer which the guests would take turns in cranking. For birthday gifts, Elvis would receive a shirt, sometimes a hand-made one using flour sack material. "Gladys was very good at sewing," Magdalene remembered. "She worked in a sewing factory. He'd wind up getting the shirt, maybe a bar of candy. Those were the good ol' times, something we will always remember."

Magdalene and Elvis planned their future together – she thought that as they were so close, they would always be together in life, singing, everything. Elvis even carved a heart on a tree trunk in the woods behind their houses, with their initials and "Love Forever" underneath the heart.

Though they were sweethearts from the end of the filth grade until Elvis moved to Memphis at the beginning of the seventh grade, their kisses were few and far between. "Just twice in three years. No, make that three," Magdalene fondly remembered. "The first time was just after he had carved that heart in the tree. The second time, we were sitting in the swing on his front porch one night while our parents were talking inside. He slowly eased his arm around me, like he didn't know if this were the thing to do or not at this stage. And then he just sort of leaned over and kissed me. I thought, 'My goodness, we're practically engaged!' You know how children were then. Of course, it's a lot different now. The third time, he sneaked a kiss in the back seat of the car while we were going to a (church) rally. I mean, that was really sneaky – just a little quick kiss.

"He never proposed marriage to me. Nothing like that. We were much too young to be thinking things like that in those days. Oh, he would say 'When we grow up, we are going to do this, do that.' At that time if you just held hands, it was very serious. And we did hold hands a lot. It was a very serious and very sweet relationship, very sweet, very clean."

Magdalene remembered Elvis' time in school saying, "He really tried his very best, but he didn't make the best of grades. He was always very well-mannered in school and never had to go to the principal's office or stand in the corner. I'm sure his mother and father helped him at times with his homework, but I never did. He was always bringing his guitar to school, and, at lunchtime, he would go sit out under a tree and pick and sing. Not just to me, to anyone who happened to be listening."

Of his clothes, Magdalene noted that Elvis mostly wore overalls and a flour sack shirt, though he did have a few better shirts. He was always neat and clean, and his clothes were always pressed. He occasionally wore jeans, but never liked wearing them.

They didn't have money to go to the movies but would sometimes go across the highway to Johnnie's Diner and drink a Coke, always accompanied by Elvis' mother.

Their main social activity with other young people was with CA (Christ's Ambassadors) which had rallies all over the area. Whichever church brought the most members to a rally got a CA banner. They could take it to their church and keep it until some other CA group did better. Magdalene and Elvis were always together at the rallies. They would go to different towns – Saltillo, Corinth and Priceville, most times on the church buses, though once or twice they rode with Aaron Kennedy, their church song leader.

She remembered the Presleys as a close-knit, loving family, saying, "He idolized his parents and they idolized him. He held a high respect for his mother and father. If they said 'no,' that meant 'no.' I know I'm prejudiced, but Elvis was just a well-mannered boy to be an only child. I'm an only child and I was spoiled rotten, and I know it. Elvis was brought up like kids should be today, from the old school, with a lot of respect, no talking back, no sassing.

"When I heard that they were moving to Memphis, I cried a good while. I missed him. I kept missing him even after I got married and had children. I loved Elvis. I will always love Elvis. There will always be a spot in my heart and Elvis will always be there."

After Elvis left town, their lives drifted apart. They would see each other again only once.

"The last time I saw Elvis, I was working with my mother in the Depot Cafe in Tupelo. Everything about him had changed, his looks, his mannerisms. But deep down, he was still the same guy." When Elvis walked into the cafe, she was taking a break, so he sat down at her table, and they talked for a while. He went over some of the music he was getting ready to sing and told her that he had been down on Beale Street in Memphis singing with some Black people and that now he had a guitar with all the strings on it, and he was really excited about what was beginning to happen in his life.

Gladys Encourages Elvis to Read

In February 1948, Gladys took Elvis to the Tupelo Public Library where he made out an application for a library card. This was quite an unusual step as a survey showed that less than one per cent of children used the library at all. Gladys only wanted the best for Elvis, and she saw that having free access to books would be a good move, as indeed it was.

Elvis was an avid reader of comics and was especially drawn to Superman, Batman, and, most of all, Captain Marvel Jr. He also loved the book "The Wizard of Oz," perhaps identifying with the story of the scary tornado at the beginning, and the theme of "somewhere over a rainbow" – that all things are possible. Now that he had access to more books, I imagine he started to read a wider variety of material. I have not been able to find any information about the books Elvis read during his teen years. However, it is recorded that during his lifetime, Elvis read over 1,000 books, mostly on spiritual topics (although he read all kinds of books, including a whole medical library). Most of his books had footnotes in his handwriting throughout them.

Elvis owned several Bibles and was given many by fans.

On his bedside table in 1960 was "The Power of Positive Thinking" by Dr Norman Vincent Peale and "How to Live 365 Days a Year" by Dr John A Schindler. He often read medical texts and was so well-versed in The Physician's Desk Reference that he more than held his own when talking to medical professionals about prescription drugs. However, as we discover later,

Elvis' knowledge of prescription drugs was not matched by his wisdom in the use of them.

Shortly before his death, Elvis had given his friend, Wanda June Hill, a list of his favourite books, saying to her that if she didn't do anything else in her lifetime, that she should read these books. The list included mostly "spiritual" books including, of course, the Bible.

Graceland archivist, Angie Marchese, recently revealed some of the hundreds of books found at Graceland in the loft, and on Elvis' bookshelves in his bedroom. They show the breadth of Elvis reading. As well as spiritual and philosophical books, there were books on karate, football, history, especially the two World Wars, the inaugural addresses of the presidents of the USA, books on music and several encyclopaedias.

Later, wherever he travelled Elvis always took a box of books with him.

Virtual Marriage

In September 1948, Elvis found his parents' marriage certificate with the back summary page blank. He pencilled in his name and Magdline (misspelling of Magdalene) Morgan as being married on 11th September 1948.

On 6th November 1948, the Presleys packed all their belongings into their 1937 Plymouth and drove the 120 miles to Memphis.

Although they suffered economic hardship, Elvis' childhood in Tupelo was indeed sweet and full of life. Elvis displayed a sweetness and innocence about which Elaine Dundy says, "that remarkable indestructible, almost *inhuman* innocence would remain with him all his life." One could say that it is indeed not human, because it is divine; it is the sweetness of the Holy Spirit.

Gallery

Contestants in the talent contest in Tupelo on 3rd October 1945. Elvis is standing next to one of the winners. Inset, close-up of Elvis (wearing spectacles) in the photo.

Elvis with his mother in the late 1940s.

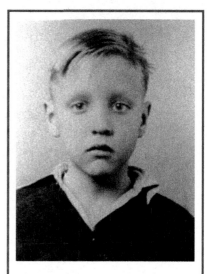

School photo around 1942.

The cabin in Tupelo where Elvis was born, taken at sunset. On the left is the statue of Elvis as a 13-year-old. (J P Wilson)

Elvis around 13 years old, with Magdalene Morgan taken one Sunday. (Photograph taken by Corene Smith, the wife of Rev. Frank Smith)

Chapter 2

Memphis Meanderings

Ask and it will be given to you; seek and you will find; knock and the door will be opened to you. For everyone who asks receives; the one who seeks finds; and to the one who knocks, the door will be opened. (Matthew 7:7& 8)

Elvis showing his natural-coloured hair.

In November 1948, Vernon, Gladys, and Elvis, along with other family members, moved to Memphis for a better life. The move was a good one for the Presley family. There were plenty of job opportunities, so they were able to sustain a reasonable income. Also, they had a welcoming church to belong to, the Church of the Lord Jesus Christ on 7th Street, where they were encouraged by the powerful preaching of Reverend Rex Dyson who baptised all three of them. Having met Reverend Dyson, interviewed him, and heard him preach, I am convinced that his passionate preaching had a great effect on the young teenage Elvis.

Elvis enrolled in the eighth grade at Humes High School, which two of the Dyson's sons also attended.

Rev. Rex Dyson remembers Vernon and Gladys more than he does Elvis, though he does recall the time Elvis came to be baptised.

When I asked him how the Presleys came to be at his church he said, "Gladys and Vernon got acquainted with me when they would come and listen to me preach every Sunday afternoon in Court Square on Main Street, all summer long. They drove up from Tupelo every weekend." (Perhaps this explains the reports that the Presleys did not attend church as regularly just before they left Tupelo to live in Memphis. Perhaps they drove up every weekend to scout for jobs and accommodation and also to look for a good church.)

I also wondered how the Presleys would know of Rex since they were in Tupelo, while he was preaching in Memphis. I later learned that, even in those days, Rex was a very well-known and respected preacher and people would travel miles to hear him. I also discovered that the evangelist Rex Humbard was named after him.

Rev. Rex Dyson had bought the First Pentecostal Church on 4th and Keele in 1936 and then, in 1949, built the church of Jesus Christ on 7th Street. He could not remember if the Presleys attended the church on 4th and Keele, but he definitely remembers that they attended the 7th Street Church for that was where he baptised Vernon, Gladys and Elvis around 1950. He says, "I baptised Vernon and Gladys first. I had them in the baptistry. Elvis came up to the baptistry and he said, "I want to be baptised." I baptised all three of them. Rex's wife, Caroline interjects, "All three were together in the baptistry, it was quite full!"

I asked how Elvis' parents came to be baptised. Rex said, "I preached them in. They didn't know anything about baptism in Jesus' name. I preached them under conviction, and they came and was baptised."

In 1950, the Dysons lived in Woodlawn Street, just opposite Humes High. Elvis, the Dyson boys and one or two other boys from the church, including a boy named Sonny Prater, went to Humes together. Caroline said, "Sonny told me many a time, he said we all just shared our lunch money and shared our lunches or whatever we had. So he [Elvis] come up poorly. He wasn't born with a silver spoon in his mouth."

Rex recalled, "During those years Elvis got him a little band, a string band, and my boy David played the guitar in Elvis' little string band. Caroline continued, "They finally ended up in the Goodwyn Institute, the place where they had musical things going on." She remembered it very well because, when her mother passed away, "Dad here had to go to the Goodwyn Institute to get our son David who was down there with Elvis playin'."

The Goodwyn Institute is remembered as the site of KWEM Radio Saturday Night Jamboree, the location of the first major public appearance by Elvis before signing with Sun Records a year later. The Jamboree was a family-oriented country music show that ran from 1953 to 1954 with a format much like that of the Grand Ole Opry. The Jamboree may be the first location where a new kind of music that would become known as Rockabilly was performed. WMC also broadcast a number of country and western artists from the

Goodwyn Institute Building and later some of the first TV programmes were broadcast from the Goodwyn. Elvis performed there several times in 1953 and 1954.

When asked if Elvis ever talked with them about what he wanted to do with his life, Caroline said, "He talked to my sons. If he did discuss that they never told us. You know how boys are. It's all kind of hush hush. They don't want anyone to know what they're talking about!"

The Dysons kept track of Elvis until he went to the army and then had no more contact, although Rex tried, as we shall discover later.

Rex speculated, "Elvis could have been a wonderful ... he could have done just as much for God as he did for the world out there if he had just lived right and done right. There's no doubt that he was called to be a preacher.

"I can say, for sure, his mother was a real Holy Ghost Christian. I don't know if Vernon ever received the baptism of the Holy Ghost or not and I don't know if Elvis did or not, he didn't whilst he was at this church. That's between them and the Lord. We are not to judge. Elvis could have done a great work for God if he would have just really lived for God, that's the whole tragedy."

Caroline added, "I always did believe that Elvis was God-minded if you know what I mean. The young people back then, they didn't talk about shooting and banging up things. They talked about church and preachers and such like. They all played music. They would get together in that trailer in our backyard and oh, all the noise with their singin'! They would really go at it! The boys that they'd hang out with were like mine, all naturally preachers. I imagine that in Elvis' mind the same thoughts were. My five boys all turned out to be preachers. It should have been the same with Elvis."

Their son, David Dyson, shared his memories of Elvis with me:

"As a fan of Elvis, I was blessed to know him as a teenager. His dad and mom attended my father's church, in 1950. They were both baptised by my dad. As they were being baptised, Elvis wanted to do the same, so my dad baptised him too. He would come to our home and, being musicians, we would jam in our travel trailer. I was able to teach him two keys on the guitar – E and B. We had lots of fun during those times. They left our church when my dad went to Israel to establish a mission. Vernon Presley told us he would leave if dad went.

"Being called of the Lord, dad knew he had to go to Israel and so they left. I did not see Elvis again until 1955. I had just got married and we were walking in downtown Memphis, and he came out of Sun records. He was telling us he had just recorded a song for his mom. That's the last time I had any contact with him. Elvis loved the Lord and his relationship with God was very important to him."

***

The Presley family's first two homes in Memphis were in rooming houses where they rented a room with a hot plate for cooking and shared a bathroom with other tenants.

In April 1949, Vernon moved from his job at Precision Tool to United Paint Company where he worked loading cans and would often see his friend Marion Carson, a painter and decorator who was also Elvis' Sunday School teacher, at 7th Street Church. Marion Carson told me that he remembered Elvis as a quiet, well-behaved young man.

High School Friends

Here is a memory from a fellow Humes High School buddy, Dwight Malone, interviewed by Bill Burk:

"Church was an important part of my family life. Even though my brother Phillip, my sister Kay and I weren't that religious during our formative years, Mama was. If the doors were open, we were there. Most sermons would slant toward 'Hellfire and Damnation,' therefore, it's understandable why the siblings in our family tried to follow the straight and narrow. Fear is a great motivator. We still go to church, but we go to one that preaches 'God is Love.'

"Elvis was different. Most boys had crew cuts and wore tee shirts and blue jeans. Elvis would appear at school in a pink jacket and yellow pants and a ducktail haircut. He was quiet, very courteous, and largely stayed to himself. I did play touch football with him on the triangle at Lauderdale Courts. He was not fast, but he had very quick movements."

Warren Gregory was another friend at that time. Warren was musically gifted. He could play the piano, the guitar, the trumpet, and any other available instrument. He never took a lesson. He could play any tune he heard and improvise the melody. During the summer months, Elvis and Warren would sit on the street curb, strumming their guitars and singing.

It was at the "Annual Minstrel" Talent Show in April 1953 that Warren realised that Elvis could really sing. He remembers his own barbershop quartet singing and Gloria Trout, a little blond dancer who was also a cheerleader. But mostly, he remembers Elvis. He says, "There were no swivel hips. His props were a chair, a guitar, and a loud costume. He put one foot on the chair, strummed the guitar and sang his heart out. To me, that was when rock 'n' roll was born. The ovation was thunderous and long. After graduation, I went into the army and was stationed in Germany. When I returned in 1956, Elvis was a huge star, and many boys were wearing pink jackets, yellow pants and ducktail haircuts."

Lauderdale Courts

In May 1949, Vernon applied to the Memphis Housing Authority for public housing. The application was approved and the home service advisor who visited them in their rented room on Poplar Avenue reported that the family was "very nice and deserving." They moved to Lauderdale Courts, 185 Winchester Street in September.

Lauderdale Courts is in the "Pinch" district in the north of Memphis. This name is a shortened form of "Pinchgut," derived from the fact that many of the people, mostly Irish, who lived there in the early 19th Century were extremely poor. They were, therefore, so thin that their stomachs were so taut that you could not pinch any loose skin, certainly not fat.

It was in the Courts that Elvis developed a close group of four friends. Vernon bought Elvis a lawnmower so that they could earn some money by going around the streets, knocking on doors, and offering to cut their grass. According to one of the four, Buzzy Forbess, they also had a rake and two sickles so one would use the push mower, two of them the sickles, and the other rake up the grass. They charged $2 for their services.

Elvis usually carried his guitar around the Courts and at school, and would sit and entertain his friends, singing their favourite songs. He would also go once a month with his friends to somewhere such as the Old Kennedy Veterans' hospital to entertain the veterans or wounded coming home from the Korean war. There they mingled with the men, talked, and maybe shot pool – anything to help them take their minds off their problems. Sometimes, they went to the

Home for Incurables. Elvis got up on stage with his guitar to sing and the others just bopped. Buzzy Forbess remembers Elvis singing his own versions of the songs.

At this time in Memphis, for families such as the Presleys, living in social housing was a Godsend, though they knew that they had to keep their homes in good condition. Farley Guy, one of the four friends in Lauderdale Courts, reports that there would be a monthly inspection of the apartments for cleanliness and the acquisition of too many material goods. If all was not in order, the families could be evicted, so many of the women worked extra hard on their housework the day before the inspection, cleaning walls and waxing floors.

Farley also says of their time in The Courts, "We were happy kids. If we wanted some spending money, we had to work. People today living in those projects go around feeling sorry for themselves, feeling the world owes them a living. Then, we looked for better days ahead, someday we would have this or that – even a job! We never had any troubles, no one had to go to Juvenile Court. We knew right from wrong. Today we hear so much about problems in the projects, but their problems of poverty are no worse than ours. We didn't form gangs, we didn't drink. If there was any trouble, I am sure our parents would have got together and dealt with it."

In 1950, Elvis was issued with his social security card, number 409-52-2002. The Government uses this number to keep track of lifetime earnings and the number of years worked. They would have noticed quite a change in Elvis' earnings over the following years!

Memphis Recording Service

In that same year, Sam Philips opened the Memphis Recording Service, known as Sun Records at 706 Union Avenue, Memphis. Sam Philips had been looking for unknown raw talent who would not have a chance on a major record label. He prized individuality, especially in the Southern blues singers. However, he also needed commercial success and felt that this would come from finding a White singer who had that raw passionate Black feeling in his voice. This search proved to be very significant in Elvis' life, though when asked how Sam Philips found Elvis, Sam said, "I didn't find Elvis – he found me."

1951 was the year that Elvis took his driving test, and his teachers and friends noticed a growing confidence in him. Elvis became part of a little band in school. Elvis' football coach, Malcolm Philips, distinctly remembers the 1951 annual school carnival in May. He was in the cafeteria below the school auditorium. The variety show had just started when he heard sounds like "be-bop-a-lula" coming from upstairs. Wanting to see who was making all that noise, he climbed up the fire escape and entered the auditorium at the side of the stage. He saw Red West playing the trumpet, Elvis playing guitar, and two or three others in the band. He said, "Elvis was a sight, believe me, his knees were a-knocking, he was singing and wiggling and wobbling all over the place. When Elvis got through singing, they [the packed audience] were yelling 'encore, encore.' He must have sung every song he knew that night!"

Also that year, Gladys started work at St Joseph's hospital as a nurses' aid – it was the best job she had ever had, and she was very proud of it.

During 1952, Elvis had several different after school and summer jobs and his father bought him a car. As well as singing with other musical teenagers in Lauderdale Courts, Elvis sang wherever he could. Johnny Burnett, a rockabilly singer/songwriter who was the same age as Elvis and lived in Lauderdale Courts at the same time, remembers, "Wherever he went he would have his guitar slung on his back. Sometimes he used to go down to the fire station and sing to the boys there, they were the only ones around Memphis who seemed to have listening time. Every now and then, he would go into one of the cafes or bars and offer to sing." (He sang for no financial reward, though he sometimes got a free hamburger.)

In many ways, 1953 was a very significant year for the Presleys. Because the family's increased income was now far above the ceiling for housing assistance, in the spring, they had to leave Lauderdale Courts. They rented a two-room apartment opposite Humes High School for only a few months, and then an apartment in a large Victorian home on Alabama Avenue, just across from Lauderdale Courts. It was here that they become very friendly with the Fruchter family in the apartment above. As Caroline Dyson says, Elvis was God-minded. He was particularly interested in the Old Testament of the Bible and the role of the Jews in God's plans. It was no surprise then that he made immediate friends with this Jewish family. Alfred Fruchter was founder of the Orthodox Memphis Hebrew Academy, and according to Larry Geller, one of Elvis' Jewish friends, Elvis' Pentecostal roots showed as he asked the Rabbi, "You don't believe in Jesus, do you?" To which the Rabbi replied, "I believe he was a great man – one of the greatest of the Jewish prophets." A puzzled

Elvis then asked, "So why don't you accept him? If he was a Rabbi and you're a Rabbi, shouldn't you stick together?"

I should imagine Elvis also had many more questions for this friendly Rabbi.

The Fruchters were a devoted Jewish family and adhered to the laws of the Sabbath which meant, on that day, that they were not allowed to work, even to switch on light switches or open locks. Elvis became their "Shabbos Goy," a Gentile who would do these small tasks for them. (When we visited Israel to research this book, the Jewish hotel we stayed in had a Shabbat lift, which, on the Sabbath, automatically stopped at every floor and the doors opened and closed themselves so that no buttons had to be pressed.)

The rest of Elvis' family also came to know and love the Fruchters and sometimes would sit down with them for their Shabbat meal. Rosella Kline Chartock in her book "The Jewish World of Elvis Presley," reports that Jeanette Fruchter described Elvis and his parents as "very poor, but very refined. They never wanted anything for nothing. They were highly respectable people. It was a beautiful relationship. Gladys and I were like sisters. When Gladys couldn't meet the heat, electric or water bill, I would lend her the money which she would always pay back." The Fruchters were considerably wealthier than the Presleys and so owned a phone and a record player. These came in very useful the following year when Elvis needed to be contacted about recording opportunities and was also able to listen at home to records.

Also, in this year, Elvis was encouraged by his appearance in his school's Annual Minstrel Show, billed as guitarist Elvis Prestly. He reportedly was, as usual, very nervous but performed so well, singing *Till I Waltz Again with You*, that he received the most applause and was allowed to do an encore. Mrs Mildred Scrivener, Elvis' teacher remembers him bringing his guitar to a class picnic at Overton Park where he entertained his classmates.

The Adventures Begin

1953 was the year that Elvis would leave school to go out into the big wide world. Now that he was 18, he could visit more places, and the clubs that he frequented in Memphis, Northern Mississippi, and West Memphis, Arkansas, were vibrant with rockabilly sounds to which he was very much attracted.

On 26th May, Elvis skipped school and hitched the four-hour drive to Meridian, Mississippi to the first Jimmie Rodgers Memorial Country Music Festival, featuring stars such as Ernest Tubb, Hank Snow, Minnie Pearl, Roy Acuff, and Red Foley. It was not to hear the singers that he had travelled so far but to take part in the talent contest for residents of Mississippi, organised at the Lamar Hotel by the Meridian Star newspaper. The musical talent contest was an attempt to showcase local artists and popularise Jimmie Rodgers' music.

The contest rules were strict, and each performer was given a maximum of four minutes to perform his song. The audience was shocked by some of the entrants, which included some teenagers singing up-tempo rockabilly songs that, according to one observer, violated all the hallowed traditions of country music.

Curtis Robison, a reporter with the newspaper, recalled his meeting with Elvis in the hotel. "There was this kid, Elvis Presley, wandering around with his guitar, looking lost. I was with my colleague, Dick Smith, and the kid told us he was from Tupelo and had hitched to get here to take part in the contest. That's right, Tupelo. If he had told us where he was really from at the time, not living in Mississippi would have disqualified him. He was flat broke; it turned out he only had 10 cents on him. Dick took pity on him and paid for his room and board. He entered the contest and won second prize." Curtis couldn't remember what Elvis sang, but he remembered that the prize was a guitar. Others remember that Elvis sang *Old Shep*.

Martha Ann Barhanovich from Biloxi, one of the young singers in the musical contest remembers, "We performed together on 26th May in Meridian at the Jimmie Rodgers Celebration. That was my birthday. He was very good looking, and he was very down to earth." What Martha also noticed was Elvis' amazing talent. She later convinced her dad, booking agent Frank Barhanovich, to bring the then-unknown star to Biloxi, which he did twice in 1955. Elvis' performance at the Slovenian Lodge on 26th June 1955 in Biloxi was the first of many gigs on the Mississippi Gulf Coast, mostly at military bases across the southeast. Martha said that everyone just thought he was wonderful and fell in love with him, and that he was a "great, great performer."

Martha lost touch with Elvis after he hired a manager. She did see him two more times when she attended his concerts. According to a report which appeared on WLOX radio website on 16th August 2013, Martha said, "I would have loved to be able to talk to him, but we couldn't get close to him after that. He was too big." However, she was looking forward to Elvis' return to Biloxi.

Her dad had booked Elvis for a show at the Coast Coliseum in November of 1977. Sadly, Elvis died in August, three months before that concert.

Seeking Full-time Employment

Having reached the age of 18, Elvis could now apply for a full-time job as he would leave school in June. He registered at the Tennessee State Employment Security office. He listed his leisure activities as singing, playing ball, working on cars, and going to movies. At the end of the form, the interviewer noted Elvis' appearance as a "rather flashily dressed playboy type, denied by the fact that he has worked hard these past three summers, wants a job dealing with people."

On 3rd June, Elvis became the first member of his immediate family to receive a high school diploma, which always occupied an honoured place in the family home. He applied for several jobs, finally obtaining a full-time job in September at Precision Tools, not dealing with people but as a sander and operator of the hand drill and drill press.

Music Still on His Mind

On 15th July, The Memphis Press Scimitar published an article about the Prisonaires singing group and their promotion by Sam Phillips. The article was entitled "Prisoners may make fame with a record they made in Memphis." With his mind still on recording, I should imagine that this article caught Elvis' attention. Later, in the summer of 1953, perhaps encouraged by the positive response to his appearance at Humes concert in April, his success at the contest in Meridian in May, and inspired by the newspaper article, Elvis ventured into Sun Studios with money borrowed from a friend. Marion Keisker, second in command to Sam Philips, was at her desk in the waiting room. She enquired what Elvis wanted, though the fact that he was carrying a guitar hinted strongly that he was there to make a recording for himself. She remembers her conversation with this shy, rather nervous young man.

Elvis said, "If you know anyone who needs a singer ..." She asked what kind of singer he was, and he replied, "I sing all kinds." She then wanted to know who he sounded like, to which Elvis replied, "I don't sound like nobody." He then made a record on which he sang *My Happiness* and *That's When Your Heartaches Begin*, accompanying himself on guitar. The recording of this rather pensive and plaintive performance cost Elvis around $5. In 2015, it sold at auction for $300,000.

Marion could certainly see that there was something different about Elvis, who popped into Sun Studios several times over the next year, including January 1954 when he recorded two ballads at his own expense. He also went in sometimes to see if she knew of any bands needing a singer. She detected a great sense of longing in him and felt he was clearly marked for success. She recognised that "he was so ingenious there was no way he could go wrong."

Israel Calls

Also in 1953, the Presley's pastor, Rev. Rex Dyson believed that the Lord had called him to Israel to set up a mission in Bethlehem. Rex says that Vernon begged him not to go, partly perhaps fearing for Rex's safety, but also not wanting to lose such a wonderful pastor. Rex was convinced of his call to Israel and went for several months. When he returned, the Presleys were no longer attending the church.

Perhaps the following extract from the introduction to an article entitled "The 'Christianization' of Israel and Jews in 1950s America" by Michelle Mart from JSTOR (a digital library founded in 1995 in New York City, United States) explains why Rex Dyson was so eager to go to Israel:

In the 1950s, the United States experienced a domestic religious revival that offered post-war Americans a framework to interpret the world and its unsettling international political problems. Moreover, the religious message of the Cold War that saw the God-fearing West against atheistic communists encouraged an unprecedented ecumenism in American history. Jews, formerly objects of indifference, if not disdain and hatred in the United States, were swept up in the ecumenical tide of "Judeo-Christian" values and identity and, essentially, "Christianized" in popular and political culture. Not surprisingly, these cultural trends affected images of the recently formed (1948) State of Israel. In the popular and political imagination, Israel was formed by the "Chosen People" and populated by prophets, warriors, and simple folk like those in Bible stories. Israelis seemed just like Americans. Americans treated the political problems of the Middle East differently than those in other parts of the world because of the religious significance of the "Holy Land".

It is here that I would like to honour Rev. Rex Dyson as a praying friend, an amazing evangelist, and lover of the Lord Jesus. I do believe that his preaching would have had a great impact, even if subliminally, on teenage Elvis. When I first met Rev. Rex Dyson in 2000, he was 100 years old, greeted me with a bear hug and spoke passionately about Jesus. Several people who have heard, but not seen him preach thought that he was a Black preacher (perhaps in the same way that some on hearing Elvis sing thought that he was a Black singer?).

When he was 23 years old Rex received the call into ministry, left his job in the mattress-making industry and began his evangelistic adventures. At one of his first meetings, he was healed of a heart condition. Over the years he preached to and baptised thousands of people. He was never concerned about finances as he knew that the Lord would always provide, which he did.

To give a flavour of Rev. Rex Dyson's travelling evangelistic activities, and how at that time in parts of USA, "religion" was very high on the agenda of many people's lives, including the Presley's, here are some stories of his ministry.

Whilst in prayer in 1929, the day Herbert Hoover won the election for President of the USA, Rev Dyson felt the Lord say, "Go West." So he set off and drove as far as Clarendon, Texas only to be told that there was no Pentecostal church in that town as they had all moved to Dallas. Thinking to ask if there were any Holy Rollers (Pentecostal Christians) in town, he was directed to a house across a field. He went over and explained he was looking for a church to host him to preach a revival. The lady who answered the door was amazed to see him as she said they had been praying for two years that God would send him to their town to help them. He stayed there a few weeks, they had a wonderful revival and then it was time to move on.

From there the call was still "Go West" so he drove as far as Amarillo, Texas. Here he was directed to the Pentecostal Church of God and warmly welcomed by the Pastor and his wife, especially by the Pastor who was startled to see him as he had seen him in his dreams, though carrying a guitar. He was therefore not surprised to find out that Rev Dyson indeed had a guitar and singing was part of his evangelistic ministry. They held revival meetings for several weeks and 49 people were baptised in the name of the Lord Jesus Christ, including the Pastor's wife.

Rev. Dyson was called to Clebit, a small logging town in Oklahoma consisting of around 200 homes. The Baptist church had built a brush arbour, and someone got their permission to invite Rev. Dyson and use it for a few nights' revival meetings. The main theme of his preaching was from the book of Acts

2:38: "Repent and be baptized, every one of you, in the name of Jesus Christ for the forgiveness of your sins. And you will receive the gift of the Holy Spirit."

This certainly had great effect and it seemed like the whole town was coming to the meetings and many, especially wives, were receiving the Holy Spirit and giving all their attention to the revival. Several of the husbands were not pleased with this and decided to try and close the meetings down. They got their shotguns, not intending to kill anyone, but just to shoot into the arbour. They hoped people would scatter, the evangelist would get scared and leave, the wives would come back home, and things would be normal again. However, before this happened, Rev. Dyson, while he was preaching, looked down at the pallet on which babies were sleeping and noticed a venomous copperhead snake, crawling over a baby's face. He immediately reached down, grabbed the snake by the tail and slung it out the back of the arbour, narrowly missing one of the men holding a shotgun. Everyone was amazed as the power of God filled the place, and the men with the shotguns went to the front and gave their hearts to the Lord.

Authors note: Rex Dyson was a Pentecostal preacher who baptised in the name of Jesus, rather than in the name of Father, Son and Holy Spirit. This is known as "Oneness" theology, which some people believe denies the Holy Trinity. Interestingly enough though, a few days after my interview with Rex Dyson, we attended a baptism at Christ the Rock Church in Memphis, and the preacher Rev. Fred Bennett, said, "I baptise you in the name of the Father, Son and Holy Spirit and even in the name of Jesus." Personally, this does not pose a problem to me as God is a mystery I do not fully understand. Three in One – Trinity/Oneness – Lord (Father), Jesus (Son), Christ (Holy Spirit) - seems fine to me. Dottie Rambo, the singer, and songwriter who wrote *If That Isn't Love* recorded by Elvis, reported that, one day, when discussing faith with Elvis, he told her that he had been baptised in the name of Jesus, as she was herself.

A New Church Community

In January 1954, Elvis started to attend the First Assemblies of God Church on McLemore, most probably because it was the church which the Blackwood Brothers, whom he greatly admired, attended. Although it was two miles from his home, the church organised transport for those without. It was there that he met Dixie Locke who became his girlfriend. Elvis regularly attended both the Sunday school and the worship service. As well as attending church, the

Presleys enjoyed the monthly all-night gospel singings at the Ellis Auditorium with the Blackwood brothers and the Statesmen, especially J D Sumner and Jake Hess. Elvis particularly liked the flamboyant stage presentation of some of the singers.

The famous Blackwood Brothers gospel group and their families, 23 people in all, had, in 1950, moved from Iowa to Memphis and started attending the First Assembly of God church on McLemore. They had also set up the Blackwood Brothers Record shop and offices on Jefferson Avenue. Having got to know Elvis at church, along with his love of gospel music, James Blackwood would take Elvis backstage to meet the groups and singers during the gospel music events at the Ellis Auditorium. James Blackwood recalls that Elvis was in the same Sunday School class at church with Cecil Blackwood and would often sing a lot in rehearsal with the gospel group the Songfellows[2] whose members included Cecil Blackwood and James Hamill, the son of the preacher at The First Assembly of God church. One of the group members was going to leave and Elvis was set to take his place, but the singer changed his mind, so Elvis just kept patiently waiting. When Cecil left the group, Elvis wanted to join, but the calling of Sun Records took precedence. In his early days at Sun, when Bob Neal was still his manager, Elvis still went to the Gospel Conventions where the Blackwoods and Statesmen would introduce him, and he would go up onstage and sing a couple of gospel songs with them harmonising behind him. Then, after Colonel Parker took over as manager, he put a stop to Elvis singing on stage for no payment. Elvis would still go up on stage, but he could only be introduced.

Sadly, later that year, Elvis and his parents, Vernon and Gladys, and Dixie Locke attended the joint funeral of R W Blackwood and bass singer Bill Lyles, members of the Blackwood Brothers Quartet, who were killed in a plane crash in Clanton, Alabama. James Blackwood recalls that Elvis told him that when he and Dixie heard of the plane crash, they drove to a park along the river and

---

[2] When I shared the Songfellows link on Facebook, Michael Scott of the Songfellows Quartet contacted me saying, "Thanks for sharing our post. This group however is a different Songfellows group than the one Elvis auditioned for. This group was formed in California in 1954. Elvis auditioned with a group around the same time out of Memphis which included Jim Hamill and Cecil Blackwood. That group never materialized. You notice in this 2016 version of our group, Elvis's long-time friend and backup singer Ed Hill is singing the baritone part for us, as he did for about 10 years until his retirement. On a side note, when Elvis was in Hollywood doing his movies in the 60s and such, he would send Charlie Hodge over to buy us lunch after our Sunday TV show. Charlie said he loved our music." (Since Mike Scott wrote this, sadly, Ed Hill has passed away. The group is now a trio consisting of Bob Jones, Tank Tackett, and Rick Strickland.)

cried for a long time. The funeral was held at Ellis Auditorium in downtown Memphis with 5,000 people reportedly in attendance. The Presley family loved the Blackwood Brothers Quartet, and they were Gladys' favourite gospel quartet. The Blackwood Brothers Quartet would later sing at Gladys' funeral in August of 1958. When the Quartet decided some weeks later to carry on, bass singer J D Sumner joined them. J D would later sing with Elvis for many years as J D Sumner and The Stamps.

In his book, "Early Elvis – The Humes Years," Bill Burk records an interview with Rev. James Hamill, the Pastor of the First Assembly of God church that Elvis attended. He told Bill that Elvis regularly attended until he started recording and touring. Although Pastor Hamill was immediately impressed by Elvis, he always thought that his hair was too long! He said, "I always thought him as a nice young kid. He was so extremely courteous and kind to everyone. He always talked to me like he was in the Military, always saying 'sir' and 'Yes, sir.' He had so many traits that I admired in an individual.

"He became good friends with my son Jimmy and Cecil Blackwood. Elvis and Jimmy would often go over to East Trigg Baptist Church to listen to the Black gospel music. They were very enthusiastic about what they heard over there. Jimmy and Elvis were totally fascinated with gospel music – they never lost their enthusiasm for it. My Jimmy was four years with the Kingsmen Quartet and up until Elvis' death, each time they were both in town, they would get together at Graceland and sing gospel until the wee hours. I remember one time Jimmy came home way past midnight. I looked at the clock and said, 'Jimmy what on earth in the world have you been doing with Elvis till 3 o'clock in the morning?' Jimmy replied, 'Singing gospel songs.'"

During those early years at First Assembly, Rev. Hamill had no idea Elvis would become what he did. He really disliked rock 'n' roll music and even gospel quartets. He liked Elvis, just not his music.

Elvis' curiosity led him to attend other churches in the area to experience their joyous music. Among these was the Centenary AME Church. According to Elvis' cousin Gene Smith, Elvis particularly enjoyed the choir at Centenary African Methodist Episcopal church on Mississippi Boulevard. The two of them, probably the only White faces in the congregation, were always welcomed though they chose to sit in the balcony out of courtesy as Black people were required to do if they attended a White church. Elvis would be swept up by the exuberant singing of the gospel choir and continued to visit the church many times.

He also visited East Trigg Baptist Church. The Church was pastored by celebrated Black gospel music composer, the Rev. William Herbert Brewster, Sr, whose songs had been recorded by Mahalia Jackson and Clara Ward, and whose stand on Civil Rights was well known in the community. He thought that Elvis' version of *Peace in the Valley* was "one of the best gospel recordings I've ever heard." He also said of Elvis that his voice agreed with the thought of Calvary, suggesting that God could use him, and that Elvis was a bundle of energy set to music, and that echo will never die.

Elvis would not be the only White face in the congregation, as Rev. Brewster's influence was substantial, reaching thousands of Memphians through radio stations WHBQ and WDIA. Memphis disc jockey Dewey Phillips of WHBQ would often interview Rev. Brewster whose sermons were broadcast on-air and both radio stations played his songs. Elvis would listen to these programmes and hear Rev. Brewster invite "Black and White" to church services at East Trigg Avenue Baptist Church.

Rev. Al Green's Full Gospel Tabernacle Church on Hale Road, just a couple of miles from Graceland is also a very lively church. It is visited by fans today who want a taste of what Elvis experienced in those Black churches. However, Al Green did not establish the church until 1974, when he was ordained as a Baptist minister, after a spiritual experience that convinced him to stop singing "secular" music and sing only gospel. As we shall discover, by 1974, Elvis was struggling and rarely went out in public, apart from his concerts and I doubt if he even knew that Al Green's church was there. They had only met once, briefly, but they did appreciate each other's music.

***

In March 1954, Elvis left his job at Precision Tool as he was not happy with the work or the ribbing he received from his workmates because of the length of his hair. In April, he took a job at Crown Electrics as a truck driver, hoping for the opportunity to train as an electrician. When he was not at work Elvis, Dixie, and their friends went to Riverside Park where Elvis played guitar and sang.

Dixie Locke

As part of my research, I interviewed Dixie Locke in January 1999. She was and still is a member of the First Assemblies of God Church, where Elvis went after Rev. Rex Dyson went to Israel.

Dixie Locke, now called Dixie Emmons, could perhaps have become Dixie Presley as she became Elvis' girlfriend in 1954 – before he became famous – and they had talked of getting married. When Elvis attended the church, it was located on McLemore Avenue. In 1962, the church relocated to North Highland Street, which is where I met Dixie who had become the Church Secretary. I phoned her, having been told that she rarely gave interviews because many writers and reporters are just wanting to "dish the dirt" on Elvis. I met her and talked for a while when my husband and I attended a Sunday evening service, and, later in the week, she very graciously granted us half an hour. She is a very pretty lady (Elvis always knew how to choose a good-looking girl!) and she shared her memories of Elvis with me.

Elvis regularly attended both the Sunday School and the worship service. Perhaps I need to explain here, that in the USA, Sunday School is not just for children, but for all ages including adults. It usually takes place before the main service, and the congregation splits into age group classes and studies the Bible. They have discussions about the meaning of the Bible and its application to life. After the Sunday School classes, everyone comes together for the service, which includes singing, preaching and prayer.

Elvis and Dixie were in different classes as Dixie is four years younger than Elvis, but they noticed each other and soon started dating. She said that most of the dates she went on with Elvis were church-related and that they talked a lot about their Christian faith. They both attended the Ellis Gospel Singings and even an Oral Roberts Crusade. She recalled that Elvis had no problems with the Gospel, and he truly believed that Jesus was the only Son of God and that he died for our sins so that we may have everlasting life.

I asked Dixie if Elvis was baptised in the Holy Spirit. She was not aware that he was, though baptism in the Holy Spirit and speaking in tongues was taught at church and they were exposed to its manifestation in others, so just expected that it would happen one day. As far as she knew, Elvis was not baptised in the Holy Spirit whilst at their church and neither of them spoke in tongues. Baptism in the Holy Spirit is not something we choose to do at a certain time and date like water baptism, which is undertaken by believers in response to Jesus' command to repent and be baptised. Rather, it is an experience direct from God, one of the manifestations of which is speaking in tongues. Dixie was not baptised in the Holy Spirit herself until she was 26 years old.

In May, Elvis discovered that there was an opening for a vocalist at the Hi-Hat Club in Memphis. Accompanied by Dixie, he attended an audition but was not offered the job as the club owners were not impressed with his singing, and maybe his sideburns, bolero jacket and pink shirt did not warm them to him.

Also in May, the United States Supreme Court decided a case that changed the course of American history. In the case of Brown v. Board of Education, the Supreme Court ruled that racial segregation of schools was unconstitutional. It was noted that such segregation, solely because of race, generated a feeling of inferiority that may affect Black people's hearts and minds in a way that might never be undone. As we shall see later, racial prejudice was very much "in the air," during Elvis' lifetime and, I may say, even today.

The Early Days at Sun Records

On 26th June 1954, after Marion Keisker's insistence that Sam have "the boy with the sideburns" try out a new song Sam had got from Nashville, Elvis was invited to Sun Studios to record the ballad *Without You*. He failed to come up with a successful cover of the song, but at least he was noticed. Just a week later, he was called into the studio for an audition as Sam Philips saw potential in Elvis and felt he would be able to coax hidden talent from within. Elvis was invited by Sam Phillips along with guitarist Scotty Moore and double bass player Bill Black, to try recording a ballad. They attempted one ballad after another with no success. Feeling pretty discouraged they had a break during which Elvis, without warning, launched into Black singer Arthur Big Boy Crudup's very up-tempo *That's All Right*. Bill and Scotty immediately joined in this jam session. Sam Philips overheard them and believed he had got what he was looking for, a White singer with a Black "feel" to his voice. When Sam asked them what they were doing, they said they didn't know, so Sam told them, "Back up, try to find a place to start and do it again." Which they did, and he recorded it.

Sam gave a copy of the one-sided acetate to Dewey Philips, DJ of the local radio station WHBQ based in the Chisca Hotel, who promised to play it on his programme. When he did, on the 8th July, the switchboard lit up with people wanting to hear it again. He played it over and over during the evening. He called the Presley's home to try and get Elvis down to the radio studios, but Elvis was at the cinema. Gladys and Vernon immediately went to the cinema, walking up and down the aisles searching for their son. He was finally located, and they sent him down to the studios, where Dewey interviewed him, not telling him till afterwards that he was live on air. This was probably a good

50

move on Dewey's part as Elvis might easily have clammed up or stuttered incoherently if he had known he was on-air.

Sam Philips knew he now needed a song for the B-side of the record in order to release it, and the boys came up with an up-tempo version of *The Blue Moon of Kentucky*. The record was released in mid-July and immediately sold well in Memphis and had sales in Mississippi, Arkansas, and even as far as New Orleans. They now needed to be playing concerts to get themselves better known and hopefully earn some money.

Elvis signed a year's contract with Sun, countersigned by his parents as, at only 19 years old, he was underage to sign legal documents. Scotty Moore became the manager and booking agent for the group, and they started performing regularly at the Bon Air and Eagle's Nest clubs in Memphis.

On 30th July, Elvis made his first appearance at the outdoor venue of the Overton Park Shell in Memphis. It was the Slim Whitman Show and Elvis was billed as Ellis Presley. (As late as 1955 his name was still sometimes misspelt, such as Alvis Presley and Elvis Pressley.) He was so nervous his leg shook, which brought appreciative screams from the girls in the audience. It could have been a sign of nervousness but, later, all his fellow musicians noticed that Elvis kept time to the music with his legs and body movements.

Of this, Norman Putnam, bass player, says of the RCA Studio B in Nashville recordings in June 1970, "We would run the song once for the engineer, and then record it with vocals. He [Elvis] would be like 'Let's get it in the first take' and start breathing like an athlete. We played to his dynamic. He was almost conducting us with his body language, and I think that's the reason those records have such a great feel."

Also, this was the way that one of Elvis' heroes performed. Jim Wetherington, known as the "Big Chief," was part of the Statesmen Quartet that Elvis would go to see at the All-Night Singings at the Ellis Auditorium in Memphis. The Big Chief shook his legs to the beat of the group's up-tempo songs. Fellow gospel singer, Jake Hess, recalled that Wetherington "went about as far as you could go in gospel music," noting that the women in the audience would go crazy over the bass singer's leg shaking.

***

While recording at Sun Studios in 1954, Elvis made the acquaintance of "The Prisonaires." Elvis later visited them in prison and became a friend of the lead singer, Johnny Bragg. This American doo-wop group had recorded their first hit, *Just Walkin' in the Rain,* in 1953 at Sun Records, while the group was incarcerated in the Tennessee State Penitentiary in Nashville.

So how did this come to be? This all-Black singing group was formed by five prisoners who were clearly very good. The group was paraded around a variety of receptions and civic functions as a demonstration of the prison's enlightened rehabilitation programme, playing a mix of blues, gospel, and pop songs under armed guard. The new Warden, James E Edwards, then arranged for two talent scouts from Sam Phillips' Sun Records to see the group. They were subsequently driven down to Memphis to record *Just Walkin' In The Rain*, which was written by two of the group, Johnny Bragg, and Robert Riley.

The record took hold, first on radio and then becoming a major seller, moving over 250,000 copies. The Prisonaires had arrived and found themselves in demand for a series of television and concert appearances. They gradually became high-status figures in Tennessee and never betrayed the trust placed in them by trying to escape their guards on their numerous forays outside the prison. A second single followed in August 1953, the spiritual *My God Is Real,* followed by *I Know* and its autobiographical B-side, *A Prisoner's Prayer.* In 1961, Elvis visited Bragg and offered to pay his legal bills, but Bragg declined, telling Elvis he would be out in a matter of months. He was released seven years later. After that, he was in and out of prison for many years. He died in 2004 aged 79.

In September, Elvis and his band released their second single *Good Rockin' Tonight/I Don't Care if the Sun Don't Shine,* which was eagerly purchased by teenagers wanting to hear more of this upbeat, lively music.

Now that Elvis was hitting the regional billboard charts, Sam Phillips was able to get him an appearance on the Grand Ole Opry country music radio programme at the Ryman Auditorium in Nashville.

The Ryman Auditorium had opened as the Union Gospel Tabernacle in 1892. Thomas Ryman owned several saloons and a fleet of riverboats and, after attending one of Samuel Porter Jones tent revivals intending to heckle, he instead became a devout Christian. He built the tabernacle so the people of Nashville could attend large-scale revivals indoors. Although it was designed as a house of worship, in order to pay off its debts it was often rented out for non-religious events. Over the years it has hosted lectures and presentations from a great variety of people, including presidents of the USA, and big names like Helen Keller, WC Fields, Bob Hope, Doris Day, and Harry Houdini.

The Grand Ole Oprey could be heard in 30 states, but people would also go to the WSM studio to watch it live. When crowds got too large for the studio, the show eventually moved to the Ryman Auditorium and had sell-out shows for the next 31 years. One of these shows, on 2nd Oct 1954, featured Elvis Presley. The Ole Opry audience gave Elvis a polite, but not effusive, reception as they did not appreciate this rockabilly approach to their beloved country music. This kind of response was repeated later in Las Vegas, as we shall see.

Again, because of the popularity of Elvis' records, the group were able to appear on the Louisiana Hayride. This was a radio and, later, television country music show broadcast from Shreveport, Louisiana, which helped to launch the careers of many singers including Hank Williams and, of course, Elvis. He performed on the radio version of the programme on 16th October 1954 and made his first television appearance on the television version on 3rd March 1955.

Sometime in mid-October Elvis, Scotty and Bill left their jobs to focus on their concert appearances. On 6th November Elvis signed, along with his parents, a one-year contract with Louisiana Hayride.

During these days Elvis was to make a connection that would be a key part of his later performances. Visiting the Ellis Auditorium backstage, he met the Jordanaires, the popular, well-respected backup singers for Eddy Arnold. The young, not-yet established Elvis naively told them that he hoped he would be able to have them sing on his records someday. A hope that was fulfilled.

Another significant relationship was about to develop. In November 1954, Colonel Tom Parker was a music promoter and manager, who, with his right-hand man Tom Diskin, had been working with popular country singer Hank Snow. He had gone into business with Hank with a 50/50 investment to form Jamboree Attractions – Hank Snow Enterprises. This company was formed not only to arrange bookings for Hank Snow, but also to provide a platform to help promote up-and-coming singers.

Elvis, Scotty, and Bill meanwhile were seriously entering the music business. They needed someone who could take over the management and bookings. For this purpose, Elvis signed a management contract with Bob Neal, the folk music disc jockey on the local WMPS radio station, who would have more contacts and time to book them further afield, even as far as Texas and Mexico.

1955 was a year of much travelling for Elvis and the band. They did 220 one-night stands throughout Texas, Arkansas, Mississippi, and Alabama, appearing in high school gyms, county courthouses, sports arenas, theatres, and baseball parks. They travelled by car with Bill Black's bass strapped to the roof. They were not yet big or even medium earners. The three of them shared a bedroom in hotels in order to have enough money for petrol. They only made enough money to cover other basic costs, sometimes not including meals, though with typical Southern hospitality, they were often given free meals in local restaurants. Fans they got to know would also invite them to eat with their families, so they were usually well fed.

It was at one of these 1955 concerts in Lubbock, Texas that Colonel Tom Parker (aka the Colonel) made his first approach to Elvis. Country singer Jimmie Snow, son of Hank Snow whom Elvis greatly admired, first met Elvis, and brought the two men together as Jimmie was the opening act for the show which was part of the Hank Snow Jamboree Tour. Jimmie passed on a letter of intent by the Colonel to Elvis and Bob Neal, as they had been discussing becoming part of Hank Snow Enterprises.

Jimmie Snow

Jimmie was bowled over by Elvis whom he saw as having something special. He said that Elvis electrified the audience, especially the women, of all ages, who would get out of their seats to dance to the joyful music. Jimmie said that he loved Elvis straight away, that he was a nice, warm, polite person, and they immediately became friends. Also appearing in the concert, at the bottom of the bill, was Buddy Holly who also noticed Elvis' energy on stage but commented that he was not impressed with some of his behaviour such as spitting out chewing gum when he arrived on stage and telling some crude, off-colour jokes which weren't funny.

On a tour later in the year, Jimmie roomed with Elvis. While Elvis always had a lot of girls around him and took some of them to his room, Jimmie felt that Elvis just liked to have the girls around and that he loved women but did not use them. The next time Jimmie met Elvis was News Year's Day 1958 when Elvis invited him to Graceland. According to Jimmie, Elvis introduced him to all his friends, and they had great fun visiting the cinema, which Elvis rented for the night, and roller-skating. Jimmie said Elvis would "sometimes get serious and sit down at the white piano and we would sing gospel songs. So, we should get serious which I didn't really want because I was fighting it. I was being tugged at that time by God to go into the ministry, get married and give up my [singing] career, but we would talk about the Lord, and he would voice his feelings, then we would go off and do more fun things."

So, what happened with the battle that Jimmie had with the Lord? Was he to continue to be a singer or become a preacher? Around the same time as Elvis and Buddy Holly, Jimmie began to rocket his way to stardom on the RCA label. But he soon learned that something that wealth and fame cannot provide is lasting peace. In front of his parents' house, Jimmie Snow committed his life to Christ and soon answered the call to preach. One of his early sermons has been featured in a PBS documentary about rock 'n' roll. The film featured a clip which is on display at the Rock and Roll Hall of Fame, of an early sermon by Jimmie Snow denouncing the evils of rock 'n' roll. Some preachers went even further and preached against Elvis as a person of bad influence on the youth.

Perhaps some of these preachers had a point. During his performance in Jacksonville, Florida on 13th May, Elvis told the screaming girls in the 1400-strong audience that he'd "see them backstage after the show," prompting a mad rush toward the stage and a riot that spilled into the streets. A group cornered Elvis in his dressing room and tore off his clothes in their competition to grab a souvenir. Elvis had to be rescued by police from what has become known as the "first Presley riot."

Elvis spoke of the riot in a 1956 interview: "Mom and Dad still haven't gotten over all this hoopla about me. Mama was down in Florida once when the girls mobbed me, and she was afraid they were hurting me. Shucks, they were only tearing my clothes. I didn't mind a bit. I told her, 'Mama, if you're going to feel that way, you'd better not come along to my shows because that stuff is going to keep right on happening – I hope.'"

Later Elvis was reported as saying, "They didn't really want to hurt me, they only wanted a piece of me for a souvenir." He also said about being mobbed and having his clothes torn off, "My fans want my shirt. They can have my shirt. They put it on my back." After another concert in Jacksonville, Elvis told reporters that "the kids took my watch, ring, coat, shirt and shoes. I got out with my pants, but the cuffs were gone."

Up until that Jacksonville concert the audiences had been enthusiastic – now they were becoming unmanageable. The Colonel noticed this powerful effect Elvis had and, by his own admission, began to plan how he could move away from Hank Snow promotions and "exploit" this phenomenon by becoming his sole manager.

On 26th May, Elvis attended the third Annual Jimmie Rodgers Memorial Celebration in Meridian, Mississippi, making his second visit to the celebration. This time he was there not for the talent contest, but to perform at the main event along with Ernest Tubb, Slim Whitman, and Hank Snow.

Elvis' Only Full Gospel Public Performance

The concert on 4th July 1955 in DeLeon, Texas, was a unique one for Elvis. James Blackwood recalled that both Elvis and the Blackwoods were booked for the annual Country and Southern Gospel Event. He said, "Elvis drove there in his Cadillac and we in our bus. When we arrived, he along with Scotty and Bill and Vernon and Gladys stayed with us in our air-conditioned bus and, when he went on stage, he announced that he was going to sing nothing but gospel – which he did."

The Statesmen opened the show, followed by the Blackwood Brothers. Elvis was the next act after the Blackwoods who had sung a touching tribute to their two fellow members who had died in the air crash the previous year. Elvis was so moved by their performance that he decided to sing only gospel songs. The audience was expecting Elvis to leap up on stage and give a lively performance of rockabilly. However, Elvis, without any of his energetic stage moves stepped slowly up to the microphone and presented a programme of melodic, old-time religious songs, including *Known Only to Him* and *Just a Closer Walk with Thee*. This was not well received by the 5,000-strong audience. The teenagers who had come to hear him were disappointed that he did not sing any of their favourite songs and the adults who had come to hear their favourite gospel groups were either unimpressed or insulted to hear their lovely songs coming out of the mouth of this hooligan.

Ironically, this is the only all-gospel public performance that Elvis ever did, and perhaps, why, initially, Elvis did not sing gospel songs in his early concerts. It is documented however that he was planning to do an all-gospel show after the concert tour in August 1977. As we know, neither the August concert tour nor the gospel show took place.

James Blackwood knew how much Elvis loved gospel and felt that, had Elvis chosen gospel music as a career he would have made it big, but not as big as he did in rock 'n' roll. James Blackwood recalled that during Elvis' later years, they were both singing in Fort Worth one night and he went over to Elvis' hotel after the show where J D Sumner took him up to Elvis' suite. Elvis had had a standing ovation that night after singing the hymn *How Great Thou Art*. James said, "After Elvis showered, we talked a long time. It was that night that Elvis told me that gospel music was his first love and he hoped one day he could devote the rest of his life to singing gospel. If he had done that, he would have been a worldwide sensation. And it wouldn't have mattered that he was an older man. I feel that, had Elvis gone into gospel he would still be alive today. He paid a terrible price."

***

On 15th August Elvis had a meeting in Memphis with his manager Bob Neal, The Colonel, and Vernon Presley at which a new contract was signed, naming the Colonel as "Special Advisor" with control of almost every aspect of the operation. Also in August, the drummer D J Fontana joined the group.

The group's income for September was $3,300 of which Elvis got $1,650.

Now that he was earning more money, Elvis paid for his own ticket the next time he attended the Blackwood Brothers All Night Singing at the Ellis Auditorium in Memphis, on 23rd September. Until then he had always been let in free by the group. When James Blackwood discovered this, he sent his apologies along with a refund cheque, not realising that Elvis could now afford it.

Pat Boone

October and November 1955 were filled with concerts around the South and Mid-South, and Pat Boone vividly remembered meeting his opening act, Elvis, in Cleveland, Ohio on 20th October. The event was a sock hop for 3,000 teenagers hosted by the renowned Bill Randle.

Here is how 86-year-old Pat Boone recalled the event to Fox News in 2020:

"Bill Randle met me at the airport and said that a new kid would be going on before me. I said, 'Is it anybody I know?' He said, 'No, you wouldn't have heard of him. Name's Elvis Presley.'" Pat said that he had seen Elvis' name on a jukebox, but that is all he knew about him.

When he finally got to meet Elvis backstage, Pat was stunned by what he saw.

"He was just a scared young kid," he recalled. "He had not had a hit record yet. He was with two or three of his buddies. His collar was turned up, his pants were long. He was wearing scuffed up white shoes like me, white bucks … I told him, 'Bill Randall thinks big things may be ahead for you.' Elvis said, 'I don't know about that, but I hope so. And he just leaned back against the wall and his buddies closed in around him. I thought to myself, 'Wow, he's nervous. He may mess up out here in front of these 3,000 kids.'" But Pat was impressed by Elvis' unique look. Unlike Pat, who was famous for his squeaky-clean image, Elvis had already embodied a bad boy persona before fame.

"He sorta' looked like the guy that their moms didn't want their kids to associate with, because he looked like the rebel at school that wasn't on the sports team and wasn't concerned about grades, maybe had a pack of cigarettes rolled up under his sleeve and laughing at the guys that were taking school seriously," Pat explained.

The first song Elvis performed at that concert was *Blue Moon of Kentucky,* a bluegrass track by Bill Monroe. For that song, Pat said the audience "gave him a nice hand." But his second one, *That's All Right Mama,* really rocked the house.

"They loved it and wanted more," Pat recalled. "But that's all he had on his record, both sides. Those two songs. So, he left. I came on and sang my three hits. I got all the screams that night and it's the last and only time we ever appeared together on stage."

Pat said that the two men became good friends and their friendship lasted over the years. He remembered another, later conversation he had with Elvis.

"I wish I could go to church like you," Elvis told Pat. When Pat told him he could, Elvis replied, "No, they wouldn't leave me alone. I would distract the minister."

Pat assured Elvis that "if they see that you are coming for the same reason that they are, all of that would ease away and you could actually worship freely like everybody else. And it would do you a world of good, Elvis." According to Pat, Elvis felt like he couldn't go anywhere in public. So, he was sort-of imprisoned. "I felt like he lived like Public Enemy number one instead of the King of Rock 'n' Roll. It stunted his social and spiritual growth.

"We were two boys from Tennessee," he said. "We were both filming movies at 20th Century Fox at the same time. And we had dinner together. We played tag football with some of my buddies, like Ricky Nelson and others. We were just two lucky kids from Tennessee, loving it."

Pat said the last time the two crossed paths was July 1977, a month before Elvis died. Pat, along with his wife and four daughters, were doing a family act together and heading to Orlando from Memphis. He remembered that the airport was all abuzz because Elvis was about to fly to Las Vegas, and he was in his Cadillac limo waiting to get on board. Pat recalled, "We waited at the gate for him to get out of the car and come up. He came up, we talked a few minutes, took a picture – I've got a picture of that meeting. And he looked like he gained weight, which he had. I smacked him on the stomach and said, 'Are you carrying your money in here or what?' He said, 'Oh I've been eating too good, boy. I'll sweat it off in Vegas.'"

Pat Boone has had a successful career as an entertainer and a marriage that lasted 65 years, only coming to an end when his wife passed away in 2019. He said, "We made our commitment in our marriage to God and each other." Whenever Elvis comes to mind, he still thinks of "the scared young kid" with big dreams to make it big – the same ones Pat had. Though they lived their lives differently, they had a lot in common as well.

The Move to RCA

RCA (The Radio Corporation of America), producer of electronic and broadcasting equipment and gramophone records, had been interested in signing Elvis, making several offers to Sam Philips. The deal with RCA was completed on 21st November 1955. The legal document for the sale of Elvis' contract and all his Sun masters was signed by Colman Tilly for RCA, Sam Phillips for Sun, The Colonel as "Special Advisor," Bob Neal, and Elvis, with Vernon Presley countersigning as Elvis was still too young to sign a legal document. The price was $35,000 – the most paid for any performer to date.

The RCA signing ushered in 1956 – Elvis' breakthrough year.

On 10th and 11th January, Elvis recorded his first sessions for RCA with his group: guitarist Scotty Moore, bassist Bill Black, and drummer D J Fontana, who had joined the band the previous August, along with Chet Atkins on guitar and Floyd Cramer on piano. It was the first time he had backup singers, who were Gordon Stoker (of the Jordanaires) with Ben and Brock Speer of the Speer family, a Southern gospel group which RCA had just signed. *I Got a Woman, Heartbreak Hotel,* and *Money Honey* were recorded without the singers; *I Was the One* and *I'm Counting on You* were recorded with the backup singers.

26th January was the first of only a few major television appearances during Elvis' lifetime. It was on the Tommy Dorsey Stage Show broadcast from studios in New York. Elvis did six TV Stage Shows in early 1956 and it was the one in February, as we shall see later, which was instrumental in getting Elvis a screen test in Hollywood.

After his third performance in Jacksonville, on 23rd February 1956, Elvis collapsed while signing autographs. He was taken to the newly opened Baptist Memorial Hospital in what was said to be an ice cream truck. The doctor said Elvis was doing as much on stage in 20 minutes as the average labourer does in 8 hours. He advised him to slow down and kept him overnight. When released, Elvis said that the nurses would not let him rest, laughing as he left. Elvis did the second of his two scheduled shows the next night, with even more vigour and energy than the night before and was quoted after the show saying he had no intention of slowing down.

Another House Move

In March, Elvis had his first Number 1 hit with *Heartbreak Hotel* and was rich enough to be able to buy his family a house, thus fulfilling one of his dreams. Elvis purchased the house, which was in a relatively wealthy area of Memphis, from the Welsh Plywood Corporation for $29,500. The house, at 1034 Audubon Drive, had been built in 1954 and had four bedrooms and two and a half bathrooms. The Presleys only stayed there for a year as the constant stream of fans meant they had very little privacy and the neighbours were beginning to complain.

When they first moved into their house, Gladys had welcomed Elvis' fans, giving them glasses of lemonade or water when they asked. And, since theirs was the only house in the street with a pool, she often invited some of the neighbours round to cool off on hot days. Some had invited the Presleys back and been thoroughly neighbourly.

When the fans began turning up in their hundreds practically setting up camp on their front lawn and tearing out clumps of grass as souvenirs, Vernon had a fence built, but the fans just climbed over it to write messages in lipstick on Elvis's growing collection of cars. Some of the girls would even climb into the garden at night and sit outside Elvis' bedroom tapping on the window, calling for him to come and talk to them.

It was hard on Elvis' parents to find themselves virtually marooned inside their home every day, with the shades permanently drawn for privacy. But what really upset Elvis was the reaction of some of his middle-management neighbours. He could sympathise with them objecting to all the noise and traffic as they hadn't reckoned on that when they'd bought their homes. But then some of them began to complain about Gladys pegging out her washing in the garden and having relations from Tupelo to stay. In other words, bringing down the neighbourhood.

Elvis continued to have studio sessions and, on 14th April, when Elvis recorded *I Want You, I Need You, I Love You* he asked Gordon Stoker if the Jordanaires would record with him. The first time the Jordanaires performed with Elvis was at a concert on 16th May 1956 at Robinson Memorial Auditorium, Little Rock, Arkansas which was recorded, but not released. Perhaps the Jordanaires wanted a practice run with Elvis before they entered the recording studio.

After that, the next time Elvis did a studio recording with the Jordanaires was 2nd July 1956 when he recorded *Hound Dog* and *Don't Be Cruel.* Subsequently, he used them on nearly every one of his recording sessions for the next 14 years. The quartet also appeared in some of his concerts, his television appearances, and his movies. However, in 1969, when Elvis was about to start performing at the Hilton in Las Vegas, the Colonel's office called for the Jordanaires to work with him in the shows. They had 35 recording sessions already booked for the dates he needed, so they could not go. The Colonel got in touch with the Imperials, who had done the background vocals for Elvis' album *How Great Thou Art* along with The Jordanaires, and they were pleased to accept the engagement.

The Door to Hollywood

On 26th March 1956, Elvis had a screen test in Hollywood. This was an unusual occurrence, for even though he was going great guns in the music industry, it certainly was not the norm of the day for singers to automatically be offered starring roles in Hollywood, especially a singer who was vilified by the established press of the day.

Elvis' film career began when film producer Hal Wallis' partner in New York, Joseph Hazen, saw Elvis on TV in the Dorsey Stage show back in February 1956. He thought that Elvis was "terrific" and phoned Hal Wallis to switch on the TV and watch. Wallis was impressed with Elvis – especially by his originality. He saw something in Elvis that he was certain would transcend to the silver screen. Elvis was a big fan of the movies, and especially admired serious actors such as James Dean and Marlon Brando, so this would be another dream coming true for him. However, this dream was not quite fulfilled the way Elvis would have wanted.

Elvis had never acted on stage before but, for the initial screen test, he read and learned the two scenes from the script of *The Rainmaker*. Both Wallis and Hazen agreed that Elvis could act. Elvis was also asked to lip sync to *Blue Suede Shoes* with a guitar that had no strings and Wallace was interested in this aspect of Elvis' talent as it was his singing that had made Elvis so popular.

Hazen thought Elvis had real potential as a serious actor, while Wallis was convinced the public would never accept Elvis as a straight actor. Hal Wallis controlled the creative side of the business so, as we shall see, he overruled Hazen and cast Elvis in musical comedies.

The Colonel continued to find Elvis singing engagements and, in April, he was booked into the New Frontier Hotel in Las Vegas for a two-week engagement, billed as an Added Attraction – "The Atomic-Powered Singer" (in a town where people could watch real atomic tests taking place in the Nevada desert nearby).

Elvis's frenetic rock 'n' roll performances, which were causing such a sensation in the rest of the country, were hardly geared for a crowd of middle-aged Vegas showgoers.

At first the crowd got what they were expecting. Freddy Martin, whose "sweet music" orchestra was known for its pop versions of classics like Tchaikovsky's Concerto in B-flat, opened the show with several of his instrumental hits and a medley of songs from the musical Oklahoma. Next came Shecky Greene, a Chicago-born comedian just gaining notoriety for his Vegas lounge act.

Elvis was the closing act. Backed by Scotty Moore, Bill Black, and D J Fontana, Elvis performed four songs and was onstage for just 12 minutes. The response was polite at best. Apparently, one member of the audience sitting near the stage got up and ran out during Elvis' act crying, "What is all this yelling and noise?" The critics weren't much kinder. "Elvis Presley, coming in on a wing of advance hoopla, doesn't hit the mark here," wrote Bill Willard in Variety. "The loud braying of the tunes which rocketed him to the big time is wearing, and the applause comes back edged with a polite sound. For the teenagers, he's a whiz; for the average Vegas spender, a fizz." Newsweek said Elvis is "like a jug of corn liquor at a champagne party." Despite this reception, overall, Elvis enjoyed his time in Vegas, and said that he wanted to go back.

Another tour followed. The concert on 13th May in St Paul, Minnesota was the first of the next tour in which, over 15 days, Elvis performed every day including Sunday, doing a total of 25 shows. The shows were not sell-outs, but there was always a need for a police presence to protect Elvis from over-enthusiastic fans storming the stage. At one venue in La Crosse Wisconsin, 20 policemen and 12 Military Policemen from the local army camp could not contain the crowd trying to get to Elvis at the end of his performance. A second line of defence at the foot of the stairs leading to Elvis' dressing room prevailed. Also, outside the auditorium, the fans built a 30-foot-high human pyramid to reach the second storey dressing room windows. The promoter said he would never invite Elvis to perform in the town again. An editor of the local newspaper was so shocked at what he heard about the show that he wrote to J Edgar Hoover, head of the FBI, saying that Elvis' performance was "the filthiest and most harmful production that ever came to Lacrosse for teenagers." Rumours also abounded that the fan club meetings were sex orgies, and that Elvis was probably a drug addict and sexual pervert. Most press coverage during the tour focused on Elvis' stage antics which were described as anything from a St Vitus dance to a striptease with clothes on.

The riotous fans were becoming a concern for Elvis' personal safety, especially in Kansas City where the newspaper headline was "Elvis Presley Flees to Car After 20 Minutes on Stage." The fans had become so excited and physical that one girl had managed to get onto the stage and give Elvis a quick hug and kiss. This emboldened many more to suddenly leap onto the stage which became awash with swarming bodies. Elvis and Scotty made a dash for the back curtains, but D J Fontana was knocked to the floor and Bill Black ended up in the orchestra pit. In the melee, the drum kit and double bass were damaged.

In such a short time, Elvis life had changed considerably. He was now doing what he had been planning to do: sing to and entertain thousands of people. However, he had not expected the commotion and disturbance he caused. His response to questions about the negative influence he seemed to have, was, "I don't even smoke or drink and I started singing as a gospel singer and I come from a Christian home."

As we shall see, the success which Elvis desired so much, was to have an enormous effect on him as a person and bring conflict into his life.

Gallery

Photos from the AoG church magazine showing members of Bill Hatton's Sunday School class and a downtown Church parade. (First AoG church Memphis)

Elvis in his In the ROTC uniform standing outside the Lauderdale Courts Apartments, Memphis – 1951. [The Reserve Officers' Training Corps (ROTC) is a college program in the United States that prepares young adults to become officers in the U.S. Military.]

Dixie Locke and Elvis at her Junior Prom in Memphis, May 6, 1955. (Getty Images)

Elvis with Sam Phillips and Marion Keisker outside Sun Studios 1956.

A lovely photo of Elvis and his parents in their Audubon Drive home. It is one of the few photos I have seen where Gladys is looking happy. She was always so concerned about her "baby".

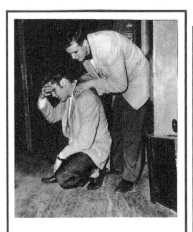

Exhausted Elvis, backstage. (Jo Tunzi)

Peter Wilson with Rev. Rex and Caroline Dyson. Rev. Rex is 100 years young in this photo. (J P Wilson)

Chapter 3

The Slippery Slope

When I said, "My foot is slipping," your unfailing love, Lord, supported me.
(Psalm 94:18)

In two short years, Elvis had shot to stardom but had become more removed from his spiritual roots. He could no longer attend church as he was travelling most Sundays and, even if he tried to, the fans would cause a commotion that Elvis felt was disrespectful to God. With this hectic lifestyle, even his prayer life and Bible reading suffered. June Juanico, his girlfriend in 1956, told me that she never saw Elvis read a religious book and they didn't pray together.

Tupelo Homecoming.

June's Story

In her book "Elvis in the Twilight of Memory" however, June wrote that they did sometimes talk about religion and that Elvis shared his faith with her. She also described the time when the Jordanaires went to Elvis' home in Audubon Drive to rehearse for the Ed Sullivan Show. She said that they practised the songs for the show until they were satisfied with their performance, and then they went on to sing just for fun. June was so thrilled hearing Elvis' rich voice harmonising with The Jordanaires that even her goosebumps had goosebumps! Gladys Presley, being the Holy Ghost Christian she was, raised her hands in the air shouting "Hallelujah!" June said that they sang every hymn she had ever heard and more. After three hours of this joyful exuberance, they all wanted to carry on, but a couple of the Jordanaires' voices were feeling the strain, so they said their farewells and departed.

Elvis spent his first-ever holiday, consisting of three weeks, mostly in Biloxi with June Juanico and her parents. It was a good time for Elvis, even though he had to be careful to avoid the fans who would turn up in their hundreds when they discovered he was in the area. Hence, in the home movie taken at the time, he does look most relaxed when they are out at sea on fishing trips!

When he returned to Memphis after this holiday, Elvis attended the Blackwood Brothers All Night Singing, joining them on stage to sing *Jesus filled my Every Need* and *You'll Never Walk Alone.*

June accompanied him on his August concert tour and saw how exhausted he became, not only from his high-energy performances on stage but also dealing with adoring fans. She also noticed that he was changing, becoming easily angered that his Hollywood career wasn't turning out to be what he had hoped. Perhaps if Elvis had not been so exhausted by the concert tours, he may have had the energy to control his anger. However, forces were at work to try to control him, and he could feel it.

June and Elvis stopped seeing each other by October 1956. Although June loved Elvis, he wanted her to be with him all the time, but she did not want to be following him around the country with all the hoopla that accompanied his public appearances, and which had invaded his private life.

In March, the next year Elvis sent a telegram to June to ask her to meet his train in a brief layover in New Orleans. It is then that she told him that she was engaged to be married. Over the next twenty years, they did keep in touch, although rarely. June attended a concert, and they had some telephone conversations.

June told how, on 4th July 1977, she had a visit from her girlfriend, Pat, whom she hadn't seen for 10 years, someone who had shared lots of her Elvis adventures, and who had kept more in touch with Elvis. This friend, as well as June, was very concerned about Elvis, noticing how much he had deteriorated. Pat was particularly concerned not only about Elvis' physical health, but also his mental health. She knew that the upcoming 14th August was the anniversary of Elvis' mother's death, and that Elvis was now 42 years old, the same age at which his mother died. She felt that Elvis would find this time particularly difficult and that she and June should go to Memphis to see if they could help at all. This was not possible for June, but she did want to see Elvis again, and her teenage daughter was nagging her to go to a concert and hopefully get backstage to meet Elvis. June saw that Elvis was coming to Biloxi for the dedication and opening of the Coast Coliseum in November of that year and she and her daughter had planned to attend. As we know, sadly, that did not come to pass.

One thing I noticed in June's book was something I had not come across before, which is Elvis describing how he felt when singing on stage. June had noticed that Elvis seemed to be a different person when he was on stage, and he agreed. He told her, "It's like your whole body gets goosebumps, but it's not goosebumps, it's not a chill either. It's more like a surge of electricity that goes right through you." This reminds me of how Billy Elliot, in that wonderful film of the same name, describes how he feels when he is dancing. Almost the same words, certainly the same experience.

Elvis Continues to be Vilified

In August 1956, in Jacksonville, Florida, Elvis was booked in for six concerts. By now he was seen as a dangerous rebel, so much so that local Juvenile Judge Marion W Gooding spoke with Elvis saying that he would have him arrested if he swivelled his hips while performing. He also told people that "this savage and his music is undermining the youth of America." Elvis was very polite and respectful of the judge but couldn't understand why his stage performance was viewed with such distaste, even horror. He complied with the judge's order and at the next night's performance he toned down his act, hardly moving his body and just wiggling his little finger, explaining what had happened with the judge and asking, "What's wrong with that?" Apparently, the crowd still went wild, most probably appreciating the humour, but also just being wooed by Elvis.

The Church also had an opinion of Elvis and rock 'n' roll. Young people at the Murray Hill Methodist Church in Jacksonville heard Elvis denounced in a sermon entitled "Hot-rods, Reefers, and Rock and Roll." Elsewhere in town, the Rev. Robert Gray, pastor of Trinity Baptist Church, offered up prayers for Elvis' salvation after declaring that the singer had "achieved a new low in spiritual degeneracy." Rev. Gray went on to say, "If he were offered his salvation tonight, he would probably say, 'No thanks, I'm on the top.'"

Despite the objections of religious and community leaders, young fans packed into the shows. All six performances in two days at the Florida Theatre sold out, with 2,200 Jacksonville teenagers at each one, separated from the stage by a line of uniformed policemen.

Elvis later confessed frustration at the Baptist preacher's actions. "I think that hurt me more than anything else at first. This man was supposed to be a religious leader, yet he acted that way without ever knowing who I was or what I was like." Elvis said. "I believe in the Bible. I believe that all good things come from God, I don't believe I'd sing the way I do if God hadn't wanted me to. My voice is God's will, not mine."

Hollywood Calls

On 16th August, Elvis flew out to LA (Los Angeles) to start on his first film, "The Reno Brothers," which was eventually renamed "Love Me Tender."

In his screen debut, Elvis sang four songs and died at the end. This was a Western film located in Texas after the Civil War. The sons in the family had conflicting politics, and Elvis and one of his brothers were in love with the same woman.

Elvis had thought that this would be a straight acting part, without songs. The script had no songs, however, the producers knew that Elvis' singing was a hit parade success, so decided to include songs in the script, much to Elvis' disappointment.

Debra Paget, who played the love interest in the film, began her motion picture career at the age of 15. While "Love Me Tender" was Elvis' first film, it was her twentieth picture. Her first meeting with Elvis was on The Milton Berle Show on 5th June 1956. "Although I usually don't form an opinion of a person until I have met him," she explained, "frankly, I looked forward to my first meeting with Elvis Presley with mixed emotions. I'd heard and read a lot about this new young singing sensation from Tennessee – and most of it was not complimentary."

However, Elvis impressed her from the very beginning. "The first thing I recall was the way he greeted us. When Mr Berle introduced us, Elvis grabbed my hand firmly and said, 'I'm glad to meet you, Miss Paget.' Then he shook my mother's hand with equal vigour, excused himself, and a couple of minutes later came back with a chair for her. We were together for only a couple of hours, but sometimes you can learn more about a person in a short span of time than in weeks of seeing one another constantly. I felt I did. From the very beginning, Elvis impressed me as a pleasant, sincere, obliging young man."

She said that when the cast of "Love Me Tender" learned that Elvis had been given a starring role in the film, at first, she sensed a great deal of apprehension on the set. But soon, Elvis won over the cast and crew as he had her. "From then on my family and I saw a lot of Elvis," she explained, "at the studio, on location, when he came over to our house for a swim on Sundays. I grew to understand him better. I also found out some things which really surprised me."

One of the things that surprised her was Elvis' sensitivity. "At first, I'd been under the impression that he was quite indifferent to the attacks made on him for the way he sings, dresses, wears his sideburns, and all the other comments. But he isn't. Not that he'd admit the fact easily to a stranger. I could tell he was deeply hurt when his performances were criticized, or when he was threatened with being banned from certain cities." She mentioned that some of her friends had asked her if Elvis had "romantic appeal." She told them, "I'm convinced he has, and that it will come across on the screen. It is certainly felt by those who meet him, although I don't think Elvis himself is conscious of it. He certainly never talks about his 'conquests.'"

Debra portrayed her own relationship with Elvis as being more family-oriented than romantic. "From the time he first came to the house," she recalled, "my folks have considered Elvis a member of the Paget clan – a feeling which, I believe, he reciprocated. I had the feeling that our closely-knit family life must resemble his own to quite an extent. And I could tell how much he missed his parents."

Elvis Meets a Soulmate

It was during the filming of "Love Me Tender" that Elvis met and became good friends with fellow actor, Nick Adams. Nick was four years older than Elvis and had had some roles in TV series and films including a small part in "Rebel Without a Cause" with James Dean. Elvis, being new to Hollywood, was pleased to have a friend with whom he could share his joys and concerns.

In his book, "The Rebel and the King," Nick relates his friendship with Elvis. As with many others, Elvis won over Nick by immediately showing interest in him. He remembered some of the parts he had seen Nick play in films, especially "Rebel Without a Cause" (which Nick refers to as 'Rebel'). Elvis, who loved the film and had watched it many times, commented on how much he had enjoyed a particular scene in the film, which he recalled in exact detail, saying what Nick had said and done. He thought Nick's acting was "real good."

Nick said of Elvis, "He was real down to earth and sincere and humble and he sure made me feel good telling me those things, because even my own family didn't notice me in 'Rebel.' I didn't think anyone had ever noticed me in 'Rebel' but standing opposite me was the hottest box office attraction in thirty years and he had remembered me and was telling me what a good job I had done."

Nick also thought that Elvis was a genuine guy, and I believe that he summed up what I have discovered in my research about Elvis, in this statement, "After you have been talking to Elvis for five minutes, you feel as though you have known him all your life and you feel good inside. He makes you feel comfortable, and he makes you feel like you belong. You never feel for one minute that you are talking to the most famous personality in showbusiness. You are talking to a nice guy from Tennessee who wants to know you. He doesn't have any phony airs about him or any conceit. He looks dead at you when he speaks and when you have something to say he listens intently."

Nick was amazed how Elvis, although he was hurt by the criticism, could forgive all the people who were vilifying him. Elvis responded to this by telling him that he could overlook it all "because God knows my heart and I can say [quoting Jesus] 'forgive them Lord for they know not what they do.'" Nick spent a lot of time with Elvis during that month of filming and they talked about many things, including the fact that they were both brought up in poverty. Elvis encouraged Nick to keep trying in his acting efforts as he could "make it" someday. Adding, again quoting Jesus, "Have faith in God because if you have the faith of a mustard seed, you can move a mountain."

Elvis told Nick that in 1953, after seeing his father sitting on the bed with his head in his hands because of their financial difficulties, he asked God to help him so he could help his father and that he "sincerely believed that a miracle would happen and sure enough it did!" That was the time in 1953, immediately after his graduation when Elvis went to the Tennessee Employment Security Office, desperate for a job, saying that he "must help his father work off financial obligation." He said that God answered his prayer so fast (August the next year) and he still didn't know where it all started.

Elvis said that he believed that "all good things come from God" and that when something good happens to them or something good is given to them, if people would just stop and think and thank God, saying "God, thank you for this wonderful blessing you have bestowed upon me," then they would have more blessings. He also said, "If tomorrow should it all [the success] come to an end, I wouldn't stop thanking Him, and I would go the rest of my life telling people what a wonderful blessing He once gave me." Elvis was very much aware that he could lose all of it, but until that day came, he would "go on enjoying it, doing my dead level best to give people something to hear and something to see that they might enjoy."

Elvis then went on to say how he thought the world could be a better place. "The thought is always bearing in mind there is a God somewhere watching you, watching every move you make. And if I do something wrong, He knows it. And somewhere, sometime, I will answer for my wrongdoings. And I don't think that I haven't done anything wrong, because somewhere along in life everybody gets off track, but it's their duty to their God and their loved ones to get back on the right track and ask for forgiveness for their mistakes. And that's why it kind of hurts me when they say I have contributed to juvenile delinquency. Because if more kids who want to do something bad, if they would only think along these same lines then maybe it would change their whole outlook on life. And maybe they would have more hopes of someday having something and being somebody and feeling that they belong. Then they wouldn't want to get into any trouble and then there would be much less juvenile delinquency. Because if I can say or do anything that might change some kid's outlook on life then I feel as though I have contributed something in the short span of life which we all live."

Nick's response to this outpouring was to realise what a wonderful person Elvis was, and to feel a little ashamed himself, so much so that he started to get on the right track again. Without too much effort, Nick was able to give up swearing, drinking and other bad habits. He said, "Little by little because of Elvis' influence on me. I've cut out all my old bad habits." Nick and Elvis remained good friends until, sadly, Nick died in 1968. His death certificate has the cause of death as "paraldehyde and promazine intoxication," both being prescription drugs. There was no alcohol in his blood. Since then, the American Medical Association has warned these two types of drugs should never be taken together.

Elvis Becomes More Acceptable

The 9th of September 1956 was Elvis' first performance on The Ed Sullivan Show. So far, Elvis had already performed on national television shows like the Dorsey Brothers' Stage Show, The Milton Berle Show and The Steve Allen Show. However, Elvis had not yet been booked on the country's most popular variety show, The Ed Sullivan Show. Elvis had a reputation among conservative leaders and parents for his performances, which they often labelled as inappropriate or even dangerous. Elvis was simply unlike any other performer they'd ever seen, and they were concerned. For this reason, Ed Sullivan initially refused to book him on his show as he wanted to distance himself from the harsh criticism that Elvis was receiving.

It was a surprise, then, when Ed announced in the summer of 1956 that Elvis would perform not just once, but three times on his show. Ed had watched Elvis' career blossom and knew that he would pull in high ratings if he allowed Elvis to perform. Elvis was to be paid $50,000 for all three performances – an unprecedented amount at the time.

A month before Elvis' appearance on his show, Ed suffered from an almost fatal automobile crash that left him hospitalised for weeks and unable to recover from his injuries quickly enough. Therefore, he was not in the studios that day for filming. British actor Charles Laughton filled in and served as host for Elvis' debut performance. The show was filmed in Hollywood rather than its usual New York as Elvis was in the middle of filming "Love Me Tender."

The show was a huge success with 60 million people, 82.6 per cent of the entire television audience, tuning in to watch Elvis perform *Don't Be Cruel, Love Me Tender, Ready Teddy,* and a few verses of *Hound Dog.* Elvis ended his performance by saying "Until we meet again, may God bless you as He has blessed me."

Elvis' second appearance on the Ed Sullivan show in October was preceded by a press conference where he was asked about his influence on teenagers. He said, "My Bible tells me that what he sows he will also reap, and if I am sowing evil and wickedness it will catch up with me." He then added, "If I did think I was bad for people I would go back to driving a truck, I really mean this."

The Battle Against a Deadly Disease

Before his performance on the Ed Sullivan show, millions of viewers watched Elvis get his polio vaccine jab. It made headlines and, critically, reportedly helped convince teens and young adults – people who thought they weren't at risk – that they needed a vaccine too, to help defeat the deadly disease.

Polio, also known as Poliomyelitis or Infantile Paralysis, was a viral disease that surged in the US during the 1940s, killing thousands of children and leaving tens of thousands paralyzed. The disease was a terrible threat to the country's children – in 1954, nearly 40,000 were infected, and 1,450 died. Many who survived were paralysed and confined to "iron lungs" which pumped breath into their bodies because their own lungs had failed. Quarantines were imposed as outbreaks appeared, parents were urged to keep their children home and travel between cities was curtailed. This likely helped slow this highly contagious disease, which was eventually eradicated after Dr Jonas Salk developed a vaccine in 1955.

The National Foundation for Infantile Paralysis, now known as the March of Dimes, decided to make polio their number one issue, at once emphasizing its danger and its curability. The organisation was founded in 1938 by President Franklin D. Roosevelt, who had contracted polio and was paralysed from the waist down. The name March of Dimes was coined by the comedian Eddie Cantor who encouraged "all persons, even the children, to show our President that they are with him in this battle against this disease by sending in a dime [a 10-cent coin], or several dimes to the White House." Bags of mail arrived, and the final amount raised was $268,000. Elvis would later often promote the March of Dimes fund raising.

After funding Jonas Salk's polio vaccine, which eradicated polio in most of the world, the organisation expanded its focus to the prevention of birth defects and infant mortality. In 2005, as preterm birth emerged as the leading cause of death for children worldwide, research and prevention of premature birth became the organisation's primary focus.

Birthplace Celebration

On 26th September, Elvis performed at the Mississippi–Alabama Fair and Dairy Show in Tupelo – the same place where he performed in public for the first time at the age of 10 when he had entered a talent contest at the fair, singing *Old Shep* and finishing in fifth place. Elvis and his band had performed at the fairgrounds in 1955 alongside artists such as Webb Pierce and Wanda Jackson, but he wasn't the star of the show.

When he returned just a year later in 1956 to do the "Homecoming" concerts at the Tupelo Fairgrounds, this East Tupelo "poor boy" had recorded and released his debut album, performed several times on national television and was filming his first movie. Elvis was Tupelo's most famous hometown boy, and the town wanted to celebrate him.

The celebrations included a parade through downtown Tupelo, which Elvis didn't attend as his manager, the Colonel, feared for Elvis' safety in such a big crowd. But the town enjoyed the parade anyway and encouraged participants to create Elvis-themed floats.

Elvis performed two shows that day. Elvis and his parents, his Memphis girlfriend Barbara Hearn, and Nick Adams all drove down from Memphis for the shows. Elvis wore a beautiful handmade blue velvet shirt for the daytime show and a red one for the evening show. These were a gift from actress Natalie Wood who knew Elvis in Hollywood and who had them made by her dressmaker. As with many of Elvis' belongings which have brought high prices at auctions, the blue velvet shirt, or one claimed to be that shirt was bought in the late 90s, at an auction in Christie's of London, by Elvis fan and British comedian, Frank Skinner, who paid £11,200. Frank did some research to authenticate his purchase, however, the conclusion was that it was Elvis' shirt, but not the one worn at the Tupelo concert.

Elvis, backed by his band and the Jordanaires, sang his hits such as *Hound Dog* and *Don't Be Cruel* to thousands of fans. As usual, many fans rushed to the stage, somehow defying the massive security team. Elvis encouraged them to be safe – which they were – and no one was hurt.

Tupelo Mayor James L Ballard gave Elvis a key to the city, which was in the shape of a guitar and featured his initials and the words "Welcome Home, Tupelo, Miss." Mississippi Governor J P Coleman presented Elvis with a certificate and called him "America's number one entertainer in the world of popular music."

Elvis told the Mayor of Tupelo: "I saw the house I was born in and 15 acres for sale. I want you to take this check back and put it to build a park for the kids of East Tupelo."

Elvis' generous habit of giving to others throughout his lifetime is a result of his upbringing and Christian beliefs, following the words of the apostle Paul, "You yourselves know that these hands of mine have ministered to my own needs and those of my companions. In everything, I showed you that by this kind of hard work we must help the weak, remembering the words of the Lord Jesus Himself: 'It is more blessed to give than to receive.'" (Acts 20: 34&35)

Consequently, when Elvis returned the following year to do a show on 27th September 1957, he donated approximately $14,000 for a youth recreation centre to be built in Tupelo.

Elvis spoke to the press in between the performances, thanking the city for honouring him and talking about his upcoming movie career. "I love it here," Elvis told reporters. "I'll come back as often as I can." And he did.

There is a home movie video showing Elvis and his friends visiting Tupelo, four years later, trying to hold up the fallen sign for the future Elvis Presley Youth Recreation Center. The building work on both the Elvis Presley Park and Youth Center construction had not even started. It wasn't until Elvis made a few phone calls, in February 1961, that things changed.

He called Mayor James Ballard and told him that if dirt wasn't moving by the end of the month there was going to be hell to pay. As a result, the next day the work started on the Elvis Presley Park and the construction of the Elvis Presley Youth Center soon followed.

The Youth Center had a pool, playground and picnic area, and school dances were held there. It was situated next to the birthplace home at 306 Old Saltillo Road (now 306 Elvis Presley Drive). When it was no longer viable as a youth centre, it was converted into the Elvis Presley Birthplace Museum and shop. Meanwhile, during the 1960s, Elvis fans began visiting the grounds of the birthplace to see the house where Elvis was born.

Over the years, Elvis visited Tupelo more often than local residents realised. When Elvis and his future wife Priscilla were dating, he took her to Tupelo several times to show her around where he grew up and went to school.

A New Girlfriend

In early December 1956, Elvis was back in Memphis with girlfriend Marilyn Evans who was a 19-year-old showgirl dancer at the New Frontier Casino in

Las Vegas, whom Elvis met whilst he was performing there. He asked her for a date, to which she agreed, and found that this gorgeous being was sweet and down to earth. Marilyn decided to tell her mother that she was dating Elvis in order to head off any trouble in case her mother saw reports of her relationship with this most "undesirable" young man. After a telephone conversation with Elvis, Marilyn's mother felt that Elvis was "a very nice young man," so Marilyn and Elvis spent time together, visiting places in Vegas, just having a good time in each other's company.

When Elvis asked Marilyn to visit him in Memphis and meet his family, she knew that she needed to get her mother's permission, which she did, though only after her mother had spoken with Gladys Presley on the phone.

In Memphis, Elvis and Marilyn spent their days riding motorcycles, going out to eat and watching rented movies at Elvis' house. "He was relaxed. He was comfortable there," she recalled. And at night she slept at his home, though "not with him. He was extremely honourable."

The Million Dollar Quartet

On 4th December, Carl Perkins, accompanied by his brothers Clayton and Jay and drummer W S "Fluke" Holland, went into Sun Record Studios in Memphis to cut some new material. Sam Phillips, the owner of Sun Records, brought in singer and piano man, Jerry Lee Lewis, still unknown outside Memphis, to play the piano on the Perkin's session.

Sometime in the early afternoon, Elvis, now at RCA, dropped in to pay a casual visit, accompanied by Marilyn. The musicians had just finished a session and were having a break when Elvis and Marilyn entered. After chatting with Sam Philips in the control room, Elvis listened to the playback of the Perkins' session, which he liked. Then he went into the studio to chat with the guys, and from this came an impromptu session. Sam Phillips left the tapes running to "capture the moment" as a souvenir and for posterity. This became known as The Million Dollar Quartet.

The gathered musicians at Sun Studio that day started by singing some of Elvis' songs, then included other popular songs. However, the highlight to them, I believe because of the comments they made and the "feel" of the songs, was the gospel songs they sang, starting with, *When The Saints Go Marchin' In* followed by *Softly and Tenderly, When God Dips His Love in My Heart, Just a Little Talk with Jesus, You Gotta Walk That Lonesome Valley, I Shall*

Not Be Moved, Peace In The Valley, Down By the Riverside, Farther Along, Blessed Jesus (Hold My Hand), On the Jericho Road, I Just Can't Make It By Myself, I Hear a Sweet Voice Calling and *Keeper of the Key.*

Elvis led on most of the songs, and during this gospel section, there is handclapping, whooping and other expressions of the joy of the Lord. You can hear comments such as "This is fun!" and "I like it", and after some lovely harmonising on *Keeper of the Key,* "beautiful." Someone also commented, "We ought to get up a quartet," which they had: Elvis Presley, Carl Perkins on guitar, Jerry Lee Lewis on piano and the drummer W S Holland. The photo, on the subsequent album of the session called the "Million Dollar Quartet," shows Elvis, Carl Perkins, Jerry Lee Lewis, and Johnny Cash. This came about because Johnny Cash popped in later, as he wanted to listen to the Carl Perkins' recordings. Sam saw a photo opportunity, so he called the local press photographer. As this was not an official recording, it was not released till several years later. In 1969, Sun Records was bought by Shelby Singleton He searched the Sun catalogue of more than 10,000 hours of tapes. He licensed much of the Sun catalogue to the English Charly label for reissue in Europe. As a result, a portion of the session came to light. This was issued in Europe in 1981 as Charly/Sun LP #1006 *The Million Dollar Quartet,* and it contained seventeen tracks, focusing on gospel/spiritual music from the session.

It is Not Only White Teenagers Who Like Elvis

Three nights after this Sun session, Elvis was invited to attend the WDIA radio station's Revue which was held every year to raise money for their Good Will Fund which was established to help "needy Negro children." This revue, held at the Ellis Auditorium, was for and by Black people. The headliners that year included Ray Charles and B B King and there was a gospel section featuring the Happy Land Blind Boys and the Spirit of Memphis Quartet. This quartet was a very popular, high-energy gospel group which continued to record throughout the '60s but, by the '70s, had all but retired. They were poised for a major comeback when they were scheduled to record some tunes with Elvis in 1977. However, Elvis was unable to do that because he was too ill.

During the show, Elvis watched from the wings as the organisers knew that if Elvis was featured during the programme, chaos may ensue. So, he made a non-singing appearance at the end of the show, and chaos ensued anyway. One report from the Pittsburgh Courier stated that "A thousand black, brown and beige teenage girls in the audience blended their alto and soprano voices in one wild crescendo that rent the rafter and then took off like scalded cats in the direction of Elvis. It took some time, and several white cops to quell the melee and protect Elvis." Apparently, many of those on Beale Street wondered how it was that coloured girls would be so enthusiastic over a Memphis white boy when they hardly let out a squeak over B B King, a Memphis coloured boy. How indeed?

Elvis Will Not Be Dissuaded

Elvis decided he would sing one of his mother's favourite songs, *Peace in the Valley*, on his third and final appearance on The Ed Sullivan Show on 6th January 1957. Also, he was filmed from the waist up only, to prevent viewers being offended at his gyrations, which he had toned down anyway for the Ed Sullivan shows.

The show's producers did not want Elvis to sing a gospel song on national television, but Elvis insisted: "No, I told my mother that I was going to do *Peace in the Valley* for her, and I'm going to do it." Ed Sullivan supported his decision and introduced the song describing Elvis' plea for people to donate to the charity Operation Safe Haven, which was a refugee relief and resettlement operation executed by the United States following the Hungarian Revolution of 1956. In a subtle attempt to explain Elvis' choice to sing a gospel song, Sullivan said Elvis was going to "sing a song he feels that this is sort of in the mood that he'd like to create." Ed also, at the end of the show, told the audience, with Elvis by his side, that Elvis was a "real decent, fine boy ... We want to say that we've never had a pleasanter experience with a big name than we've had with you."

The network's hesitation with Elvis singing gospel was proved wrong by the positive response to the performance – one writer described it as "terrific". This prompted RCA to support a four-song gospel EP called "Peace in the Valley" which was released a few months later in April. The songs recorded were *(There Will Be) Peace in the Valley (For Me,) It is no Secret (What God Can Do), I Believe* and *Take My Hand, Precious Lord.* This EP initially sold over half a million copies (and ultimately going Platinum), prompting RCA to encourage Elvis to do his first gospel album a few years later. We can conclude from this that going for the gospel is not harmful but is of benefit. It is interesting to note that Elvis was awarded only three Grammys for his recordings, and they were all for his gospel music.

Back To Hollywood

In February 1957, Elvis started work on his second film, "Loving You" He played a small-town country boy who is discovered and makes it big as a singer (a fictionalised account of his own career). His mother and father are seen as extras in the audience.

Hal Kanter, the film's director, described Elvis as pleasant, courteous, and talented, with a lovely unsophisticated sense of humour and a native shrewdness. As he got to know Elvis, the more he saw in him "the sweetness, the poetry and vulnerability that was the true essence of his character."

In Hal Wallis' "Producer to the Stars" biography, Bernard F Dick evaluated Elvis' co-star, Lizabeth Scott's, and Elvis' work in "Loving You" as follows:

"But what was even more impressive about Lizabeth's performance was her rapport with Elvis, which revealed deep respect for him and his talent. Elvis' character, falling in love with Lizabeth's might have seemed strained in the script, yet Lizabeth and Elvis interacted so well with each other that theirs became the natural attraction of a protégé toward a patron."

Elvis' love interest in the film was played by Dolores Hart. Billed as the "next Grace Kelly", she was just 19 when she made her movie debut in "Loving You". She said, "I had no idea who Elvis Presley was. When I first met him, he was just a charming young boy with long sideburns. He couldn't have been more gracious. He jumped to his feet and said, 'Good afternoon, Miss Dolores.' He and Gary Cooper were the only ones in Hollywood who called me that."

She was very much aware of his sexuality saying, "Elvis has a way of being that, in itself was very innocent, even though from the waist down there was serious invitation." Elvis wanted to date her, but although she liked him, she refused, giving the reason that her 5am calls to set every morning made going out at night impossible.

A Difficult Confrontation

On 23rd March, Elvis attended an All-Night Singing at the Ellis Auditorium in Memphis. This couldn't have come at a better time for Elvis as he must have needed something to give him peace. The previous day, in downtown Memphis, Elvis was accused of pulling a gun on Private Hershel Nixon, a 19-year-old Marine, who claimed that Elvis insulted his wife. Two days later Elvis sent a rambling six-page telegram to Private Nixon after which they met up and the incident was amicably resolved. The telegram, containing an apology and explanation, describes some of the difficulties Elvis had been encountering and his philosophy about them, as follows:

TO: PFC HERSCHEL NIXON – NAVAL AIR TECHNICAL TRAINING CENTER

I read in the paper that you wanted an apology, and I am willing to give you an apology. In fact I think we owe each other one. The whole thing is kind of uncalled for. I would like to straighten out another rumor that started out there a few months ago. Somebody started the rumor that I didn't like marines or sailors and it was for a while that every time I got out, there was some marine or sailor that tried to cause trouble with me. And also somebody started a rumor in Mexico that I didn't like Mexicans and a lot of Mexicans got mad at me and then here in Memphis the rumor got out that I didn't like colored people and God knows that I have never said that I didn't like anybody. It's just that rumors like that get started and there is nothing I can do about it. The marines and the navy and the army and the air force protect our country and they have been around for a long time protecting us so who am I to say that I don't like anybody because God created everybody equal, and I would never say that I don't like anybody. I'm not saying this because I'm afraid, heaven knows I am not a least bit afraid, but I just don't want anybody thinking I said things like that when I never even thought about it. I got a lucky break in life, and I am very thankful but there are a few people who want to take shots at me. The majority of the people all over the world are very nice. But there are a few who want to prove something. I have talked my way out of trouble so many times that I couldn't even count them. Not because I was afraid, but just because I was always the type of person that I never did believe in fighting and all that kind of stuff unless I thought it was absolutely necessary. And about the instance the other night and about the gun. The gun is a Hollywood prop gun and I brought it home because a lot of people ask me about how movies are made and about the guns and so on. I had about six of those guns with me and I was showing them to some people, and you called me over there. Many times there have been people who come up to me and stick out their hands to shake hands and they hit me. And I have had guys come up and ask for autographs and hit me and take off for no reason at all. I never laid eyes on them before. I said many, actually there were very few, but I have had it happen to me, so when you and your friends called me off the other night and you started that stuff about me bumping into your wife, I didn't know what you

82

were going to do. I'm just like you, if a guy can do something to protect himself
he should do it. Again I say I am sorry the whole thing came up. I hope you
have the best of luck in the future and I would like to add that some of my best
friends are marines and some are sailors and the army and the air force and
so on. And I think that they are all great outfits because if it wasn't for them
and if it wasn't for God, where would our country be.

So long, Elvis Presley

Sam Phillip's Faith

On 20th April, Elvis, and Yvonne Lime, whom he had met on the set of "Loving
You" and had invited to spend time with him in Memphis, attended an Easter
Eve party at Sam Philips' home. The night ended with early morning breakfast
and gospel songs sung by the pool.

Sam Phillips had a strong Christian faith, which is revealed on a recording of
him having a discussion with Jerry Lee Lewis. In this recorded conversation,
and I use the word conversation lightly because Jerry Lee spends most of the
time shouting excitedly and interrupting Sam, whereas Sam spoke calmly and
strongly – when he got the opportunity, Sam tells Jerry, "Jesus Christ is just as
real today as then."

Jerry Lee was brought up as a Christian and almost became a preacher himself,
enrolling at the Southwestern Bible Institute in Texas. But rock 'n' roll got the
better of him. He was concerned that as he had turned away from the church
and embraced rock 'n' roll that he had the devil in him. Sam was trying to
encourage him about his faith. Even in his later years, according to a report in
the Guardian newspaper in 2015, Jerry Lee continued to be worried about
whether he is going to heaven or hell. Of course, he needn't have as if he was
a Christian in the sense that he accepted Jesus as his Saviour, he would know
that he was going to heaven, even if he had done wrong in his life, for Jesus
gave him a new life.

The Slippery Slope

By now, Elvis was feeling the slippery slope. As he began recording and
touring and making films in Hollywood, he was no longer able to regularly
attend church, but clearly felt the needed to visit his home church. On Easter
Sunday, after the party at Sam Phillips' house, Elvis and his girlfriend,
Yvonne, attended a service at the First Assemblies of God church. He passed

a note to one of the ushers to give to his pastor, Rev Hamill, to ask him if he could meet him in his office after the service. Elvis was shown to the office and waited for Rev. Hamill, who recalled, "When I walked into my office, Elvis was sitting down, but he quickly got up. He said 'Pastor I am the most miserable young man you have ever seen. I have got more money than I can ever spend. I have thousands of fans out there and a lot of people who call themselves my friends. But I am miserable. I am not doing a lot of things you taught me, and I am doing the things that you have taught me not to do.'

"I could see Elvis was terribly troubled, so I sat and prayed with him for well over an hour. He prayed, we prayed. He prayed and wept. He asked me to forgive him for his sins. He didn't say what they were, and I didn't know what they were.

"He had brought a little Hollywood starlet [Yvonne Lime] and a couple of his fellows with him and all during this time they stayed outside. The girl had only recently become a Christian and my wife visited with her while Elvis was in my office."

Rev. Hamill wanted to help Elvis, so told him he would find the address of a pastor friend of his in Hollywood, to whom he could go in times of trouble. Elvis did receive the address, but never got in touch with the pastor. Rev. Hamill heard later that when Elvis returned to Hollywood, the Colonel read him the riot act, telling him that it was OK if he had feelings about religion and sang a few religious songs, but that he could not get real religion as he had a lot of contracts to fulfil.

Rev. Hamill believed that was when Elvis decided to focus on his career rather than his faith. He did see Elvis several more times, once when he took Gladys' funeral service in 1958 when he spent a lot of time one-to-one counselling Elvis. He said that, later, Elvis stopped seeking his advice. He felt that it may have been because when Elvis came to ask him to perform the marriage of his widowed father to Dee Stanley, he refused as his church would not allow him to marry a divorced person. He was told that Elvis was deeply hurt by his decision, though he didn't think Elvis ever fully understood the philosophical ramifications. (Interestingly, most reports about this say that Elvis did not approve of his father's remarriage. However, perhaps he was being gracious, wanting the best for this father and, therefore, a minister whom he admired and respected to conduct the wedding.)

Elvis had also more publicly expressed his dissatisfaction at the way he was perceived by some, in an interview with Photoplay magazine in which he said, "I never expected to be anyone important. Maybe I am not now, but whoever I am, whatever I become will be what God has chosen for me. Some people I know can't figure out how Elvis Presley happened. I don't blame them for wondering that. I sometimes wonder it myself. But no matter what I do, I don't forget about God. I feel he is watching every move I make and in a way it's good for me. I'll never feel comfortable taking strong drink and I never feel easy smoking a cigarette. I just don't think those things are right for me. I just want to let a few people know that the way I live, is by doing what I think God wants me to do. I want someone to understand."

The Strain is Beginning to Show

In May, Elvis started work on the film "Jailhouse Rock." Elvis' character, Vince, learns to play the guitar while in prison and becomes a star (with a conniving manager) when he gets out. Then, a former cellmate comes calling. The film includes the famous scene of Elvis dancing to the title song, which dancer Gene Kelly watched and applauded during the filming.

Elvis was used to recording all his songs, including the soundtracks, in a recording studio. However, for these next sessions RCA, apparently in order to save money, wanted him to record on the movie lot soundstage. Elvis was not comfortable with this as he liked the intimacy and the quality of the sound bouncing off the close walls of a studio whereas the soundstage was a huge room. Elvis agreed, though he felt he needed time to warm up and get in the mood, so he sat at the piano and started singing gospel songs. At 10am he had the Jordanaires come and sing around him. By noon they were still singing gospel and not a single soundtrack song had been recorded.

They stopped for lunch and, when they all returned to the soundstage, Elvis headed straight for the piano and started to sing another gospel song. He was puzzled when the Jordanaires did not join him and so he asked them why that was. At their reply that the studio people had told them not to sing gospel with him because they wanted him to get on with the session, Elvis exploded. He insisted that they join him, which they did and sang gospel for another four hours until it was time to finish for the day. Again, not a single soundtrack song had been recorded.

According to George Klein, who had joined Elvis' travelling companions in March that year, Elvis was in a black mood for the rest of the evening, which

85

expressed itself by him trashing one of the dens in the Presidential Suite of the Beverly Wilshire Hotel where he was staying. The room, as well as beautiful paintings and objets d'art, contained a small pool table. Elvis, who was very good at pool, directed all his shots, not to go into the billiard table pockets, but to fly off the table and smash anything breakable in the room, including a wall-length mirror. Finally, he turned over the billiard table and smashed as much of that as he could before retiring to his room.

His companions watched in horror as they knew that Elvis had a bit of a temper, but none of them had ever seen anything like this. They ran out of the room to avoid the flying broken glass and, being very concerned, called the Colonel who told them not to tell anyone about the incident. The Colonel then approached the hotel management and offered to pay for all the damage.

The next day, Elvis turned up at the soundstage, and to the dismay of the studio staff sat at the piano and started playing a gospel song. However, after just a few songs he was ready and went on to put in a full day of hard work and finish recording the soundtrack to "Jailhouse Rock."

Just a few days after completing production on this film, the actress Judy Tyler, who had played her first big role as Elvis' love interest in the movie, was killed with her husband in a gruesome car accident in Wyoming. She was only 24. Elvis was devastated at hearing the news. He asked George Klein to join him as he drove around Memphis all day on 4th July trying to cope with the loss. According to George, Elvis "kept talking about how good a person Judy was. He drove and talked for hours reminiscing about every moment he'd shared with her."

"Nothing has hurt me as bad in my life," Elvis said publicly about Judy's death. "All of us boys really loved that girl … I don't believe I can stand to see that movie we made together now, just don't believe I can."

Elvis had considered going to the Tylers' funeral but decided against it in order not to disrupt the service. Although he took his parents to a private screening of the film, many believe that Elvis never watched the film again because of Judy.

Time To Move On

Because it was not tenable for the Presleys to stay in Audubon Drive, Elvis bought Graceland, situated in the Southern outskirts of Memphis with plenty of land and more privacy. On 16th May 1957, Vernon and Gladys moved into Graceland while Elvis was still filming in Hollywood.

Graceland is an eight-bedroom mansion designed and built in 1939 by Dr. and Mrs. Moore in the Whitehaven District of Memphis. It was named after Grace Toof, Mrs. Moore's aunt. The house was designed and planned with music in mind for their daughter Ruth Marie who played the piano and harp, and who eventually joined the Memphis Symphony Orchestra. The living rooms were built large enough to hold musical soirees. The Moores moved out in 1957 and, when Elvis went to see the property, it was being used for meetings by Graceland Christian Church. When Elvis moved into Graceland, the Church built another property next door on land given to them by Mrs Moore. Later, the church moved to another part of Memphis and the building now houses the headquarters of Elvis Presley Enterprises Inc. It seems that Elvis could not escape his musical nor his Christian roots; even his new home was a church! It was certainly a haven of rest for Elvis, though most often a hive of activity as Elvis had, by his own choice, his extended family including his parents, grandmother and aunt and some friends living there.

Elvis knew that his mother had worked hard all her life and now he wanted her to rest and be able to buy whatever she wanted, but Gladys, who couldn't do nothing, found this change of lifestyle very difficult. Even though they had had a maid when they lived in Audubon Drive, Gladys still did some of the cooking. When they moved to Graceland they had privacy, but she couldn't buy her own groceries nor go to the movies nor visit the neighbours. They had a maid and a cook but, above all, now that Elvis was away most of the time on concert tours or filming, she missed her beloved son and was concerned for his welfare. She had initially been delighted at the idea of living at Graceland with its 13-acre estate and Elvis had hired a tractor and cleared some land so that she could plant corn, which she did. Elvis also bought her some chickens and she enjoyed feeding them and collecting the eggs. However, she stopped doing that as she had been informed that all this farmyard activity "would not be good for Elvis' image." She told her family and friends, on one of the few times she was able to go to Tupelo, that she was the most miserable woman in the world.

Was Elvis a Racist?

In August 1957, Elvis was accused of racism. Elvis' supposed "racist comment" that is often bandied about but has never been verified, seems highly unlikely considering Elvis' deep love of and involvement with the Black music of the era. The word spread in the African American community that Elvis had declared, either at a personal appearance in Boston or on Edward R Murrow's "Person to Person" television programme, "The only thing Negroes can do for me is buy my records and shine my shoes." Interestingly, Elvis had never been to Boston nor appeared on the Ed Murrow show.

Ironically, back in the mid-50s Elvis was one of the few artists who refused to play to segregated crowds. It is a shame that this champion of racial integration was branded a racist by those whose culture and music he not only admired but also for whom he wanted equality.

On the set of "Jailhouse Rock," Elvis was directly challenged about the statement by reporter Louie Robinson from the prominent Black newspaper, Jet. Elvis replied, "I never said anything like that, and people who know me know that I wouldn't have said it." Satisfied with the sincerity in Elvis' eyes and the tone of his voice, Robinson came away from the meeting convinced it was an outright lie. Robinson found Elvis only guilty of one thing: "judging people regardless of race, colour or creed."

This was just an early tabloid smear of the type that would sadly continue way past his death.

If Elvis was a racist, then I wonder why so many Black people loved and respected him.

Here is what some Black artists who knew Elvis have said:

Little Richard – "Elvis was an integrator. Elvis was a blessing. They wouldn't let Black music through. He opened the door for Black music. I thank God for Elvis Presley. I thank the Lord for sending Elvis to open that door so I could walk down the road, you understand?!"

Sammy Davis Jnr. – "On a scale of one to ten, I would rate Elvis eleven. Early on somebody told me that Elvis was Black. And I said, 'No, he's White but he's down-home.' And that is what it's all about. Not being Black or White, it's being 'down-home' and which part of down-home you come from."

The depth of racism in the USA at that time was conveyed by the fact that, in 1960, even in the supposedly egalitarian atmosphere of the Democratic Convention in Mississippi, Sammy Davis Jnr. was booed while singing the national anthem – an incident that left him near tears. His offence was not only that he was Black, but that he had dared to become engaged to a White woman, actress May Britt. Sammy Davis Jnr. was even asked by the Democrats to postpone his marriage until after the election, which he did. But even then, he was snubbed and asked not to attend President Kennedy's inauguration. Sammy was a long-term friend of Elvis and details like these help our understanding of the political and racist pressure in this era, even on well-known celebrities.

B B King – "I knew Elvis before he was popular. He used to come around and be around us a lot. I can remember once or twice when we met down at Club Handy on Beale Street. Even then, I knew this kid had a tremendous talent. He was a dynamic young boy. His phraseology, his way of looking at a song, was as unique as Sinatra's. I was a tremendous fan and, had Elvis lived, there would have been no end to his inventiveness. Elvis, at heart, was very religious and I think that throughout his career he couldn't help but let it come out and you can hear it. With Elvis there was not a drop of racism in that man and when I say that, believe me, I should know!"

Myrna Smith, a member of the Sweet Inspirations, one of Elvis' backing groups – "I know that no matter what colour I was, Elvis would have loved me the same. As far as he treated me, there was not a racial bone in his body."

Cissy Houston, another member of the Sweet Inspirations – "Elvis loved gospel music. He was raised on it. And he really did know what he was talking about. He was singing gospel all the time – almost anything he did had that flavour. You can't get away from what your roots are."

James Brown – "I wasn't just a fan; I was his brother. Last time I saw Elvis alive was at Graceland. We sang *Old Blind Barnabas* together, a gospel song. I love him and hope to see him in heaven. There'll never be another like that soul brother. We were friends for a long time, for twenty years. And he told me, he'd ride around Memphis, around the streets he'd come up in, all alone at night. Ride around on his motorcycle when he was sure the rest of the world was asleep, just kind of hauntin' them places he hung around in as a kid. He was a country boy."

James Brown was so moved by Elvis' death that he requested, and was allowed, time alone with Elvis' body lying in his coffin at Graceland. James Brown was also the first entertainer to arrive at Elvis' funeral. After Elvis' death he released a heartfelt tribute to his friend – his version of *Love Me Tender*.

Al Green – "Elvis had an influence on everybody with his musical approach. He broke the ice for all of us."

Muhammad Ali – "Elvis was my close personal friend. He came to my Deer Lake training camp about two years before he died. He told us he didn't want nobody to bother us. He wanted peace and quiet and I gave him a cabin in my camp, and nobody even knew it. When the cameras started watching me train, he was up on the hill sleeping in the cabin. Elvis had a robe made for me. I don't admire nobody, but Elvis Presley was the sweetest, most humble and nicest man you'd want to know."

Elvis said about his alleged misappropriation of Black music:

"A lot of people seem to think I started this business. But rock 'n' roll was here a long time before I came along. Nobody can sing that kind of music like coloured people. Let's face it: I can't sing like Fats Domino can. I know that."

It is surprising that Elvis did not have any colour prejudice, as the Southern States were still segregated into the sixties. It is easy to forget that it wasn't until the mid-sixties that The Civil Rights March and Martin Luther King's "I Have a Dream" speech occurred. It is a sad historical fact that even after The Beatles and the new "freedom of the sixties," President Lyndon Johnson still had to force the Civil Rights Act of 1964 through Congress over fierce opposition from Southern legislators. This was the political atmosphere in which Elvis was living.

Early on in Elvis' recording career, it was, of course, his respect and understanding of local Black music and culture that made him and Sam Phillips such kindred spirits. Although obviously rare for that era and the Southern States region, both had beliefs in Black culture and the equality of man. Sam Phillips said, "The lack of prejudice on the part of Elvis Presley had to be one of the biggest things that could have happened to us."

Throughout the years, Elvis always showed his appreciation for his Black musical roots. In his 1954 Sun Studio "Million Dollar Quartet" session Elvis spoke about his admiration of singer Jackie Wilson who Elvis believed had outdone him with a better version of *Don't Be Cruel*. Elvis later acknowledged Wilson's style and footwork when he filmed *Return to Sender* for the film "Girls, Girls, Girls."

Jackie Wilson said, "A lot of people have accused Elvis of stealing the Black man's music, when in fact, almost every Black solo entertainer copied his stage mannerisms from Elvis." When Jackie had a stroke in 1975, leaving him unable to perform and hospitalised, Elvis covered a substantial proportion of his medical bills.

Elvis in Canada

In April 1957, Elvis had concerts in Toronto and Ottawa, the first time he had performed outside of the USA and the only foreign country in which he ever performed publicly. The Montreal booking was cancelled because of a combination of civic concern and pressure from local Roman Catholic officials.

At a press conference before this second visit to Canada in August, Elvis told reporters that his first love was "old-coloured spirituals" and that he knew practically every religious song that had been written.

The show, which was held in a stadium with a temporary stage at one end, had to be stopped twice as fans from the 26,500-strong audience came onto the pitch and surrounded the stage. Eventually, when threatened with the show's cancellation, they calmed down. At the end of the concert, however, when the performers dashed off to escape into their cars, the fans descended onto the stage for souvenirs, including broken bits of wood, music gear and sheet music. The stage was demolished.

Final Concert Tour?

On 26th October, Elvis started a short concert tour in California, performing his first concert in Los Angeles. The press response was "Elvis Presley Will Have To Clean Up His Act Or Go To Jail." He did tone down his act for the next performance after a warning from the LA Vice Squad. This second LA concert was meant to be the last one of the tour, however, Australian booking agent Lee Gordon had been conversing with the Colonel. Gordon was desperate to get Elvis over to Australia and had managed to persuade the Colonel to add two extra dates to this tour, in Hawaii, which he felt was like getting Elvis at least halfway there. Apparently, he often talked with the Colonel about getting Elvis to perform in Australia but was unsuccessful with his persuasions.

The two concerts in Hawaii, in Honolulu and Pearl Harbour, were Elvis' last public performances for a while as the Colonel decided that Elvis would no longer do live performances as it could lead to overexposure.

There was also another reason that he would not be able to perform concerts. On 20th December, Elvis received his draft notice and every branch of the military, except for the marines, bid for his services. He decided on the army who were willing to defer his induction so that he could complete the filming of "King Creole." Elvis had requested a deferment "so that these folks [Paramount Pictures] will not lose so much money with all they have done so far."

First Christmas at Graceland – With Two Special Gifts

This was the first Christmas Elvis spent at his new home, Graceland. Although Elvis stopped going to church regularly in the 1950s, he maintained that he was still a Christian, telling reporters, "All good things come from God. You don't have to go to church to know right from wrong … you can be a Christian so long as you have a Christian heart."

Two of the gifts Elvis received were Bibles and one wonders if his friends and relatives had bought him those to remind him of his Christian faith and inspire him to stay close to the Lord.

Elvis' friend Gary Pepper, who continuously rose above the challenges that he faced in life, not the least of which was cerebral palsy, was also a Christian. Gary had a zest for life and a passion for helping others, values that the two men had in common. Gary and his family and Elvis became acquainted as Gary, a huge fan of Elvis, discovered that Elvis' mother, Gladys, was keeping a scrapbook of Elvis so he began clipping all mentions of Elvis from the newspapers and sending them to her.

Moved by Gary's story, Gladys invited the Pepper family to a Christmas Eve party at Graceland where only close friends and relatives of the Presleys would be in attendance. That is where Gary presented Elvis with the Bible. Gary and his family formed a lovely relationship with the entire Presley family. Elvis even employed Gary's father as a guard at Graceland.

The Bible, given by Gary, was auctioned in Chicago on 16th January 2021 for $9,200.

The Auction notes read:

The white Bible shows signs of heavy use with wear and the interior pages are also heavily marked, creased, and worn. The considerable wear reflects a well-used tome. The Bible has every sign of being well-loved with frequent use. It has Holy Bible embossed in gold in the center and "Elvis A Presley" embossed in gold in the lower right corner of the cover. Under "presented to," the brightly colored title page lists "Elvis Presley / Gary Pepper / Dec. 25, 1957.

The other Bible that we know was given to Elvis this Christmas was from his Uncle Vester and Aunt Clettes Presley.

The Bible, which is black leather-bound with gold lettering, and 1600 pages long, was purchased at an auction in the UK by an American in 2012 for £59,000.

The Auctioneers notes for this are as follows:

The Bible, embossed in gold on a black leather cover has annotations in the margin of the Bible, which was gifted to him by his uncle Vester and Aunt Clettes Presley for Christmas in 1957, reveals something of the depth of Elvis' personal convictions, and give an insight as to how he must have found the criticism he faced at that time. One note reads: "To judge a man by his weakest link or deed is like judging the power of the ocean by one wave."

On another page, Elvis wrote: "For what is a man advantaged if he gain the whole world and lose himself or be cast away."

Elsewhere he jotted: "There is a season for everything, patience will reward you and reveal all answers to your questions." And on another page, he simply prays: "May our souls join the spirit of One God."

Elvis showed his trust in the Lord by jotting below Psalm 11:1: "In the Lord I place my trust and He will guide me." Also, Psalm 43:3 is underlined with a note at the top of the page reading, "Lord send me light to guide me."

Jotted at the bottom of page 670, in reference to Psalm 137, are the words, "Trust in the Lord, not man."

The American owner of the Bible loaned it to The Museum of the Bible in Washington DC for some time, where several of the staff were able to carefully study it.

Norm Conrad, the Curator of American and Biblical Imprints for the Museum of the Bible, is convinced the Bible belonged to Elvis because the notes are in Elvis' handwriting.

He said that the underlines and notes reflect themes of trusting God. "They definitely lean to 'I will trust God. I can trust God. God is in control.'" While not an expert on Elvis, Conrad believes the writings show that Elvis was a believer. "If he was not a man of faith, then he was a man seeking a relationship with God. I believe both. I believe he was a man of faith. My gut tells me that."

The Bible is very fragile and was obviously well-used. The cover shows signs of its age and use, but both the cover and pages are intact. There are many pages with sections underlined and around 20–30 annotations throughout.

Steven Bickley, Museum of the Bible, Vice President of Marketing, said that Elvis is a prime example of the unparalleled influence of the Bible. "His life may have taken a few twists and turns along the way, but it's clear, as evidenced by his own handwritten notes, that the Bible had a profound impact on him."

He also commented that "It's apparent that Elvis looked to the Bible for inspiration for his music, for example, jotted below Psalm 81, Elvis wrote, 'Sing the Lord Praises' and in reference to Psalm 149:3 - 6, Elvis wrote, 'The highest graces of music flow from the feelings of the heart and soul.'" Various other phrases and words are also underlined in Psalm 149 and the words "Sing for the Glory of God" are written in Elvis' handwriting at the end of the Book of Psalms.

Others from the museum, having studied the Bible said, "It appears that Elvis' favourite book was the book of Psalms. He had a lot of writings in that book. The book of Psalms is basically a book of songs. In the back of the Bible, he wrote some notes, poems, and parts of songs. It seems he wrote about what inspired him from the Bible."

Dr Jeffrey Kloha, the Chief Curatorial Officer at the museum said, "Musicians have always found inspiration in the Psalms. Like Elvis, J S Bach, for example, wrote notes in his Bible throughout the Psalms. This is because the Psalms themselves are intended to be sung and have been sung in churches and synagogues for centuries."

Bible Giving Continued Throughout Elvis' Life

Elvis received many Bibles from fans during his lifetime, especially it seems, nearer the end of his life. Some would be mailed to him, but some would be given at concerts, placed on the stage during the performance along with other gifts. J D Sumner remembers picking up Bibles from the stage after concerts to give to Elvis.

Another of Elvis' Bibles that made its way to the Bible Museum is one from a fan, Pat Hyder of Cowpens, South Carolina, dated 20th February 1977. It is a black leather-covered Bible with the words "Holy Bible" and "Dictionary Concordance" embossed in gold on the front. This kind of Bible is very useful for people studying the Bible as the concordance is an alphabetical list of significant words and phrases in the Bible with notes of the chapters and verses where they can be found.

Also, on the front of this Bible is inscribed "Elvis Aron Presley." This raises the continuing debate as to the correct spelling of Elvis' middle name. Is it Aron or Aaron? Considering that the inscription on his gravestone, overseen by his father, the spelling is Aaron and that this Bible-based family would know the name from the Bible, which is always spelt Aaron, for me, it has to be Aaron.

Another copy of a Bible gifted to Elvis Presley by fans during his final concert tour is a blue Bicentennial Bible with an embossed Liberty Bell image on the cover. The title page indicates that the Bible was presented to Elvis on May 28th 1977, by Tom and Judy Davidson. It was accompanied by a letter from the Davidsons saying they were sorry not to present the Bible in person and asking for an autograph. They also wrote, "We hope that this Bible becomes a blessing to your heart and may the Lord be a lamp unto your feet and a light unto your pathway."

Elvis also gave Bibles as gifts as he felt led. On one occasion, however, he was asked for one.

Dottie Rambo, singer-songwriter, and member of The Rambos, a Southern gospel music group that was formed in the 1960s, was a good friend of Elvis. He had even recorded some of her songs. She remembered, one time in 1974, being in Las Vegas with Elvis and some friends in the early hours of the morning, singing, eating, and chatting endlessly. She was concerned about Elvis' health and was questioning him. He attempted to distract her by offering to buy her a car. She refused his offer, and, exasperated, Elvis said, "Name it and I'll give you anything." She replied, "I'd like to have your Bible." He went into his bedroom and returned with a Bible, saying, "For all the Bibles I have had this is the only one I've really been able to listen to. It speaks to me. You might as well read it in the way I read it." He then handed her the Bible with a pair of reading glasses in a case.

She opened it and found a red bookmark Elvis had made for himself. Elvis then took the Bible and signed on an inner page, "Dottie, you are special, love you forever, love Elvis Presley."

This Bible is The Living Bible, a paraphrase, published by Tyndale in 1971. Kenneth N Taylor, who wrote the personal paraphrase, explained the inspiration for preparing The Living Bible. He says:

"The children were one of the chief inspirations for producing the Living Bible. Our family devotions were tough going because of the difficulty we had understanding the King James Version, which we were then using, or the Revised Standard Version, which we used later. All too often I would ask questions to be sure the children understood, and they would shrug their shoulders – they didn't know what the passage was talking about. So, I would explain it. I would paraphrase it for them and give them the thought. It suddenly occurred to me one afternoon that I should write out the reading for that evening thought by thought, rather than doing it on the spot during our devotional time. So, I did and read the chapter to the family that evening with exciting results – they knew the answers to all the questions I asked!"

This Bible was treasured by Dottie for many years and, when she died, she left it to her grandson Israel Anthem. In 2018, it was auctioned for $10,000. This is also the version that Joe Moscheo gave to Elvis in 1976, as we shall see later.

**

By the end of December Elvis had earned £629, 988 from RCA in royalties from record sales.

More Support for March of Dimes

Part of Elvis' 23rd birthday on 8th January 1958 was spent with Mary Kosloski, an eight-year-old from Collierville, Tennessee, who had been the national March of Dimes poster child in 1955. She had been invited to Graceland to meet Elvis. Despite keeping her waiting for almost two hours, Elvis was forgiven for the delay when he appeared and said to Mary, "If you were 10 years older, honey, I wouldn't let you go." Mary was enchanted and asked Elvis to sign her autograph book on the page opposite President Eisenhower's signature. Elvis and Mary were photographed for the local papers on the staircase at Graceland surrounded by teddy bears that Elvis was donating to the March of Dimes fundraiser on 20th January. Elvis had a vast collection of teddy bears donated to him by fans since his recording of the song *Teddy Bear,* earlier that year.

Elvis' favourite Film?

In February Elvis started work on the film "King Creole." Apparently, of the films he made, "King Creole" was his favourite. It is based on the novel "A Stone for Danny Fisher." Set in New Orleans, Elvis becomes a nightclub singer who gets drawn into the criminal world. The role was originally conceived for James Dean, who died at the age of 24 in a car crash, and whose acting Elvis admired.

Jan Shepard, who played Elvis' sister in the movie, enjoyed working with Elvis and they developed a brother-sister relationship as they got on so well. She recalled their first meeting, which was yet another example of how Elvis made others feel at ease, often with a sense of humour. She was in the Doctor's office on the set (all actors had to have a medical before they were signed on) when Elvis walked in. They both looked at each other and burst out laughing as Jan was wearing slacks of the same colour and material as Elvis' jacket. He said that she had to give him her slacks or she had to have his jacket.

In a 2007 interview with Joe Krein, Jan Shepard provided some insight into Elvis's character and personality during the five weeks spent shooting in Hollywood. "He was never in his dressing room. He was always out with a group and having fun and playing the guitar," she recalled. "Elvis never had a dime on him. He would follow me to the apple machine. 'You want an apple, right?' 'Yes, please,' he'd say.'"

Jan also described how Elvis reacted differently to two fellow stars at Paramount. "One day, Pat Boone came walking onto the set. Elvis spotted him and he started to sing *April Love,* just the way Pat would sing it. Pat just grinned from ear to ear."

Jan says that Elvis reacted quite differently when another actor walked into the Paramount commissary while they were eating lunch. When she saw Marlon Brando come in, she told Elvis, but he was too excited and nervous to turn around. When Brando noticed Elvis, he walked over and sat in an empty chair right behind Elvis. Jan then whispered to Elvis, "When you get up your chair is going to hit his. So just say 'Hi' to him." When this happened, Marlon stood up and the two of them shook hands and then they did a little small talking. Jan said, "Elvis acted cool until they were outside the commissary. Then he erupted with excitement over meeting Brando."

Dolores Hart had already appeared in a film with Elvis in "Loving You." In both films, she played essentially the same role, that of the girl who's sweet and innocent, but (especially in "King Creole") somewhat wise to the ways of the world. This is her memory of the filming:

"When we were making "King Creole," he had so many people after him you couldn't walk through the streets in New Orleans. It was like a circus. You would not believe the crowds. Policemen were everywhere. We had to go to hotel rooms to wait in between scenes. When we finally got to the site, we were ushered into the elevator and into the hotel rooms. There would be boards built from one hotel to another. We crossed over to another hotel and would go down the elevator and enter another room. They'd bring us sandwiches. Elvis would open the Gideon Bible, as that was the version placed in the hotel rooms. Whatever passage he'd open it to, we would talk about it. He would ask me, 'What do you think of this passage?'"

She then said, "On 22nd March, it was Jan Shepherd's birthday, and we had a party for her at my house. Elvis came to the birthday party. I played the clarinet and Elvis sat down and played the piano. We played a few tunes for Jan's birthday."

She said of Elvis, "He is a young man with an enormous capacity of love, but I don't think he has found his happiness. I think he is terribly lonely."

She also commented later, "Elvis was quite a gentleman, a quality of simplicity, humour, and shyness about him. It was very much his persona at that time."

Jan Shepard was Godmother to Dolores Hart when, in 1963, she gave up her acting career and became a nun in the Benedictine Abbey of Regina Laudis in Bethlehem, Connecticut. I correspond with Mother Dolores and she and her community faithfully pray for us at Elvis Gospel, and our reaching out to fans with the Gospel of Jesus Christ.

On 24th March 1958, Elvis was inducted into the army.

August 1956. Baptist preacher Robert Gray denounces Elvis in his church service.

A cropped version of this photo is used on the Million Dollar Quartet album cover. The girl sitting on the piano is Elvis' girlfriend Marylin Evans. (Colin Escott)

Elvis with Mohammed Ali who is wearing the jewelled robe Elvis gave him.

Elvis was a great supporter of the March of Dimes fund raiser.

Elvis receiving the polio jab on the Ed Sullivan Show.

Elvis in front of Graceland.

Christmas gift Bible from Elvis' Uncle Vester and Aunt Clettes.

Chapter 4

Military Manoeuvres

Fight the good fight of the faith. Take hold of the eternal life to which you were called. (1 Timothy 6:12)

At 6.35am on Monday 24th March 1958, Elvis reported to the Memphis draft board with twelve other recruits to begin his processing into the army. After a medical check-up, the group of recruits were bussed to Fort Chaffee in Arkansas where they received a haircut, their uniform and were sworn in. It was on this bus that Elvis met Rex Mansfield who became a good friend.

Elvis in his army uniform with his parents, a few months before Gladys' death.

In his book, "Sergeant Presley," Rex Mansfield evocatively describes his response to the first time he saw Elvis, who was not what he expected him to be. "He was sitting resolutely by himself in a front-row chair in the induction room dressed in a multi-colored, checkered sports coat. He reminded me of the Bible's description of a young Joseph, all decked out in his coat of many colors." At that moment Rex also had a feeling that he immediately wanted to protect Elvis but did not understand why. We later will find out that it was Elvis who protected Rex.

This draft process was, of course, quite unusual because of Elvis' fame. The bus taking the recruits to Fort Chaffee was not usually followed by cars full of desperate fans wanting to have a last glimpse of their idol before he is absorbed into the army. Neither did the other recruits have more than fifty reporters and photographers watching them having their military haircut. Elvis was not fazed by all this public attention, which was now part of his life, and in his usual fun-loving way, as his famous quiff and sideburns disappeared, he commented, "Hair today, gone tomorrow."

Elvis was stationed at Fort Hood, Killeen, Texas for basic training and was assigned to the Second Armored Division's "Hell on Wheels" unit (once led by General George Patton). During his basic training, Elvis earned a marksman's medal with a carbine and achieved a sharpshooter level with a pistol and was named as acting Assistant Squad Leader. With his wanting-to-please personality and determination to do the best he could at whatever he attempted, Elvis soon won the respect of his fellow GIs and officers. He did not expect, nor did he receive, any special privileges because of his fame. The army, however, had to spend extra planning time and resources to cope with the many fans who arrived at the base asking to see Elvis. They also had to monitor the many phone calls for him, as soldiers were only allowed family phone calls. In this instance, The Colonel was considered family. The press was also told in no uncertain terms that access to Elvis was off-limits. The army introduced operation Teddy Bear, where they kept Elvis' location in the barracks and his daily routine a closely guarded secret. However, they were no match for Elvis' fans who got to know his schedule. Wherever he marched or stood guard they were there, watching and waving.

The basic training day started at 5am and finished at 7pm. It consisted of gruelling physical exercises, including 15-mile marches carrying a 70-pound backpack and, more regularly, plenty of press-ups, 100 at a time, which were also used as punishment if anyone failed in their duty. Face-to-face armed combat with bayonets was included alongside housekeeping tasks such as cleaning and kitchen duties as well as classroom studies. Apparently, the most challenging was an exercise called "confidence training," where they had to crawl on their backs then fronts over jagged rocks under a barbed wire "ceiling" whilst a salvo of machine-gun fire was shot a couple of feet over their heads. Less strenuous was the hour of marching on parade in which Elvis' musical ability came in useful as each company needed a drummer to help them keep time and Elvis was the only one in his company who could do this.

Just in case there were some soldiers who did not appreciate Elvis being in the army, Hy Gardener an American entertainment reporter who had interviewed Elvis on the TV in 1956, wrote a newspaper column in the form of a letter to Elvis' fellow soldiers proclaiming Elvis' credit to his country:

"Where else could a nobody become a somebody so quickly and in what other nation in the world would such a rich and famous man serve alongside you and other draftees without trying to use his influence to buy his way out? In my book, this is American democracy at its best – the blessed way of life for whose protection you and Elvis have been called upon to contribute eighteen to twenty-four months of your young lives. I hope you go along with my sentiments."

A Renewed Friendship

During these early weeks, Elvis renewed his friendship with Waco businessman Eddie Fadal whom he met during a Texas concert tour in 1956 when Elvis was invited to Eddie's home for meals. At Elvis' invitation, Eddie gave up his job as a DJ and accompanied him on several concert tours in 1956, but only as a trusted friend and travelling companion, never on the payroll.

Eddie said, "My relationship with Elvis began in February 1956. I was a disc jockey at KRLD in Dallas, Texas, and Elvis was making the rounds. Texas was one of his stomping grounds in those days. He had a lot of success in Texas, and I met him at the radio station where he was promoting some records. I'd been spinning his records and liked his voice and thought he had great promise ... and was hoping someday that I'd meet him. I was just in the right place at the right time."

When, in 1958, Eddie learned that Elvis was stationed nearby, he tried to reach him, and eventually succeeded in getting through the red tape but was not sure if Elvis would remember him. However, Elvis greeted him like a long-lost friend. Eddie offered him a home from home, including a room which he had built on to his house and customised for Elvis, even before this reunion, as he had an intuition that he would, at some stage, be seeing Elvis again to renew the friendship. Eddie gave an open invite to Elvis to "come to the house for a spell and kick your boots off."

Once Elvis was allowed off base, he visited the Fadals every weekend from where he made tearful phone calls to his mother. Although Elvis had come to terms with being in the army, he was sure his removal from public life, not being able to sing and make films, would be the end of his career, his fans would forget him, and nobody would know him. It was all over. (How wrong he was!) Eddie encouraged him with "Elvis it's not all over, it's just the beginning, you're never going to be forgotten." (How right he was!) Eddie's home became a haven for Elvis to chat, eat, play games, listen to records, and even accompany their little daughter on the piano when she played her scales. Eddie reports that they also did a lot of singing around the piano with Elvis mostly singing gospel. Before meals, Eddie would sometimes ask Elvis to give thanks to the Lord.

The custom room they had built on their house for Elvis included recording equipment which Elvis used to record him singing with the family, the children singing their off-key Jordanaires impression. Elvis also used the stereo player in the room to listen to the latest releases and keep up with what was happening in the music industry in his absence. Elvis certainly treated their place as a home from home, as they wished, and would sometimes turn up unexpectedly mid-week if he had got some time off and just fit into whatever was going on in the house.

Eddie's relationship with Elvis was quite unusual as he would not accept large gifts from him, such as a new car that they could well afford to buy themselves. Elvis appreciated that and referred to Eddie as "the only friend I have that doesn't need me."

Eddie also spent time with Elvis at his home, Graceland, and noticed that preachers would flock to his door when he was in Memphis. No one was turned away by him and they usually left with a hefty donation for their church.

Many of the preachers tried to encourage Elvis to "go into religious work" but Elvis' reply was always "Not yet, Sir, but I am praying over it." Eddie himself asked Elvis if he would like to start off in some small way by speaking at a chapel service at Baylor University in Waco or by just giving his testimony at any Waco church but Elvis said, "Not yet Eddie, later." Eddie could tell by his voice that the was giving much thought and prayer to the idea. Later, when a young evangelical group from Fort Worth had heard that Elvis was "leaning towards religious work" Eddie arranged for them to meet Elvis in Waco to discuss the idea with them, but his reply to them was "Not yet, but maybe later."

Eddie remembers that on one occasion in Memphis, when a local minister had called to see him, that after they had all prayed together the Minister asked if he would like to work for the Lord. Elvis replied, "Yes, but I have many other things I must do first!"

He also remembers that sometimes, on an evening, Elvis would call down to the gates of Graceland to see how many fans there were, and if it was not too many perhaps 'only' 50, he would invite them in, give them a tour of his home, then get them to get in their cars and lead them to a movie theatre or fairground he had hired out. Entrance and all concessions were on Elvis.

Elvis' parents were regular visitors to the Fadal's, and they could see that it really was home from home for Elvis, with nothing expected of him, but just to be there and be looked after.

Anita Wood

Several of Elvis' friends also visited the Fadals, including Anita Wood, Elvis' girlfriend whom he met in 1957. Anita recalls, "I was on Top 10 Dance Party on WHBQ radio and television in Memphis at the time. It was a popular dance show that they had every Saturday afternoon. The teenagers would come along and dance, and Wink Martindale and I would introduce the songs. Elvis watched that show a lot, and one Saturday after the show, he had Lamar Fike call me on the phone, and he wanted a date to see me that night. Well, I already had a date, and I wouldn't break the date and Lamar went ballistic. I mean he just could not believe – 'You won't break a date to go with Elvis Presley. Are you crazy?' I mean, you know, he just really went wild. And I said, 'Well, I don't believe Elvis would like that if I did that to him if I had a date with him and broke it.'"

Eventually, Anita did have a date with Elvis and, although at the time she was not particularly an Elvis fan, she did admit that he was very good looking. On their first date, he drove her round Memphis with some of his friends and went back to Graceland to meet his parents. They did manage to have some time alone together in Elvis' office and while they were talking Elvis kissed her. She says, "You know, in those days, people didn't kiss on their first date, not ever. So, you know, that was just – I didn't want to be like that. Because I don't care who he was, you know, and then he began to try to get a little fresh with me. And I said, 'Oh, no. That won't work. You know you're gonna have to take me home.' So he said, 'Okay' and he took me downstairs and took me home. He was a gentleman about it. He was very nice. But he did try to get fresh the first date, but he didn't get to first base. It didn't work." Then as she got to meet him and know him, she discovered that he had a very good personality – funny, pulling pranks and laughing.

She said that at that time Elvis was more like a normal guy. He didn't have any dye in his hair, he was just like the guy next door. When Anita was at Graceland she spent a lot of time with Gladys, who she could see dearly loved Elvis and wanted him to "settle down" and get married and have a family. Anita says, "She would talk to me about how she wanted us to get married and she wanted us to have a little boy and to name him Elvis Jr. And she said, 'I can just see him running up and down the driveway in his little bare feet, this little blonde-headed boy.' We talked about things like that a lot."

Anita thought that Elvis was deeply religious. They went to a lot of gospel singings, and she remembers sitting backstage all night long in Memphis and Nashville. Anita says "You know, he just loved to sing religious songs. We talked about the fact that Elvis told me that he was saved. Because I was. He told me that he was a Christian. I think later in his life, I don't know what happened with the books and the other kind of religions and everything. But when I knew him, he told me – he assured me that he did know Jesus as his Savior and that he was a Christian, because I certainly was. And I was of the Baptist faith. But he was of the Assembly of God."

They only once attended a church service, the reason being Elvis' presence caused such a commotion. Anita remembered when they went to the AoG church, going up into the balcony after the service started so as not to be noticed, but they had to leave before the service was over as people just wanted to look at Elvis and not listen to the sermon. Elvis felt very bad about that. So, they didn't go any more. They did however visit with the preacher Rev. James Hamill a few times.

When she first visited Elvis at Fort Hood, Anita stayed with Sergeant Richard and Ali Norwood who lived on the base. She said that she and Elvis would go and sit in the backyard and look up at the sky and talk about all the things they were planning on doing, like getting married. Anita says that it was the greatest time that she ever spent with him. "He was a soldier boy, and I was his girlfriend from back home and we were in love, and we were together with friends. We had a wonderful time – we just had a normal relationship during those days."

Sergeant Norwood could see that Elvis was homesick for his mother and needed someone to look out for him. That is most probably one of the reasons that he let Anita stay at his home on base when she visited Elvis. He would have had more opportunity to see Elvis as a whole person, not just the soldier. William Norwood, the master sergeant, advised Elvis, "When you come in my house, you can let it all out. But when you walk out of my front door, you are now Elvis Presley. You're an actor. You're a soldier. So, by God, I want you to act! Don't let anybody know how you feel on the inside." Sergeant Norwood was aware of the extra pressures on Elvis because of his fame, so when GIs from other companies derided or heckled Elvis during marches, Sergeant Norwood would stop the proceedings and dress down the offender.

Elvis wanted Anita to go to Germany with him and had got her passport and all the shots ready. She agreed, but just before she was going to leave Elvis called her and said that the Colonel had put a stop to that, as he thought that if she went over there, the press would have them engaged or getting married and Elvis did not need to have that kind of publicity. Consequently, Anita did not go, but they continued to communicate by phone and letters. In these letters, Anita says, "He swore he loved me, how we would get married, how there was so no one else, how I need to stay true to him and remain and wait for him. How he was afraid I would not. I don't know why Elvis thought so little of himself. He was so jealous. I don't know why. I can't imagine why."

After Elvis returned to the USA from Germany where he had met Priscilla, his wife-to-be (though he did not know it then), Anita realised that she may have a rival. Eventually, in early 1962, she decided to break off their relationship, not only because of Priscilla, but also as Anita once said, "There were always people around Elvis, guys. Okay, that's one reason why I could never have married Elvis, when you really get down to it because you were not alone very often. There were very few times in our life that we were totally alone for very long at a time. They were always there. They lived with him, they took care of him, they did everything he said, and they were always there. And they were always going to be there."

Furlough With Friends

The 1st of June was the start of a two-week furlough when Elvis returned home to Graceland with his new army friends Rex Mansfield and William Norvell. William remembers well his friendship with Elvis (who doesn't!):

"I had met Elvis before at my church in North Memphis," William says. "All my friends over there went to Humes." The press had found out that William knew Elvis and had offered him money to tell them about his friendship with Elvis. He was concerned and asked Elvis about it, saying, 'Elvis, I think this is trying to get into your private life. This is what they want to do. And I am not going to do it.' Elvis replied, 'They will take everything you say and rearrange it.'

"They were offering me $25 a statement. We only made between my wife and me $97 a month. I still wouldn't do it. So we became good friends after that for a long time. We went all the way through basic training, and we remained friends." Norvell and Elvis were assigned bunks, with Norvell on the top bunk. Norvell remembers that one night he dropped his wedding ring and Elvis crawled around in the dark helping his friend find that wedding band. "Elvis did not sing," Norvell said. "He wouldn't sing for anybody. But he did play the piano. He would play the piano like you couldn't believe. They put on some shows. We met one guy named Charlie Hodge out of Nashville. Charlie, Elvis and I got to be good friends on the ship."

Between married life, flying planes, designing train layouts, and running Norvell's Millington Body Works, Norvell made time to hang out with his friend. "I used to go to Graceland and see him all the time," he said. "Then he got so busy. I used to go to his house and carried my children. We were regular visitors to Graceland, and I had a secret way to get into Graceland."

Elvis spent this furlough time in Memphis with his family and friends hiring the Rollerdrome and fairgrounds. He also took time to go to Nashville to record a single, *Hard Headed Woman,* which was the last professional recording session he had for two years.

After basic training, every soldier could apply to live off base with his dependents, usually a wife and children. In Elvis' case, he applied for and was granted permission to live off base with his dependents, his mother and father. His grandmother Minnie and his friend Lamar Fike also took up residence in the trailer home Elvis hired. It soon became too cramped, so Elvis leased a house in nearby Killeen where his cousins Gene and Junior Smith also joined the expanding household.

Tragedy Strikes

All through the summer of 1958 Gladys had been feeling ill, with loss of appetite, poor colour, and depression. As her condition worsened, on 8th of August, Elvis insisted that she went back to Memphis to see her own physician, so she and Vernon took the train back home. The next day she was admitted to hospital where her condition was reported as grave. Elvis felt he needed to be at his mother's side, so he pulled out all the stops to get emergency leave and flew back to Memphis with Lamar Fike on 12th August, going straight to the hospital.

Vernon stayed at his wife's bedside, with Elvis visiting again next morning and afternoon, staying till near midnight. On 14th August at around 3.15am, Gladys Love Presley, aged 46, passed away with Vernon at her side. Vernon phoned his son, who knew what the phone call was before he answered. Elvis immediately joined his father at the hospital and as so eloquently put by biographer Elaine Dundy, "piercing the night-time silence of the hospital and reverberating through its corridors, the wild despairing wails of Vernon and Elvis were heard as they wept and prayed long and hard over Gladys' lifeless body."

It is here I need to re-introduce someone we have already met, Rev. Rex Dyson, the pastor of the first church the Presleys attended on arriving in Memphis.

On 9th August 1958, the day that Gladys Presley was admitted to hospital, Rev. Rex Dyson had just returned from a Revival in Dallas and was staying in West Memphis. That evening he had a very vivid dream about Vernon and Gladys, he says "as real as if they were in the room with me." The next morning, he went to buy a newspaper and saw Gladys' picture and a report that she had been taken into hospital. At church that day, Rex spoke to Marion Carson, Elvis' former Sunday School teacher, and told him that Gladys was in hospital. Rex felt very strongly that he needed to go and visit her in hospital and Marion said, "I will go if you will."

Rex explained to me that he had not been in contact with the Presleys since he returned from his mission in Israel and Elvis had become very rich. "I have a complex about rich people," he confessed. Anyhow, Rex and Marion arranged to meet at 9am the next day to go to the hospital. Marion did not turn up, although Rex waited for some time, so Rex decided not to go on his own. He said, "I am sorry I didn't go – I should have went." He saw Marion later in the week, who apologised that he had got tied up and was not able to get there. Consequently, they arranged to meet up the next day and go. Next morning, Rex went to the filling station to get a newspaper and saw that Gladys had passed away. He said, "I was falling out of my shoes when I read that. I felt I had failed God. If I had gone to the hospital, I would have had Elvis, Gladys and Vernon all together and could have spoken to them."

I wonder how things might have developed had Rex been able to see the Presley family together at that time. Rex tried later to get to Vernon, just before Vernon died. He went to the Baptist hospital to visit Vernon but was not allowed to see him. He learned later that Vernon's nurse asked Vernon why he was not baptised in Jesus' name and Vernon said, "I am by Pastor Rex Dyson."

This reminds me that, in 1975, Rev. Frank Smith, the Presleys' Pastor in Tupelo felt a compulsion to visit Elvis and encourage him to become a more positive role model. He never acted on this, and I wonder how many other pastors had this compulsion and tried to get to Elvis. Elvis, however, did seek out Christian ministers later in his life.

The Practicalities of Death

Elvis had his mother's body moved to Graceland on the Thursday and opened the doors to friends for a last look at his "best girl-friend." Many people came to console Elvis and his father at Graceland and there were hundreds of fans keeping vigil at the gate.

Elvis wanted the funeral conducted at the house, but the Colonel convinced Elvis that it would not be possible to effectively maintain security, so arrangements were made to have the service at The Memphis Funeral Home on 15th August. Elvis had arranged for Gladys' favourite gospel group, the Blackwood Brothers, to sing at the service. They were flown in from a concert tour in North Carolina at Elvis' expense. They were scheduled to sing three or four songs, but Elvis would not let them stop, (according to J D Sumner they sang about twelve songs) and they went on for so long that they had to charter a plane to make it back for their next engagement.

During the service, Elvis and Vernon sobbed so much they nearly collapsed several times.

Elvis' former girlfriend, Dixie Locke, married and a mother by then, attended the funeral and, before the service, went up to Elvis and his father to pay her respects. She says Elvis "just burst up out of his chair and grabbed me, saying 'Look Dad here's Dixie' like I was going to save the world." He asked her to go to Graceland that evening, saying "I just need to talk to you."

Elvis had asked his pastor, Rev. James Hamill, to conduct the ceremony in which he said, "Women can succeed in most any field these days, but the most important job of all is being a good wife and a good mother. Mrs. Presley was such a woman. I would be foolish to tell this father and this son 'Don't worry, don't grieve, don't be sorrowful. Of course, you will miss her, but I can say with Paul 'sorrow not as those who have no hope'" After the burial, Pastor Hamill also spent a lot of time one-to-one counselling Elvis.

When the entourage moved to the Forest Hill Cemetery gravesite to bury Gladys, there were over 500 onlookers and Elvis was even more inconsolable, crying out, "Oh God, everything I have is gone." Elvis leant over the grave, crying out, inconsolably, "Goodbye, darling, goodbye. I love you so much. You know how much I lived my whole life just for you."

Many of Elvis' fans were upset on his behalf – they sent him more than 100,000 cards and letters, around 500 telegrams, and more than 200 floral arrangements to express their sympathy for his loss.

Dixie Locke did go to Graceland that evening, and even though the place was chaotic with so many people milling around, Elvis arranged that they would have some quiet time together. Dixie says that they talked about his mother and rehashed the time she had met her and all the things that they had done that were funny and silly. Elvis expressed how special it was just to be with somebody you knew from those many days back that loved you and accepted you for just what you were. He told Dixie that he felt that most of his current friends were looking for something from him. He then went on to tell Dixie about one of the guys who was singing backup for him, (that would be Hugh Jarrett) who had just given his life to the Lord. He had been "in the world" for a long time and was just really messed up. Hugh told Elvis that he was having to walk away from the life that he was leading, and Elvis said, "I wish I could do that." Dixie said, "Why don't you too?" to which Elvis replied, "It's too late for that, there are too many people that depend on me, I am too far in to get out."

A large, white marble cross with a statue of Jesus with open arms, two angels and PRESLEY carved at the base was placed at the head of Gladys' grave in March 1959. Elvis' father had ordered the statuary before he left for Germany. The footstone, designed by Elvis, features the Star of David to represent Gladys' Jewish heritage, and, as well as Gladys' name and dates there is an inscription which says, "The Sunshine of Our Home." The inscription on the front of the footstone says, "NOT MINE BUT THY WILL BE DONE." Elvis would have been very familiar with this scripture, as it is what Jesus prayed in the garden of Gethsemane, the night before his crucifixion. Jesus knew what was going to happen to him and was struggling with the contemplation of the pain, both physical and spiritual, which he would endure. Jesus, like us, was human and had free will, but He chose to submit to God's will (for Him to be crucified, thus setting all men free from the bondage of sin and therefore able to have a loving relationship with their maker.) Perhaps Elvis was reminding himself that whatever happened in life, he would always try to obey God's will.

Elvis was so distraught after his mother's funeral that his leave was extended for another five days. Many people were concerned for him and tried to help. Even the Memphis Highway Patrol tried to cheer him up by giving him a helicopter ride over Graceland and the city.

He returned to Fort Hood on 24th August, for eight more weeks of training, this time learning everything there was to know about tanks. Everyone noticed how Elvis' demeanour had changed from happy-go-lucky, to more serious and grief-stricken. Elvis, however, still took his training seriously. When he wasn't training, he would do everything to keep himself busy and he invited people, including Fan Club Presidents to the Fadal's home.

On returning to Fort Hood, Elvis spoke briefly with an Associated Press reporter in Dallas. "One of the last things Mom said was that Dad and I should always be together. I'll report back to Fort Hood Monday morning. Wherever they send me, Dad will go too."

The European Adventure Begins

On 11th September, Elvis found that he was assigned to the Third Army Division in Germany.

The evening before his departure to Germany, he spent an emotional farewell time at the Fadal's house in Killeen with family and friends. They ended the evening by praying, each one contributing in their own way (known as extemporary prayer.) The next day, on 20th September, Elvis joined the other trainees on the troop train to Brooklyn Army Terminal in New York.

It was on this train he met fellow GI Charlie Hodge who was a singer with the gospel group, the Foggy River Boys, a group which later Jim Hamill, a friend of Elvis and the son of Elvis' Pastor at Assemblies of God, joined. Charlie knew that Elvis was on the train and sought him out as he felt he was meant to meet him. In fact, Charlie, a diminutive five foot three inches tall, was a Godsend, as not only was he a Southerner and a gospel singer, but he had a winning personality and a great sense of humour and made everyone laugh with his jokes and tales, something they all, especially Elvis, needed. Elvis and Charlie hit it off straight away and became good friends. Charlie joined Elvis' entourage in 1960 and was with Elvis till the end, including singing with him in his concerts.

In New York, at a press conference, Elvis expressed his fervent hope that his fans would not forget him and that he was looking forward to coming back to entertain them. When asked for his idea of the ideal girl, Elvis' witty reply of "Female, sir" had the reporters roaring with laughter. Later, on a more serious note, a reporter expressed sympathy for the death of his mother and asked Elvis if he would like to say a few words of tribute as to how she had helped him in his life. He replied, "Yes, sir, I certainly would." He continued to say that, as he was an only child, they were closer than usual and that she was always with him. She was a friend, a companion, someone to talk to any hour of the night and, if he was troubled, she would get up and try to help him. He also mentioned that growing up he used to get very angry with her when she wouldn't let him do some things, thinking "what's wrong with you?" Later on he found out that she was right and was only doing it to protect him and stop him from getting into trouble. He was very happy that she had been strict with him and that it had worked out the way it did.

When it was time for him to board the SS Randall, he did so eight times, toting a borrowed duffel bag as his had already been taken on board, so that the many assembled cameramen and reporters could get a good shot.

During the daytimes of this nine-day sail to Bremerhaven, the troops received instruction about duties to come and what was expected of them during their spare time off base in a foreign county. In order to relieve the boredom of their evenings, as well as watching movies and playing cards, they organised a talent show. Elvis was appointed producer and director, with Charlie Hodge as MC. Elvis played piano to accompany some of the singers, though, as per strict instruction of the Colonel, did not sing. The show was of high quality and a great success, with Elvis receiving a standing ovation for his part in producing the show.

On 1st October, the boat arrived in Bremerhaven, greeted by hundreds of screaming fans and a virtual army of press. This was a surprise and revelation to Elvis, as until then he had not realised that he had such celebrity status outside of the USA. Elvis' battalion boarded a troop train which took them to Ray Barracks in Friedberg. It had once been home to Hitler's SS troops and was very grey and drab, not helped by the common foggy weather conditions. After an army press conference the next day, when the press was told Elvis was now off-limits, the work began in earnest.

Elvis was assigned to a Scout Platoon where he was trained to go ahead of tanks, set up roadblocks, direct traffic and give enemy positions. Elvis' platoon

Sergeant was Ira Jones, a veteran of WW2, who took over the role held by Sergeant Norwood at Fort Hood as a father figure for Elvis. In his book, "Soldier Boy Elvis," Ira Jones describes his friendship with Elvis and recalls first meeting him on the train journey from Bremerhaven to the base. Sergeant Jones suddenly realised, "I had no idea what he looked like!" He quickly found that Elvis was "just like any other soldier." When told that on the train ride South he should sit and keep his window closed, Elvis merely replied, "Yes, sir" and did just that. When the cooks on the train served a hot meal, Elvis thanked them.

Elvis drove Sergeant Jones in a jeep for nine months while serving in the Scout Platoon, 1st Medium Tank Battalion, 32nd Armor, of the 3rd Armored Division, part of the US Seventh Army. Many a confidence was shared between them during those lonely hours on patrol and Sergeant Jones remembers several emotional conversations he had with Elvis, telling Ira how much he missed his mother and how much he missed his beloved Graceland while tears flowed down his face. When Sergeant Jones eventually retired, Elvis threw a farewell party for him, the likes of which the army had never seen before ... nor since.

It was good that Elvis had Sergeant Jones as his new father figure, however Sergeant Norwood from Fort Hood still kept in touch and later wrote to Elvis in Germany. In November 1958, Elvis replied saying:

"Well I am writing a letter for the first time in years. I received your letter and was glad to hear everything is ok. I am in a scout platoon and believe me we are on the move all the time. We are up at a place called Grafenwoehr. I'm sure you've heard of it. It's miserable up here and we are here for 6 wks. The German people are very nice and friendly but there is no place like the good ole U. S. I am with a good bunch of boys and Sgts. although I would have given anything to stay at Ft. Hood with you guys. I talk to Anita every so often and she writes me all the time. I sure miss her along with 50 million others ha. Boy I'll tell you something I will be so thankful when my time is up. I can hardly wait to get back home and entertain folks and make movies and everything. Well it will come someday soon. All of us were separated over here. Nowell and Mansfield are in other companies, but there is a lot of good boys in this outfit. Well tell Olly and the kids hello for me. Also tell Sgt. Wallace and Lt. Meister hello for me and if I get a chance, I will write to them. Tell Sgt. Wallace to write me sometime so I will know to write him. Well when it's over we will

get together again, and it'll be like old times. Well I have to go now so you all take care and write again."

Meanwhile Elvis' father Vernon, Grandma Minnie Mae, Lamar Fike and Red West had arrived in Germany and moved into the famous Ritter's Park Hotel in Bad Homburg. Elvis applied for and received permission to live off base with his family. It was all very strange for them, and they were struggling to adjust, especially as Elvis and his father were still grieving the loss of Gladys.

Next, they all moved into the Hilbert's Park Hotel in Bad Nauheim, and, on his first weekend leave, Charlie Hodge, whom Elvis had befriended on the SS Randall, turned up and raised everyone's mood by telling his jokes and tales. Vernon, Red and Lamar immediately liked Charlie and they all harmonised acapella on some old gospel songs, which no doubt raised their spirits too. As they settled in, the lads relieved their boredom by playing some hijinks, much to the annoyance of the other residents and management. They were consequently asked to leave, and they moved to the Hotel Grunewald where Elvis rented the entire top floor.

Elvis Was Not the Only Singer Who Caused Disturbances

On 23rd October Elvis attended the Bill Haley and the Comets concert in Frankfurt and visited him backstage. He also attended Bill Haley's concert in Stuttgart on 29th October. Both times he was not actually in the audience, as already Bill Haley concerts resulted in riots, and it was felt that the presence of Elvis would add to the problem. From film taken at the time, it appears that most of the fans in the packed sports arena were young men who stayed in their seats enjoying the music. It is when they were leaving that the battles began. The police were there in force including those on horses, and there were many fights taking place as well as seats in the auditorium being smashed. There was a lot of testosterone around! As a result, thirty people were injured and there was property damage of 12,000 Deutsche Marks. These violent incidents, which were sharply criticised in the Western press as well, were viewed in the communist German Democratic Republic as the result of a conscious ideological strategy on the part of the US and the West German government to rob young people of their critical faculties in order to lay the groundwork for nuclear war.

Field Training – No Walk in the Park

On 3rd November 1958, Elvis' battalion was sent to Grafenwoehr for field and weapon training. When training in the field, Elvis suffered the same harsh, wet, cold, tent-sleeping conditions as everyone else and proved himself to be very adept at reconnaissance manoeuvres. On one occasion his team took by surprise and captured several 'enemy' officers, thus winning the day.

This field training was especially important considering the serious political situation at the time. On 10th November, whilst Elvis was in the field, Soviet Premier Nikita Khrushchev demanded that the United States and its allies relinquish their occupation roles in Berlin. He also declared that if they did not sign an agreement to this effect within six months, the Soviet Union would no longer honour their post-war agreement and would enter a separate treaty with East Germany. US President Dwight D Eisenhower refused Khrushchev's demands, insisting that their Berlin agreement still held. On 27th November, the day that Elvis was promoted to Private, First Class, the Soviet Union announced that it had rejected the post-war agreements concerning the occupation and governance of Germany and West Berlin. Khrushchev also proposed that Berlin become a free city. Although Khrushchev did not indicate that the Soviet Union would use military force if the United States did not comply, it was widely understood that the Soviet Union intended to back up its demands.

As part of their training, the men had been taught about the relationship between the USA and the USSR and its possible consequences, so there was a lot of serious discussion amongst the men about this potentially hazardous situation. There was great concern that should the Third World War break out, their battalion, being so close, would be among the first units to take on a Soviet attack.

The Grafenwoehr Training Area is known today as the largest US Army training area in Europe, a place where artillery manoeuvres take place alongside tanks and infantry. It is the largest NATO training base in Europe, which means allies come from all over to train there. It was originally built by the Bavarian Army between 1907 and 1915, and after World War II, it became a jointly run base between the US and Germany. It is also situated in one of the largest nature reserves in Bavaria.

Operation Winter Shield

Another major training exercise Elvis undertook during his time in Germany was in January/February 1960 when Elvis' outfit joined many others to begin the two-week Operation Winter Shield. This was the most intense training they had undergone. Not only was it to test their combat readiness, but also to train for warfare in extreme cold conditions. It took place in the middle of the Black Forest which is in Southwest Germany on the border of Switzerland. It was literally freezing cold with two feet of snow. During the days they had to keep themselves and the equipment camouflaged so they couldn't be spotted by 'the enemy' and at night they were on blackout manoeuvres travelling without any lights using only night vison equipment. Many soldiers got frostbite. It was indeed a miserable time for all. Elvis' tasks included reconnaissance, gathering information on the enemy and the terrain. He also assessed weight limitations of bridges, considering they would have to be able to take the weight of some very heavy machinery and vehicles.

Each exercise saw the participation of some 60,000 troops and about 15,000 vehicles. The use of nuclear weapons was given a decisive role in Winter Shield I. They were meant to serve as a deterrence as the military forces in the East were getting stronger and stronger. Both exercises were conducted under the motto: "Train as you fight." Commanding officers were veterans of recently fought wars – US officers had seen action during the Korean War while many German commanders had gained their experience on the Eastern Front during World War Two.

As we now know, The United States and Britain refused to agree to the Soviet demands, arguing that a free Berlin, with no guaranteed access to the West, would soon be controlled by communist East Germany. Multiple attempts to find a diplomatic solution were fruitless, but a solution was reached unilaterally on the night of August 12–13, 1961, when the East German government, backed by the Soviet Union, began to build a barrier, "The Berlin Wall", between East Berlin (the Soviet-occupied sector) and West Berlin. The United States did not intervene because the Soviet Union was exercising control over its sector. A major outcome of the Berlin crisis was that, without military intervention, a new understanding between the United States and the Soviet Union came about. The Soviet Union would continue to have dominance over its eastern European allies and East Berlin, while the United States and its allies would claim western Europe, West Germany, and West Berlin within their sphere of influence.

A New Love Interest

When Elvis was in the barracks at Grafenwoehr, he spent much of his free time at the Tower Theatre on base, watching movies. It was here that he met Elisabeth Stefaniak who lived on the base with her family. Elisabeth was an Elvis fan and hung around in the cinema foyer hoping to get a glimpse of him. Rex Mansfield who accompanied Elvis to the cinema had noticed Elisabeth, especially how beautiful she was, and it was Rex whom Elvis sent into the foyer to bring Elisabeth into the cinema to sit next to him when he heard that she had wanted an autograph. As Rex says in his book, *"Living the moments, My Journey with Elvis, Elisabeth and Jesus,"* it was not the only time he walked down an aisle with Elisabeth.

Elisabeth got more than she had ever hoped, not only an autograph, but Elvis walked her home after the film and gave her a goodnight kiss. Elvis was clearly taken with Elisabeth as he took her to the theatre for the next six nights, and on Thanksgiving, his first without his mother, he called on the family unannounced. The only people in the apartment were her five-year-old sister, Linda, and her father who was asleep. Linda answered the door and had no idea who Elvis was, except that he was a stranger, and she did not allow him in. Fortunately, a neighbour across the hall had overheard this and invited Elvis in to wait until Elisabeth and her mother came back from shopping. Elvis was, of course, invited in and spent time with the family talking about his family, especially his mother. He also showed interest in their family and Germany and asked many questions. Elvis soon became a favourite with all the family and visited often, as he felt so comfortable with them. As Elisabeth says, he became a fixture in their house, even turning up for breakfast which her mother would cook just as he liked.

Elvis also visited the Mickey Bar, the 'happening place' in Grafenwoehr town where international bands performed. It was run by the local Feiner family, who allowed Elvis' father and friends to stay in the apartment upstairs. As a way to say thank you, Elvis performed a concert for the Feiner family and German workers at the Mickey Bar, singing such hits as *Hound Dog* and *My Happiness*. This was the only concert, albeit private, that Elvis performed whilst in the army.

Elvis returned to Bad Nauheim on 20th December with a promise from Elisabeth that she would come to work for him as his secretary. Elisabeth spoke both German and English so was an ideal person to deal with all the mail from German fans, also to help with any other translations the Presleys may need.

Elisabeth's room in the hotel doubled as an office and was already half full of bags of mail. She was so curious that she stayed up the whole of the first night reading the mail. She found that most people asked for signed pictures, some asked for financial assistance and there were many love letters and letters telling Elvis how much they enjoyed his music. A few letters were hate-mail from jealous boyfriends and husbands and some fans had sent Elvis St. Christopher medallions. St. Christopher is the patron saint of travellers, so this was most probably seen as an appropriate gift at this time.

A New Home

Staying in hotels was not ideal, neither for Elvis' family, nor his friends. They needed somewhere more private that they could call "home."

Elvis finally found a house suitable for them all, and they moved into Goethestrasse 14, Bad Nauheim, on 3rd February 1959. It was a five-bedroom house, and the owner Frau Pieper insisted on remaining in the house, occupying a bedroom on the top floor.

Each workday, Elvis would rise at 5.30 in the morning for his standard breakfast of slightly burned bacon, hard-fried eggs, peaches, and homemade Southern baked biscuits with butter and jam, prepared by his grandma. He washed it down with coffee before driving to the base at 6.30 – at first in his black Mercedes, later in two different BMW two-seaters. Most days, if he was not away on manoeuvres, he would come home for lunch. In the evening, he would return from the base in time for dinner with the household. Of course, the fans soon discovered his new abode and would gather outside the house, just for a glimpse of Elvis as he came and went, also hoping to get an autograph. To control this situation a sign was put outside the house that Elvis would be signing autographs between 7.30 and 8pm.

Frau Piper and Elvis' Grandma, Minnie Mae shared the kitchen and, considering they could not speak each other's language, got along fine most of the time. One wonders if Minnie Mae's strong Christian faith helped her in this. It must certainly have helped Elvis to have her continuing wisdom and strength at hand, as I can find no record of his attending church services whilst he was in Germany, though I assume that the army base had a chapel. I do not know if he contacted the Army Chaplain at all. Elvis chose to spend his Sunday afternoons playing football. The passing of his mother, leading to the dearth of such close Christian fellowship in his life, would certainly have made it more difficult for him to keep to his Christian principles.

In order that he could continue enjoying live music, especially gospel, as well as listening to records, Elvis hired a piano, and the house occupants were treated to many private performances. Elisabeth remembers the great times they had singing gospel in the Goethestrasse house. She says that Elvis loved Roy Hamilton's version of *I Believe* and *You'll Never Walk Alone*. He would play the songs on the piano by ear, and have Red, Rex, Lamar, and Charlie sing along with him.

He also enjoyed listening to the Statesmen gospel quartet who had a powerful influence on him. Elvis admired and imitated Jake Hess' vocal styling and Bill Wetherington's movements and gyrations on stage. In an interview with songwriter Bill Gaither, Jake Hess remembered seeing young Elvis coming to Statesmen shows in Tupelo when Elvis was only nine or ten. Hess said that the serious young Elvis would ask him, "How do you make a record?" or "How many suits you got?" On the Gaither Homecoming video, "Oh My Glory," Hess recalls Elvis, (before the Colonel came along) attending Statesmen concerts and being invited up onstage to sing lead in his place on a couple of handpicked numbers. Another favourite of Elvis was the Harmonising Four, a Black gospel group from Richmond, Virginia. Two of their songs he especially liked were *Only Believe* and *When I've Done the Best I Can*. His favourite song of theirs was *Farther Along*. Elvis was amazed by the deep voice of the bass singer and showed his friends that the lowest note that he sang was off the piano keyboard. Elvis was fascinated by the human singing voice and later on he would get some of his backing singers on stage to do solos in order to "show them off."

It was Gordon Stoker of the Jordanaires who kept in touch with Elvis while he was in Germany and, among other things, sent him the album by the Harmonising Four. This Black gospel group was a relative anomaly of the post-war period as most of their contemporaries modernized their sound, rejecting the traditional jubilee style. The Harmonising Four remained true to their roots, focusing on the spirituals and hymns of a time gone by, honing their smooth lyrical harmony style to perfection. Gordon says that "When I finally saw him after his return, I asked him if he liked the album - he said, 'Are you kidding? I wore it out!'"

"The greatest thing that ever happened was when Elvis asked us to work for him," Gordon said. Elvis insisted that The Jordanaires' name be placed on the record labels, and the recognition they received opened doors to other opportunities. "Elvis opened the door for everybody," he said. "You could hardly find a guitar picker anywhere in those days. Now there is one on every corner. Elvis has inspired the world to sing and play."

The Colonel Encourages

We know that Elvis was afraid of losing his fans while he was away in the army, but the Colonel dealt with that by working tirelessly to promote Elvis, setting up future film commitments, negotiating other deals with RCA and discussing possible songs for recording with Elvis' music publisher Freddie Beinstock. He also organised some promotional events in Germany, including one in which he cooperated with a German magazine resulting in Elvis hosting afternoon tea at his home for four German teenage girls who won a competition.

There was no need to worry about whether people had remembered Elvis while he was away. Just before Elvis left the army, *Billboard* magazine, a US magazine which researches record sales, reported that Elvis had sold 18 million singles to date, a feat accomplished by no other artist in history at that time. The Guinness Book of Records, at the time of writing, says that "Elvis Presley (USA) is the best-selling solo artist, with one billion sales worldwide."

The Colonel had also been regularly writing encouraging, newsy letters to Elvis and, in a letter dated 9th January 1959, asked him to get a tape recorder and record some homemade music, using a piano or guitar. He thought that Elvis' voice would be more prominent than on some of the latest releases on which he felt that his voice was drowned out by the instrumental music. He advised Elvis, "... if you could do this in your own time without any publicity, without letting anyone know. You could work on this until you thought they were good enough for editing and mail them on to me here. I could try to make a couple of releases or EPs of them as a special set up with RCA." The Colonel especially asked Elvis to record "more sacred songs." In particular, he mentioned *Just a Closer Walk With Thee* and "about three more sacred songs that you like yourself and could do in your own style any way you thought best. Also, some other songs that you like."

He encouraged Elvis by saying that he was sure he would do a very good job of it and that the kids would love the more pared back style. He clearly wanted to follow up on the success of the *Peace in the Valley* EP released in April 1957. However, nothing came of this, and the home-recorded tapes were only discovered and released in 1983 after Elvis' death. One third of the songs recorded are gospel songs, and the remainder give an insight into other songs that Elvis was interested in at the time. Perhaps a little reminiscent of the Million Dollar Quartet session.

Prescription Drugs

It was in Germany that Elvis was introduced, by one of the sergeants, to prescription drugs – "uppers" – to keep awake during the bitter winter night watches at the Russian front. Known as the "magic little white pills," these amphetamines are classed as stimulants which change the amounts of certain natural substances in the brain. They can help increase ability to pay attention, stay focused on an activity, and control behaviour problems. They may also help to organise tasks and improve listening skills. Elvis liked the way the pills made him feel and continued their use for the remainder of his life. Not only that, he wanted to share the wonderful experience with others, so many of his friends were also introduced. As they were prescription drugs, Elvis considered them harmless, especially as his mother had been prescribed them for diet control to help her lose weight.

Rex Mansfield was one of those to whom Elvis offered the drug. Perhaps "offered" is not a strong enough word. Elvis very much encouraged people to take Dexedrine. Some refused, though by this time it was very difficult to say "no" to Elvis. Some pretended to swallow them then got rid of them, and others took them. Rex readily took the pills, encouraged by Elvis that they were completely harmless as truck drivers took them to stay awake on long trips. He describes the effect of taking his first pill, "I actually felt the hair on my head standing up and a surge of energy bolting through my body. The pill gave me an abundance of strength and energy I didn't know I had. I was astonished that after taking only one pill I could easily go 24 hours without food or sleep. And they were harmless!" Of course, they are harmless if taken in the correct dosage, but the body soon gets used to them, so the temptation is to take two rather than one, and then more, to get the same effect which leads to addiction. How Elvis came by such large supplies of Dexedrine, not only for his own use but also to give away, is not clear except that as already mentioned, it was getting very difficult for most people to say "no" to Elvis and that could have then, and later did, included medical doctors.

Christmas Greetings

The 19th December 1958 was the final day of training for the year, and, back in Bad Nauheim, Elvis threw himself into preparations for a Christmas party at the local orphanage, to which he had also made a generous financial donation. Also, his platoon was designated to clean the company area and decorate the Christmas tree for any visitors that may come over the holidays. At the end of the day when everyone was getting ready to leave one of the soldiers picked up a guitar and started to sing Christmas songs. Others soon joined in.

According to Ira Jones, when Elvis was asked if he would like to join in, he gave a subdued "Yeah, all right" and then led the soldiers in some more carols. At the end he started singing *Silent Night,* singing as if in a trance, oblivious to his surroundings. No one joined in but listened quietly. Other soldiers passing by did not interrupt, but walked silently past Elvis, touching his shoulder. Not a word was spoken after the song had ended until Elvis broke the spell with "Merry Christmas everyone" to which they replied in unison "Merry Christmas Elvis!"

The Christmas celebrations at the Grunewald Hotel were very subdued. Personally, it was difficult for Elvis' family being the first Christmas without Gladys, but also Germany was still struggling to get over the financial impact of the Second World War and, even for the hotel, it was a low-key affair.

Munich Visit

On 3rd March 1959, accompanied by friends Red West and Lamar Fike, Elvis travelled to Munich to visit Vera Tschescowa, an actress whom he had met in January doing publicity shots for the March of Dimes. Elvis bought up all the tickets for a performance of a play that she was acting in with a small experimental theatre group. Elvis, Red and Lamar had no idea what the play was about as it was performed in German. Afterwards they all went out to dinner with some theatrical friends of Vera. I wonder if they asked about the play and what other conversations they had. This three-day leave seemed to be fairly quiet with Elvis going on a boat ride with Vera and visiting a film set of a Viking movie being made at a local film studio.

On 1st June, Elvis was promoted to specialist 4th class raising his salary to $122.30 per month. He would stand in line to receive his pay and, many times, money could be seen changing hands as Elvis received back the loans which he had handed out to those struggling to manage on their pay. Most paid him back, though some didn't, but he didn't complain because he said he knew their need and was happy to help them out.

Due to tonsillitis and a high fever, Elvis was admitted to the 97th General Hospital in Frankfurt on 3rd June. He was discharged six days later.

Munich and Paris

A 14-day furlough started on 13th June when Elvis spent two nights in Munich with Charlie Hodge, Lamar Fike and Rex Mansfield. They mainly spent their time visiting night clubs, and it was here that Rex Mansfield, who had had that initial feeling of wanting to protect Elvis, was rescued by Elvis. The event took place at the Moulin Rouge nightclub where the boys were sitting with some girls in separate booths. Rex was enjoying the company of his girl when a large German man came up and spoke to the girl. It looked as though he was her boyfriend and was asking her to leave and go with him, but she refused, wanting to stay with Rex. This did not please the German and he grabbed the girl, pulled her out of the booth and pushed her down the hallway. Rex objected to this treatment of her, so he challenged the man and grabbed him by the shoulder, at which point, the man spun round and punched Rex on the jaw. They continued to exchange blows until Elvis intervened by shouting, "OK men, now let's break it up." He then grabbed the man by his arms and pinned him against the wall in order that Rex could plant a knockout blow, which he did, so that when Elvis let go of his arms, he slid down the wall. The club manager had been called, and when he enquired what had been happening Elvis replied, "I sure do apologise for this situation, Sir, but this guy got a little out of hand and one of my boys had to put him in his place." This elicited an apology from the manager for any inconvenience caused.

The group then arrived in Paris on the 15th of June where Elvis gave a press conference. This was the first time Rex had witnessed one of these and was amazed at how Elvis handled the questions. He could see that he was a "consummate professional" and that "off stage he was just one of the boys, but when in the spotlight he was transformed."

The reporters had told Elvis that Paris was the most international city in the world and that celebrities could be seen walking down the street without being bothered or even noticed, much less mobbed by fans. Encouraged by this, Elvis and his friends decided to try it out. They walked out of the hotel into the Champs-Élysées, and they were able to walk down peaceably for three blocks with some people stopping and staring, but no more. Elvis was delighted and decided to stop at a pavement café and sit down for refreshments and do some people watching. Suddenly they were mobbed by hundreds of people trying to get to Elvis. Rex, who had not seen anything like this before, found it very frightening, but on the instruction of Lamar who knew what was happening, they surrounded Elvis and managed to get him away, running as fast as they could back to the hotel. Daytime sightseeing was hence taken off the agenda and Elvis slept in the daytime and went to clubs at night.

The furlough expired at midnight on Friday 26th June. According to Rex, though, Elvis decided they would miss the train back to Frankfurt that day and spend another night in Paris. At that time, the army had a day-of-grace policy concerning leaves, so they knew that as long as they were back at Friedberg by midnight on the 27th, they would not be AWOL. It cost Elvis $800 to hire a limousine to take them back to Germany. Elvis later told Rex he had spent $10,000 on the trip to Paris, and that it was worth every cent of it.

Hollywood in Germany

Although Elvis was 100 per cent committed to the Army, he was still under contract with the movie industry in Hollywood. Consequently, in August that year, producer Hal Wallis visited him to discuss the script of his next film, "GI Blues," and to shoot the exteriors and army footage. For long shots featuring Elvis, a stand-in from the 143rd Signal Battalion was used. The close-up scenes with Elvis were filmed later back in the USA as Elvis was not allowed to and did not want to take time out to film. In Germany, he was Elvis the soldier, not Elvis the actor.

This film contract ensured that Elvis received 50% of the gross income plus $250,000 in advance for signing the contract and $100,000 for expenses while the movie was being filmed. He also received a cheque for $279,000 for just three months record sales. This makes his army salary of $122.30 per month somewhat pale into insignificance.

Enter Priscilla

Priscilla Ann Beaulieu was a 14-year-old Elvis fan, whose stepfather, Airforce Captain Beaulieu (her own father had died when she was only 5 months old), had, in August 1959, been transferred from the USA to the US Base at Wiesbaden, about a one-hour drive from Bad Nauheim. Priscilla met Currie

Grant at the Eagle Force Community Center in Wiesbaden and discovered that he regularly visited Elvis' home. According to Currie, Priscilla asked him if he would take her to meet Elvis, which he did on 13th September 1959. When she arrived at the house everyone noticed what a beautiful young girl she was. Although she was demure, petite, and quiet, she seemed to be more sophisticated than other girls her age. For Elvis it seemed to be love at first sight as he could hardly take his eyes off her all evening. A few days later, Elvis phoned her parents to ask if she could visit again, assuring them that he would treat their daughter with total respect and that there would always be a chaperone with them. They agreed as long as the set curfew was observed.

Priscilla visited most weekends when she would sit in the living room with the "gang" talking, laughing, and listening to music, with Elvis making every effort to impress her, including showing off his newly obtained karate skills. Eventually for some privacy Elvis took Priscilla up to his bedroom where they would indulge in pillow fights, tearful conversations about his mother and stillborn brother and more romantic conversations about his love and respect for Priscilla. There was some sexual activity, but Elvis knew that she was under-age for sexual intercourse, and being overall a law-abiding citizen, he would not break that law. Also, he had promised her parents that he would not take advantage of her.

Vernon's Love Interest

Soon after his arrival in Germany Elvis had a call from Dee Stanley, the wife of an American Sergeant stationed in Frankfurt, inviting him and his family to dinner with her family. As Elvis was about to go on manoeuvres, he sidestepped the invitation and his father went alone, starting a series of events which did not please Elvis.

Vernon started spending most of his time with Dee Stanley. Since meeting her, he spent more and more time with her and her husband at their home and military clubs on base. As the relationship developed, three became a crowd and Dee's marriage fell apart, so they separated. Dee took her three young sons over to the USA to live with her sister until she returned to the States. When she returned to Germany, she and Vernon started dating and she moved in with him.

Elvis was not pleased about this as he thought that it was too soon after his mother's death for his father to be looking for another partner. Also, he wasn't sure if Dee was just after the fame and the money. However, he never criticised his father, whom he loved and respected, and he was always polite and gracious towards Dee. The love between Elvis and Priscilla and Vernon and Dee were not the only romances in that household. Rex was beginning to fall for Elisabeth, though, as she was officially one of Elvis' girlfriends, she was out of bounds for anyone else. This caused problems as Rex and Elisabeth had to meet somewhere Elvis would not find them, and this was at a friend's house on base. The subterfuge and guilt of meeting behind Elvis' back like this was a strain on them both, but the situation was resolved as we shall see later.

A Happier Christmas for Elvis, But Not for Rex

As Christmas approached, Elvis bought gifts for his family and friends, including arranging for a poodle to be sent to Anita Wood, his girlfriend in the States. He also gave a donation of $1500 to a local orphanage. The donation made it possible for the owner, Hermann Schaub, to buy gifts for all 115 children in the orphanage. Although Elvis had asked him not to make the donation public, he was so overwhelmed by Elvis' generosity that he informed the local newspaper, publicly thanking him, saying that he didn't understand his music, but thought that he was a terrific person. "Never in the history of the orphanage has anyone treated the children so well," he told a reporter.

On Friday 25th December, Elvis hosted a large Christmas party for family and friends and fellow soldiers. Gifts were exchanged, but Elvis' most treasured gift was one which had arrived at the house some time before Christmas. Initially he was suspicious of this large crate with no return address delivered to his home. It could be anything, including a bomb, so it was very carefully opened to reveal a living Christmas tree with pine needles still intact and adorned with suitable decorations. He assumed it was from a fan and was delighted, saying what wonderful fans he had. The tree took pride of place in the living room.

Two of the guests at the party were Rex Mansfield and Elisabeth Stefaniak who were in love and still meeting secretly behind Elvis' back. They found it very hard not to be able to be seen as "being together." Rex was particularly devastated when, at the end of the party, Elvis told him goodnight and to make himself at home, and then took Elisabeth upstairs to his bedroom. Rex had never felt so lonely. He had already had a few of the "little white pills" to make him feel better and downed a few more. As he was waiting for them to kick in, he thought he would listen to a record that might lift his spirits. He picked up the first album he reached which was, he noted, one of Elvis' favourites, the

Harmonising Four. Rex says that the song *Only Believe* reached out to him. He had heard it many times before but this time it seemed to speak to him personally:

Only believe, only believe,
All things are possible if you'll only believe,
My Lordy, only believe, yes, only believe,
All things are possible if you'll only believe.
I met God one morning, my soul feeling bad,
Heart heavy laden, I felt tired and down.
He lifted all my burdens,
Yeah, right now I'm feeling glad,
All things are possible if you'll only believe.
I believe, yeah, I believe.
All things are possible if you'll only believe.

Rex was in an impossible predicament: in love with the girl of a close friend, and not yet ready to tell Elvis and face up to the consequences. As the amphetamines kicked in, his mind began a torturous hallucinatory journey and he wanted to start running and screaming his head off. He said, "What saved me that night was the song by the Harmonising Four. Like so many people in the world I only turned to God when things became unbearable. The song had ministered to my heart in ways I would only understand much in later life." He said he went to God on his knees in prayer right there in Elvis' living room and that God had brought him through a night of hell on earth. He said, "For the first and last time in my life, thank God, I was happy to see the day after Christmas and felt relieved to be back in my barracks." Later, in their book, Rex and Elisabeth mention that they are especially fond of Elvis' gospel records, especially *You'll Never Walk Alone, I Believe, Where No One Stands Alone, Precious Lord, Without Him* and *He Touched Me,* with Rex recalling Elvis singing them at the house in Germany and the many times he joined in.

The 8th of January 1960 was Elvis' 25th birthday and he threw a party for over 200 guests including Joe Esposito who had been inducted into the army the same time as Elvis and trained at Fort Hood but had only met him in Germany on the base, playing touch football in a field behind Elvis' house. From the first meeting Joe said that something clicked, and they immediately liked each other. From then on, they became good friends, with Joe becoming Elvis' Road Manager and being with him till the very end.

Karate and Gospel in Paris

Later in January, Elvis started a five-day furlough in Paris. It was here that he took private lessons with Tetsugio Murakami, one of Japan's top shotokan stylists, who would help pioneer shotokan in Europe. He spent the five days studying for several hours each day with Murakami. Elvis was first exposed to karate in Germany. His first instructor was a German shotokan stylist named Juergen Seydel who was considered the father of karate in Germany. Elvis would also spend hours training with Rex Mansfield.

Always eager to seek out gospel singers, Elvis went to a concert where the Golden Gate Quartet opened for Line Renaud at the Casino de Paris, with her review "Plaisirs." At the end of the show, Elvis joined the group backstage, where he discovered a Selmer guitar and started a jam session with the Golden Gate Quartet, in front of an audience of his two friends, Line Renaud and her husband, their driver, a dresser and the concierge. At the invitation of Loulou Gasté, Line Renaud's husband, Elvis and the Quartet moved on to their apartment and sang gospel songs until around 6am. Elvis was in his element, singing his first love in music. Unfortunately, this jam session has never been properly documented as there were no cameras nor audio equipment. To my mind, this jam session was just as historic as when Elvis jammed with the Beatles – maybe more so!

The reason the American group the Golden Gate Quartet was based in Paris was because, in 1955, they decided to revive their career by touring Europe for the first time, where they became widely popular. They moved to Paris in 1959 and continued touring, primarily in Europe. The quartet is still active today, albeit with different members. Like many singing groups, they have kept their name and changed members throughout the years, replacing those who have retired. Elvis and the Jordanaires recorded *Swing Down Sweet Chariot* about six months after his Paris jam session with the Golden Gate Quartet. Orlandus Wilson, one of the members of the group, judged their rendition "very well done … close to the Golden Gate Quartet. If you're not sharp enough, when you hear it, you think it's the Gates." Elvis's first LP following his military service, "Elvis Is Back!", includes a version of the Golden Gate's secular hit, *I Will Be Home Again.*

The songs Elvis recorded, apart from the ones in the films, were his own choice. He told reporters that "It would be a bad mistake if I had someone telling me what to record and how to record it, because I work on instinct and impulse. I choose songs with the public in mind. I try to visualise as though I am buying the record myself."

One critic says that one of Elvis' most endearing artistic qualities was his identification with southern vernacular music and his genuine appreciation of African American musicians and that Elvis's methods seem practically reverential, and never descend into parody or minstrel-mockery.

In February, Elvis was promoted to Sergeant and threw a party to celebrate. He was very proud of this promotion, and rightly so as not many people enter the Army in peacetime as Private E-1 and come out of the army two years later as Sergeant E-5.

Bill Taylor Remembers

According to William (Bill) Taylor, who was a 25-year-old first lieutenant in the same battalion as Elvis, in his book "Elvis in the Army," Elvis opened up to him about some regrets he had about his mother. Elvis said, "Lord knows I wish I could go back and change some things. You know, if I hadn't been on the road so much, I could've taken care of my family better. Spent too much time thinkin' 'bout myself." Bill was stunned because he saw how much Elvis cared for Vernon and Minnie, then realised Elvis was talking about his mother.

From one of their other conversations, Bill gained a significant insight into Elvis' way of thinking about his life. Elvis told him, "I do the best I can. Somehow, it's never good enough for somebody. Sometimes I feel like just quittin.' Screw 'em all. But can't do that. Too many people dependin' on me. Too many people think I'm goin' places. Too damn many people!" From that Bill observed, "It's revealing that he didn't talk about what he wanted: he talked about the others who depended on him and what they wanted and expected of him." Taylor continues writing, "Elvis sounded as if others were driving him towards goals and objectives without his deciding whether these goals and objectives were the right ones for him, and whether he would know how to get there."

Bill also tells about how the girls always knew how to find Elvis. He writes, "So help me, the local girls had an intelligence network that was almost infallible. They were like hummingbirds attracted to a flower. They could almost always find Elvis, and their presence almost always disrupted scout platoon road march operations." He continues writing, "I saw a horde of girls jumping up and down, waving notepads in their hands, and pressing in on the jeep … How did they know it was Elvis? … they found him. They always did."

Bill sums up Elvis' army career as he observed it in Germany. He did not see any evidence of Elvis taking drugs or drinking alcohol. In fact, he says that Elvis did his assigned job well, he pulled his weight and used his head. He was one of them, he cared about them, and he got back the respect and friendship he gave everyone else. He saw sparks of leadership in Elvis and wondered that he could have induced men to follow him in combat, just as his music caused millions of young people to follow him. He admired Elvis, not only for his efforts as a soldier, but the way that he handled the results of his fame. He felt that Elvis was a young soldier of character and professionalism, a selfless team player, a man of self-reflection, tempered by humour.

Another soldier who remembers meeting Elvis just once, so not getting to know him, was Colin Powell, an American politician, diplomat, and retired four-star general who served as the 65th United States Secretary of State and was a respected statesman until his death in 2021. In his memoirs "My American Journal," he tells of relating his army stories to his children "who only perked up at one story." The story was of his serving in Germany as an army Lieutenant in 1960.

He recalled one day on manoeuvres: "'Hey, Lieutenant' one of my men shouted. 'Come on over. Look who's here.' I walked over to the jeep, where a grimy, weary-looking sergeant saluted me and put out his hand. It was Elvis Presley. That their father had shaken the King's hand astonished my kids. What impressed me at the time was that instead of seeking celebrity treatment, Elvis had done his two-year hitch, uncomplainingly, as an ordinary GI, even rising to the responsibility of an NCO."

The Problem of "Being on Show"

Elvis' life was, as it is with us all, a battle, though, in Elvis' case as we have already seen, the pressures he was under were more than many have to deal with. The death of his beloved mother at such a young age was probably the worst thing that ever happened to him.

However, as we can see, Elvis was very much respected, especially by those who worked with him in the army. Over time many pressures had been building up which challenged him immensely, and amongst his family and friends it was not unknown for him to lose his temper if he thought people were trying to control him. Also, he would ignore people for a while if he felt they had slighted him. Rex Mansfield says, "Let me give you a little insight because, keep in mind, Elvis was under tremendous pressure. He had to put up this front to a point. He had to be careful of everything he said and, even though he was in the army and protected to some extent, we had some close calls. So, Elvis had to be nice to everybody all the time, and so his friends were the ones that he was able to take it out on – and they'd still love him. So, it was Lamar, Charlie and Red etc. who bore the brunt of it."

Time to Depart

On 1st March 1960, the Army held a press conference in the barracks at Friedberg which was attended by over a hundred reporters and photographers. Elvis was presented with a certificate of merit, citing his "Cheerfulness and drive and continually outstanding leadership ability." Elvis told reporters that he wanted to have more serious acting roles. He felt that his time in the army had helped him in his personal life and his career as he had made a lot of friends, had some good experiences and (laughing) some bad ones. He had learned to rough it and put himself to the test to see if he could take it.

During the question time, Elvis interrupted the meeting to say "hello" to one of the few women in the room. With the eyes of everyone upon him, Elvis approached an information officer named Air Force Captain Marion Keisker MacInnes, embraced her warmly, and thanked her for helping him to become a worldwide musical icon. Elvis told everyone that she was the entire reason the press conference was happening.

Marion was the person who had encouraged (nagged?) Sam Phillips to listen to the personal recording Elvis had done at Sun Studios nearly seven years ago. Marion had left Sun Records in 1957 and joined the US Air Force. Elvis hadn't seen her since then and, when he saw her in the audience, in his usual spur of the moment way, just had to go and greet her. Elvis told her, "I don't know whether to kiss you or salute!" She responded, "In that order." Apparently, she later was reprimanded for over-familiarity in public with a non-commissioned officer.

Elvis spotted her in another crowd in January 1971. It was at a luncheon in Memphis honouring the U.S. Jaycees Ten Outstanding Young Men of America of 1970 – one of several activities leading up to an evening awards banquet. Elvis was one of the ten. This time he grabbed Marion and took her to his table and introduced her to his wife, Priscilla, and the guys in his entourage, telling them, "… she's the one who made it all possible. Without her I wouldn't even be here."

On 2nd March, one of the many people at the airport to wave goodbye to Elvis was Priscilla Beaulieu. She was captured by a Life magazine photographer and the photo appeared in the 14th of March edition captioned "The girl he left behind."

Elvis in the UK

The only publicly recorded time that Elvis set foot in the UK was when his plane landed at Prestwick Airport in Scotland for a two-hour stopover to refuel.

In those days, Prestwick was home to the 1631 USAF unit. Despite a massive security clampdown, the news leaked out that a mystery VIP was flying in and when Sergeant Presley stepped off the plane, local fans rushed to greet him. A relaxed Elvis mingled with them and also held an impromptu press conference.

Fewer than 200 people saw him, but for some, such as Ann Murphy, then aged 16, it changed their lives. Here, she tells about her historic meeting.

"I used to babysit for Sergeant Phelps at the US airbase. I was at work one day when he turned up at my house and told my mum that Elvis would be at the airbase that night and I should go if I wanted to see him. My mum ran to a phone box to call me at work. I couldn't believe it. I loved Elvis. I had all his records. On the bus home, I was telling everyone I was going to see Elvis that night, but they all thought it was just a rumour. They probably thought I was crazy. I changed into my American jeans, lumber jacket, bobby socks and blue suede shoes and cycled the three miles to the airport base.

"I dropped in at my friend Muriel's and she said she would come too. When we got to the base there was a small group of people already there, standing at the barrier in front of two huge Cadillac cars. Muriel and I were right at the barrier. We were so excited and suddenly the plane was in front of us. The door opened and there was Elvis. He was so handsome in his uniform. He waved and we started screaming. He shouted: 'Where am I?' and people shouted back: 'Prestwick' – but I was shouting: 'I love you.'

"He came down the stairs and looked fantastic with that beautiful smile. We could hardly believe we were looking at him. We could nearly touch him. The next thing we knew, he was away. We went to the cafe where the young folk hung out and told people we had seen Elvis. They were all laughing at us, but the papers the next day proved it.

"I suppose that day changed my life. I went on to marry my own Elvis. I met my late husband Andy at dances, and he was a great jiver. He had a black quiff hairstyle and was known as the Prestwick Elvis. He used to sing Elvis songs all the time and won a talent contest as Elvis. When I had a win on the football coupons in 1997, I took Andy on a surprise trip to America. We went to Nashville, and he made a couple of records – *Blue Suede Shoes* and *All Shook Up* – then we went to Graceland and Las Vegas. He was like a wee boy.

"Looking back, it was as if I was meant to win that money because Andy died nine months later. He was buried in his midnight blue suit and his blue suede shoes.

"So, my daughters – Angela and Andrea – were really brought up by Elvis. They're both big fans and so are my grandchildren. I'll never forget the day I saw my idol face-to-face. I might have been a naive, Scottish 16-year-old, but it changed my life forever. It might have been 50 years ago, but it feels like yesterday."

One of the black and white photographs taken during this short visit to Prestwick shows a journalist sitting next to Elvis, taking notes. The reporter in the photo is Ian Nelson, believed to be one of only two journalists who had an audience with Elvis that night, and the only one to be photographed with him.

Apparently, Elvis avoided questions about Priscilla, but when Ian asked him if he would perform in Scotland, Elvis said: "I kind of like the idea of Scotland. I'm going to do a European tour and it would be nice to come back here."

This stopover in Prestwick is the only photographed time that Elvis set foot on British soil. However, theatre producer and Elvis fan, Bill Kenwright claimed that Elvis went sightseeing with Cockney singer Tommy Steele during a trip that took in the Houses of Parliament. In 2008, he told BBC Radio's Ken Bruce, "Elvis came to England. Nobody thinks he did, and I hope Tommy doesn't go mad when I tell you."

Tommy Steele confirmed that the trip did occur, and that he did take Elvis Presley on a trip around London in 1958, but said he regrets the news leaking to the press. In a note to the Daily Mail, he said he "swore never to divulge publicly" what happened. "I can only hope he can forgive me," he wrote. "It was an event shared by two young men sharing the same love of their music and the same thrill of achieving something unimaginable." He confirmed that Elvis was flown in from Germany by the army, picked up in a limo and driven around London with Tommy as his guide. No "buddies" involved – as far as they were concerned, he was out on manoeuvres in Germany for the day.

Before this trip, Elvis had phoned Tommy, whom he knew of as a kind of rival (Tommy had been billed as Britain's answer to Elvis), but not met personally. Bill Kenwright, reports, "Tommy got a phone call one night which said: 'They tell me you're good' and Tommy replied: 'Who's this?' The caller said: 'It's Elvis,' Tommy said: 'Get outta here.' And Elvis said: 'Are you as good as me?' And they talked, and they got a friendship. Elvis flew in for a day. And Tommy showed him round London. He showed him the Houses of Parliament and spent the day with him."

Personally, I can see this happening, and why the secrecy. Elvis wanted to be treated like any other GI and did not want any special privileges, but I can believe that he was keen to visit London and, in one of his spurs of the moment ideas, asked if he could get on one of the military flights to Northolt, the secure UK military airport in London, where there would be no press nor 'outsiders'. It would be easy to hire a limo, and then be driven round London for a couple of hours where no-one would see him. As for food and the toilet, all that could take place at Northolt before and after the limo trip. Elvis would have sworn Tommy to secrecy because it would not be good if it had got out that he had had this special privilege.

As well as being a military base, Northolt is also used by civilian aeroplanes, and celebrities today, such as Arnold Schwarzenegger, Madonna and Tom Jones choose to fly to and from there to be out of sight and mind of the public and press.

A spokesman for Elvis's Graceland Estate said: "To the best of our knowledge there was only the one stopover at Scotland. We are researching our archives. There are some undocumented areas of Elvis's life."

Back in the USA

On 3rd March, Elvis arrived at McGuire Airforce Base near Fort Dix where hundreds of fans and press welcomed him. Among the official welcoming group were the Colonel and Nancy Sinatra, who presented him with a gift of a couple of formal lace-front shirts. Then, yet another press conference.

Elvis said of his time in the army, "I was in a funny position. Actually, that's the only way it could be. People were expecting me to mess up, to goof up in one way or another. They thought I couldn't take it and so forth, and I was determined to go to any limits to prove otherwise, not only to the people who were wondering, but to myself. The hardest part of the entire military service was being away from the fans and just being away from show business altogether." He said, "That was the hardest part of all – it wasn't the army, it wasn't the other men, it was that. It stayed on my mind. I kept thinking about the past all the time, contemplating the future, that was the hardest part."

These press conferences again showed Elvis' sense of humour. When asked if two years of sobering army life had changed his mind about rock 'n' roll, he replied, "No it hasn't because I was in tanks for a long time, and they rocked and rolled quite a lot."

Elvis spent two days at Fort Dix going through the routine discharge procedure, after which he was honourably discharged from active duty on 5th March, receiving a mustering-out check of $109.54. He took the train to Memphis with the Colonel, Lamar Fike and Rex Mansfield. Meanwhile Vernon had arrived home at Graceland with Minnie Mae, Dee Stanley, and Elisabeth.

Elisabeth had come over to the USA to continue her work as Elvis' secretary and Rex Mansfield had been offered a job by Elvis to be his number one aide. The next few days were crucial for them both. Elvis still did not know of their dating but when they arrived back in Memphis, he told Elisabeth that she was free to date other men. She told Rex this and that she had decided to be with him. Rex declined Elvis' job offer and went back to his home in Dresden, Tennessee, and Elisabeth planned a trip to her parent's home in Florida, later telling Elvis that she could not continue as his secretary, to which he replied she was always welcome back if she ever needed a job. They both left Graceland separately and never returned. Apparently, Elvis never knew of their subterfuge, and they were never in contact with him again, though they did invite him to their wedding, an invitation to which he did not reply. Rex and Elisabeth had a very happy marriage, adopting a son, Don. The marriage only ended when Rex passed away 26th August 2018.

On 7th March, when Elvis arrived back at Graceland, he held a Press Conference in his father's office at the rear of the house. When asked about any romances or hearts he had left behind Elvis said that over the last few months he had been seeing a little girl whose father was in the Air Force, but it was no big romance, commenting, "I have to be careful when I answer questions like that." (laughing). He also advised any young man going into the army to do their service, to play it straight and do their best otherwise they would have two years of misery. He also said that he had no plans to leave Memphis and would keep Graceland as long as he could.

Before he returned to Hollywood, he had some other things to attend to. The first thing he did the day after his return to Memphis was to visit his mother's grave at Forest Hills Cemetery where he saw the large statue of Jesus which his father had ordered and placed there during their time in Germany.

On 21st March, Elvis returned to Nashville to record songs for a single and the album "Elvis is Back!" He then took a train to Miami, where, on 26th March, The Frank Sinatra Timex Show "Welcome Home Elvis" TV show was recorded.

Frank Sinatra and Elvis had been musical rivals since the 1950s, and on occasion they had each been asked their opinions on the other. Frank had said of rock 'n' roll music as "sung, played and written for the most part by cretinous goons and by means of its almost imbecilic reiterations and sly, lewd – in plain fact, dirty – lyrics, and as I said before, it manages to be the martial music of every side-burned delinquent on the face of the earth … this rancid smelling aphrodisiac I deplore." When asked his reaction to hearing this, Elvis responded, "He has a right to his opinion, but I can't see him knocking it for no good reason. I admire him as a performer and an actor, but I think he's badly mistaken about this. If I remember correctly, he was also part of a trend. I don't see how he can call the youth of today immoral and delinquent." Of course, Elvis' image had now changed, and on the show, they had nothing but good things to say about each other and appeared to really enjoy singing together, smiling, and laughing. As they harmonised on *Love Me Tender* Frank interjected "Man, that's pretty!"

During April, Elvis had a garage at Graceland converted into an apartment for his father and Dee and her three boys.

On 21st April, Elvis returned to Hollywood with his entourage of his cousin Gene Smith, Joe Esposito, Charlie Hodge, Lamar Fike and Sonny West to start work on "GI Blues."

Gallery

Elvis' mother's grave in Forest Hills Cemetery, Memphis. (Jim Reid)

Breakfast time in Goethestrasse. Elvis with his father Vernon and Grandma Minnie Mae who is holding a plate of homemade biscuits.

Whilst serving in the army, Elvis kept up with the latest popular music, and of course listened to gospel recordings.

Elvis briefing his team during a Winter Shield Cold (in both senses of the word!) War exercise in February 1960 in the Grafenwöhr training area (USA National Archives)

Showing off his Sergeant's stripes

Priscilla waving farewell to Elvis as he leaves Germany.

Elvis and Frank Sinatra enjoying singing together on Sinatra's Welcome Home Elvis TV show.

Elvis interview at Prestwick airport, Scotland. (Daily Record)

Chapter 5

Hollywood Highlights

Trust in the Lord with all your heart and lean not on your own understanding; in all your ways submit to him and he will make your paths straight. (Proverbs 3:5-6)

Elvis on the set of Change of Habit with Mahalia Jackson and actress Barbara McNair who played one of the nuns.

It seems that when Elvis returned to Hollywood in 1960, making what many describe as rubbish movies, life was just as difficult spiritually and emotionally for him as were the later fifties. Despite his own difficulties, Elvis prayed for many people during these years, he prayed for healing and people were healed, he counselled and prayed for people who were having marriage difficulties or who were depressed and feeling lonely. He would tell them of God's great love for them and how they could enjoy life if they just trusted the Lord. He had the Meditation Garden built at Graceland in 1965, a peaceful place (even today with hundreds of fans milling around). His entourage, "The Memphis Mafia," although not on the whole partaking in Elvis' love of the Gospel, certainly recognised his zeal and enthusiasm and bought him a statue of Jesus for the Meditation Garden.

Elvis' relentless search for "the Truth," led him into studying other philosophies and religions, which only served to confuse him even more. There were some highlights, however among them he was able to have a few gospel songs included in the movies and he recorded two gospel albums, *His Hand in Mine* in 1960 and *How Great Thou Art* in 1966. He also married and sired a beautiful daughter.

In April 1960, work started on the film "G.I. Blues" in which Elvis played a guitar-playing soldier stationed in West Germany who makes a bet that he can date a cabaret dancer played by Juliet Prowse. The German location shots and army manoeuvres had already been filmed in Germany.

The director, Norman Taurog, directed eight other Elvis films and he felt that Elvis was a natural for the movies as he was "the most relaxed boy you could want." He also said that Elvis was a good listener and "when you have a good listener, you have a good actor." Many felt that Norman Taurog was one of the nicest and kindest people in Hollywood and Elvis certainly liked him and working with him. He regarded him as a kind of father figure as he really cared about Elvis personally and his well-being.

Marriage Material?

We know that Elvis was attracted to beautiful young women and had many relationships with them, most, I would say, being "just good friends." I have Dan Wooding to thank for this story of Sandy Martindale remembering dating Elvis while he was filming "G.I. Blues."

Dan Wooding was a pioneering journalist who interviewed many people and attended many events. One such event was The Media Fellowship International Praise Brunch held in Beverly Hills in 2011, where the speaker was American radio and television personality, Wink Martindale, who was a friend of Elvis' and who had interviewed him on his radio show in Memphis in 1956. Wink told the audience that his wife, Sandy Ferra Martindale, had once dated Elvis Presley.

Dan interviewed Sandy after the event when she offered some insights about Elvis' faith. "He knew the Bible from cover to cover and was a very religious person," she said. "Elvis once told me about the time, when he was younger, that he was driving across the desert in Texas when he said he saw a vision of Christ."

In reference to that unusual incident, Elvis told Sandy, "You know, I believe that God has something big for me to do, but I don't know what it is." Sandy felt that Elvis didn't realise what was going to take place after his death, for that is when they released much of his gospel music, she noted. "He had no idea at the time, as he was kind of like my husband, a Tennessee boy, who was very shy and who didn't know how talented and valuable he was."

Sandy went on to say Elvis loved to sing hymns and added, "In fact, during a lot of our dates, he'd just be at the piano in the den of our home and begin singing gospel songs." She then said that, even though Elvis was fighting many demons in his later years, he held on to his great love for the Bible. "What a lot of people don't know is that he could quote the Bible from cover to cover. He believed deeply," she said.

Sandy first met Elvis when he visited the Cross Bow, her father's nightclub in Panorama City, California. "Elvis had just got out of the army and one day he came into my dad's club and saw my picture in the office, and said, 'I'd like to meet your daughter,'" she recalled.

"So, Elvis called me, and because it was a school night and my mother wouldn't drive me up to the nightclub, he said he could come back the next week and he asked me if I could meet him there. In the meantime, my dad came home and told me that he [Elvis] was a "gorgeous guy" because at the time, I didn't know who Elvis Presley was." Sandy explained that Elvis didn't visit the club to sing, but just for recreation.

"So, the next week my mother said she would drive me to the club. Elvis had a date with a beautiful actress, and I just sat there with my little ponytail and frilly dress. He kissed me on the cheek and then later he called and told my mother he wanted to date me, and my mother said, 'I don't care if you're King Farouk; my daughter's only 14 and she can't go out with you.' So, Elvis said to my mother, 'Well, you can come on the date,' so she came on our first three dates.

Elvis was living at the Beverly Wilshire Hotel, so Sandy and her mother and he would go there and have pizza, hot fudge sundaes, banana splits, as well as watch television and talk and dance. After these first three dates when Elvis promised her mother that he'd be a "gentleman" and "take good care" of Sandy, her mother said it was OK for them to date without her being there. Sandy says "He stuck to his word and was a perfect gentleman. He loved and respected my parents and was a wonderful part of my life."

They talked about marriage, and Sandy knew that she was the kind of a girl he wanted to marry, but also knew that he had met Priscilla in Germany two months before he met her, and when Priscilla moved over to Memphis, with her parents still living in Germany, Elvis felt responsible for her. Alongside this, Sandy's mother would not let her go over and spend the night with Elvis. Sandy felt that Priscilla and Elvis forged a much stronger bond than was possible between them, with Elvis falling deeply in love with Priscilla and eventually marrying her.

About the traumas in Elvis' life, Sandy said, "After his mother Gladys died, Elvis kind of lost his way. But then when Pricilla left him, he just wanted to forget reality because he had chosen her for his queen, and he believed in marriage as an institution; that it was meant to be 'till death do us part' and that kind of broke his heart.

"God had a plan, and this [marriage to Wink Martindale] was the plan God had for me. If I had stayed with Elvis, I may have been able to save him, but you know, I'm not God, so maybe, also I may not have been able to save him."

Ed Parker

Elvis met Ed Parker at a karate demonstration at the Beverly Hills Hotel in May 1960. Ed, a Hawaiian, had developed a more flexible street fighting technique which interested Elvis.

Ed and Elvis become good friends and Elvis felt comfortable confiding in Ed, whom he knew would understand his spiritual yearnings, as they both recognised Jesus as Saviour. Ed felt that Elvis did not fully realise the vast extent of the influence he had. In his book, "Inside Elvis," Ed says of Elvis "Only one other, greater than all of us, was instantly known by his first name only, our Savior Jesus Christ." Ed says that he is not trying to parallel the lives of Elvis and Jesus, as Elvis had very human flaws, but that Elvis loved the Lord and tried to follow him. He said, "Elvis was a missionary without realising it. His gospel singing and generosity had planted the seed of Christianity into the souls of thousands that heard him. He was also instrumental in cultivating those seeds in many souls. His efforts made it possible for preachers and pastors to reap the benefit of the harvest."

Ed described Elvis as "impulsive, unpredictable, amiable, forgiving, loyal, very observant and a good judge of character. He was also genuine, sincere, radiating raw human magnetism, unselfish, giving and forgiving. He had a great sense of ESP [Extra Sensory Perception – knowing what people were thinking] and a desire to excel. He was a mixture of bold determination and self-doubt."

He also felt that the love affair that Elvis had with his fans was what killed him because of his desire to please them and a fear of losing them. Ed believed that Elvis felt he was a prisoner of his own environment, but that he accepted having to be "Elvis" with style and dignity.

***

After completing the filming of "G.I. Blues," Elvis returned to Memphis on 30th June.

The next day his father married Dee Stanley in Arkansas. Elvis did not attend the wedding. In an interview with Memphis Press-Scimitar, Elvis said of his new stepmother, "She seems pretty nice," then added, "I only had one mother and that's it. There'll never be another, as long as she understands that there won't be any trouble." Of his father, he said, "He's all I've got left in the world. I'll never go against him or stand in his way. He stood by me all these years and sacrificed things he wanted so that I could have clothes and lunch money to go to school."

Back in Hollywood for the filming of "Flaming Star," Elvis and his entourage were, as before, staying at the Beverly Wilshire Hotel. After several disruptive incidents, they were asked to leave, and Elvis rented a house in Bel Air which he used on and off the next five years.

After completing the film, he returned to Memphis in mid-October.

More Gospel Recordings

On 30th October, Elvis attended RCA studios in Nashville where he recorded fourteen gospel songs for his upcoming LP "His Hand In Mine." It represented the heart and soul of Elvis and his lifelong love of gospel music. The entire album was recorded in one 14-hour session with The Jordanaires supplying backup vocals. The album reached #14 on the Billboard Hot 200 chart and was later certified Platinum.

The recording session was attended by Sonny West, and, although he had heard Elvis sing gospel in private, he said of this session that a transformation came over Elvis and that "his majestic voice and unique interpretation just blew me away." He had never seen anything like it beforehand. To him, it seemed that the Lord was using Elvis as a conduit of his love and power, with

Elvis giving his all. He was not only trying to sound technically perfect but to get the feeling.

Al Pachuki, a recording engineer with RCA, says of recording with Elvis that he was a dream come true, that he motivated everyone, including the person making the coffee, to go above and beyond their capabilities. He said that the recordings never started as soon as Elvis went into the studio, but there was always an hour or so of chatter, asking how everyone was, and lots of laughter, just like a family gathering. When the recording began Elvis always put a lot of emphasis on the feeling of the music. Sometimes, if that feeling wasn't there Elvis would call off the session and say that they would pick it up the next day. The whole studio worked as one. Al says, "Right now I am sitting here with a big smile and a wonderful feeling recalling those great moments in my life. When Elvis came into the studio, it wasn't work, it was pure unadulterated pleasure." He also recommends that people not be sad at Elvis' passing, but rather thank God Almighty for the time he gave us Elvis Presley.

Signs That All Is Not Well

During the filming of "Wild in the Country" in November, members of Elvis' entourage noticed mood swings and fits of temper, maybe brought on by the character he was playing in the film, though they were concerned when Elvis, during a trip to San Francisco, pulled a gun on a group of guys whom he believed had insulted him.

Christmas 1960 was Elvis' first Christmas back home after the army. His father and his new wife, Dee, and her sons were living in the converted garage apartment built for them at Graceland. Although Elvis was not happy with this arrangement, he continued to be gracious to his father's new family especially the boys, Billy (7), Rick (6) and David (4) whom he readily accepted as his new brothers.

The Boys Meet Their New Brother

When they first arrived at Graceland after their mother had married Vernon, and collected them from the boarding school, the brothers must have thought they had arrived in heaven. Rick Stanley says in his book "Caught in A Trap," that their time at the boarding school, while their mother was in Germany with Vernon, was not good. The school was on an impressive estate on the banks of a river, but they slept in a cold, dark dormitory. Because David was a different age, only three, he slept in a separate dormitory, across the corridor. This was traumatic for them, as not only were they separated from their mother, but also from each other. When the lights went out, they could hear David crying and would sometimes crawl into bed with him until he went to sleep. If they were caught, they were punished by having tabasco sauce poured into their mouths. This was also the punishment for other minor offences.

When the boys awoke on their first morning at Graceland there was an array of toys, including bikes, trikes, scooters and even a swing set in the yard. As well as the gifts, they found that Elvis was very indulgent with them and would not get cross when they behaved rather boisterously, even waking him up. Rick also remembers how much he enjoyed being with Elvis' Grandma, Minnie Mae, and would spend many hours with her in her room. She was a source of stability for him in that rather hectic household. When they grew up the brothers became part of Elvis' entourage and lived at Graceland with him and toured with his concerts for most of the next 17 years.

Letter to Ireland

On 18th January 1961, Elvis wrote a hand-written letter to Maureen Colgan in Swords, Ireland. Maureen married Maurice Colgan in 1951 after they had first met at a nightclub. Maurice was not even meant to be there as he was on a boy's night out when he heard the sound of Elvis blaring out from a nightclub. He went inside and met Maureen and they enjoyed their first dance to a romantic Elvis slow song. In January 1961, while pregnant Maureen became critically ill and went on the danger list in the hospital. Maurice wanted to do what he could to keep up her spirits so he wrote to Elvis seeking a get-well message for his wife, not even sure if it would bear any fruit. Maureen was delighted when a handwritten letter from Elvis arrived for her at the hospital.

The letter reads, *"Just a short note to say I hope you are feeling much better. Take care of yourself and don't worry – everything will be alright. Sincerely, Elvis Presley."* Elvis went even further and sent Maurice a note to their home to say that he had written to his wife. Maurice's letter reads, *"I sent your wife a get well message. Take care of her and yourself. May God bless you both. EP."* (Both letters have been authenticated by Sotheby's.)

***

Elvis' cousin Junior Smith, died of alcohol poisoning on 4th February. He had not been right since suffering shell shock in the Korean war. Elvis was distraught, though could not attend the funeral as he was called back to Hollywood to reshoot the ending of "Wild in the Country," as preview audiences did not like the suicide of one of the characters.

Elvis Becomes an Honorary Colonel

Elvis addressed the Tennessee State Legislature in Nashville in March and accepted the title of "Honorary Colonel." The honour was bestowed to recognise all the work Elvis had done not only in putting Tennessee on the map for music, but also for the tourism factor that Tennessee was hoping to be able to build.

Here is what Ann Ellington, daughter of Tennessee Governor Buford Ellington, says of the event. "When we got there, the Jordanaires were present, and they were seated around the table with my dad. We had been there for quite some time waiting for Elvis and his entourage to arrive. There were people everywhere. The whole of Capitol Hill was filled with cars and people standing outside waiting to get a glance of this car pulling in, and then Elvis Presley getting out of the car.

"So, we were sitting around the table and talking about the various things that the Jordanaires had been doing, when this entity was standing in the doorway, this black suit on, and every hair immaculately combed. There was absolutely a dead silence in the room. It was just like somebody had sucked all the air out of it. And he came in and stood behind a chair, and Dad got up and walked around and shook hands with him, and he sat down at the end of the table. And there was a lot of chat about what was going on and what was coming up in the future." Ann said that as they entered the legislature, which was packed with people, the sound of everyone cheering and calling to Elvis was overwhelming. Even the gavel, loudly banged for attention, could not be heard. It was not until Elvis stood up and spoke that the place became quiet.

Ann really felt a kinship with Elvis and said that any female who had an opportunity to sit down and meet him, just even for five minutes, would find a love for him that words cannot describe. In their case, she said, "I don't know how to exactly express this, but I wasn't looking to be an affair or in a fling or a romantic situation. I think all girls at that age have that feeling. But it was a momentary thing that developed into a lasting friendship that I feel very, very blessed to have had."

She said of Elvis' charisma, "I don't know if anybody could ever put a name to it. There was just an aura about him that for an instant he just absolutely consumed the area that he was in and everybody that was in it. It was a look, it was a demeanour about him, the way he held himself. The way he would look at you eye-to-eye when he talked to you. He made you feel like you were the most important person in the world for that moment. And you walked away with that feeling."

***

In March, work started on the film "Blue Hawaii" followed in July by "Follow That Dream," which is one of my favourite Elvis films. It is a "David and Goliath" story about the battle between a family and the government as they establish themselves on untitled land. The film is very amusing, telling a great story, and I believe that the character Elvis plays is very close to his own, in terms of his naivety and ingenuity. My favourite scene in the film is the court case where not-so-bright Toby Quimper, played by Elvis, wins the day by a rather clever ruse that exposes the prejudice of the plaintiff.

In November, work started on "Kid Galahad," and, partly due to the overrunning of the filming, Elvis spent Christmas of 1961 in California. Meanwhile, on 28th December, Vernon and his new family moved to a house he had bought in Hermitage Drive, a street behind Graceland, where they resided until 1965.

On 8th January 1962, Elvis celebrated his birthday at the Sahara Hotel in Las Vegas.

A Very Dedicated Fan

In February and March, Elvis was at home in Memphis, then returned to Hollywood to begin work on "Girls! Girls! Girls!"

As the title suggests, Elvis is chased by many beautiful girls. The problem is, he has trouble choosing just one. This really is a musical, with twelve songs. Filmed in Hawaii it is very much in the mould of "Blue Hawaii" and, as such, did well enough at the box office to convince studio executives that they had nailed down the blueprint for an Elvis Presley film, featuring Elvis as an entertainer rather than a serious actor, a formula they would see no need to change in the future.

It is here that I would like to introduce you to Sue Wiegert, who first met Elvis on the set of "Girl, Girls, Girls." Sue became an Elvis fan in 1956 and attended her first concert in 1957 when she was 12 years old. She immediately felt a connection to Elvis and wanted to be his friend. She saw that Elvis had a fun time, laughing and fooling around and he talked to the audience as though he liked them. She was not screaming like all the other girls as she saw him more as a brother rather than a potential boyfriend. She wanted to meet Elvis and become his friend. She believed that would happen. Well, the doors certainly opened for Sue. The next year, in 1958, travelling back to St Louis from Florida, she persuaded her parents to go via Memphis and go to Graceland. Although she would not see Elvis, as he was in the army and his parents were visiting him in Fort Hood, she just wanted to see Elvis' home. Elvis' Uncle Travis was on guard at the front gate, and he invited them in to walk up the driveway to the front of the house.

Uncle Travis was the first one of Elvis' relatives that Sue met, and she saw in him the same down to earth friendliness and warmth as she detected in Elvis. Later that year when she heard that Elvis' mother had died, she wrote to Elvis offering her condolences and then continued to write to him every week. She avidly watched his movies many times and, in 1962, she visited Graceland again. Passing through Hollywood on her way back to Hawaii where she then lived, she called in at the Colonel's office to find out when and where Elvis would be filming next. Sue was delighted to hear that Elvis would be filming in Hawaii and that she may get an opportunity to meet him.

By driving up to the film location and giving notes to people, even though the security guards had been told not to let any fans on the set, she was allowed onto the set to watch the filming. And that is when she met Elvis for the first time. From reading her accounts of her adventures with Elvis, I can see why Sue found it easy to get access to Elvis. She was shy and patient (she waited for three days near the film set before being taken to meet Elvis) and did not want to cause any bother. That was the start of a beautiful friendship. Sue visited Elvis at his homes in LA and at Graceland, was invited to Elvis' New Year parties, got to know, and was respected by, Elvis' entourage and family. Most of their conversations were in the open at the house gates as Elvis came and went, but they were frank and quite deep at times.

Sue knew that Elvis loved the Lord, and she gave him a gift of a painting of Christ for which he thanked her several times. On another occasion, she asked him, "Elvis did you ever have the experience of the Pentecost?" Elvis said,

"Sure that's my faith, I was raised in the Pentecost church." Sue said, "I know, but have you ever had the experience of being filled with the Holy Spirit and speaking in tongues?" After some thought Elvis replied, "No, but I guess you could kinda say I was raised in the Holy Spirit, being raised in a church like I was." (As we know from Rev. Rex Dyson, Elvis' mother was a "Holy Ghost Christian.")

Another time when she got serious with Elvis was into Spring of 1968. She had just come out of college and was very idealistic. When one of Elvis' relatives told her that although he liked black people and had black friends, he did not think they were equal to white people and that Elvis felt the same way, she did not believe that was the case, but needed to know. So, she drove from Memphis to LA to ask Elvis. She knew that Elvis' family were all Southerners – and had probably all been raised with the inbred bigotry that goes so deep, which they never questioned nor thought needed fixing. However, she couldn't believe that Elvis thought that black people were inferior to whites. Elvis told her that although he dearly loved his uncle, he had no right to speak for him and that he did not agree with him.

Much of the time though, Sue and other fans (calling themselves the Bel Air Bums) who used to wait at the gates just had fun with Elvis and he seemed to enjoy their company, being able to relax with people who dearly loved and admired him and demanded nothing from him.

One fan, however, got more than she expected from her meeting with Elvis. A group of them had taken a cake inscribed "We love you Elvis" to Elvis' house and, when he came to receive it, she blurted out, "Elvis, we love you more than God." Elvis was visibly shaken and instantly responded, "Please don't ever say that again!" He was not himself after that and soon went back into his house. Jillayne Stark Readon had witnessed this and was so impacted by it that she decided to investigate Elvis' religious roots. She reports that she visited an AoG church, and her life was touched by the God who had made such a lasting impression on Elvis. For that, she will always be thankful.

Sue was genuinely concerned for Elvis' welfare and, as time went on, she could see that all was not well. She saw that Elvis suffered from hyperactivity, but also the making of the movies was causing him some bother as he wanted to have meatier roles and not always have to sing some, often, inane songs. She knew that he was obliged by contract to do three movies a year and was presented with the scripts and expected to do them. Although in his early rock 'n' roll years, Elvis was portrayed as being rebellious, she could see that he

151

was, in many respects, very compliant, with obedience to elders being ingrained in him during his childhood. The films were very lucrative, so the studio and the Colonel put a lot of pressure on Elvis to accept the scripts. Sue and her friend Cricket Coulter were interviewed and appear in the documentary film, "Elvis – That's The Way It Is (1970)."

Back in Memphis

On 6th August, Anita Wood, living at Graceland and patiently waiting for Elvis, moved out and returned home to Jackson, Tennessee, as she realised that Elvis was not yet ready to settle down.

For the remainder of summer and autumn, Elvis worked on the film "It Happened at The World's Fair," based in Seattle.

Priscilla, who had already had a two-week visit with Elvis in Los Angeles in June, arrived in Memphis from Germany on 19th December for a three-week stay. She missed the first two days of her visit because of the pills Elvis gave her to help her sleep on the first night. They had a Christmas Day party at Graceland and a New Year's Eve fireworks display.

Priscilla returned to the USA with her father in March the next year to meet with Elvis and conclude the arrangements for her to live in Memphis with Vernon and Dee and complete her Senior Year at Immaculate Conception High School. She graduated from the school on 29th May 1963 and moved into Graceland.

In April, to feed his eclectic reading habit Elvis purchased 29 books from the Readin'& Ritin' shop in Memphis. Titles included: Eye Witness History of World War II, First 100 Days of the Kennedy Administration, Exploring the Earth, Giants of Medicine, World Philosophy, East of Eden, Joke Dictionary for the John, Antique Guns, Right to Privacy, Lonely Life, Vocabulary Builder, and I Owe Russia $1200 by Bob Hope.

Kindred Souls

In July 1963 filming began on "Viva Las Vegas." It is clear to see from the body language that Elvis and Ann-Margret, his co-star, were kindred souls. They soon became "an item" and thereafter life-long friends. Ann-Margret says of Elvis, "We had a strong, real, serious relationship for a year." She is very angry at all the negative things written about Elvis and with those who made fun of him. Although she recognises all the good things written about Elvis after his death, it grieves her that these were not written in his lifetime, which would have been an encouragement and given Elvis more self-confidence. She only wants to cherish the memory of this very talented and sensitive man. She remembered one time when she was living with her parents in an apartment. The Danish landlords lived in an apartment above, and the husband passed away just before the birthday of his wife. Knowing this, Elvis suggested that they go up and see the lady to wish her a happy birthday. Ann-Margret fondly remembers that Elvis was so sensitive and considerate with this grieving lady.

Wanda June Hill

It was during the filming of "Kissin' Cousins" that Wanda June Hill met Elvis and they became lifelong friends.

Wanda had been raised in a strict Pentecostal (AoG) church whose pastor had given many a sermon on Elvis being "the devil's child" sent to destroy the youth of America.

Her husband, who was an Elvis fan, worked nights and slept days and they lived near the beach where she took their young daughter so he could sleep. Often on the way home, she would stop off and do their laundry. One day in late summer, her daughter found a playmate at the laundry and his mother and Wanda talked while the clothes dried and the kids played. This mother was an actress who had made two films with Elvis and said that she was just finishing one with him. She had just moved down to Huntington Beach for her son's health and didn't know anyone, so she invited Wanda and her daughter to come by her place saying that Elvis was supposed to call her, and she didn't want to miss the call as she thought he was going to ask her to come up to his house.

Wanda was curious so went home with her. Elvis did call and after their conversation the actress asked Elvis if he would say "hello" to Wanda, explaining that she had just moved out to California and hadn't met or seen any movie stars. Elvis did say "hello" and they talked for about 35 minutes.

Wanda never worked for Elvis but volunteered to help him when he said he had so many letters to answer – all of which were from handicapped young persons and people he wanted to respond to personally. Some months later Elvis told her that he was so busy he couldn't keep up and accepted the offer of her help to type the letters if he would dictate his response on a cassette. She

153

dropped by his home in Bel Air to collect the tapes and drop off the letters. She always returned his recorded cassettes with the letters. The first time she gave him the cassettes back, she said that he seemed surprised. "I think he thought I would keep them, and I said, 'Elvis, these are personal correspondence – you need to keep them safe.' I won't ever forget the look on his face, it was priceless, and he leaned over and kissed me on the cheek as he said, 'I'll remember that.'"

Along with so many who observed Elvis, Wanda remembers incidences of Elvis' kindness and generosity. She recalls, "When our daughter was seven years old and fell from a swing, she severely broke her elbow and spent several weeks lying in traction in the Children's Hospital in Orange. When Elvis found out, he began sending stuffed toys with flower arrangements every other day to his 'little Julie'. He also called the nurses' station when he couldn't catch me by phone as I was spending all my time with my daughter.

"When Elvis discovered that there was a little girl from Mexico sharing the room with Julie, he was upset, as he had been showering the one child with things and this little girl didn't even have her family there with her. She had been born with an abnormal opening at the base of her spine and had never walked, she was about 12 years old. I thought he was going to cry when I told him about her."

Wanda reported that the next day, and for some time after, when Julie got her stuffed animal and flowers, the little girl roommate got some too, from her "secret admirer." The little girl was thrilled. Elvis also gave some money to buy her some pretty nightgowns and things she would like.

One of the nurses told Wanda that Elvis located the girl's family, paid their travel to see her, put them up in a hotel room nearby, and, when she left the hospital, paid her hospital bill. Elvis also asked a florist to get a large potted plant, with elves and fairies in the branches for the children's floor and corsages for all the nurses.

Wanda's husband, Jimmie, was not jealous of Elvis. In fact, he was an Elvis fan and was the reason that Elvis came into their lives. As she says, "I would not have gone with the young woman from the laundry had it not been for Jimmie's love of Elvis – I thought he'd get a kick out of me getting to say hello to Elvis Presley! He did! And he got to be his friend also."

Wanda says that Elvis gave Jimmie a couple of his shirts, a ring, and a Bible that Elvis had used and then signed and gave to Jimmie for his birthday. Inside the Bible was an inscription Elvis wrote, saying: "For Jim, in the love of Jesus and the faith of God in my heart. May God guide your search. E Presley 1– 1976."

Sadness and Fun

When President Kennedy was assassinated on 22nd November, Ann-Margaret and Elvis watched the news on TV together at Elvis' home in LA. They discussed the ramifications of this, and they prayed together for the future of their country.

After dating for a year Elvis and Ann-Margret both realised that, for various reasons, their relationship as it was could not continue. However, they remained friends and, when Ann Margret started doing a nightclub act, Elvis sent her a bouquet of flowers in the shape of a guitar, which he did for every one of her opening nights until his death. It was during one of these nightclub acts that Elvis delighted her with one of his "spurs of the moment" activities.

Ann-Margret was walking round the audience singing and talking with them when she spotted Elvis in a booth and introduced him. "I am sure you know who this is," she said when the spotlight fell on him. Elvis stood up and improvised a short dance with her. She says, "As I made my way back to the front, he somehow got backstage and as I finished up, he ran on and slid halfway across the stage, stopping right at my feet. The audience went wild. Pretending it was nothing extraordinary, I said 'I didn't know you could do a knee slide.' Elvis laughed harder than anyone." By this time Ann-Margret was married to Roger Smith, but he was not at all jealous of Elvis' friendship with his wife.

In December, Elvis spent Christmas at home at Graceland and, as usual, donated to several local Memphis charities. This year the amount was $55,000

Stuck in a Frustrating Rut but Still (Mostly) Gracious

In February 1964, work started on the film "Roustabout."

Hal Wallis felt he had defined the template for success and didn't want to break it. Around the time "Roustabout" was filmed, Wallis told a journalist that "To do the artistic pictures, [such as "Becket" which won many awards] it is necessary to do the commercially successful Presley pictures."

That remark stung Elvis who challenged the producer. "Mr Wallis, when do I get to do my 'Becket'?" he asked. Also, Elvis and director John Rich never saw eye to eye. But the suspicion that Elvis' movies were subsidising Wallis's pitch for an Oscar may have fuelled Elvis' disaffection with his director. When Rich said the Jordanaires could not accompany Elvis as he sang on his motorcycle because "where would we put the backing singers?" Elvis replied: "Same damn place you put the band."

Terry Garr, one of the dancers in the film, remembers Elvis as a real gentleman. She recalls the time when she was dancing in a chorus wearing a watermelon costume. She says, "Well, I never really fit into the chorus girl thing. I was always a little bit off, a little bit wrong. Anyway, they're starting to roll this thing, okay, action, and we're rolling. And this director, his name was John Rich, would go, 'Oh, cut, cut, cut. Who is that dumb broad on the left? Honey, get it together, okay? Roll, action.' We'd start again and he said, 'No, honey, God, that stupid bitch.' And he was just so mean to me, and he was about to fire me, and Elvis said, 'Excuse me, sir, but this broad ...'". He stood up and defended me."

Elvis was the first person Terry worked with in a movie, and he had a big influence on her. She says, "maybe it was me that made it up, but I thought, he's a person, I'm a person. If he can do it, I can do it. And he made you feel like that, too. You know, he made you be an equal. And I think that really was an incredible catalyst for me. I mean, you're working with Elvis Presley, and he thinks that you guys are alike so maybe if he can do it, you can do it. So, then something like that, it's a subliminal subconscious incredible influence he had on me."

Another actress who remembers Elvis as someone who looked after her is Mary Ann Mobley who worked with Elvis on "Girl Happy." It was her first film, and she was very nervous. Elvis noticed this and took her under his wing. She said of the films that it wasn't really serious acting – they were just having fun. Of Elvis she said, "This is an odd thing to say about Elvis Presley, but it was like I was working with my brother. We never dated. We were just two people from the same state. The first day I came on the set of "Girl Happy," Elvis got up and he came to me, and he said, 'Hi, I'm Elvis.' Like I didn't know! Elvis said, 'Where is Mary Ann's chair?' All of a sudden, a chair appeared with my name on it. That was the beginning of our friendship."

Enter Larry Geller

On 30th April 1964, Larry Geller received a phone call that would change his life – he was invited to Elvis' home in LA to style his hair, as a replacement for Elvis' regular hairdresser. Lengthy conversations took place after the styling as Elvis discovered that Larry was very interested in spiritual matters and, like Elvis, he was a 'searcher.' During their conversation, Larry had mentioned several spiritual books and Elvis was so fired up by this encounter, that he would not let Larry go until he had promised to leave his current job and go to work for him, bringing some of the books he had been talking about to the film studio in the morning. One of the books Larry brought along the next day was "The Impersonal Life," published in 1917. It is this book, I believe, which did the most damage as it proposes the view that each person's divinity lies within himself, and that God is in fact "the Divine I." In the Bible, God calls himself the great "I AM," who is a separate being who created the universe for his own pleasure and to have a loving relationship with human beings created in his image. The only way in which people have divinity within themselves is when they become believers in Jesus as Saviour and the Son of God, and the Holy Spirit comes to dwell within that person as a constant help and companion.

In July and August, Elvis became very involved with Larry, reading his books, and discussing spiritual matters with him. The Colonel became concerned at this recent "religious kick" of Elvis and had a private word with him which annoyed Elvis, who told his entourage that the Colonel did not know anything about him.

Elvis and his entourage, now including Larry Geller, departed for Memphis and spent the next six weeks there doing the usual things of renting the Memphian Theatre and the Fairgrounds, and riding around Memphis, as well as Elvis continuing his studies with Larry. Films that Elvis watched that summer included "Dr Strangelove," "King of Kings," "The Robe," "A Shot in the Dark," "The Great Escape" and "Marnie."

The Tables Are Turned

Elvis, as ever, was always willing to welcome strangers into his house, whom he thought he could help. Larry Geller remembers one incident in the Autumn of 1964.

Larry and Elvis were sitting in the living room at Graceland when Vernon came in and told Elvis about a young boy and his mother who had just arrived from Sweden. The young boy's recently deceased grandfather had left him $500,000 plus two hotels and a jewellery store, and he wanted to give it all to Elvis.

Elvis was shocked at this and asked his father to tell them thank you, but that he did not need any money. Vernon persuaded Elvis to speak to the boy, as the mother was frantic, saying her son was threatening to commit suicide unless Elvis accepted the gifts.

The next day the boy and his mother went to Graceland. When the boy saw Elvis, he was overwhelmed and his voice cracked as he told Elvis how much Elvis had done for him, and that now he had to do something for Elvis. His mother told Elvis that her son said that he couldn't live if he didn't accept the gift. She also revealed that his older brother had committed suicide a year earlier, and the boy was all she had left.

Elvis took the boy off to the music room. About fifteen minutes later they emerged, both looking very happy. "It's alright, he understands how I feel. He gave me this gold ring and that's how we're going to leave it for now. Ma'am, I told your son I wanted him to stay in touch with me and let me know how he is doing." Elvis put his arm around the boy's shoulders. "We're friends now." Elvis explained later that he couldn't have the boy outdoing him [in giving], so he told him that he could best please him by going back to Sweden to take care of his mother, and by spending that money to get an education for himself, and to help other people. He told him that he had more money than he could spend, and his gift would only give him problems.

***

Elvis received a Golden Laurel Award for The Best Male Actor in a Musical Film for his performance in "Tickle Me" which was the last film he worked on that year. The Golden Laurels were an industry award that had no ceremony and names of winners were published in the Motion Picture Exhibitor Magazine.

In October, Vernon and his new family moved to a house on Dolan Drive, just behind Graceland, backing onto the grounds.

Tree of Life

The 8th of January 1965 was Elvis' 30th birthday and the guys gave him a gold Tree of Life pendant designed by Marty Lacker.

I contacted Marty Lacker on Facebook and he told me this: "One night in early December 1964, when my family lived at Graceland I couldn't sleep, so I started doodling on a piece of paper and without any preconceived idea I started drawing a tree with bare branches. I wrote Elvis' name down the trunk and then using a letter from his name, I wrote the name of the guys that were working for him at the time on each of the branches. The concept was that he was the tree to which we were all attached. That's what happens when you have pills in you. All of a sudden, I got artistic and able to draw. I showed it to him the next day and he loved it." As well as Elvis Presley engraved down the trunk, the names, Billy Smith, Alan Fortas, Joe Esposito, Richard Davis, Mike Keeton, Red West, Larry Geller, Jerry Schilling, and Marty Lacker, formed the limbs that intersected with the letters on the trunk. Inscribed above the tree is part of a Bible verse from Psalm 1, "like a tree planted by the water that bringeth forth fruit in his season." The rest of this verse 3 is "his leaf also shall not wither; and whatsoever he doeth shall prosper."

On the reverse of this rectangular pendant is inscribed one of Elvis' favourite Bible verses 'AND YE SHALL KNOW THE TRUTH AND THE TRUTH SHALL MAKE YOU FREE,' written in English, Hebrew and Latin and taken from the Gospel of John, chapter 8 verse 32. Marty said that he chose the Scriptures for the pendant and that he chose English, Hebrew, and Latin to represent the nationalities of the Memphis Mafia at the time. Marty Lacker was Jewish but would go to East Trigg Baptist Church in Memphis to hear the wonderful gospel music. Marty said, "It didn't matter what you were, if that music didn't move you then you had to be dead."

The Face of Jesus

In March 1965, Elvis was driving his van somewhere outside Flagstaff on his way to Hollywood to start work on the movie "Harum Scarum." As they were behind schedule, the crew members took turns driving the bus straight through, with hairdresser Larry Geller riding shotgun. Larry recalls in his book, "If I Can Dream, Elvis' Own Story," that in the distance mountains loomed in the fading light and an iridescent blue sky seemed to colour everything in view with a peaceful, heavenly shade when, without warning, Elvis shouted, "Whoa!"

Elvis was staring at a mass of clouds building over the San Francisco Peaks. "Do you see what I see?" he asked Larry, who looked up and instantly recognized the face of Joseph Stalin in the clouds. They watched it change shape and disappear, but Elvis continued to gaze upward. Suddenly he hit the brakes and pulled off the highway. Jumping out, he took off running into the desert and told Larry to follow. "It's God! It's God!" he shouted. "It's love. God is love!" He hugged Larry, laughing, and crying, overcome by what had happened. Elvis initially wondered why he had seen the face of Stalin and thought that the Lord was telling him that he was evil, so he asked God to destroy him if he was evil. He then saw the face of Stalin turn into the face of Jesus who was smiling at him. No wonder he hit the brakes! He told Larry, "He smiled at me, and every fibre of my being felt it. For the first time in my life, God and Christ are a living reality." Elvis then paused and wondered, "Can you imagine what the fans would think if they saw me like this?"

Gospel Success

At Easter time in April, Elvis' first gospel single, *Crying in the Chapel/I Believe in the Man in the Sky* was released. It reached #3 in the States and #1 in the UK charts. It was Elvis' first Top 10 hit since October 1963. This success encouraged the release of more gospel singles at Easter time in the following years.

In May, the Colonel arranged for a special Mother's Day radio show to be broadcast on stations throughout the country, featuring the gospel songs *Crying in the Chapel* and *His Hand in Mine*. Also this month, work began on "Frankie and Johnny." As in most of Elvis' films, there were now 12 songs, this time one being the gospel songs *Down by the Riverside/When the Saints Go Marching In*.

Jewish Elvis

As part of his discussions with Larry Geller, who is Jewish, Elvis had become more interested in Judaism. He was aware of the role of the Jewish people in God's plans from his study of the Bible. He would have known that Jesus was Jewish, but I am not sure how much he understood that, according to Jewish law, he himself was Jewish, having a Jewish great-great-grandmother, Nancy Burdine. Elvis started to wear a Chai pendant, a Hebrew word meaning "life," and, with Marty Lacker, designed and had manufactured by Harry Levitch Jewelers of Memphis a watch fashioned so that the image of the Star of David with a Christian cross appeared on the face every 20 seconds. Elvis gave these watches as gifts to his closest friends and the cast and crew of "Harum Scarum."

***

On 27th August, at Elvis' Perugia Way home in Los Angeles, the legendary meeting between Elvis and The Beatles took place. After a rather awkward start, they just chilled out and chatted and played music.

The Strain is Showing, but Others Still Come First

Work began on "Paradise Hawaiian Style" in August. Jan Shepard, who played Betty Kohana in this film, immediately noticed a difference in Elvis from when she was with him in "King Creole." Jan says, "He kept to himself between takes, mostly going off to hide in his dressing room. He was now surrounded by an entourage and seemed very within himself, not as outgoing and fun-loving as before. He was preoccupied with theology books and seemed to be questioning his role in the scheme of things. But in the quiet moments, he was still very sweet when we reminisced about 'Creole.'"

Suzanna Leigh, Elvis' co-star in this film, had a wealthy, but not particularly loving background and had little self-esteem though she appeared confident enough. Elvis could see this and became her friend and gave her a sense of her own self-worth. They also discussed religion. Suzanna could see that Elvis was still searching spiritually, looking for answers to many questions. Suzanna's mother was not at all loving towards her, in fact very cruel at times, and she felt very much unloved. Even at her convent school she was physically beaten. When Elvis asked her why being beaten most Sunday evenings at the convent hadn't put her off religion, she replied that it had made her faith stronger, and she would ask Jesus to take away the pain. Suzanna suggested to Elvis that he should spread "word" (of the Gospel) through his songs, and he replied, "Maybe one day Baby, but right now I gotta kiss the girl or knock the guy out and then sing to 'em."

Tom Jones

It was during the shooting of this film that Tom Jones first met Elvis. Tom says that Elvis inspired him in his earliest days singing at working men's clubs in Wales. "I was singing Elvis Presley songs in these clubs and pubs, and they'd say, 'Wow that's as good as Elvis Presley.' And I said, 'Well, I'll tell him when I meet him.' They said, 'Elvis Presley, are you joking?' and I said, 'No, I think I will meet him.'

"So, when I met him and he was walking towards me, I could see these fellas. I'm ready to tell him how much he's influenced me, and he's walking towards me singing my song, *With These Hands*. It was a ballad. And I went, 'Wow, Elvis Presley.'" Tom and Elvis became good friends and spent many hours singing together.

When Elvis arrived back at Graceland in October, it was the first time he had been home for seven months and he was able to see the progress that had been made on the Meditation Garden. Its design was influenced by the Self-Realization Park in Pacific Palisades, which he liked because of its peaceful atmosphere. The garden has a curved wall with stained glass panels, Italian marble pillars and a fountain with underwater lighting.

In December, Elvis made his annual donation of around $50,000 to local Memphis charities. He gave gifts of jewellery to his family and friends and his entourage bought him a statue of Jesus for the Meditation Garden.

More Gospel Recordings

In February 1966, after the great success of the gospel single released for Easter the year before, RCA released two gospel singles, *Joshua Fit the Battle/Known Only to Him* and *Milky White Way/Swing Down Sweet Chariot*. Sadly, these had little commercial success.

Starting in February till about mid-1966, Red West did some home recordings at Elvis' house in Bel Air. Elvis and Charlie Hodge played guitar, piano and sang. About a quarter of the songs sung were gospel including *Hide Thou Me, Oh How I Love Jesus, Show Me Thy Ways Oh Lord* and *I John*. Some of the tapes were discovered during the 1980s, the remainder in 1996 at Graceland.

To fulfil his new contract with RCA to produce two singles, a Christmas single and a religious album, back at home in Graceland Elvis continued to work with Red West and Charlie Hodge to produce a list of gospel songs for the new album. More than half of the material Elvis approved was from his own collection of records, including *Lord, I Need You Again Today,* by the Statesmen, *Room at the Cross,* by the Blackwood Brothers, *Wasted Years,* by Stuart Hamblen, *He* by Roy Hamilton, *Don't Knock,* by The Staple Singers, and *You Better Run* and *Run On* by the Golden Gate Quartet. Also on the list were *How Great Thou Art, Walk that Lonesome Valley, Where No-one Stands Alone, By and By, I'll Tell It Where I Go.* Elvis particularly liked bass singers and had wanted Jimmy Jones of the Harmonizing Four to join the recording session, but he was not available, so the gospel group the Imperials Quartet, then led by Jake Hess, were employed instead.

Elvis, the Consummate Producer

The gospel recordings took place from 25th to 27th May at RCA Studio B in Nashville. The final round-up of singers to accompany Elvis was The Jordanaires, The Imperials, Millie Kirkham, June Page and Dolores Edgin. The producer on this album, Felton Jarvis, was new to Elvis, however, Elvis was not new to him. Felton was a big Elvis fan and had previously recorded a "talking" single, *Don't Knock Elvis,* in which he encouraged people to look at the good aspects of Elvis and not just dismiss him as a person who was corrupting the youth of the nation. Also, Felton was a very upbeat person and was happy to take part in the all-night recording sessions, usually 10pm till 7am.

By now, many people recognised that Elvis was a consummate producer in the recording studio. He knew exactly the sound and feeling he wanted, and although he had no professional musical training, he would instruct the singers how and when to sing, what instruments he wanted highlighting, the tempo, repeats – in fact, everything which goes into making the right sound. Felton understood Elvis and what he wanted in a mix. He knew Elvis wanted the instruments to be louder and that he wanted his records to have a "bigger sound." He would advise Elvis on certain aspects and make suggestions. One of his roles was to encourage Elvis to keep trying if he was struggling with a song. Felton could perhaps see more than Elvis could that there was much more left in him and not to give up.

They made a good team and Felton worked with Elvis until the end of Elvis' life. In June of 1970, he quit RCA and became an independent contractor, working exclusively with Elvis on his studio recordings as well as live concert recordings. Three years later, in July 1971, Felton became very ill and started experiencing kidney failure. He supervised Elvis' live recordings of February 1972 in Las Vegas, although he required dialysis several times a week. Elvis arranged and paid for a kidney transplant for Felton in October 1972. Sadly though, Felton died at the age of 46 in January 1981 after having suffered a stroke.

Many people believe that the recording of the *How Great Thou Art* album was a Godsend for Elvis. He had been working in Hollywood on the very lucrative musical comedies and had, as always, done a good job, though emotionally and spiritually he was at his lowest ebb. It has been said that working on the movies artistically castrated Elvis. To him, it had become just a job and he suffered several bouts of illness. Many have said that Elvis should have just given it all up and gone back to singing, but he had signed an agreement and was contractually obliged for four more years to do these movies.

Jerry Schilling vividly remembers these *How Great Thou Art* sessions. As usual, Elvis spent over an hour just hanging out with everyone and getting in the mood. The studio was part social club and part sanctuary, somewhere Elvis could feel at home and just be himself, expressing his deepest longings, hopes and joys through his music. He would sing the vocals separately if he had to, with the instruments and backing singers added later, but he preferred to record the whole sound together. This is what happened with the recording of *How Great Thou Art*. Elvis' facial expressions showed the intensity he felt whilst singing the song. After the dramatic finish of the song, Jerry says that there was a strange hush in the room as though no-one seemed to want to break the spell. At the end of the take, Elvis was as white as a ghost and thoroughly exhausted. He was hunched over, almost on his knees, as if he had been touched by something amazing. Elvis looked up and saw Jerry looking at him and smiled as though to recognise that Jerry had witnessed something special. As indeed it was, not only did it win a Grammy for Elvis, but it had, and continues to have, amazing effects on others, including this remembered by Larry Geller:

In his book, "Leaves of Elvis' Garden," Larry tells of the time, ten years after the recording, that he met a fan who had a story to tell of the power of Elvis' singing *How Great Thou Art*. She believed that this had saved her life. This lady, Darlene, had a disfigured body caused by a childhood spinal injury. She was in constant pain and felt that she would never be able to get married and have a family. When she could no longer cope with it, she "just wanted out." She wrote a note for her family and had the painkillers and a glass of water ready to do the deed. As she reached to turn off her radio, she suddenly heard Elvis singing *How Great Thou Art*. She told Larry that she burst out crying and fell to her knees. She said that it was the way Elvis sang it, that all the love of God seemed to come through him. She "felt I could actually reach out and touch God. He felt that close to me in that room." Darlene had no doubt that

God had chosen that moment to send Elvis to help her. She wanted now to help and protect Elvis and to live for him and for God.

Circle G Ranch

One February morning in 1967, at dawn, Elvis, along with Priscilla and three of his entourage had driven out to Lennox Farms to purchase a Tennessee Walking Horse for Elvis' father, Vernon. They were driving back to Graceland when Elvis noticed a beautiful, enormous white cross overlooking a lake. There was also a For Sale sign. They pulled the car over and Elvis, being Elvis, had to have it there and then. He asked Alan Fortas to knock on the door of the farmhouse. The property's owner, Jack Adams, asked $437,000 for the house, cattle, farm equipment and land. Elvis agreed to the price and, within a day or so, his crew began moving in. It was rechristened the Circle G Ranch ("G" for Graceland, according to most accounts, though some say the "G" was for Elvis' mother, Gladys).

The property is a 163-acre tract located about 10 miles south of Graceland, in Walls, Mississippi. Soon after the purchase of Circle G, Elvis stocked the stables with 40 horses and began buying mobile homes for some of this entourage, such as Alan Fortas, Elvis' cousin Billy Smith and his wife Jo, Stevie and Larry Geller, Joanie and Joe Esposito, Richard Davis, and Jerry and Sandy Schilling. He also bought trucks for everyone to get around this expansive country estate, as well as tractors and all sorts of gear for their newfound country lifestyle. Within a few weeks, Elvis had spent nearly a million dollars.

After the initial spending spree was over, it did turn into the peaceful, communal refuge Elvis intended. They did target shooting, frog hunts and picnics near the lake. As well as those living on the ranch, other members of his entourage spent a lot of time at Circle G riding horses.

Dr George Nichopoulos was called during this time to treat Elvis for saddle pain and was taken on as Elvis' full-time doctor in 1970 until Elvis' death in 1977. He was always referred to as "Dr. Nick."

***

In March, the filming of "Clambake" was plagued by misfortune and chaos even before shooting started, and much of it was due to Elvis' total disinterest in doing the film. By the time "Clambake" rolled around, the guys seemed to be out of control. Pie-throwings, firecracker fights and water bombardments on the set were a common occurrence to alleviate the boredom. Also, Elvis experienced a major weight gain. United Artists demanded he take off the extra poundage. On the first day of scheduled shooting, Elvis slipped on his bathroom floor and hit his head. After a private conference with the Colonel, the doctor declared that Elvis had suffered a concussion and could not work. Shooting was delayed for more than two weeks. Vernon and Priscilla flew out from Memphis to be with Elvis and the Colonel took the opportunity to upbraid Elvis and the guys for behaviour which could jeopardise Elvis' film career. He also had a special word for Larry Geller whom he saw as a real threat, leading Elvis into more "religious kicks." He told Larry that there must be no more religious discussions and no more books – the current religious books must be removed.

Later on, at Graceland, just after their wedding (to which Larry had not been invited), Priscilla persuaded Elvis to make a bonfire of the books and magazines that the Colonel had banned.

It was around this time that the Colonel tried to persuade MGM to come up with a good hard-hitting story for Elvis' next film as he could see the harm that the "cash cow" pictures were doing to Elvis' self-confidence and general attitude. However, his efforts were to no avail as the next film "Speedway" was the same kind of musical comedy with seven songs and the addition of some high-speed car racing to give it a bit more "action."

Wedding Belle

On May 1st 1967 Elvis married his beautiful sweetheart, Priscilla Beaulieu, at the Aladdin Hotel in Las Vegas. There were no fans in sight, but there were members of the press, who were invited by the Colonel to a press conference between the ceremony and the champagne breakfast for 100 that followed.

The wedding was arranged by the Colonel, who gathered the wedding party in Palm Springs in advance of the big day. George Klein recalled, "Just after midnight on May 1st, the wedding party snuck out the back door of Elvis's Palm Springs home, climbed over the backyard wall and got into a car to head to the airport. Elvis had been loaned Frank Sinatra's private jet for the occasion." A second chartered plane carried the rest of the guests. On arrival in Las Vegas, the party was taken to the Aladdin Hotel, where they used the rear entrance to avoid detection.

In the early morning hours, Elvis and Priscilla were issued a marriage license at the Las Vegas Courthouse. Just before 10am, Nevada Supreme Court Judge David Zenoff married the couple in a flower and candle-filled suite at the Aladdin Hotel in front of about 14 people. Elvis's best men were Joe Esposito and Marty Lacker; Priscilla's maid of honour was her sister, Michelle. "My wedding was very unusual," said Priscilla "It was the people closest to us, and private, and that's how we wanted it. We didn't want a fan club. We didn't want a circus."

After spending two nights in Las Vegas, they returned to Memphis and the Circle G Ranch, staying in the small farmhouse on the property. Because many of their friends were excluded from the celebration on 1st May, they held a second reception at Graceland on 29th May.

In her book, "Elvis and Me," Priscilla reminisced about the ranch and its unassuming farmhouse. "I pictured us saddling our own horses and riding in the early evening or at dusk. My picture was of us alone, without an entourage," she wrote. But Elvis saw it as the best of both worlds. He could hang with the group when he wanted and have his alone time with Priscilla, which she really appreciated. She wrote, "It turned out to be very romantic. I loved playing house. I personally washed all his clothes, along with the towels and sheets, and took pride in ironing his shirts and rolling up his socks the way my mother had taught me. Here was an opportunity to take care of him myself. No maids or housekeepers to pamper us."

In October, "Stay Away, Joe" was filmed in the Arizona town of Sedona and it was one of the rare times that Priscilla and the wives of his entourage attended a location shoot. This was also the last film the Jordanaires backed Elvis. They decided to stay home in Nashville as they had a steady workload as studio musicians.

Although Elvis loved the refuge of the Circle G Ranch, with lots of space for himself and his expanded "family," the spending started getting out of hand and Elvis' interest in the place waned as his commitments to making films and recordings took up much of his time. In November 1967, Elvis started selling off the ranch equipment, by the end of the year, the operation was shut down and the remaining horses taken back to Graceland. In May 1969, the North Mississippi Gun Club bought the ranch for $440,000.

Elvis Encourages Lanny

On 5th December 1967, Elvis wrote his first letter to Lanny Smith. Lanny was a Christian and a singer/songwriter. I met him whilst doing research in the USA in 2005. Lanny had a friend who knew Elvis and so he wrote to Elvis hoping for a reply. Elvis did indeed reply, and Lanny gave me photocopies of the letters, typed and signed by Elvis. This one has a hand-written PS. I have copied the letter exactly as it is written. Elvis' grammar and punctuation are not perfect, but it does not detract from the observation that he is eager to share his thoughts and to help and advise others. Lanny also had several telephone conversations with Elvis.

Dear Mr. Smith,

I have just talked to your lady Friend Mrs Stroud, of Hermitage and she told me you had written to me but not received and answer. I would like to say I am sorry about that. I have an office full of girls who answer my mail and they try to get to everyone who asks questions of the standard kind and you letter is most likely in the bag meant for me to get around to. I am way behind even with my friends helping me. I hope this letter will do for now.

I have just completed the film we have been working on for Metro Goldwyn Mayer. It will be the first of a new image for Elvis Presley. At thirty two it seems I should grow up some. I am very excited about making the more adult films, just because I am fed up with all the fluff we have been doing. It just seemed that nothing was coming from it and I think a man ought to feel some sort of reward in his efforts. I don't mean material reward, but the inner kind that lifts the spirit and freshens the air. Lord knows I have all the material reward that any person could ever hope for and I am very grateful to all the wonderful people and our God for providing the chance I was given. Therefore I try to help or advise anyone who asks me, in any way that I can, If I see they are honestly trying to be someone worthwhile. A man is only as great as his motives and so I try to have the best possible and when I meet those who feel the same, I try to help. Now as you can see my typing is no great shakes, but my penmanship is even worse.

I am in Mississippi at the moment but will be in New York tomorrow. Have to go to discuss my next album with RCA. It will be country western at the last count. I enjoy doing those, but seldom get the chance to really sing the blues for there. My wife is here too, she is one of the greater blessings of my life and soon we will have the greatest of all blessings, our own child. Feb 8-11th

probably. We can hardly wait. Priscilla and I have known each other since 1959 and I decided then she would be the one I wanted. She is all that I had hoped for and more. It means a lot to have a woman who will wait for you to settle down and one who knows that a man must be free to be happy. And she understands all this. Well sorry about all that, I just have to brag when I can.

You may write to me and I will receive it...at c/o 222 Avocado Street, Costa Mesa, Calif. This is the address of your friends granddaughter who knows where I am and how to reach me at all times. She forwards a lot of personal mail to me, so feel free to write at anytime.

If there are any questions or remarks you wish to ask or express, I am at your service, so to speak. I really do like to hear from the folks who see my films and hear my songs. I have learned a lot from them and their opinions. So fire one at me at your convenience.

Sincerely Elvis Presley

P.S. I got a lot of relatives named Smith – Mississippi, Oklahoma

Elvis spent most of December and January in Memphis.

On 9th January 1968, Elvis wrote again to Lanny Smith in reply to a letter and tape received:

Dear Lanny, Just finished listening to your singing and would like to inform you of my thoughts while they are fresh I my mind. First off I was much impressed with the simple, direct manner with which you presented your talents. That alone was evidence of your quality of personality and responsible maturity. Now I am no scholar, so don't expect any flowery phrases coming from me. You won't get nothing except what you deserve. Alright.

I like your accompaniment very much... you sure pump a fine pedal.. and to have no one joining you it sounded quite perfect for the whole bit. And the selections were pretty well rounded to show your ability. I think your voice range is best suited for the ballad tyle of song and the more popular tunes as in mine unless I have help. Which I do Incidentally – often. I do want to you to sit down when you have the time and write off the words to "Hills of Yesterday" as I feel that is that one has the most chance of being picked up and made off. In fact if my p&r man likes it I might record it myself with your ok of course. I wouldn't do nothing without that. I am taking the liberty of bring your tape with me to NY and letting my pal Charley "Red" West listen

169

to you. He has a small recording company in LA and presses a few of the newer artist and newcomers. BackBeat, Smash, Epic, Commondore are a few of his labels...one artist you might recall that did well on BackBeat.. Roy Head... from Texas and around Arkansas. He is a fellow that I run into and liked so he proved he had the nerve and the rest is up to him. He had a run of bad luck with nodules on his pipes, May have to cut out singing altogether later on since they keep on growing back. That comes from straining your voice & without the proper breath control, it's easy to do. Anyway while I am recording in NY my P&R man can listen to you and if he thinks you have possible public interest he will give red the ok and then red will be in touch with you about making some demo recordings If your considered good enough he might just make a master and press a few to see how goes it. Roy started by making demos for bigger artists to listen to and then he got a lucky break when I picked up one of his and spun it - it could happen to you. I already like your style probable because it is so near like my own. Try and come up with a distinction of your own whenever you can. I admit I copied several artists and then blended in my own ideas. Gene Austin, Red Foley, Hank Williams. If Rd and Mr Shoals like your sound you will hear from them and in the meantime practice, practice, practice and capture an audience every chance you get. I used to sing on street corners and folks would throw money to me. Yeah, begging but it gave me insight. The public is a fickle lover...they woo you with hot passion one day and like as not chill you with icy breath the next. Just when you think you own the world you find you been dreaming. But I think anyone who'd go through the extent that you have should have a chance to be heard. That's all I will do for you Lanny, just offer a chance. I have never lent my name or my recommendation to anyone and I never will. If I can open a door fine, and Lanny you just got your foot in the door so sit tight and don't get jumpy. I can't promise, but I will do what I can. Things that come too easy are often not fully appreciated. Its been said that I was an overnight success....well that's stretching the truth quire a bit. It was more like a three year long night with hungrey days an many many hours of thinking what the use. There were times when we five would split a dollar for food cause that's all we had and if we bought gas and at time we bought gas and did without food cause we had to reach the next town for a one night stand an maybe play to an audience of 12-20 and make just enough to get to the next town. I remember times when we stole food another times when we just starved it out. But to see the light in my loved one's eyes when they look around and see the nice things we have I'd do it all again. I think the most important thing I am gladdest about is the things we have been able to do to help others who have nothing but pain and trouble. That brings joy to my heart. And the warm friendly letters we receive makes it all worth it.......even worth the crank letters and phone calls and all the nasty barbs I get. I want you to know that success isn't all peaches and cream girls, fancy cars and big houses. For every minute of that kind of thing you have an hour of misery and mental anguish over something or other that happened or is said or just can't be helped. And when your on top as I have been it sometimes seems the whole world is against you. Folks who wish you success and fame turn on you when you get cause you made it...they didnt. And then those met after fame. You never knew if they like you or your money till you lose it...then its too late....your alone again.

I am going to give you some advice....you may already know and do it.

If you wan to add depth to your voice go out somewhere each day and practise speaking as loudly as you can without straining ad breath deeply each time. Read aloud to your self and practise speaking as many words as you can without breathing in between Sit before a mirror and speak to your self so you can see if your mouth is opening wide enough. Sing to your self before a mirror. And get a full length one so you can see the overall picture you make. I have a mirror on my ceiling over my bed and I lie on it and practice all the time I seldom a chance to relax and when I do I have to take full advantage of the time. And being actor I have to practice making faces. I used to get the feeling like an idiot but it is necessary to become a narrcisist in this business. My wife doesn't care for the mirror much and I get teased a lot about it always did...even before getting married. May West gave me the mirror she has one over her bed and he told me "It was to see if I am doing it right". That always cracked folks up. But that's the truth...to see if your doing it right... And I'm dead serious about that. Practise makes perfect... My diction is terrible being from the south and I have to really work on it each time I return work after being home. You try to expand your lung power and youll see the difference when you sing. You do ok now, but theres always room for improvement. I do this each day, no matter how busy I am. I just get up early enough. I go thru the scales 12 times and I read the Bible aloud for 30 minutes before I go to work. If I miss a day I notice it. My voice gets tight. I never had a voice lesson but I did have breathing lessons...made lots of difference...listen to me before 1960 and after. It shows. To get a new sound in your songs try recording in the bathroom with the doors closed...like a shower stall. I did a Bob Dylan tune that way (Its on my Spinout album...Tomorrow is a long Time) and they never touched it when they made a master. oh they added volume and bass but that's all. They said I couldn't do a tune like that so I did it on my own and they liked it. Sometimes even the gist of us get told no! When you send in songs get copies and get witnesses to sign them. Dates and names...every time. There are lots of con merchants in the business...no sense in losing your royalties. If I do your tune I will buy the rights from you...first. Any time that you are made int a Demo it is at the companys expense and you don't get a thing until someone decides to record it or the company will buy your song from you. Red usually buys all songs and rights or the writer gets a 5% on the dollar royalties. It mounts up over several thousand. By being on a demo several hundred artist and producers will have a chance to hear you. Demos are available to all the major studios.

Now I hope you are not disappointed in me for not doing more. But I just can't do it or else I will have to stop and devote myself to nothing else. ..there are just too many folk wanting this kind of help. I wish I could help each and every one have ever thing I got thats good by I can't so no use trying or crying about it I hope you make it and ...I will sure see you get heard but that's all I can offer now. I will say this.....you want to write song.........s I will listen and if I feel they fit me or someone I know I will see they get heard. I use alot of material myself fand am always looking for new ones If you want to send tapes fine. That lets more of the song show thru rather than just words on paper...I can't read music anyway. Don't forget to make copies of anything you do and get signed witnesses. I'm in a kind of hurry and my typing shows it....this isn't the best typewriter in town either but it is small land handy in the car or wherever and serves the purpose ok.

Always me, Elvis

PS. The last song on your tape sold me....just thought you'd like to know that idea payed off. Until then you hadn't really sounded any better or any worse than a lot of the other kids who send into me. I liked you but nothing special until I heard it and it remined me of myself... that always gets a guy, when he sees or hears himself. Good luck Buddy.

There is a PPS in Elvis' handwriting which says *Send me your birthdate. Time of day place year month. Its important too.*

New Life

Elvis and Priscilla's daughter, Lisa Marie, was born on 1st February exactly nine months after their wedding. Elvis and Priscilla were delighted with their little bundle of joy.

Elvis gave power of attorney to his father on 6th February 1968, putting him in charge of all his business activities. Later in the month, Elvis, Priscilla and Lisa Marie flew out to Los Angeles to their new home, 1174 Hillcrest Drive. The four-bedroom French Regency home has spectacular panoramic city to ocean views and had more privacy than Elvis' other homes in LA, and with only Charlie Hodge and Gee Gee and Patsy Gambill residing with them.

In time for Easter, another gospel single was released, *You'll Never Walk Alone/We Call on Him.* Although it was not a chart hit, it was nominated for a Grammy for the best Sacred Performance, losing out to *Beautiful Isle of Somewhere* by Jake Hess who was one of Elvis' favourite gospel singers.

Another Assassination

Elvis was in Hollywood on 4th April 1968 filming "Live A Little, Love A Little." This was the day Dr. Martin Luther King Jr was assassinated in Memphis at the Lorraine Motel. Celeste Yarnall, who had a small role in the film was with Elvis when he heard of the assassination.

She remembered, "It was during filming, and we went back to his dressing room to have lunch. He was so upset, and he started by standing up singing *Amazing Grace* before breaking down and sobbing in my arms. Elvis was truly devastated by Martin Luther King's assassination. Elvis felt such an integral part of the Memphis and Black community and he felt that they had taken a brother from him, and it happened in his hometown. We both cried together, it was so emotional and wrong. It was a truly touching experience to go through that together and feel the same." They later watched Dr. Martin Luther King's funeral together in Elvis' trailer.

Celeste says, "I adored Elvis. When I met him for the first time, he immediately put me at ease. We had to film our kissing first and neither of us heard the director say, 'Cut!' For me, it was love at first kiss! We became very good friends. He was warm and kind and full of love. He had this tremendous desire to please people. I was so lucky to spend time with Elvis, I couldn't believe how much charisma he had and how nice he was with everybody who was working with him. Elvis was so understanding, so kind and so generous. Meeting and working with Elvis really was one of the highlights of my life. I'll never forget being with Elvis, he was so special. Elvis hid his feelings from lots of people but inside he was a very kind and very precious person."

The '68 Comeback Special

In June and July, Elvis worked on the recording for the Christmas TV show sponsored by the Singer Sewing Machine Company for which, earlier in the year, the Colonel had made a deal with NBC. The producer of the show, Steve Binder, could see the potential in Elvis for doing more than just singing a few Christmas songs, which is what the Colonel wanted. This would be Elvis' first live performance for seven years. To accommodate Elvis' love of gospel music, there was a whole section devoted to gospel songs that included vigorous dancing and lots of tambourines, expressing the joy of the Lord. The songs sung were *Sometimes I Feel Like a Motherless Child, Where Could I Go But To The Lord, Up Above My Head (There's Music In The Air)* and *Saved,* all of which Elvis would be able to identify with, and especially the latter in which he pronounces several times, with great gusto, "I'm saved!" In the same show, however, he also sang, "I'm evil," from the song *Trouble.* Perhaps a reflection of the spiritual confusion that was inside?

If I Can Dream, which Elvis sang as the finale of the show, was written at the last minute by the show's musical director W Earl Brown, at the request of the producer Steve Binder, to replace *I'll Be Home for Christmas.* He wrote it as a response to the assassination of Martin Luther King. Dr. Martin Luther King's speech "I Have a Dream" was one of Elvis' favourite speeches, and, as we know, Elvis was very troubled by Dr. King's assassination, especially that it happened in his hometown of Memphis. Elvis sings this song with such vigour, expressing the yearning for "a better land where brothers walk hand in hand, where doubt and fear are blown away." This song is describing heaven! Yet, I believe that the song parts company with the gospel when it proclaims that, "as long as a man has the strength to dream, then he can redeem his soul and fly." Elvis would know that man cannot be redeemed through his own efforts, and yet he sings this with such passion, one thinks he might actually burst. He certainly looks as though he is drained of energy at the end of the song.

If I Can Dream writer Earl Brown said of the song "I wanted to let the world know that here was a guy who was not prejudiced, who was raised in the heart of prejudice, but who was really above all that."

This show originally titled Singer Presents Elvis is now usually accepted as the '68 Comeback Special. Much of the show is performed on a stage the size of a boxing ring, with Elvis surrounded by an audience, mostly of young women. It did indeed seem that Elvis had come back from the mire of those films he so hated and was back in front of his fans again, with whom he had such a great rapport. He now knew that he wanted to be back performing in concert.

Darlene Love, one of the members of the Blossoms gospel group that sang in the gospel section remembers Elvis as being "a little shy, very introverted" during the rehearsals. "He was very nervous because he hadn't performed in years," she said. "When you talked gospel with him, though, he was just like a friend sitting down talking. Also, they would chill out, singing with Elvis. "Yes! Whatever song he knew – *Amazing Grace* or *River of Jordan* or *Heaven Is a Wonderful Place, Sweet Hour of Prayer* or *Pass Me Not, O Gentle Savior.* We'd harmonize with him. There's something we had with Elvis that others didn't have. It was fun to be wanted by someone like Elvis Presley."

She felt that he was very nervous because he had become a movie star and hoped the performance would be all right. She said, "He was very concerned about, 'How do I look? Do I look all right?' He was just like a normal person, but he was Elvis Presley. So how could you be normal?"

***

On 20th July, Elvis' Uncle Johnny Smith died of a kidney ailment at the age of 46. Later, in 1973, Elvis was diagnosed with the hereditary liver ailment that killed his mother and his Uncle Travis Smith.

On 27th August 1968, Elvis wrote another letter to Lanny Smith:

Dear Lanny. I am really sorry to have waited so long to correspond with you in reply to your letters. I have received them but just can't seem to get the time to set myself down and write or even think long enough on one thing to dictate a letter. I am going to right now while I get my boots shined up some, I really am a luck dog. Here I sit getting polished and looking at the cutest little gal sitting here typing for me. I just embarrassed her till she made a mistake. She is about 5 foot and a size 10. Well she refuses to type what I said about her so we will dispense with her other charms. They're charming!! I don't just know what has been done with your tapes. Except you got some darn good ideas and considerable talent. I wish you all the luck and I will do what I can to help you as long as I can stand clear. My friend Wanda told me how much she liked you and what a nice guy you be. She as much as said she thought you sexy and that you'd do well with the girls…you've got to sell your sex appeal to the public. It helps if your born lucky but most of us aren't and then it is a darn hard job to convince the people you have it. Wanda – I respect her judgement. She is usually right on all accounts. Thanks for helping her out. This studio typ(writer)e isn't such a good one Making this little girl nervous more than she normally is. I shake her up she says. Too bad I'm married....Sometimes I find that hard to remember around here with so much so free so easy. She informs she is not. I guess she isn't (NO!)

I have to be moving out so until my next free moment. I also understand you can sound identical to me. I'd like to hear some of that. Elvis.

A More Enjoyable Film

In September work started on "The Trouble With Girls – (And How To Get Into It)." The film had four songs, one of which was a gospel song *Swing Down Sweet Chariot*. Elvis's character deputises for a gospel group member with laryngitis in *Swing Down Sweet Chariot* and he certainly swings, acting as the gospel singer onstage, as he loved to in real life.

Although this film is not the "serious one" that Elvis was hoping for, he really seemed to enjoy it, as I believe it catered to his playfulness. Co-actress, Marlyn Mason, said that she never saw Elvis lose his temper, on set, or with his entourage as he was enjoying just having fun (and being paid a lot for it!). Also, he had just recorded the '68 Comeback Special, in which he was able to flex his creative muscles, so was in good form both physically and emotionally.

On 3rd December, the '68 Comeback Special was aired. It was seen by 42 per cent of the viewing audience, giving NBC the biggest TV ratings of the year. Critically it was received very well with the comment, "Elvis is back!"

On 13th January 1969 Elvis began 14 days of recording sessions, which were held in the American Studios in Memphis, rather than in Nashville. These sessions featured only secular songs, but Glen Spreen one of the arrangers was impressed with Elvis soulfulness and his ability to make a song live. He said, "It was almost like going to church." Chips Moman, the producer who was known for tolerating nothing less than total commitment, said Elvis was "One of the most hard-working artists I have ever been associated with."

The Last Movie

In March, work began on "Change of Habit," Elvis' last movie. This is a crime-drama musical about three Catholic nuns, preparing for their final vows, who are sent to a rough inner-city neighbourhood dressed as lay missionaries to work at a clinic run by a young doctor. Their lives become complicated by the realities they face in the inner city, such as racial prejudice, financial strife, drugs, and the effects of addiction on a community and the lack of knowledge and workings of medical conditions such as autism, further complicated by Dr. Carpenter, played by Elvis, falling in love with one of the nuns.

The film includes the gospel song *Let Us Pray,* which Elvis sings in the final scene at a church service, where we see the nun that he has fallen in love with, contemplating whether to stay a nun or leave the order and marry him.

Barbara McNair, who played one of the nuns, recalls gospel singer Mahalia Jackson visiting Elvis on set: "Elvis and I were sitting there together, and Mahalia came on the set, and she asked Elvis if he would participate in a fund-raiser that she was going to organize. Elvis was so gracious, 'Oh, Mrs Jackson, I am so happy to meet you, I would love to do it, but I still have to ask the Colonel.' So, after she left, he said to me, 'I'll never do it, the Colonel won't let me.' But he was so gracious to her, he knew all the time the Colonel would not let him do it."

William Graham, the director of the film initially thought that Elvis was not the right casting for the movie, however with a bit of rewriting, he was happy to go ahead.

He found that Elvis could handle humour quite well and could do an argument very well. Also, he could handle a fight scene. However, in certain other areas, for example, a love scene or if there was some subtlety that was called for, Graham found that Elvis was a little self-conscious. So he decided to teach him some of the elements of The Method style of acting. Apparently, Elvis really enjoyed that and responded to the input he was getting from Graham. They did improvisations – simple action problems. An example of this was that Priscilla would be in the bedroom taking a nap. Elvis' assignment in that 'scene' would be to sneak into the bedroom, to crawl on his hands and knees around the foot of the bed and go up and see if he could steal her gold Rolex off the bedside table without her waking up. However, the Colonel heard about this Method teaching and called Graham into his office. Graham recounts their conversation:

"The Colonel said, 'I hear you've been going up to Elvis' Sonny.' And I said, 'Yeah, that's right. I've been working with him. We've been working on the acting and he's really coming along very well.' So he said, 'Well listen, Sonny, let me tell you something. We make these movies for a certain price, and they make a certain amount of money, no less and no more. Don't you be goin' for no Oscar, Sonny, because we ain't got no tuxedos.'"

However, Graham kept on going up to see Elvis, and took the movie off in a little bit different direction from Elvis' normal stock in trade. He felt that if he had met Elvis earlier in his career that it might have taken a different turn.

Regarding autism, which is dealt with in the film, Graham said that the little girl actress was not autistic, she was just playing the part. To try to understand the condition, they had gone to see a doctor up in San Jose who had a way of treating autism that he called rage reduction and it was very controversial. Not everybody believed in it – people then believed that there was no treatment for autism. The actress, Mary Tyler Moore, was very concerned about the way they were handling the scenes. It involved Elvis holding the child in his arms and letting the child struggle because she felt contained, and going into a rage, but he would still hold her and continue to hold her until finally, she would quiet down. The doctor in San Jose said he had successfully treated many children with this method.

On 29th April 1969, Elvis movie career was over as he was released from "Change of Habit." However, since the success of the '68 Special TV show, Elvis was eager to get back on the stage in front of his fans. The Colonel agreed and negotiated a deal for Elvis to do a series of concerts at the yet-to-be-completed International Hotel in Las Vegas in August that year. Elvis would receive a salary of $100,000 a week, out of which he would pay for his band and backing singers.

Gallery

Elvis and Priscilla's wedding. (Getty images)

Billy, Rick and David Stanley and their mother Dee, with Elvis.

Dancing scene from the Gospel medley of the '68 Special (Graceland)

The cross which attracted Elvis to the Circle G Ranch.

Always me,

Elvis

P.S. The last song on your tape sold me..just thought you'd like to know that idea payed off. Untill then you hadn't really sounded any better or any worse than a lot of theother kids who send in to me. I liked you but nothing special until I heard it and it reminded me of myself..that always gets a guy..when he sees or hears himself in someone else. Good luck Buddy

PPS. send me you Birthdate - Time of day - place - day - year - month -

It's important Too.

Final part of a letter to Lanny Smith – notice Elvis' interest in Lanny's birth date. Elvis was very much into numerology at the time.

Tree of Life pendant designed by Marty Lacker.

The gold tone watch is designed so that the image of the Star of David with a Christian cross appears on the face every 20 seconds. Elvis had these made and gave them to his closest friends and the cast and crew of "Harum Sacrum".

Chapter 6

The Concert Years – Part 1

I will sing to the Lord all my life; I will sing praise to my God as long as I live. (Psalm 104:33)

Concert from Hawaii, via satellite. Elvis' jump suit emblazoned with the American eagle.

As he went back into his favoured professional activity of being a singing entertainer, connecting with live audiences, Elvis continued to pray for and counsel his family, friends and even fans, though after the initial triumph of the first three years or so back on tour, it became clear that it was Elvis himself who was very much in need of prayer. As well as his family and friends who prayed for him, there were many fans who also undertook this task.

Elvis did pray for himself, especially just before he went on stage. He prayed that he would please his audience. On one occasion before a concert when he was to sing *How Great Thou Art* but was concerned at not being able to hit the high notes, Kathy Westmoreland, one of his backup singers, suggested they kneel down and asked the Lord to help him. When the time came for the song, Elvis hit the notes perfectly and he turned round to Kathy and gave her a wink. An instant answer to prayer is always gratifying!

On 4th May 1969, Elvis flew to Hawaii with Priscilla, Lisa Marie, and friends for a three-week holiday.

In July Elvis came to an agreement with the Graceland Christian Church next door for him to use their driveway, from which he had access to Graceland, when he needed to avoid the fans at his gates. He paid a nominal fee of $10 as well as the cost of resurfacing the driveway and promised not to use any motor vehicles during Sunday Church services "unless absolutely necessary."

For the remainder of this month Elvis worked with Charlie Hodge to gather songs for the upcoming shows at the newly built International Hotel in Las Vegas. He also contacted many of the musicians he knew to get together a band and backing singers.

Elvis would have liked the Jordanaires, as he really appreciated them, not only for their singing ability, but also for their encouragement. He told them, "If there had not been the Jordanaires I guess there wouldn't have been me. You guys took an interest in me and when I didn't care you helped me with bad material [referring to the movie songs] and just when I did not want to record." Gordon Stoker said, "We did it because of our love for him!"

As we know, the Jordanaires stopped working with Elvis near the end of his movie career and now had plenty of work of their own. Also, they knew that the late night/early morning shows in Las Vegas were not for them.

The band Elvis gathered comprised James Burton on lead guitar, pianist Larry Muhoberac, drummer Ronnie Tutt, bass player Jerry Scheff and rhythm guitarist John Wilkinson. He had asked Scotty Moore and D J Fontana, but they were not available. For his backing singers he wanted the Blossoms, but they were also unavailable, so he chose the Black rhythm and blues group, the Sweet Inspirations who had recently released a gospel album. Members of the Sweet Inspirations were, Cissy Houston (mother of Whitney), Myrna Smith, Sylvia Shemwell and Estelle Brown. For his male backing singers, Elvis chose the Imperials whose members were, Armond Morales, Joe Moscheo, Jim Murray, Terry Blackwood, and Roger Wiles. Elvis also hired soprano Millie Kirkham with whom he had previously worked. The International Hotel provided a 30-piece orchestra.

The first rehearsal was also the first time that Elvis had met the Sweet Inspirations as he had not required an audition. As with all of the musicians he liked, he had carefully listened to their records and knew well their repertoire and performances. Myrna Smith says of that first meeting, "Well, we were starting rehearsals in July of 1969, and we were all on the stage and Elvis hadn't arrived yet, nor his entourage. We were sitting there waiting for him to come in and all of a sudden, he walks onto the stage, walks right over to us and plants a kiss on each one of us. That's how we met him. He had on a chocolate-coloured suit. He had a tan, and he looked absolutely gorgeous. He walked over to us and introduced himself – like we didn't know who he was: 'Hi, I'm Elvis Presley.' (Cissy literally fell off her stool.) From then on, whenever he'd see us, it was always a kiss. He had so much energy. His voice was a lot more remarkable than it ever came off on record. He was just a much better singer than could ever be captured. Some great singers' voices are just too big. Elvis was like that."

Stage Fright Overcome

If the '68 Comeback Special was a triumph, then Elvis' first public stage appearance in over 11 years on 31st July was phenomenal. The Sweet Inspirations opened the show, followed by comedian Sammy Shore. Elvis suffered a bad case of stage fright before he went on, but once he had started his first song, there was no stopping him.

The invited audience included many celebrities such as Cary Grant, Sammy Davies Jnr, Pat Boone, Fats Domino, Tom Jones, Paul Anka and Ann-Margret. Also present was Sam Phillips from Sun Records. Mac Davis, the singer-songwriter who had written *In the Ghetto* for Elvis was also in the audience and reported, "I never saw anything like it in my life. You couldn't take your eyes off the guy. It was just crazy. Women rushing the stage, people clamouring over each other. I couldn't wipe the grin off my face the entire time."

Billboard's review said, "It was not the Elvis with the rough edges of the middle 1950s on stage, it was a polished, confident and talented artist, knowing exactly what he was going to do and when." Rolling Stone magazine said, "Elvis was supernatural. His own resurrection," and commented that Elvis worked so hard that many of the audience thought that he would collapse.

The remainder of the shows were equally successful, all sell-outs with rave reviews. When Elvis closed at the International on 28th August 1969, he had, during the engagement's 29 shows, broken Las Vegas attendance records. Following this, the International was very happy to sign a new contract for Elvis to do two engagements a year for the next five years, raising his salary to $125,000 per week, giving him a guaranteed $1million a year for just eight weeks work.

Throughout the engagement, Elvis invited friends and celebrities to his suite after the shows and he sang with the Imperials as often as he could, and with Tom Jones. These after show singings of mostly gospel songs continued throughout the years after nearly every concert.

From 1st September 1969 until January 1970, when he was scheduled to return to Las Vegas, Elvis had nothing on his calendar. He spent the time traveling between his Memphis and Palm Springs homes and his favourite holiday spots. He did this without Priscilla and Lisa Marie and rumours started that their marriage was in difficulties. He did, however, spend Christmas in Memphis, arriving there on 18th December.

Elvis Loved Jewellery

Lowell Hayes remembers Elvis buying Christmas gifts from him. Lowell says, "I grew up in Memphis with Elvis but did not meet him until 1969. I was born into the jewellery business which my father had established in 1937. The night I met Elvis he was shooting at a target on the side of his dad's office. It was raining, and Elvis was wearing a full-length ranch mink coat. Over the period of that year, I got to know Elvis. We went to movies and football games together."

"In December 1969, he called me on Christmas Eve and wanted to do his Christmas shopping at around 10:00 or 11:00 at night. I took my briefcase to the Memphian Theatre, a movie house in Memphis where I met him. He sat down, went through my jewellery briefcase and very carefully selected pieces of jewellery for friends, family, his aunt, and his dad. From then on, I was Elvis' jeweller. He invited me to go on the tours with him, with one requirement that I bring along a case full of jewellery. He loved to give gifts to people he met along the way. Elvis bought a small garnet cross from me. He had it with him when we were in Jackson, Mississippi at a concert, and someone told him about a little boy who was dying. It was a Make-A-Wish Foundation request, and he wanted to see Elvis. So, Elvis agreed, and we took the limo to the hospital where the little boy was staying. Elvis visited with him awhile and then gave him that very cross I had made for Elvis. The parents were there, and we all said some prayers.

"One night in Asheville, Elvis came over, reached down in my case, got out a ring, and walked over to this girl that was standing there with a rose in her hand. He handed her the ring, and the crowd just went wild. Elvis was in one of those giving away moods. Afterwards I told Elvis that I was embarrassed and wished I hadn't been there so he wouldn't have lost so much money, but Elvis looked at me and said, 'I'm going to have to sing five minutes longer tomorrow night to pay for that jewellery,' and he laughed."

Among the pieces Lowell made for Elvis during his career were the TCB ring, the Aloha ring, the Maltese Cross, and the lion necklace. He says that "Elvis was a very giving person who had wonderful, yet expensive taste in jewellery. He loved his fans, friends, and family, and he tried to give everything he could back to them. I was honoured to be able to work with him."

In January 1970, Elvis had two rooms and a bathroom at Graceland converted into an apartment for Charlie Hodge.

Healing Prayer

For his second engagement at the Hilton in Las Vegas in January, Glen D Hardin had replaced Larry Muhoberac as Elvis' pianist. Glen stayed with Elvis' band until 1976. For these performances Elvis was much more confident and relaxed. He knew he was a hit. The band and backing singers were now like extended family. Myrna Smith of the Sweet Inspirations (aka The Sweets) remembers that straight after the shows, Elvis would go to their dressing room to let off steam with pillow and water fights and discussions about his life, religion and almost anything. On one occasion Elvis found out that a member of the group, Sylvia Shemwell, had been diagnosed with cancer. He had noticed after a performance that the women were upset, and he asked why. When he found out, he immediately requested that they go to the dressing-room area, where he asked them all to join him in prayer. He prayed, touched Sylvia's stomach, and asked God to take away whatever it was. The next morning, when Sylvia reported to the Sunrise Hospital in Las Vegas and underwent tests for cancer, the disease was gone.

The Sweets were invited to his suite for the after-show parties, but they only went a few times as they were not comfortable with all the people milling around and wondering if and when they were supposed to speak with Elvis.

"No Sweets – No Elvis"

February saw Priscilla and Lisa Marie flying out to Las Vegas to attend the dinner show on 1st February for Lisa Marie's second birthday. Also, Elvis was now ready to go out and try other venues. The Colonel arranged for him to appear at the Houston Astrodome, holding over 67,000 audience and more suited to indoor rodeo performances than concerts. However, again Elvis was a hit, with a "masterful performance."

It so happened that Elvis may not have appeared there if the promoters had not had a change of heart. They had sent a message to Elvis that they were thrilled that he was coming, but not to bring "those Black girls" (the Sweet Inspirations). They had nothing against the girls as such but did not want them appearing on stage with white folk. Needless to say, Elvis was infuriated by this and told the promoters in no uncertain terms, "No Sweets, no Elvis." The Sweets only found out about this later as the guys didn't want their feelings to be hurt.

The Houston Livestock Association gave a gold Rolex watch to Elvis for breaking attendance records at the Houston Astrodome. Elvis net income for the Las Vegas and Houston shows was $351,000.

***

In March, Elvis and Priscilla spent two weeks in Palm Springs looking for a house to purchase. They eventually settled on 845 West Chino Canyon Road. Elvis purchased the house from the Kroc family for $105,000 and he, Priscilla and Lisa Marie lived there for several months a year, before the couple's divorce in 1973.

Elvis spent five days recording at RCA studio B in Nashville in June. Of these songs, *Bridge Over Troubled Water, Life* and *Only Believe* were gospel.

Rehearsals began in July for the next shows in Las Vegas, promoted as the "Elvis Presley Summer Festival." These rehearsals were filmed for the documentary "That's the Way It Is." This is when Joe Guercio started working with Elvis, conducting the orchestra. He continued in this role until Elvis' death.

Something New for Joe Guercio

Joe was not a fan of Elvis and was initially dismayed at what he saw as the disorganised state of Elvis' written musical arrangements and rather amateurish approach to the whole show. However, he was totally confident of Elvis' star quality. Although he thought that Elvis was not very disciplined, Joe recognised that what makes a star is charisma. He said that Elvis was a happening. He could walk across a stage and not even open his mouth for people to be enamoured and hooked straightaway.

Joe said about the concert years with Elvis, "He had chosen the best musicians and backing singers, whom he really appreciated and respected."

They all worked together very well, and they had to be on their toes as, although they rehearsed and knew many songs, there was no set list for the shows. Elvis sang whatever he felt at the time. As Joe said, "He would just want to pull a tune out and sing it. And it was great because everybody behind him was his immediate group. He'd say, so and so, and they'd turn around, and they'd start. Well, you can say that to five guys. I'm sitting up there with 32. You know, when am I going to start? So, it was always a scuffle. Let's do this and bam and suddenly I'd say, 'Here we go, guys. Bar 12.' And I'd bring him in on bar 12, and we'd be locked in. And the first couple of times I did that, he really turned around and acknowledged it because, you know, we didn't leave him in the desert. We just jumped in the pool, a little late, but we jumped in the pool."

Later when somebody asked Joe how he enjoyed conducting for Elvis, he said, "It's like a marble rolling down concrete steps, you know, dinkle, dinkle, dinkle. You know, one of those kinds of things." This must have been reported to Elvis because, the next day, when Joe opened his dressing room door, he heard a strange noise. He turned on the lights to reveal marbles all over the floor, marbles in every one of his pockets, marbles piled high in the sink and the sign on the mirror saying, "Follow the marble. E.P."

It was Joe Guercio who suggested that Elvis' shows open with the theme from the film "2001 – A Space Odyssey." This theme is the initial fanfare, *Sunrise* from *Also Sprach Zarathustra* by Richard Strauss. The inspiration for this came when Joe and his wife saw the movie. When the music began, Mrs. Guercio whispered to her husband "You'd think Elvis was about to enter."

New Love Interest

Also, for these shows at the International, Kathy Westmoreland replaced Millie Kirkham, Elvis introduced her to the audience as "the little girl with the beautiful high voice." Although Elvis was married, he insisted that it was an "open" marriage, so it was OK for him to have sexual relations with other women. He did not force himself on her, but eventually they became lovers and dated for a while, remaining close after it ended. Elvis continued to ask her to share his bed as friends for comfort, and she continued to work with him until his death.

187

Kathy explained: "I dated him for about six months on a regular basis, it was fun. He was very thoughtful. Almost motherly. Then it became obvious to me that there were other women." Like many others, she described how Elvis hated to be alone at night. On tour he would call her up to his room just to keep him company. "He suffered from insomnia. I think a lot of geniuses are like that, 'I just can't turn it off,' is what he would say."

August was quite a traumatic month for Elvis, as not only did he have to deal with a paternity suit (which took four years to conclude that Elvis was not the father of the child), but he also received a death threat that he would be killed during his Saturday night show. Extra security was provided as well as an ambulance and standby doctors. All of the guys including Elvis had a gun packed in each boot. Thankfully, the threat came to nothing, but Elvis was clearly shaken by these events. Perhaps this explains a change in his demeanour. Several people noticed that he became boastful and less caring in some ways, though he continued to give stellar performances on stage.

The Norwegian Connection

This character observation reminds me of something which Pål Granlund mentioned when I interviewed him in 2002. Pål had been an Elvis fan since he was a child and had formed the Norwegian Elvis Fan Club, "Flaming Star."

Pål met Elvis several times, but it was his first meeting that surprised Pål – and me when he told me. He initially met Elvis in 1970 for a short while at the gates of Graceland and when I asked him how he felt about that meeting, he replied, "Disappointed." He said that Elvis was twice as good looking as he imagined and that no photo could ever catch his beauty. However, he felt that he was very different from his current image, he was tougher, cooler. Also, he was surprised to see Elvis kissing the girls that had gathered at the gate and thought to himself, "You're married." After meeting Elvis five more times, he developed a fuller picture and could now describe Elvis as so many do: kind, sweet, polite, fun-loving, etc. Pål is quite outspoken, and one-time asked Elvis if everything was OK with his marriage and was there anything in the rumours. To which Elvis replied, "There's nothing to it, son. We get along fine." He last saw Elvis in 1976 when Elvis invited him to Graceland the next time that he was over in the USA. Sadly, Elvis passed away before Pål could visit again.

I like to find out what it is about Elvis that people love. For Pål, Elvis touched him like no one else ever had, he was larger than life. He never gets tired of listening to him, and it helped him when he felt down. Elvis was a kind of medicine, and even like one of Jesus' disciples. Pål has clearly been inspired by Elvis, but Elvis also indirectly helped him build a very successful publishing business. Pål had no formal business education but, having run the fan club for several years, he had all he needed to know to start and run a successful business.

The Touring Starts

Elvis started a six city "pilot" tour, in November, beginning in Phoenix, Arizona. This tour was a great success, the tickets for almost all the dates were sold out within hours of going on sale. Back home in Memphis he was able to attend the Gospel Quartet Convention in October and had an impromptu "quartet" sing backstage with James Blackwood, J D Sumner, and Statesman founder Hovie Lister.

This month was when Elvis had 14 of the famous TCB pendants, which he and Priscilla had designed, made up in 14 carat gold for his entourage. The design consists of the letters TCB above a zigzag lightning bolt, conveying "Taking Care of Business in a flash." Over the years he gave many to his friends and people he admired. Certainly, the members of his band and backing singers were recipients. Later he also had some made for ladies, where the TCB is replaced by TLC, "Tender Loving Care." These pendants sometimes come up for auction and sell for over $50,000.

For the remainder of the year Elvis spent most of his time at his homes in Memphis and Palm Springs, touring one night stand concerts, and attending friends' weddings.

Karate in Memphis

In December, Wayne Carman, a black belt martial artist who trained at the Kang Rhee Institute in Memphis, received a telephone call which, at first, he thought was a hoax. It was Red West saying that Elvis wanted his security staff to have lessons in martial arts. Wayne had been recommended by a mutual contact at The Memphis Police Supply. Over the next few months, he gave Red and others lessons, and then Elvis would come to some karate workouts, often accompanied by an audience of friends and family. Wayne, a Christian, became friends with Elvis and felt that it was the Holy Spirit who empowered him, not only in his entertaining and karate, but also in his generosity and blessing of others.

Elvis had expressed that he wanted to show the students that he was attending class as a martial artist, not as an entertainer, so he asked if he could demonstrate a variety of self-defence techniques. He demonstrated several defences at close range and then stepped back. He was about to demonstrate a defence against a gun technique from more than five feet away. He slowly straightened his uniform, then dropped to his knees and put his hands together. After a minute's silence, someone asked him what he was doing. "Praying," Elvis answered, smiling. "When someone is standing 10 feet away from you with a drawn gun, that's when you pray." All the spectators laughed and clapped. Toward the end of the demonstration, Kang Rhee himself requested that Elvis offer a prayer for the students, which he said was "very moving and beautiful."

Elvis trained from 1970–1974 under Master Kang Rhee and was awarded 7th Degree Black Belt in 1973. Master Rhee said, "Elvis was very humble. In many ways, Elvis taught me more than I taught him. He was a deeply religious person, he presented me with a Bible as a gift." This was not only a healthy pastime for Elvis, but he used several of the karate moves to enhance his stage show.

A Presidential Appointment

Elvis had been on a spending spree, purchasing many firearms for himself and others, as well as a house for Joe Esposito and his wife, and a Mercedes car for Jerry Schilling. On 19th December, when Vernon and Priscilla confronted Elvis with his extravagant spending, Elvis was furious and left Graceland, driving to the airport where he boarded a flight for Washington DC. Thus began one of the most bizarre events of Elvis' life.

After arriving in Washington, Elvis checked into a hotel, then flew on to Los Angeles where he persuaded Jerry Schilling to fly back to Washington with him. He also arranged for Sonny West in Memphis to join them in Washington and to tell Vernon and Priscilla that he was safe, but with strict instructions not to disclose his whereabouts. On the plane to Washington, Elvis penned a five-page letter on American Airlines paper to President Nixon offering his services to combat illicit drug use. A sincere offer, with the hope of obtaining a Bureau of Narcotics and Dangerous Drugs badge, as Elvis was an avid collector of Police badges. Here is a transcript of that letter:

Dear Mr. President.

First, I would like to introduce myself. I am Elvis Presley and admire you and have great respect for your office. I talked to Vice President Agnew in Palm Springs three weeks ago and expressed my concern for our country. The drug culture, the hippie elements, the SDS, Black Panthers, etc. do not consider me as their enemy or as they call it the establishment. I call it America and I love it. Sir, I can and will be of any service that I can to help the country out. I have no concern or motives other than helping the country out.

So I wish not to be given a title or an appointed position. I can and will do more good if I were made a Federal Agent at Large and I will help out by doing it my way through my communications with people of all ages. First and foremost, I am an entertainer, but all I need is the Federal credentials. I am on this plane with Senator George Murphy and we have been discussing the problems that our country is faced with.

Sir, I am staying at the Washington Hotel, Room 505-506-507. I have two men who work with me by the name of Jerry Schilling and Sonny West. I am registered under the name of Jon Burrows. I will be here for as long as long as it takes to get the credentials of a Federal Agent. I have done an in-depth study of drug abuse and Communist brainwashing techniques and I am right in the middle of the whole thing where I can and will do the most good.

I am Glad to help just so long as it is kept very private. You can have your staff or whomever call me anytime today, tonight, or tomorrow. I was nominated this coming year one of America's Ten Most Outstanding Young Men. That will be in January 18 in my hometown of Memphis, Tennessee. I am sending you the short autobiography about myself so you can better understand this approach. I would love to meet you just to say hello if you're not too busy.

Respectfully,

Elvis Presley

P. S. I believe that you, Sir, were one of the Top Ten Outstanding Men of America also.

I have a personal gift for you which I would like to present to you, and you can accept it or I will keep it for you until you can take it.

Elvis finished the letter by giving the President all his private telephone numbers and the hotel number.

When they landed, Elvis and Jerry dropped off the letter at an entrance gate to the White House at about 6.30am. After checking in at the hotel, Elvis left for the offices of the Bureau of Narcotics and Dangerous Drugs where he got to meet a deputy director, but not approval for a Bureau badge. Meanwhile, his letter was delivered to Nixon aide, Egil "Bud" Krogh, who happened to be an avid Elvis fan. Egil loved the idea of a Nixon-Presley summit and persuaded his bosses to make it happen, which they did as they could see that their anti-drugs campaign was not credible to young people and that Elvis could possibly help.

Around noon, Elvis arrived at the White House with Jerry Schilling and Sonny West, who'd just arrived from Memphis. He was wearing a purple velvet suit with a huge gold belt buckle and amber sunglasses, not the standard attire for male guests to meet President Nixon in the White House. Elvis was also bearing a gift – a Colt .45 pistol with seven silver bullets mounted in a display case. This was intercepted at the gate house and taken from Elvis with the explanation that weapons were not allowed in the Oval Office, but that it would be given to the President.

At the beginning of the meeting with President Nixon, Elvis showed him photos of Priscilla and Lisa Marie and some of his collection of police badges. There was then discussion about Elvis helping with the anti-drugs campaign during which Elvis asked, "Mr. President, can you get me a badge from the Bureau of Narcotics and Dangerous Drugs?" When the answer was in the affirmative, Elvis was ecstatic. "In a surprising, spontaneous gesture," Egil Krogh reported, "Elvis put his left arm around the President and hugged him. President hugging was not, at least in my limited experience, a common occurrence in the Oval Office." This gesture caught the President off guard, but he recovered from his surprise and patted Elvis on the shoulder while expressing his appreciation of Elvis' offer of help.

Then Elvis, being Elvis, couldn't resist sharing his Presidential moment with his friends, so he asked if Jerry and Sonny could also meet the President. This was agreed although the timing was tight. As is usual -about the only thing that was usual in this meeting - the President walked round to his desk and opened a drawer containing gifts with the Presidential seal, such as pins, tie clasps, cuff links and golf balls. He picked out some tie clasps. At this point, overcome with curiosity, Elvis joined the President in rummaging through the drawer for suitable gifts.

After Elvis collected his coveted badge, he and his guys left the White House very satisfied and somewhat bemused with their visit, though no doubt not as bemused as President Nixon.

In January 1995, there was a TV documentary based on the book "The Day Elvis Met Nixon" by Egil "Bud" Krogh as part of the celebration of Elvis' 60th birthday. This documentary was one of the programmes I watched that week which made me realise how amazing Elvis was and I became a fan. My enduring memory of the programme is the description of Elvis joining the President in rummaging through the drawer to find suitable gifts. I fell in love with his childlike innocence and enthusiasm.

Elvis returned to Graceland bearing gifts for Lisa Marie and Priscilla and with many stories to tell. Elvis and his family spent a quiet Christmas at Graceland, with Elvis visiting Memphis Police Headquarters in the early hours of Christmas day to say "Hello" and "Happy Christmas" to the men and women who had to work over Christmas.

An Outstanding Young Man

On 16th January 1971, Elvis accepted the award of being one of the Ten Outstanding Young Men in the USA, by the United States Junior Chamber, or the Jaycees. The Ten Outstanding Young Americans programme is an annual award given to ten Americans between 18 and 40 years of age who "exemplify the best attributes of the nation's young people." This national honour has been given each year since the late 1930s and recognizes young men who have made great achievements in their field of endeavour, illustrating the opportunities available in the free enterprise system. It also applauds humanitarianism and community service. Scientists, inventors, performers, film makers, politicians bound for the Presidency, and men of greatness in all fields, have been selected for this award over the years, including John F Kennedy, Gerald Ford, Charles Lindburgh, Orson Welles, Howard Hughes, and Bill Gates.

It was the only award he carried with him everywhere he went for the rest of his life.

Elvis attended a day of functions, culminating in an evening awards banquet where he and nine others accepted the honour.

Of Elvis' arrival at the Jaycee prayer breakfast held at the Holiday Inn-Rivermount in Memphis, the host, Harold Sterling said, "I was just not ready for someone that theatrical, he had all these diamonds on, and his hair was long. Charlie Hodge was drinking and laughing, Red West and his wife were there. Priscilla had long jet-black hair. He was a taskmaster, people jumped, he had ideas on what he wanted and the impression he wanted to give, but he was a benevolent tyrant, he was so good, but he was demanding too. His entrance into the dining room was electrifying, the most staid of businessmen and society wives all stopped their conversations to watch him enter the room. Just as he and Priscilla sat down, photographers rushed to their table. Graciously Elvis allowed a couple of quick pictures, then he asked the newsmen to leave."

A private question and answer session followed the breakfast at which Ron Ziegler, Press Secretary to President Nixon, who was also receiving the award sat next to Elvis and conversed. This is his memory of that conversation; "I think he [Elvis] was very pleased to receive the award, and it was an honour to him, and he so indicated, he was expressing a little discomfort of how he was going to react and to relate to the other people who were there, so we talked about that a little bit. It appeared to me at that time that he wanted to reach out and talk to someone different to that what he could find in his entourage. I didn't get the impression that he was limited or dull witted, I found him to be a somewhat articulate and poised individual, I did sense however an individual who was withdrawn and an individual who was somewhat shy. I think all of us were moved by Elvis. He was a natural nice man, I liked him."

This meeting was without the press, but other reports say that Elvis spoke about religion and its importance to his life, in the sense that he called on God many times for strength. He also said "Yes, I don't go along with music advocating drugs and desecration of the flag. I think an entertainer is for entertaining and to make people happy."

In the afternoon, at 5.00pm Elvis hosted a cocktail reception at Graceland for the honourees and members of the Jaycees.

Elvis was nervous about his acceptance speech. After a two-thousand-dollar-a-plate banquet, Elvis gave his address in which he quoted a favourite Roy Hamilton tune, *Without A Song:*

"When I was a child, ladies, and gentlemen, I was a dreamer. I read comic books, and I was the hero of the comic book. I saw movies, and I was the hero in the movie. So, every dream I ever dreamed has come true a hundred times. These gentlemen over there, these are the type who care, are dedicated. You realize that it's possible that they might be building the Kingdom, it's not far-fetched from reality. I learned very early in life that: Without a song, the day would never end; without a song, a man ain't got a friend; without a song, the road would never bend, without a song. So, I keep singing a song. Goodnight. Thank you."

Another award Elvis received this year was Grammy Lifetime Achievement Award. It is a special Grammy that is awarded by The Recording Academy to "performers who, during their lifetimes, have made creative contributions of outstanding artistic significance to the field of recording." This award is distinct from the Grammy Hall of Fame Award, (of which Elvis received three) which honours specific recordings rather than individuals, and the Grammy Trustees Award, which honours non-performers. Elvis, at the age of 36, was the youngest living artist to receive a Lifetime Achievement Award.

The awards kept coming, and the following year he received a Lifetime Achievement Award from the National Academy of Recording Arts and Sciences. (NARAS). Until then, there had been only five other recipients of the award: Bing Crosby, Frank Sinatra, Duke Ellington, Ella Fitzgerald, and Irving Berlin.

***

On 26th January Elvis started four weeks of concerts at the International Hotel in Las Vegas with Lisa Marie attending the dinner show on her third birthday. He developed a high fever and 'flu but carried on, completing the engagements. A revue in Variety magazine said, "He comes on stronger than before. The programming is better with amounts of the goldies along the past 15 years spaced out well, interlaced with contemporary fare and – the stroke of a master planner – a couple of his gospel hits."

Over the next few months, RCA wanted Elvis to produce several singles, a pop album, a gospel album, and a new Christmas album. He started on this in March in a two-day recording session in Nashville. The only gospel song he recorded was *Amazing Grace*. During this time Elvis had discomfort in his eye and was admitted to hospital for three days where a diagnosis of iritis and secondary glaucoma was confirmed. Elvis spent Easter with his immediate family and friends in Palm Springs.

May saw more recording sessions in Nashville. Gospel/Christmas songs which were recorded are *Miracle of the Rosary, Padre, The Lord's Prayer, O Come*

All Ye Faithful, Lead Me Guide Me, He Touched Me, I've Got Confidence, An Evening Prayer and *Seeing is Believing.*

Even though he no longer had contact with Larry Geller, who introduced him to the place, Elvis visited the Self Realisation Center on 12th May, as he was still on his spiritual quest.

There were more recording sessions in June, including the gospel songs, *Put Your Hand in the Hand, Reach Out To Jesus, He is My Everything, There's No God But God, I John* and *Bosom of Abraham.*

Elvis Presley Boulevard came into being on 29th June, when the Memphis City Council renamed part of Highway 51 South on which Graceland is situated.

Elvis Needed Female Company

With Elvis being so much away from Memphis, and therefore Priscilla, he still had need of female company. It seems that in order to help in this, his entourage would contact women in whom Elvis had shown an interest and invite them to meet him. One such person was actress Peggy Lipton. She was taken to the aeroplane in which Elvis was to travel to Lake Tahoe and stayed with him in a hotel overnight. They met several other times too. She was very nervous, but found Elvis very attractive, almost overwhelming, and very different from her. He showed great interest in her and wanted to know all about her. She felt that she even began to like him. She said that he smelled good and kissed like a god with very warm, wet, and passionate kisses. It was so wonderful that at one point she didn't want him to stop kissing her. When they moved on to the "next stage" Elvis was not able to "perform" which she put down to his drug abuse. She said that she could make him laugh, which would have been attractive to Elvis. Although sex was the main agenda as far as she was originally concerned, Peggy became more interested in Elvis' heart and soul. She thought that he was a kind and beautiful person and a type of Peter Pan – the boy who never grew up.

***

Elvis' two-week engagement at Lake Tahoe in July was to sell-out crowds. Many people who saw the opening show felt that Elvis had never looked better and that the gospel number *Bridge Over Trouble Water* was the hit of the concert.

Bridge Over Troubled Water

Here I would like to have a closer look at this song. Once, at an Elvis Tribute Artist (ETA) concert, I requested *Bridge Over Troubled Water,* commenting that it was a gospel song. The ETA did not look convinced of that fact, as it not usually thought of as a gospel song. However, when Paul Simon, who is a Christian, wrote it, he said that it was "a humble little gospel hymn with two verses and a simple guitar behind it." That at least is how it sounds on the demo, but the final product was much more grandiose. Apparently one of the main influences for the song was a line that Paul heard on the radio in 1957. He was listening to the Swan Silvertone's version of *Oh, Mary Don't You Weep*, and heard Claude Jeter singing a line of scat midway through: "I'll be your bridge over deep water if you trust in My name." "My name", of course, refers to the name of Jesus, which the Bible says is "the name above all names".

I wonder how many people the song has influenced to become Christian. One of our relatives told me that when she was 'searching' and becoming interested in Christianity this song had a profound effect on her. She was listening to it one day and suddenly realised that Jesus is the bridge over troubled water, and that the words of the song could be taken as the words of Jesus to us. A short time later she accepted Jesus as her Lord and Saviour.

There are certainly biblical references in the song. As we know, Jesus "laid down" his life for us, "he took our part" so that we may not perish but have everlasting life. (John 3:16.) Also, the Lord promises to dry our tears "The sovereign Lord will wipe away the tears from all faces" (Isaiah 25:8). And, of course, the Lord is our friend and comforter. The reference to "your time has come to shine" is found in Isaiah 60.

When asked what he thought of Elvis' version of the song, Paul Simon said this. "It was in his Las Vegas period and done with conventional thinking. He sang it well, but it would have been nice to hear him do it gospel because he did so many gospel albums and was a good white gospel singer. It would have been nice to hear him do it that way, to take it back – as opposed to the big ending; he seemed to end everything with a karate chop and an explosion. So he didn't really add anything to the song. It's not nearly as significant as the Aretha Franklin recording. It's just a pleasure for me that Elvis Presley recorded one of my songs before he died."

Signs of Struggle

Three days after closing at Lake Tahoe, Elvis started his summer engagement at the Las Vegas Hilton. The reviewer from the Hollywood Reporter was not impressed with the opening show which he called "sloppy, hurriedly rehearsed, mundanely lit, poorly amplified, occasionally monotonous, often silly and haphazardly coordinated." He commented that Elvis looked drawn and tired and noticeably heavier. He also noticed that "the audience couldn't have cared less. They absolutely loved, honored and obeyed his every whim."

For most of this engagement, Elvis suffered from throat problems and, although he carried on, he was struggling. For one concert, he was onstage for only 30 minutes, rather than the usual one hour. Although still tired, his health did improve, and he could still excel. In the concert on 27th August, he received such a tumultuous applause for *Bridge Over Troubled Water* that he repeated the last verse, "Sail on silver girl," and was rewarded with an even louder ovation.

Times of Change – Not All Good

Elvis spent his time in September and October resting in Memphis and LA before he started the 12 one-night stand concert tour in November. Due to scheduling conflicts, the Imperials were not available for this series of concerts, and they decided to stop performing with Elvis, most probably also because they wanted to concentrate on singing gospel.

Their place was taken by J D Sumner and the Stamps comprising, at the time, Ed Enoch, Donnie Sumner, Bill Baize and Richard Sterben. Over the next few years, the membership of the group would change and others who joined and sang with Elvis were Ed Hill, Rick Strickland, Dave Rowland, Tony Brown, and Larry Strickland.

The November concert tour was a great success with Elvis in good health and on top form. He had by now introduced *How Great Thou Art* into his show and throughout his rendition of this in Dallas, the audience punctuated his singing by shouting "Hallelujah."

Christmas was spent at home in Memphis with his family and, of course, some of his entourage.

On 30th December, Priscilla and Lisa Marie returned to LA and Elvis announced that she was leaving him, though she hadn't told him why.

So, why did Priscilla end her married relationship with Elvis? She dearly loved him, and he loved her, however she found that being his wife was too demanding. He wouldn't let her have a career or a life of her own, which often left her feeling incredibly isolated.

When interviewed in 2016 Priscilla explained. The pair "didn't go out" and "truly lived in a bubble." She said, "I just kind of followed what he did. You lived his life. You really kind of lost yourself." Not even alone with Elvis could she be entirely herself. "He taught me, even in having a relationship, about always having a mystique – never revealing everything." For example, he did not like to see her without her make up on, and he never wanted to see her getting dressed. He wanted to see the result of getting dressed. While her teenage years were "fun," she didn't experience them "as a normal girl." Only when she began attending a dance class did she realize how unusual their relationship was. "I left because I needed to find out what the world was like," she said. "I didn't really know who I was."

Elvis Loved an Adventure

In January 1972, Elvis began his four-week engagement at the Las Vegas Hilton, introducing the song *American Trilogy* which is also known as *Mine Eyes Have Seen the Glory,* outside of the United States. It is a powerful melding of *Dixie, The Battle Hymn of the Republic,* and the Black spiritual *All My Trials.* This mixture of patriotism and gospel, sung with great fervour by Elvis became one of his fan's favourites. As usual, after the late show he would have guests up to his suite and start singing gospel. His backing singers, the Stamps, would be there, as well as, sometimes, members of the Imperials if they were in Las Vegas backing other singers.

Joe Moscheo remembers well one such session. It was about 3 o'clock in the morning and they were standing round the piano singing gospel when the telephone rang. Sonny West whispered in Joe's ear that his wife was on the phone. Now Joe, his wife and four children were staying in an apartment in a motel whilst Joe was in Las Vegas. The call was to tell Joe that their house in Nashville had been broken into and she was panicking. Joe had a quiet word with one of the guys to say that he needed to leave and went out of the suite to the lift. While he was waiting for the lift, Elvis burst out of his apartment and demanded of Joe, "Moscheo, where are you going?" Joe explained that he had a little family problem. Elvis wanted to know all the details and, to the concern of his entourage, all of whom by now had come into the corridor, Elvis said,

"I'm going with you, we need to get to the bottom of this. I'll sort it out." Joe insisted that it was OK, that he could deal with it, but by now Elvis was on a roll, sensing an adventure. He started giving out orders, to get the cars, the plane, "we're going to Nashville."

By the time Joe got down to the front door, there were four white limousines ready to take Elvis and his entourage back to Joe's motel. Joe says he felt quite embarrassed leading this convoy with his little hire car. On arriving at the motel, everyone followed Joe into his apartment where they were greeted by his wife wearing a dressing gown with her hair in rollers. All 20 of the visitors piled into the small living area, Joe's wife was crying so Elvis hugged her and told her he was there to take care of things. This commotion of course had woken the children who were peeking round their bedroom door to see what was going on. Elvis saw them and went into their bedroom and sat on the bed with them. He told them the reason he was there, and that if anything of theirs, bicycles etc that they especially loved, had been stolen, to write him a note and he would replace it better than what they had.

Joe's take on this bizarre series of events is that it displayed Elvis love, care and concern for others and his need to help. Apparently, Joe's children, now grown up with families of their own, still talk about the time Elvis Presley came into their bedroom in the middle of the night. I guess Elvis is quite unforgettable!

Separate Ways

Elvis and Priscilla separated on 23rd February 1972 and later filed for legal separation on 26th July. To avoid Priscilla having to make her home address available on the public records and therefore risking the security of both her and Lisa Marie, Elvis filed for divorce on his 38th birthday, 8th January 1973.

Elvis took a long time to accept that Priscilla wanted to leave him. He couldn't really understand why, as he had given her everything he could. She only had to ask, and he would get things for her. One of Elvis' main ways of showing love was by providing material wealth, especially for those who really need it. That is why, when he started earning a lot of money, he spent it on his parents and family who had struggled financially most of their lives.

When his mother died, it was a natural occurrence, not controlled by man. As already mentioned, Elvis did recognise that he might have tried to spend more time with his mother, as she worried about him so much, but he was committed to travelling away for home much of the time. When he lost Priscilla, it was by her choice. This was a great blow to his ego, perhaps from which he never really recovered.

A Revealing Documentary

MGM commissioned another documentary, *Elvis on Tour*, which began filming in March. Three tours were performed by Elvis in 1972. MGM and RCA technicians accompanied them to record shows. The documentary gives close ups of not only Elvis, but also the band, the singers, and the audience, as well as informal off-stage times which reveal Elvis' love of gospel songs.

One of these informal times is when Elvis and some of his entourage and band and gospel singers were gathered round a piano singing gospel songs. The first song is *The Lighthouse,* during which Elvis doesn't sing but listens intently and is visibly moved, gently shaking his head in wonderment. What I also notice about this is that some of his entourage are not joining in and seem to be bored. They do, after all, hear Elvis singing a lot of gospel before his shows, after his shows and whenever he can. Elvis was never bored with gospel singing.

Here are some of the words of this song which Elvis so loved:

I thank God for the lighthouse,
I owe my life to him.
For Jesus is the lighthouse,
And from the rocks of sin,
He has shone the light around me
That I might clearly see
If it wasn't for the lighthouse
Tell me where would this ship be?

After this session Elvis gave an interview that focussed on his love of gospel music and performing. Of gospel music he says, "it more or less puts your mind at ease, at least it does mine."

When asked how there is such a special feeling between the members of the group on stage, Elvis replied by saying, "I think it is because we constantly enjoy this music. We never let it get old. Every time is like we do it for the first time, and that's one of the secrets." Elvis was aware that although he had sung the songs many times, for most of the fans at his concerts it was the first time they had heard him sing live, and he wanted to honour that by making the experience for them as fresh as possible.

Elvis greatly admired Bill Baize's tenor voice (he could hit very high notes) and during the concert would ask him to sing *When its's My Time (To Call Upon the Lord)*. This song is not very well known, but Elvis would have identified with it as he would have called upon the Lord many times. Here are some of the lyrics:

When it's my time for tears and trials,
When it's my time to carry a heavy load,
When this old heart of mine starts to tremble,
Then it's my time to call upon my Lord.
There's nothing like the sweetness of Jesus being near.
There's nothing like his presence to dry my every tear.

Elvis' father, Vernon, asked Bill to sing this at Elvis' funeral.

Another song which Elvis did not sing in his concerts, but asked the Stamps to sing, is *Sweet, Sweet Spirit,* written by Doris Akers. This was always sung acapella:

There's a sweet, sweet spirit in this place
And I know that it's the spirit of the Lord.
There are sweet expressions on each face
And I know they feel the presence of the Lord.
Sweet Holy Spirit, Sweet heavenly dove
Stay right here with us, filling us with your love.
And for these blessings we lift our hearts in praise.
Without a doubt we'll know that we have been revived when we shall leave this place.

On introducing the song, Elvis says, "I do not sing in this song, just listen to them, please." There are indeed sweet expressions on Elvis' face as it is clear he feels the presence of the Lord. Sometimes his eyes are closed, or he is smiling as he shakes his head, or he mouths the words along with the Stamps.

I clearly remember experiencing the effect of hearing this song sung live when I was at an Elvis event in Knokke in Belgium in November 2008, where guests were Ed Hill, Bill Baize and Shaun Neilson. After dinner, they responded to a request to sing *Sweet, Sweet Spirit* and, along with five other singers present, gathered in a space between the tables and sang. Beautiful!

It Is Not Only Gospel Songs Which Inspire

One of the songs filmed for this MGM documentary is *Always on My Mind*, which I believe is inspirational for several reasons. It is not a gospel song but, sung by Elvis so sorrowfully, it can bring to mind any regrets we may have in our own lives and how to cope with them. Here is a story I find very encouraging.

August 1997 marked the 20th anniversary of the death of Elvis, and earlier in the year *Always on My Mind* was re-released as a single and entered the charts at number 13. Most people on hearing the song and knowing that Elvis' marriage was on the rocks, believe that Elvis had Priscilla in mind when he sang the song. It is this which gives the song such authenticity and depth, and one cannot help but be moved by it, especially when also seeing Elvis facial expression on video as he sings it.

This song had a profound effect on a member of my family. This person is the mother of three children, now all adults. Sometime in late August in 1997, one of her daughters suddenly confided in her mother that as a teenager she had felt very insecure and "not good enough." That was a surprise for the mother as her daughter had always been very outgoing and vivacious. Also, she was somewhat concerned as she had always thought of their family as being very close and loving and yet she had not noticed her daughter's unhappiness in those years. Because she was an Elvis fan, she had recently purchased the recording and a few days later she was led to carefully listen to the words of *Always on My Mind* again. While she was listening, she shed many tears, mostly of regret, that she hadn't always treated her daughter "as good as I should have," that "I didn't take the time to tell her that I am so happy that she is mine," or to "hold her in all those lonely, lonely times." She was "so sorry that I was blind and made her feel second best."

Having shed the tears and feeling a release, she then wrote out the words of the song and sent them to her daughter, with a note saying that that was how she felt about their relationship, and that she was and always will be on her heart and mind.

The wonderful result is that although they were close, a barrier was broken down and their relationship changed. They became much closer and able to confide in each other to keep their relationship full of love and commitment. The mother said that she wanted to thank the songwriters, Carson, James, and Christopher for the powerful words of the song, Elvis for the powerful singing of the song, but most of all, Jesus Christ for the power of forgiveness. She also wanted to encourage anyone who has someone who is "their" wife, husband, mother, father, brother, sister, daughter, son, friend, neighbour, or colleague to regularly inspect their relationship with the words of this song in mind, and if there are any causes of regret, to share them with the person, and stand back and watch the healing take place!

Denise's Dying Wish

Elvis' concert at Tingley Coliseum in Albuquerque, New Mexico on 19th April was attended by Denise Sanchez, an eight-year-old little girl from Santa Fe, New Mexico who had been a big fan of Elvis since she was four years old. After the Christmas holidays of 1971, Denise was diagnosed with cancer. Her leg had to be amputated, along with part of her hip to block the extension of the cancer. In no time, the cancer spread to her lungs. The doctors stopped Denise's chemotherapy after ruling that there was nothing more they could do for her. Several months later, Denise's mother Trudi, discovered that Elvis would perform a concert in Albuquerque. She managed to obtain two tickets. The day of the concert was near, when Denise unfortunately had a relapse and was given the terrible news that in her condition, she could not withstand the 65-mile trip to see Elvis. Denise cried for several days and prayed for her mother to take her to the show because she wanted to see Elvis in person before she died. Eventually her mother and the doctor decided to please her by taking her to Elvis' show.

Two days before the show Mrs. Sanchez was called by the Albuquerque Journal who arranged a meeting with Colonel Parker, who then arranged for Denise and some of her family to meet Elvis in his dressing room before the show. Denise was anxious and afraid of Elvis' reaction to her missing leg and her hip, and some parts of her head without hair. Denise had nothing to worry about. Elvis looked at Denise and he knelt before her and kissed her on the cheek. Denise said that Elvis was "very pretty," and her mother Trudi began to cry. She could not believe how Elvis was so tender with her daughter and how he made her feel happy and alive. Denise timidly unrolled a poster of Elvis and asked him for an autograph. Elvis signed it: "To Denise – Love You, Elvis Presley" and, afterwards, Denise asked him to sing a song for her in concert. During the concert, Elvis dedicated *You Gave Me A Mountain* to

Denise. He explained to the audience, "This song is for a very special little girl I just met backstage." Elvis remembered the request and he also sang *Love Me Tender*. Denise was thrilled and cried during the whole song.

When Denise returned home, she told her mother she was not washing her face because she did not want to remove "the Elvis kisses." Her mother let her keep the kisses for four days, then insisted that she wash her face. Denise passed away four months later, in August that year. Elvis for a brief time had made Denise's life more beautiful with this demonstration of love to make her feel better and relieve her pain.

The Big Apple – A Dream Come True

Elvis visited 11 cities in his 1972 June tour, including New York, where his last appearance had been in 1957 on TV in the Ed Sullivan Show. These four concerts (the fourth one being added last minute because of the number of fans still wanting tickets) at Madison Square Gardens were a big hit with 80,000 fans and grossed $730,000. The New York Times described Elvis, "Like a Prince from Another Planet." As someone in whose hands the way a thing is done is more important than the thing itself. "He stood there at the end, his arms outstretched, the great gold cloak giving him wings – the only one in his class."

During the Madison Square Press Conference, when Elvis was asked, "Will you be continuing to do more live work in the future?" he replied, "I think so. There are so many places I haven't been yet. Like, I've never played New York [before now]. I've never been to Britain either."

Elvis' appearance at Madison Square Gardens was very significant for Jerry Weintraub, one of the first independent producers to be honoured with a star on the Hollywood Walk of Fame. He began his career as a talent scout in the 1950s. He formed Management III in 1965 and, from a quite modest beginning (two partners, three clients, a small backing), became a leading concert promoter and handled such clients as Frank Sinatra, Bob Dylan, Led Zeppelin, the Beach Boys and Elvis Presley. And it was Elvis who, unknowingly, made his dream come true.

So how did it come about that he worked with Elvis and his dream came true? Here is his unusual and inspiring story:

Jerry was in business at RCA records, doing shows with some artists around the country. He was living in New York and, one night, around 1969, he woke up at three o'clock in the morning having had a dream in which he saw a sign in front of Madison Square Gardens that said, "Jerry Weintraub presents Elvis." On hearing this his wife said, "That's crazy. That's nuts. You know, you don't know Elvis. You don't know Colonel Parker. You know, how do you expect to do this?" to which he replied, "I'm telling you. God sent me a sign that I was gonna do this." Jerry reports that he does believe in God, very strongly and that he talks to him all the time. He tells how he went about trying to get to be Elvis' concert promoter:

"I started to call Tom Parker. I used to call him every morning, saying that I wanted to take Elvis on tour. He would reply telling me that I was crazy and that I would never take Elvis on tour. This went on for one year. Finally, one morning he said to me, 'You still want to take my boy on tour?' I said, 'Yes.' He said, 'Okay, you be in Vegas tomorrow morning at 11 o'clock with a million dollars and we'll talk a deal.'"

So, all Jerry had to do was find a million dollars by the next day! That seemed highly unlikely as he already owed the bank $65,000, but he told the Colonel, "Okay I'll get it and I'll be there." Somehow, he knew that he would get it – and he did. He says that he went to all the people that might lend him the money, saying "Loan me some money. I have this deal with Elvis Presley. I need a million dollars." He said that most people thought that he was either on drugs or crazy, as he was just a young man. However, one person, Lester Smith, who was a huge Elvis fan and who owned radio stations, did agree to lend him the money which had to be in cash to give to the Colonel. Lester, who did not know Jerry must have been very trusting, as he transferred funds to a bank in Las Vegas without any signed agreement or contract.

Instant Millionaire

Jerry was nervous walking into the Royal Bank of Las Vegas, as he says, "I walked in and asked for the million dollars – they thought I was nuts. I said, 'I'm Jerry Weintraub. I have a million dollars coming.' You know, I was young, I had long hair and sideburns. I was wearing a pair of jeans and cowboy boots. I looked as much like I had a million dollars coming as the man on the moon. I thought that they figured I was gonna rob the place." The startled cashiers contacted the President of the bank who confirmed his claim, and Jerry was able to meet the Colonel with a million dollars in his hand.

Jerry says, "I was so excited, I was only young, but I knew that my life had changed, that my life was never gonna be the same. I hadn't signed any contracts yet, but I now was gonna be in business with the biggest star that had ever been. I had a lot of wonderful artists, and I was working with a lot of people, but there was only one Elvis Presley. It was like a bolt from heaven, and I knew my life would never be the same."

Jerry never forgot his first meeting with Elvis, which also included the Colonel, Joe Esposito, and some others of Elvis' entourage. The Colonel introduced Jerry saying, "'Elvis, this is your new promoter, Mr. Weintraub, he has just given a million dollars for you." Jerry was somewhat surprised and delighted when Elvis, who was only two years older than him, addressed him as "Sir" saying, "Oh, thank you, sir. That's really great, you know." They shook hands and the deal was done with Elvis emphasising that he wanted all the seats filling and stipulating that he wanted the 20 front rows for fans and not reserved for the big shots.

So, this was how Jerry became Elvis' concert promoter, with Elvis' first concert tour since 1957 staring on September 9th, 1970, in Phoenix.

Jerry says, "It was a hell of a ride and three weeks after I started a tour with Elvis, I was a millionaire and my life had changed."

However, Elvis still hadn't played New York. When Jerry approached him about it, Elvis told him, "I'm not a New York City kind of artist. You know, they're not gonna like me in New York City. They like me in Alabama and Georgia and Tennessee, you know, but I don't want to go to New York City, Jerry. You're gonna have trouble selling shows in New York City." As we know, Elvis eventually accepted the challenge and in 1972 New York was booked. 80,000 people saw the shows, and many of them slept outside Madison Square Gardens to get tickets.

Jerry concludes "So, God was right, and he blessed me, and he blessed me with knowing Elvis. And I have only great memories of him. The bad memories that I have when it was near the end and he got very heavy and so on and so forth, I've put out of my mind. And I don't really know anything bad about him. You know, I don't know about the drug stuff and if I did, I wouldn't talk about it. But I could only tell you that in my dealings with him, he was bright, articulate, a brilliant musician, and a nice man, and one of the things that attracted me so much was his camaraderie and his loyalty with his friends."

New Love Interest

In July, Elvis met Linda Thompson in Memphis. She was 22 years old and the current Miss Tennessee. She was clearly very beautiful, but Elvis was also attracted by her sense of humour. Later in the month she flew out to be with Elvis in Las Vegas where she stayed until they returned to Memphis at the beginning of October.

November saw Elvis on tour, accompanied by Linda. Then, in December Elvis, Linda, Lisa Marie, and several of his entourage as well as Dr Nick, and the Stanley brothers flew out to Hawaii in preparation for the live satellite broadcast. They returned to Memphis for Christmas, which is the first one of four which Elvis celebrated with Linda.

Aloha Hawaii Five-O

On 14th January 1973, the "Aloha from Hawaii" TV show was a first for Elvis. He performed at the Honolulu International Center in a concert that would simultaneously be beamed by satellite to audiences in Asia and Oceania and with a delay in 28 European countries. In the United States, to avoid a programming conflict with Super Bowl VII, NBC opted to air a ninety-minute television special on the concert airing on 4th April. The total estimated audience was well over one billion and the concert costing was $2.5 million.

Elvis was a great admirer of Jack Lord who appeared in the TV series, Hawaii Five-O. Elvis most probably started watching and enjoying the series as it was about a special police major crimes task force and, as we know, Elvis was very interested in the police, including collecting forces badges. He had never met Jack so invited him to the concert on 14th January. Shortly before the day of the concert, Colonel Parker had personally gone to the Lords' home and delivered a message inviting them to be Elvis' guests at the Aloha concert. Afterwards, they went backstage and met Elvis for the first time. Jack would later say, "The moment we met and shook hands it was as if we had known each other all our lives." He also said of the concert that he had never heard such dramatic music in his life.

Elvis then told Jack and Marie that he'd love to see them before he left Hawaii, which he did, arriving promptly at their home at 8pm. Marie says that when she opened the door there was "a slim Adonis, looking gorgeous in a white suit with a white silk shirt that had a ruffled collar and cuffs." He kissed her as he went in – bringing seven members of his entourage. Elvis gave Marie a gift of a ring and Jack a gun. Jack gave Elvis a rare banjo after he admired it in their home.

In February, on a short break from the Hawaii Five-O series, Jack and Marie went to Las Vegas to see Elvis in concert, letting the Colonel know that they were coming. The day they arrived in Las Vegas was one they will never forget. As they walked off the plane, there, standing at the foot of the ramp, was a tall Hawaiian man holding garlands of fresh flower leis to greet the Lords. When they arrived at their hotel and walked into their suite, Marie remembers that they could hardly move around for all the flower baskets that surrounded them.

That night, when the lights went down and the curtains opened there, on centre stage with a spotlight beaming down on it, was the six-string banjo that Jack had given Elvis, Elvis then introduced the Lords saying, "I was in Hawaii recently and this great star and his wife took me into their home." Marie commented later, "He said it like he was some poor little orphan we had adopted. Then he called out Jack's name, and Jack stood up. The applause was tremendous. Elvis grinned and said, 'Sit down, Jack, you're getting more applause than I am.' Everyone laughed."

There were subsequent meetings and exchange of correspondence between the Lords and Elvis. There were phone conversations, and yet they only knew Elvis for such a short time. In fact, Elvis once said rather longingly, "Gee, Jack, I wish I'd met you many years ago." Jack and Marie clearly remember hearing of Elvis' passing, as Jack was writing Elvis a letter and getting ready to mail him a package when his secretary came in and gave them the news.

Cancelled Shows

During his annual Las Vegas engagement, Elvis was ill. In one show early on, not feeling well he had to leave the stage, but the Stamps carried on the show, singing *Walk the Lonesome Road, Sweet, Sweet Spirit, When It's My Time, How Great Though Art* and *I Should Have Been Crucified.* Charlie Hodge filled in with some comedy and was about to close the show, when Elvis returned to the stage, apologising, and finished the show. After this, several shows had to be cancelled.

The Wisdom of J D Sumner

In the early hours of 19th February, at the end of the show, cleverly avoiding the security, four men jumped on the stage and approached Elvis. Security rushed to remove them, though they did not appear to be wanting to harm Elvis. However, Elvis was convinced that Priscilla's karate instructor and lover, Mike Stone had sent the men to attack him. He was furious and he resolved to have Mike Stone killed.

This is where J D Sumner stepped in. Elvis and J D became good friends and Elvis not only admired his voice but, as J D was older than Elvis, he sometimes sought him out as a father figure for advice. This time, however, Elvis did not want advice, but J D felt strongly that he had to proffer it.

Elvis' plot to have Mike Stone killed involved telling some of his entourage to do it. However, none were willing, which made him even more angry than he already was, and he fired them all. In desperation, Joe Esposito asked J D to come up to Elvis' suite. He explained the situation and J D went in to see Elvis, who reiterated that he wanted Mike Stone dead. J D, then, rather cunningly, offered to do the job for him if Elvis gave him his gun and told him where Mike Stone lived, saying that he would be dead by the morning.

Elvis did not want J D to do that, at which point J D told him that the only one who could help him in this situation was God. He then suggested that they pray to which Elvis eventually agreed. All his entourage were called in to Elvis' bedroom to take part, with J D telling them all to get round the bed on their knees and hold hands. J D then prayed that God would help Elvis in this situation. After the prayer, Elvis looked up and apologised to the guys, telling them that he loved them and that he could now get to sleep. The next morning, Joe Esposito called up J D again asking for help. Not only was Elvis at peace having decided to forgive Mike Stone and no longer wanting him killed, but he wanted to give him a TCB pendant. Everyone agreed this this was a step too far, so Elvis dropped the idea.

***

On 20th February, Variety magazine reported that Elvis has been offered half a million dollars for six concerts at the Earl's Court Stadium in London. This is one of the many offers the Colonel received from overseas promotors. He did not feel the need for Elvis to tour abroad, as Elvis could make enough money just touring the USA. Also, Charles Stone, booking agent for Elvis' concert tours had told Elvis that no guns, nor large quantities of (even prescription) drugs would be allowed overseas, so Elvis was not too keen either. However, Elvis was aware of his great popularity in Europe and so eventually agreed to consider at least going to Europe. Charles Stone says that the day Elvis died, he had in his pocket a ticket to fly to London to check out the venue.

Lacklustre Performances

In April, Elvis performed eight concerts on the West Coast.

Elvis only performed the first of his 17-day May engagement in Sahara Tahoe. A review of the show said that Elvis was "some thirty pounds overweight, puffy, white-faced and blinking against the light" and that "his voice is weak, delivery is flabby." His friends and family were concerned about his abuse of prescription drugs, and an attorney was hired to investigate who was providing Elvis with the seemingly endless supply of drugs. Four physicians were identified, but as Elvis was unwilling to cooperate in legally prohibiting these supplies, they keep on coming.

Elvis performed 14 concerts, in June and July, two of which were extra ones added on in Atlanta, Georgia because the demand for tickets for original shows was so high. The rest of the summer was taken up with Elvis recording songs for RCA.

August was time for his annual "Summer Festival" in Las Vegas. Sadly, again it was noticed that Elvis was not at his best. The Hollywood Reporter said of Elvis' opening night, "His personality was lost in one of the most ill-prepared, unsteady and most disheartening performances of his Las Vegas career." None the less, near the end of the engagement, Elvis performed a special 3am show "by popular demand."

In the first two weeks of September Elvis had a significant disagreement with the Colonel and fired him, though it came to naught as, by the 16th, they were reconciled.

"Voice"

During this time Elvis flew a gospel group out of Nashville to LA for Tom Jones to use in his show as he was having difficulties with his backing singers. That did not work out, but Elvis liked their voices, so he signed Donnie

Sumner, Sherrill Nielsen, and Tim Baty to be his personal gospel group and he changed their name to "Voice." Shaun (Sherrill) tells the story: "Elvis had written it [the proposed contract] on a sheet of toilet tissue, and it was for the sum of $100,000 for which we'd travel with him, write songs for his music company, and work with him." They were delighted at the proposition and eagerly accepted.

Trying to Get to Elvis

Just as in Elvis' early days, fans wanted to get close to him and "have a piece of him." Perhaps that is why he started to give out scarves in his shows. Sometimes he would hand them out individually, accompanied with a kiss, and sometimes he threw them into the crowd of fans who had been able to get to the front. Consequently, in all of these concerts, there had to be plenty of security to prevent anyone being hurt. Though people were sometimes hurt if the crowd at the stage got too large, and there were sometimes fights over the scarves.

Something else fans would do is to try to get to Elvis before he drove away after the concert. Here is one fan's report of her attempt:

"I'll never forget the day his black limo almost ran over me. I had observed that every time they said, 'Elvis has left the building' his limo would be long gone before anybody got out of the concert. So, I got this big idea to get out of the concert before Elvis did and stand in the driveway where the limo would be coming out. When the limo did come it was flying down so fast that when it saw me the driver had to stop suddenly. He missed me by an inch otherwise I wouldn't be telling this story.

"Elvis called for me, I was near the window; he rolled down the window and in a very calm voice said, 'I know you consider me your king, but I am not worth dying for, there is a bigger King who is God whom you should be preparing yourself for.' I got pimples all over my body. I remember it as if it were yesterday."

Elvis always hated being called the king and would correct the comment. On one time, during a concert, a group of girls had a row of seats in the middle of the stalls, and they stood up holding a large banner "Elvis You're the King." He stopped what he was doing and told them, "No I am not the king, there is only one king and that is Jesus Christ. I'm just an entertainer."

Elvis' and Pricilla's divorce was finalised on 9th October 1973. The settlement gave shared custody of Lisa Marie, a cash payment of $725,000 to Priscilla plus over $10,000 a month spouse and child support, 5 per cent of the publishing companies profits and half of the sale of their Hillcrest house. The hearing took only twenty minutes, and they left the courthouse hand in hand and remained friends for the rest of Elvis' life. Of the divorce Elvis said, "The thing I'm trying to get across is, we're the very best of friends and we always have been. Our divorce came about not because of another man, or another woman, but because of the circumstances involving my career. I was traveling too much, I was gone too much, and it was just an agreement. I didn't think it was fair to her, that I was gone too much. We just made an agreement to always be friends and be close and care because we have a daughter to raise."

Two days after the divorce was finalised, Elvis had trouble breathing. He returned to Memphis with Linda and was soon admitted to hospital for two weeks observation. It was concluded that the problem has been caused by Elvis' daily injections of Demerol (Pethidine), an opioid painkiller, during his "acupuncture" sessions in California.

Elvis had recording sessions at Stax records in Memphis in December which included two gospel songs, *Help Me* and Dottie Rambo's If *That Isn't Love.* Wanting a fuller sound, he had increased his backing singers to eleven – almost a choir! The sessions went well and at the end of a year of great highs and lows, Elvis felt more hopeful and confident about his future.

Elvis showing pictures of his family to President Nixon in the Oval Office. (USA National Archives)

Elvis in his finery at one of the Madison Square Gardens Concert in New York.

Elvis giving his acceptance speech at the Jacyees Award Ceremony.

Proud parents with new-born
Lisa Marie.

More fun with daddy.

Having fun with daddy.

Elvis in a pensive mood.

Elvis and Priscilla
leaving court after the
divorce proceedings.

Chapter 7

The Concert Years – Part 2

I will sing of the LORD's great love forever; with my mouth I will make your faithfulness known through all generations. I will declare that your love stands firm forever, that you established your faithfulness in heaven itself. (Psalm 89:1)

During his lifetime, Elvis received 14 Grammy nominations and won three awards (pictured above), for the gospel recordings "How Great Thou Art," "He Touched Me" and the live recording of "How Great Thou Art." (Graceland)

As we have already seen, not only did the fans enjoy Elvis' concerts, so did his fellow musicians. Here are some more recollections of working with Elvis.

Jerry Scheff – Bass Guitar

"Elvis had a big impact on my career. It was like going to school. There was just something about the way he sang, and the way he'd interact, that was really, really good. It was the musical communication and personal communication. He was just really nice to us. It was fun to play, you know.

216

'Let's do this,' clowning around, 'Let's play that.' I don't remember him ever saying to any of us: 'I don't like that, don't play that. Play it this way.' I think the reason he liked the band was that we sort of listened to each other, we listened to him, and we instinctively picked up on what should be there. And me, not having any background in this music, I just listened to what everybody else was doing."

Jerry said that it was never boring as Elvis never did the same thing twice. "We always had to keep our eye on him. You never could just, you know, relax (laughs), you had to pay attention. You never knew what he was gonna do. Never."

"When Elvis sang a song, you just KNEW that the song was going through his mind. It wasn't just coming out of his mouth, but it was going through his mind and affected his emotions when he sang. So many singers sing a song, and they're thinking about the way they're going to sing – the projection, the phrasing and so forth. When Elvis sang a song, it was just going through him, and it came out to the people that way. He was probably better at that than anybody that ever lived."

Jerry also remembers one time when Elvis had invited Ronnie Tutt and himself up to his suite after the show, but they were not allowed in.

He said, "One night Charlie Hodge came down to the dressing-room, and said: 'You know, Elvis is really bummed out because you guys don't wanna see him.' And Ronnie and I said: 'Charlie, we have been down there to see him, but these guys always say: 'Oh, Elvis is busy.' So Charlie went back and told Elvis that, and Elvis hit the ceiling. Charlie came back and told us that Elvis just blew a stack. So there was that kind of stuff. I'm sure that all these people fulfilled some need that Elvis had, and I don't mean to question their motives. They just did what they thought would be best for him. So I don't try to judge that. But I do know that Elvis was always there for me."

Ronnie Tutt – Drums

Ronne didn't see Elvis too often – he said that he didn't want to be associated with the hangers-on, the guys that were constantly laughing at all his jokes – he had too much respect for him. They saw each other anytime karate people were around when Elvis would call him up to be involved. He would also sometimes go to Elvis' place in LA and when they were in Memphis they

217

would hang out at Graceland and a few very precious times at Christmas. He remembers how Elvis loved to bless people and how crazy he was!

Ronnie tells of the time he was at his mother's house, and he was thinking of Elvis, so he called him. "I told him that I was at my mother's house, and he said: 'Well, is she there?' I said: 'Yeah' and he said: 'Well, let me wish her a Merry Christmas,' because he had met her once before. So he was very gracious with that. My mother was thrilled that Elvis wanted to talk to her and wish her a Merry Christmas. She just thought that was the greatest thing in the world. "He was that way to my father later. When we'd go and play in Texas, my father would go and see the show. Elvis would talk to him, and my dad was so proud! He was so honored. Elvis was wonderful at those things. He had a great ability to be able to keep those kinds of things important and sacred in people's lives. We miss his humor, just the laughing and the craziness. He was just like a big kid, you know. One year, he was doing those ol' movies, he was 'playing' cowboy. We always called it he was 'playing' something, just like he was playing karate. He was playing cowboy that year, so he had dirt brought in from Texas around Graceland! Real dirt from Texas! And then he'd buy everybody golf carts, and then he'd do this, and then he'd do that. He was just like any of us would be if money was no object, and we had a circle of friends – and we'd just have a good time all the time. That's the way he did it, you know."

On a more serious note, Ronnie remembers Elvis inviting him out to his place because he was very concerned about what was going on with his divorce. Because Ronnie had been through a divorce, Elvis wanted his companionship. Ronnie says, "That's one thing I always prided myself in, I always tried to tell Elvis: 'Whatever you ask me, I'll give you my best answer I could possibly give you.' I wouldn't say just what I thought he wanted to hear. So, with that in mind, I told him what I think he needed to hear. He was very, very concerned about the divorce. He couldn't understand why a woman would want to divorce him when he was the idol of millions of women all over the world. He said: 'I can't, I just can't understand it.' And I said: 'Well hey, sometimes that's the way it goes.'"

Ronnie felt that Elvis was one of the most resilient men he ever knew. He remembered that there were many times where Elvis would be out of shape with only two weeks before a tour and his musicians were concerned, but sure enough, two weeks later he'd show up the first night, he'd come out and look just great. He says, "It was like he'd jumped in a convenient telephone booth and put on his 'Elvis Presley Uniform' just like Superman. He'd be great, 'up' and just wonderful, however, by 1977 it had all become too much."

Ray Walker (Jordanaires)

Ray, who joined the Jordanaires in 1958, remembers that everyone was nervous during his first Jordanaires session with Elvis. "We were looking the other way when Elvis came in. When I turned around, he stuck his hand out and said, 'I'm Elvis Presley.' I said, 'I know who you are. I'm Ray Walker.' Elvis replied to me, 'And I know who you are.' We stood there and talked, and the minute I looked into his face all his fame left. I saw one of the nicest guys. I'm not really one to keep my mouth shut most of the time, as long as I know there's no harm, so during that all-night session, I said to him, 'You know, your heart's going to take a beating in this business. And I've only been in it three weeks' (Laughs) I really liked him right off. There was just an aura about him – you knew he was around – and he was one of the most impressive people I have ever met in my life. He knew exactly what he wanted but would not go past what he could do – he would while he was playing around but would never put it on a record. He was just a good man, and I never changed my opinion of him."

J D Sumner

Elvis had first heard John Daniel Sumner in Memphis when, as a teenager, he attended the gospel singings at the Ellis Auditorium, so it is no surprise that Elvis eventually employed J D and the Stamps on his recordings and as part of his stage shows.

J D later, was the recipient of advice from Elvis. J D had got into heavy drinking, even drinking neat whisky on stage, convincing Elvis that the whisky helped him reach those low notes. (Elvis was sometimes too naive and trusting!) He never appeared to be drunk but knew that his addiction to alcohol was taking its toll on his career, his marriage, and his life. When he confided in Elvis about this, he says that Elvis urged him to get help for his alcoholism. He eventually heeded Elvis' advice, got the help he needed to quit drinking, and turned his life around for the better.

Wanting to promote gospel singing as much as he could, J D asked Elvis if he would do a benefit for the Gospel Music Hall of Fame so that they could build a building to house the Hall of Fame. Elvis arranged a conference call with himself, J D and the Colonel explaining that he wanted to do the concert and for Joe Esposito to arrange it. He wanted it all gospel and a worldwide satellite show. Nothing but gospel music he emphasised. J D knew that Elvis always wanted to do an all-gospel show, and this was a good excuse, but as J D commented, "Time ran out before it could be done."

Donnie Sumner (Stamps Quartet)

This is how Donnie Sumner describes his career in music. "Everything that I have, I'll ever be, what I've got and all I'll ever have, I have to say thanks be to God for it all, because when I found him, I had nothing. My life was totally ruined." All his life he wanted to be in a southern gospel quartet. He got through college, but his heart was in quartets and that is how he came to be singing on stage with Elvis in 1971. However, all the success which that brought could not deal with Donnie's inner turmoil. The more success Donnie had, the deeper and darker his life became. It was during his time with Elvis that the turnaround came.

Elvis made sure that each of the performers in his entourage were well taken care of, which meant they had anything and everything at their fingertips. Donnie says, "I will tell you flat out, one of the liabilities of the entertainment industry is your removal from the normal life of home, church and friends. It's kind of a world of fantasy. There's no such thing as a superstar, it's all in the audience's mind. Reality is home, church and friends." He commented that, after a while, you begin to believe it and you can turn into the kind of person you shouldn't be, because you think you're better than everybody else. Even when performing in a southern gospel group, temptation is still there."

Donnie said, "I had been involved in the drug culture ever since I entered the industry. It was more or less a social thing for the first few years, and it progressed. When I was with Elvis, I had plenty of money, plenty of safety, plenty of access to anything I wanted. I hate to say it, but I turned into a stone drug addict."

However, he does remember that the informal gospel singings they had with Elvis helped at the time. He remembers one occasion singing all four verses of *In the Sweet By and By* 18 times in a row at Elvis' bidding. "We'd be wired most of the time. But when we'd sing for him, it was like throwing a bucket of cold water on a fire. It was a cleansing of emotions. He'd get so relaxed and peaceful."

In 1976, Donnie was doing $200 of cocaine and a handful of Quaaludes a day. He tried to overdose on cocaine twice, attempting suicide three times. Finally, it all came to a head.

On the Saturday morning before Labour Day in 1976, he stood on the balcony outside Elvis' suite trying to get the nerve to jump. "I cried out for some help and didn't really expect any, but the good Lord was walking around in heaven that morning and heard me as I said, 'I believe I'll do it.' Suddenly the lyric of a song I used to sing as a kid came into my mind. 'Jesus loves me this I know 'cos the Bible tells me so.' Then, 'Little ones to Him belong, they are weak, but He is strong!'" Donnie started crying as he felt the love of God embrace him, and, rather than jumping, he cried his way back to the room for a brand-new beginning. Deciding that he needed to leave the tour and enter rehab, Donnie first had to tell Elvis, who was in the hospital at the time. On hearing the news, Elvis told Donnie that he was proud of him and said that he wished that he could go somewhere and start over but "I guess I got to keep on being Elvis."

That was the last time Donnie talked to Elvis face to face. Donnie cleaned up his life and took a long break from performing. Music was in his blood and eventually he returned to the stage. Over the years, Donnie has served as a minister and evangelist, taking his message all over the country. As a changed man, Donnie brings a new message of hope. "My emphasis is really on just one simple thing," he said. "I sing fast songs, slow songs, old songs, new songs, funny songs, and sad songs. In the end, every one of my songs says that no matter where you're at or what you're involved in, you can make it. Jesus is a new life; Jesus is an abundant life and Jesus is everlasting life. That's my story and that's my song."

Sherrill Neilsen (Stamps Quartet)

Sherrill said, "Yeah, I remember the first time I met him, that was at Studio B in Nashville. He walked in the door, and he was dressed in a black Superfly outfit. He purchased it in Beale Street, where all the R&B artists were. He walked over to me, stuck out his hand and said: 'Hi, I'm Elvis Presley. I've got all your records. You're one of my favorite singers.' That was my intro to him. I didn't realise that he was aware of me, but he watched our early morning TV show. It came on at six every morning, and he'd stay up and watch that before he went to bed. So that's how he knew about me and the group. Then he asked the producer to have us sing on the session."

Larry Strickland (Stamps Quartet)

Larry kindly wrote this for us: "As a member of J D Sumner and The Stamps quartet I toured and recorded with Elvis the last three years of his life. During that time, I was on more than 200 concerts and four records. Lots of people have ask me through the years if Elvis was a Christian. My answer to that: he was without a doubt a believer, loved God and through his music had a special spiritual connection. Elvis grew up loving gospel music. You wouldn't listen to that kind of music just by happenstance. You seek it out because it moves you and it's not going to move you if you don't believe. Of the over 200 concerts that I was a part of, Elvis sang gospel music on each and every one. *How Great Thou Art* was sung every night, and no one has ever sung that song with more intensity and passion than Elvis did. You don't do that if you aren't moved or feeling something when you sing it. He also had us, The Stamps quartet, sing an acapella spiritual song titled *Sweet, Sweet Spirit*, on every show. Elvis would stand close to us, with his eyes closed the entire time we sang it. You don't do that if you don't feel it. In his own way, I believe that Elvis was a very strong believer and had a heart for God. He expressed that in a lot of different ways."

Larry remembers his first performance with Elvis was on stage at The International Hilton in Las Vegas. He writes, "I was concentrating so hard learning my parts that I have very little memory of the show. I do remember being awe-struck. The crowd was wild and screaming. The orchestra was huge, and the sound was heavenly, unlike anything I had ever heard live. The background singers, of which I was a part, were all tight and the harmonies were magnificent. And then there was the man himself, Elvis. How do you put into words what he looked and sounded like? It feels strange for me, as a man, to say he was beautiful but it's the truth. His outfit, his hair, his face, his demeanour, his voice was all something unique and beautiful. I would never get over being in awe and star-struck whenever he came on stage or walked into the room."

The Imperials

As well as working with Elvis in Las Vegas, the Imperials also worked as backup singers for the country singer Jimmy Dean. When they stopped working with Elvis because of scheduling conflicts with the tours, they continued to work with Jimmy Dean in Las Vegas. Whenever Elvis was in Las

Vegas at the same time he would seek out the Imperials and ask them to join him in his suite for singings.

Here is a lovely story from Jimmy Dean, who was also a friend of Elvis. Jimmy was starting his show in Vegas as he usually did, walking around the audience, chatting with them. He says, "I had a portable microphone that was cutting out. I didn't know he [Elvis] was anywhere around. I said, 'Would somebody get me another microphone?' Then I went on and talked a little bit and said, 'Where is that microphone?' And Elvis went on stage with a microphone and said, 'Was this the item you were looking for Mr. Dean?' Naturally, my show was shot. Hell, Elvis was in the house!"

"He used to come over quite often when he was working in Vegas. He would come over after the last show. The vocal group that was working with me were his favorite singers. He used to call up and say, 'Hey Dean, hang around for a little bit after the last show and let's sing a little. 'I'm gonna cut a few numbers. I'll probably be there by the time you get off stage.' I know that many times I saw him while I was finishing my show, standing backstage. We'd go down and sing and he'd sing with The Imperials. Nothing but gospel. All gospel songs."

Joe Moscheo (Imperials)

We have already met Joe telling us of some of his times with Elvis. Of fellow gospel singers, he says, "Each of us had our own individual beliefs and faith. I don't think any of us regarded ourselves as super-spiritual, and we certainly did not go around quoting scripture at each other. But we did share a common language and a common heritage – the same heritage that gave rise to gospel music. That heritage was nowhere stronger and more important than in the mind and heart of the man who brought us all together to make music – Elvis Presley." We shall discover more about Joe and his care for Elvis later.

***

In August 2001, I was privileged to interview members of the Imperials: Terry Blackwood, Jim Murray, and Sherman Andrus at an event that Elvis Gospel Fan Club hosted in the Center for Southern Folklore in Memphis. When asked if Elvis ever discussed spiritual matters with them, they said, "All the time!" He would love to discuss Bible passages with them, especially ones which might be difficult to interpret. Of course, they also sang a lot with Elvis and said that he sang more off stage than he did on stage. He would often break into a song walking along or riding in an elevator. That is why he was such a good singer. Some people they had worked with only sang at rehearsals and on stage or in the studio.

These members of the Imperials shared many thoughts and stories with us. Here are a few:

Sherman Andrus

Sherman joined The Imperials in February 1972, so did not sing on stage with Elvis, but sang informally with him in Las Vegas. In fact, by joining the Imperials he helped to break the colour barrier in southern gospel music. As far as we know, Sherman was the first Black man, to ever be in a southern gospel quartet.

When Sherman first met Elvis, he was surprised and delighted that Elvis knew exactly who he was and about his music and had made himself a scrapbook of news articles about Sherman joining the Imperials. He told us, "Elvis made me feel so special. I didn't think he would be as outgoing with me as he was. But he was just like a big country boy. He welcomed me the minute the guys brought me to his suite. He said, 'Now you're one of us. You're a member of the family.' And I joked around with him, and I said, 'Yeah, but all the guys that you say are part of the family, you give these TCB chains to. And I don't have one.' [The other Imperials had already been given one]. Elvis said 'I'm gonna get you one.' A few nights later we were all at the Desert Inn backing up Jimmy Dean. Elvis waited until the curtains were almost opened, and he put these jewellery boxes in each of our hands. So when the curtain opened, there we stood with jewellery boxes in our hands. We did our little segment and went back to the green room, and when we checked our boxes, everybody had a bracelet. Except for me. I had a bracelet and a TCB necklace."

One of Sherman's favourite memories of Elvis is the incident in 2002, already mentioned, when Joe Moscheo's house in Nashville was broken into. Elvis wanted so much to find out who had done it and to help Joe. Sherman said that Elvis was really motivated and excited, like a little child. He set up a "command centre" from where he phoned as many people as possible in Nashville, including all the karate back belts he knew, to discover the culprits and deal with them. Sherman commented that the telephone bill must have been very high!

Sherman could also see that Elvis was not only very anointed but was also appointed. He believes that God appoints people to certain positions in order to bless others. He said that he talked to Elvis about that, saying, "I have never seen anybody loved the way you are." People just loved him. He told him, "It's not a natural thing. That's a God-given thing. That's not something a man could give to you. They love you because God's hand is on you." Elvis agreed with him. When asked if Elvis understood the purpose of that appointment, Sherman said that he thought Elvis went to his grave without realising how much he had meant to gospel music, making it acceptable to so many non-Christians.

Mentioning some of the gospel songs that Elvis sang, Sherman said that he felt the way Elvis sang *I've Got Confidence,* conveying that he totally believed it, he made it his own. At that time, in 1971, the Imperials had just released an LP containing a song, *Jesus Made Me Higher,* and Elvis loved the song so much he listened to it many times, totally engrossed. This was also the song that was very popular with the Imperials' audiences and when the opportunity arose, Sherman would talk about the importance of a love relationship with Jesus as the gateway to spiritual growth.

Sherman also told us that he was saved when he was 15 but knew from the age of five that he would be a singer who would travel all over the world singing to the Lord. He had never seen anybody do that, but he told all his friends and family that was what he was going to do, and he did. He has always found God so faithful, and he is living a victorious life. He says that we will hear no sad stories from him.

If Sherman could say something to Elvis, he would thank him for his kindness, generosity, and openness in being so welcoming to Sherman and his wife and son.

Jim Murray

Jim Murray had always attended church, he knew how to do church and speak the lingo, but says he wasn't saved until 1982 when he was 38 years old. He was a deacon, an established member of the church and everything was OK until he heard a preach about Judas, who openly recognised Jesus, but denied him in his heart. He realised that he was a Judas who had not accepted Jesus into his heart, so he did that, and found his life changed for the better. He says that if he had known what he knows now, he would have asked Elvis where he was spiritually, and perhaps have been able to help him on his Christian journey.

Jim could see that Elvis was very spiritual and loved to discuss the Bible and its meaning. He remembers an example of Elvis' spiritual insight when they were quietly standing in a circle with Elvis considering what to discuss and Jim had the thought that he would like to ask Elvis what he thought about heaven. Elvis immediately said, "Jim, we'll get to that in a minute." When Jim asked what he meant. Elvis replied that Jim had just been thinking about heaven.

Terry Blackwood

Terry was brought up in a gospel singing family and was saved at the age of 12. He first met Elvis in the mid-fifties, when his father, gospel singer Doyle Blackwood, was running for the state representative position in Tennessee. Elvis loaned his father his pink Cadillac to take part in a parade in downtown Memphis.

It was in 1969 that he met Elvis professionally when the Imperials joined him on stage in Las Vegas. To begin with, Terry was very shy and uncomfortable on stage until he discovered his purpose and calling in life, which is serving Christ, using the talent he has been given to glorify and thank the Lord. This gives him a reason for being. He loves to sing of the good news of Jesus, as he is aware that hurting people need to hear good news. He has known disappointment and discouragement, just as the Bible warns that we will have trials and tribulations in this life but, with Jesus, we will overcome and be victorious. When Terry's first wife left him and the devil stole his song, it took him six years to heal, and now he is very happily married with three wonderful children. He knows that if we keep our eyes on Jesus, Satan cannot defeat us. He encouraged us to never give up on God, for all things work together for the good of those who love the Lord. With Jesus, there is always tomorrow and redemption to look forward to.

1974 – A Year of Ups and Downs

1974 was a busy year with four tours, two Las Vegas engagements and two Tahoe engagements for a total of 158 concerts.

January saw Elvis back in Las Vegas for his regular two-week concert engagement at the Hilton. He introduced two more gospel songs into his show, *Why Me Lord,* and *Help Me.*

Elvis' friends noticed and were concerned about the fact that, perhaps still feeling the shock of the divorce, Elvis' personal behaviour became more erratic and he "let off steam" by shooting out a chandelier and several television sets.

The first two concert tours were pretty good, but Elvis was showing signs of his poor condition. He was overweight, had memory lapses, sometimes slurred his speech and seemed to be barely awake at all. However, the fans still flocked to see him at sell-out shows and overall were not disappointed as he was still in good voice and covered up his mistakes with his sense of humour.

By February it was becoming clear that Elvis was not coping well with life. He could not be persuaded to go into a recording studio, so arrangements were made to record the songs for his next LP in the Jungle Room at Graceland. It was noticed that Elvis' behaviour was somewhat erratic and distracted, even verging on delusionary paranoia. On one occasion he disappeared into his bedroom with Red and Sonny West to plan the demise of all the drug dealers in Memphis. He certainly had the ability, owning several guns. Red and Sonny were able to persuade him that it would not be a wise thing to do.

On 1st March 1974, Elvis met with TV evangelist Oral Roberts backstage at the McAbee Center, in the Oral Roberts University, Tulsa. I cannot find any information about what happened during that meeting, but assume they discussed the Bible and Elvis' faith and prayed together. I would hope that it was an encouragement to Elvis.

The 20-day tour in March grossed $2,310,553.50 of which, after expenses and the Colonel's cut of $394,510.86, Elvis took home $789,021.72. Financially, touring was much more rewarding than the Las Vegas engagements. The 18-day tour in June/July grossed almost $3 million, leaving Elvis and the Colonel almost $2million as their 65% share.

When he was not touring nor involved in concerts, Elvis spent his time between Memphis, Los Angeles, and Palm Springs, most of the time with Linda, who looked after Lisa Marie when she had her allotted time with her father.

Still Praising God

Now that Elvis was divorced, he made several changes to his lifestyle including physical changes to his home at 845 West Chino Canyon Road in Palm Springs. When Elvis and Priscilla bought the house in 1970 it was 3,500 square feet. When Elvis and Priscilla divorced in 1973, Priscilla gave up her rights to the house, so Elvis expanded the house, adding a party room, a sauna, a new bedroom and two bathrooms. The expansion of the property enabled the transition from a family atmosphere to more of a boys' club feel.

Girls were invited and the guys 'had a good time' with them. However, some fans who went to the Palm Springs house noticed that Elvis liked to talk with girls, to spend time discussing things or playing music or swimming in the pool. He seemed to like women around him more for companionship than for sex. From stories I have read by some of Elvis girlfriends, I have come to the same conclusion. Some of the women he knew and made love to, maybe because it was expected, genuinely wanted to befriend Elvis and so they came to a mutual agreement that they would be 'just good friends'.

Elvis enjoyed Palm Springs because of the perfect night-time temperature of the desert. He would spend an average of about three months there every year. The extremely hot temperatures during the day didn't bother Elvis because he would be sleeping until the late afternoon, even putting tin foil on the windows to keep out the daytime sun.

Apparently, there is a large flat rock behind the house where Elvis would lie at night and look at the stars. He told his friends, "This is where I can talk to God."

Sandi Miller, who met Elvis in California in the 1960s and became a friend (rather than a girlfriend) remembers:

"One of my favorite moments of all time was an Easter morning in Palm Springs. Elvis had been up all night and the sun was rising over the mountains. All but a couple of people had gone to bed. He quietly sat down at the piano and started singing gospel songs, just him and the piano and his thoughts. He threw his head back, closed his eyes, and just sang his heart out, all by himself. We had tears streaming down our faces, and so did he. It was a religious experience if ever there was one! Those people snoring in their rooms down the hall never had any idea what they missed out on!"

Dolly Parton

This is the year that Dolly Parton released her song, *I Will Always Love You.* Elvis wanted to record the song and Dolly had been invited down to the studio for the recording. She said that was the most exciting thing that had happened to her. Saying, "Who doesn't love Elvis!" However, the afternoon before the recording session, The Colonel called her. This is how Dolly remembers the conversation: the Colonel said, "You do know we have to have at least half the publishing on any song that Elvis records?" to which Dolly answered, "No, I did not know that." The Colonel then said, "Well, it's just a rule." Dolly replied, "Well, it's not my rule" So Elvis did not record the song. Dolly cried all night long because she was so disappointed. She said, "It wasn't Elvis, I loved Elvis. And I'm sure he was as disappointed as I was because he had it all worked up and ready to go, he said. I know he loved the song."

She went on to say that she has written a song called *I Dreamed About Elvis Last Night.* Dolly said: "I had an Elvis soundalike sing it with me and we actually sing *I Will Always Love You* in it." Dolly went on to say that if she could have a last conversation with anyone in history, it would be Elvis. "I'd probably talk about *I Will Always Love You* and say 'Hey, I bet you were as disappointed as I was about all that and I still dream about you singing that song.'"

Another Girlfriend

In August, Elvis met Sheila Ryan whom he dated while continuing his relationship with Linda Thompson. Sheila says:

"Elvis had qualities that no other human being has, had, will have. Some of them are so hard to describe because the charisma, the qualities that he had were almost not of this world, you know. They were, a lot of times, angelic. He knew things before I knew things. He knew things that I was feeling before I was feeling them. He was very much a little boy, had that little boy quality and I've often said, you know, before I met him, he had that smile, and everyone interpreted that smile to be his sexy look. And it wasn't that at all. It wasn't a sexy look. It was his innocence, his vulnerability. It wasn't at all something that he turned on and off. Let's face it. The man was just not normal, you know. The biggest joy that he had was in giving and I didn't really understand it that much at the time. But it was what brought most joy to him was to give."

Also in August, Elvis heard of the illness from cancer of Ivory Joe Hunter, a singer/songwriter who had written some of Elvis' songs. He sent a financial donation to the Ivory Joe Hunter Fund to help with medical costs with a note which said, "I am very sorry to hear of Joe's illness. I have been a long-time admirer of Ivory Joe and his talent. Please tell Joe for me that I wish him a speedy recovery. Joe is a great talent and has been an inspiration to many artists that have come along. It hurts me deeply to hear of his condition. I sincerely hope that this check will be of some help. Thank you for letting me know about Joe. Sincerely, Elvis Presley."

By the time of the 1974 Summer Festival in Las Vegas, Elvis had lost some weight and made some changes to his programme, omitting some of his earlier hits and concentrating more on ballads. The Hollywood Reporter certainly approved of the opening show, saying, "The best show in at least three years. He looks great, is singing better than he has in years and was so comfortable with his show – almost all new songs – the packed Hilton Showroom gave him several ovations."

Linda Thompson, as usual, was present at the opening night, but Sheila Ryan took her place for most of the rest of the engagement.

While in Las Vegas Elvis attended several of Tom Jones concerts with Sheila Ryan, and on one occasion, he went on stage with Tom, though there are no reports of him singing. However, as we know they did sing together, informally, many times.

During the show on 24th August, on introducing The Stamps, Elvis told the audience that he had always wanted to be a gospel singer. He said, "I tried, I really did. But can you see me in the middle of four guys." He then demonstrated his 1950s wiggle, saying "bodies flying everywhere!"

In this engagement, two of Elvis' performances were cancelled because he had a high temperature, and in the final show he indulged in some incoherent ramblings about personal matters, including his divorce and reported drug-taking. He introduced Sheila Ryan and got her to show off a ring he had given her. Priscilla and Lisa Marie were in the audience, and one wonders how much more complicated Elvis' life could become.

Karate Film, Generosity, and Jokes

For most of September, Elvis was in Memphis concentrating on his karate which included planning, with Linda, a film. He personally found karate empowering with its mental discipline and physical benefits which he said, "helps a person to help themselves." Being Elvis, he wanted to share that with others by making a film. The film was intended to promote an idealised world in which "good conquers evil and the strong help the weak and oppressed of all classes regardless of colour creed or religion." The final scene showed Elvis standing on a solitary hill in fighting stance with many karate practitioners behind him doing the moves with him as he conveys the Lord's Prayer in Indian sign language. The movie ends with "The Beginning" written across the screen.

On 1st October, when Elvis was taking his bows at the conclusion of a concert in South Bend Indiana, he spontaneously removed a diamond ring from his finger and flung it into a wildly cheering audience. Elvis didn't wait to see who caught such a valuable gift. He quickly spun around the moment he tossed the ring, exiting the stage.

When he got back to his hotel room, someone blurted out, "I can't believe you did that! That ring was worth about thirty thousand dollars, it was one of your favorites." Elvis said, "Well, I tell you, I didn't plan it, that's for sure. It was what I felt at the moment. Something in me told me that someone was in big trouble out there; that they needed that ring much more than I do. I just knew the right person got it. Hey, I can buy all the rings I want. But when that voice within tells me what to do, I follow it, it's as simple as that."

The show on 14th October at the Sahara Tahoe was the final one of that year and was apparently full of practical jokes, one even being played on Elvis, no doubt to try to cheer him up. Towards the end of *The Hawaiian Wedding Song,* Elvis moved close to Kathy Westmoreland, as with her high voice she would join him in singing the ending. As she opened her mouth to sing, instead of her voice, J D Sumner's deep bass voice came out. Elvis was flabbergasted and laughed so hard he couldn't continue. Sherill Nielsen fell off his stool and ended on the floor laughing.

The next week, Elvis put himself under the care of Dr Ghanem who had attended him during his Las Vegas engagements. He had a series of tests to discover the cause of medical problems, and the doctor recommended spending time under sedated "sleep rest" before returning to Memphis on 11th

231

November. On 3rd December Elvis flew back to LA for more "sleep rest" at Dr Ghanem's "celebrity" wing and returned to Memphis for a quiet Christmas at Graceland. It was clear to all that Elvis was not well and the Colonel, understanding that Elvis was in no fit state to perform, cancelled the upcoming January engagement in Las Vegas.

In 1974, Elvis received his third and last Grammy Award for a live recording of *How Great Thou Art* for the Best Inspirational Song. This award is presented by the Recording Academy to recognize achievement in the music industry. The two previous awards Elvis received were for *How Great Thou Art* (1967) for Best Sacred Album and *He Touched Me* (1972) for Best Inspirational Album.

1975 – Fat and Forty?

In January 1975, Elvis spent his 40th birthday in seclusion. Only Linda and Elvis' cousin, Billy, were allowed unannounced in his bedroom. One wonders if reaching this landmark age, he was reflecting on his life so far and wondering what came next now that he was "Fat and Forty" as so many tabloids were proclaiming.

The next day, the Colonel read of a tornado that had hit McComb in Mississippi causing injuries, deaths, and much destruction. Seeing the opportunity to mobilise Elvis and get him back on the road, he persuaded him to do a benefit concert for the tornado victims as part of a two-week April-May concert tour.

On 29th January, Elvis struggled for breath and was taken to the Baptist Memorial Hospital in Memphis, staying there for over two weeks. This is where Marian Cocke first met Elvis and became his personal nurse at Graceland. She says:

"I have thought of Elvis and the hours we spent upstairs with our long talks, having the cook fix his breakfast for him, giving him a back rub; just reliving the moments. You know, the day Dr. Nick called me and said he wanted to admit him to my floor that night my first reaction was to tell him that I didn't want him on my floor. I had 52 patients on my floor, and I made total rounds on every patient every morning and the sicker ones every afternoon and I didn't have time or patience for a celebrity on my floor who wanted a lot of attention! Dr. Nick assured me that this man would not be like that, and you know what? He wasn't and he came in that night and at Dr. Nick's request I

232

went in to admit him and the rest was sort of history! Here was one of the nicest, least assuming young men I had ever met, and the chemistry was there, and we clicked right away. Here was an extremely polite young man who called me 'Miss Cocke,' said 'yes ma'am and no ma'am' and was nothing but a pure joy to take care of. There was never a time that he used his celebrity status and never was he anything other than a polite young gentleman. It has been many years now since our meeting, me taking care of him and our often-all-night conversations and he is as vivid in my mind, thoughts, and prayers as he still is; just a nice, respectful, and truly GOOD young man. That he, even many years after his death is still loved, honored and yes, cherished, is not a surprise to me at all."

A Birthday Surprise

Elvis was still in hospital on 31st January, at the same time as Judy McDonald was celebrating her birthday with her family at home. Judy received a business-like telephone call asking if she would be available to receive a long-distance call. She said she would, assuming it would be a relative calling to wish her happy birthday. Twenty minutes later she answered the phone with a "Hello" and a voice said "Hello Judy? I wanted to wish you a happy birthday." She didn't recognise the voice and asked who it was. In a kidding, disappointed voice the reply came "Judy, don't you know who this is?" She had a quick rethink about who it might be but had no idea. The voice then said, "Well, who is your favourite singer?" Astounded, she said, "Is this Elvis?" After the affirmative reply, they had a conversation when Elvis explained that he was in hospital reading mail and came across her letter asking for a birthday card so that she could have his autograph. Elvis explained his phone call by telling her that his mother told him never to forget his fans who made him so successful. Elvis asked her not to call newspapers nor make a big deal about it. He thanked her several times and then finished with "Well, I have to go now, I just called to wish you a happy birthday and God bless you."

As well as honouring his fans, I believe that this is yet another indication as to how Elvis so much desired to have a "normal life" with everyday conversations with regular people. Throughout my research, I have discovered that Elvis used the telephone a lot when he was alone in his bedroom at home, or on tour and even in hospital. It was a way of his having some privacy away from his entourage who, although they loved and cared for him, did not always understand his needs.

Things are Looking Up

In March, Elvis returned to LA for rehearsals for the Las Vegas shows and recording for RCA.

Most of the shows were well-received, though people noticed that Elvis was "chubby" and that he did not undertake so many karate moves. However, there was so much fooling around on stage it sometimes seemed almost like a comedy show.

The May benefit concert for the tornado brought in over $113,000.

In June/July Elvis was in good spirits, joking and interacting with the audience, clearly enjoying himself. Ending his shows with "It's been a pleasure working for you, so 'til we see you again, take care, God bless you."

The concert on 5th June in Houston was considered to be one of the best concerts of the tour with people noticing that Elvis had lost weight and was "beautiful." One fan said of Elvis' singing *How Great Thou Art, "*It made me shiver. During the chorus, most of the people were clapping, and half the audience was standing. Everyone was standing when he finished the song. They would not stop applauding!"

The next show in Dallas, on 6th June, received this review in the Dallas Morning News, "More than 10,000 chanting believers took part in a rock and roll revival ministered by the King – Elvis. The congregation was filled with people from every walk of life gathered to hear the Hound Dog gospel preached in a song by the man they idolise. Hysterically they jumped, waved, and cried trying to get one of the sacred scarves from their master's neck. They put as much as $10 in his collection plate before the sermon and more contributions came at the souvenir stands. As the show wore on periodically a believer would feel the spirit and jump up shouting and crying."

This rather tongue-in-cheek description of an Elvis concert has more than a grain of truth in it as many people were ministered to by Elvis at his concerts, though it was not the Hound Dog gospel that Elvis preached, but the gospel of love.

On 8th July, Sheila Ryan realised that she could not continue her relationship with Elvis. Like so many of his girlfriends, she continued to love him but could not cope with the demanding lifestyle of his wanting her to always be on call to accompany him whenever he needed her.

Two Very Different Concerts

On 20th July, Elvis had two concerts in Norfolk, Virginia. In the afternoon show, he saw a little girl standing on the far left of the stage. She was 7-year-old Linda, a devoted fan who had been brought to her first Elvis concert by her mother. Elvis walked over and knelt in front of her. Realizing she was blind, he lowered his microphone and held her hands and spoke to her for a few minutes. According to Charlie Hodge who was in earshot, the little girl told Elvis that she listened to his songs every night before she went to sleep. She also said that her mother had told her that he was very handsome and that she wanted to feel his face to find out. Elvis was very moved by this and told her that if she wanted to know what handsome or beauty was, she needed to feel her own face. Elvis took a scarf which Charlie Hodge handed to him, kissed it, touched her eyes with it and put it round her neck. According to Kathy Westmoreland, he had Dr. Nick put her parents in touch with a paediatric specialist who said she needed corrective surgery which Elvis paid for in full. He also arranged for her and her family to have tickets for every future concert and to cover the cost of transport and hotels. Reportedly, she went on to do computer graphic work for a company on the West coast.

The evening show was very different. During the recent shows, Elvis had been 'jokingly' saying not very complimentary things about some of his female singers. In this show, he said something which annoyed them and, after apologising, said that if they couldn't take it, then to leave, at which point three of them walked off the stage. They did return for the next concert, but Elvis was so concerned that they may not be there, that he asked J D and the Stamps to do an up-front spot on the next show, which was in Greensborough, North Carolina. J D was thrilled and chose the gospel songs, *You'll Never Walk Alone, When the Saints Go Marching, I'll Have a New Song* and *Just a Closer Walk With Thee*. J D reports that these were very well received, including a standing ovation. This encouraged Elvis to ask them to do more up-front gospel songs in his shows. Thus, J D had a dream come true, to sing gospel songs to tens of thousands of people.

Perhaps to make up for his rather ungallant behaviour onstage Elvis went on a spending spree, buying gifts for whoever came to mind. In one week, he spent $85,680 on jewellery and, back in Memphis $140,000 for fourteen Cadillacs. He also gave the Colonel a Gulfstream business aeroplane, a gift the Colonel declined to accept as he had no need of it and could not afford to run it.

More Cancelled Shows and More Spending

By the opening of his Las Vegas engagement in August, Elvis was overweight, appeared tired and had to sit down for most of the performances which were reported as being lacklustre. The last two shows were cancelled due to his illness, and he returned to Memphis Baptist Hospital with continuing intestinal and bowel problems, fatty liver, and high cholesterol count. However, Dr. Nick was more concerned about Elvis' increasingly depressed state.

On release from hospital, around the clock care was arranged for him with nurses Marian Cocke, Kathy Seamon and Tish Henley, sharing the assignment.

By the middle of September, Elvis was feeling much better and was out and about on his three-wheeled motorbike. He also started spending again, paying over $30,000 on decorating bills for the house he bought for Linda Thompson. He paid $250,000 for a Convair 880 aeroplane, which he named the Lisa Marie, and which was customized with a bedroom, an executive bathroom with gold taps and a gold washbasin, a videotape system linked to four TVs, a stereo system, and a conference room finished in teak. This recent spending spree, which also included jewellery, aeroplanes, a racquetball court for Graceland and medical bills, left Elvis in need of cash, so he arranged a loan of $350,000 from the National Bank of Commerce in Memphis.

Elvis opened his two-week "Pre-Holiday Jubilee" engagement at the Las Vegas Hilton on 2nd December. Lisa Marie was also there with Linda Thompson and attended several of the shows.

Following his earlier period of rest in the Autumn, Elvis was in good spirits and the sell-out shows were well received with, unusually, Elvis asking for requests from the audience, performing songs that he had not sung onstage for a while. The musicians and backup singers were of course able to cope with this, as by then, they were a very tight unit that could follow Elvis' every whim.

Elvis and his team returned to Memphis for Christmas. Marian Cocke, who was on duty caring for Elvis on Christmas Eve, remembers that Elvis awoke from a dream in which he had gone broke and found himself deserted by all his friends. The dream was so real that Elvis woke in a rage and would not go downstairs until all the people who had been waiting for him to appear, went home.

On New Year's Eve, Elvis performed a concert in Pontiac, Michigan. The show was certainly a financial success, grossing over $800,000, the highest ever brought in by a single artist for a one-night appearance. The performance itself, however, was not one of Elvis' best. Immediately after the show he returned to Memphis to celebrate the New Year with his father, Lisa Marie and Linda watching tapes of old Monty Python shows.

A Vivid Memory from 1975

David Stanley, one of Elvis' stepbrothers, vividly remembers something Elvis did, in which he was involved, during a concert in 1975.

Part of David's responsibilities while on tour with Elvis was to make sure security was in place at the front of the concert stage before his performances. On this evening he noticed a group of people in a reserved VIP area. One young man caught his eye, he was in a wheelchair, his arms twisted in, and his legs turned inward. In his hands he had a frame with the words to a song, *Impossible Dream,* underneath which was written, "My impossible dream is to meet Elvis Presley."

David knew that this was one dream that he could make come true. He walked up to the young man in the chair, placed a backstage pass on his shirt, and informed his parents he was taking him to see Elvis. He went to Elvis' dressing room and, although Elvis was just about to go on stage so was not wanting to see anyone, David persuaded him and brought the boy in. This is how David describes that meeting:

"When the boy saw Elvis, his eyes lit up. His disease-riddled body began to shake. With every ounce of energy that he could muster up, he slurred 'ELVIS.'

"When Elvis saw him, he was so overcome with emotion he simply walked over, fell on his knees next to the boy, dropped his head in his lap and began to weep. Still grasping the frame, the young man began stroking Elvis' hair with his crippled hand.

"This was the most beautiful sight that I had ever witnessed. Elvis had met politicians, royalty, celebrities, and spiritual leaders but, despite all that, he was most humbled by what he saw in this incredible young man."

Elvis had to leave to go on stage and David kept the boy with him, so he had the best seat in the house. When Elvis started to sing *The Impossible Dream* the smile on the young man's face grew bigger. David had an assistant help pick the boy's wheelchair up and place it on the corner of the stage so that he could be nearer to Elvis. When Elvis glimpsed the young man, he walked over and sang directly to him. Tears rolled down his face as his impossible dream was coming true. He held up the frame with the handwritten phrase, "My impossible dream is to meet Elvis Presley." Elvis took the frame from the boy's hands as he sang the last lyric, "to reach the unreachable star."

David says, "In the hundreds of concerts that I had done with Elvis Presley, there had never been a time where the audience did not give a standing ovation after one of his songs. On this night, instead of applause, the only thing that could be heard was the sound of tears from 20,000 people dropping on the concrete floor of the sold-out concert hall. The love that Elvis showed that night toward that young man was as Christ-like as anything I had ever seen in my life. In that moment, Elvis saw the perfection of this crippled man. What's more, this young man felt his own perfection and saw himself as Christ would see him. He experienced Elvis's gift of healing first-hand. As a result, his life would never be the same again. This was the side of Elvis Presley that the public was drawn to."

That young man was Stephen Green, from Nuthall, Nottingham, in England, born with Downs Syndrome. Stephen was able to return to the USA to visit Graceland. Also in 2012, aged 47, Stephen became the first person with Down's Syndrome in England to be elected to a Parish Council, and he served on the Council for over two years. It is possible to believe that his time with Elvis had such a positive effect on him, that he is still leading a joyful and meaningful life. Stephen was 56 years old, as of 8th February 2021.

David Stanley also remembers Elvis reading the Bible on stage. A member of the audience went up to the stage and handed Elvis a book, he shook her hand, entered the spotlight on the stage and told the audience he wanted to read to them for just a minute. The audience became very quiet as Elvis flipped the pages and read from John 3:16, "For God so love the world that he gave his only begotten son, that whosoever believeth in him shall not perish but have everlasting life" He also read from Psalm 23, "Yea though I walk through the valley of the shadow of death I will fear no evil." David could feel the emotion with which Elvis read, as so could the audience as they sat enraptured, hanging on every word. Elvis then turned to the orchestra and announced that he was going to sing *How Great Thou Art*. David says that from his vantage point he thought that at the end of the song Elvis was weeping, he says "I know I was."

Interview With David Stanley

I was pleased to be able to interview David Stanley at the opening of the Fingerprints of Elvis Exhibition in Liverpool, England on 14th June 2003.

After ascertaining that David's favourite Elvis songs were *Jailhouse Rock* and *Memories,* that he didn't like Elvis singing *Hey Jude,* and that he thought Elvis' best years were 1969-1972, the interview proceeded as follows:

Madeleine Wilson (MW): You have said that one of the problems with Elvis was that he had no accountability, no one to answer to. Do you think that he was aware of that and, if so, what sort of person do you think he could have been accountable to?

David Stanley (DS): I think Elvis was this prototype person; he was the first rock star. There was no one before him. Professionally it was hard for him to communicate with somebody who had similar success. There had been Frank Sinatra, Dean Martin, but this young kid Elvis just broke out of the mould. There was no solid advice on how to be a rock star.

As far as accountability throughout his life – because he was a superstar, not only on stage, but as a person, he was a very powerful presence, it was hard to tell him what to do, I would look at Elvis and make a suggestion. I'm 47 years old now and the way I am answering these questions, would be a lot different to that then. He was very humble and grateful that God had given him these incredible gifts of music and charisma and presence, but there was not a lot of people who could relate to him, to get at that level of what it's like to be an icon. Whether you are good or bad, people still love you. Elvis was just loved. We all have things in our lives that we are not proud of. We've all sat down and said, "How can anyone really care about me?" Including Elvis. People did love him. He didn't comprehend that. So it was hard to discuss those kinds of things, to let someone advise him. In my opinion.

MW: So, you don't think he looked for some accountability?

DS: Elvis used to talk to preachers. He met with Rex Humbard and Oral Roberts, people like that. Elvis had a tremendous faith and that was instilled in him by his mother. But it was kind of like, "Who can understand where I am coming from?" Does that make sense? It's like me doing this interview on a smaller level. We can talk about Elvis, but who can really understand what it was like to be in that whirlwind with Elvis Presley?

MW: God can.

DS: Of course. When I say accountability, I mean no one could really tell him what to do. He had his own mindset. I think Elvis' conscience caught up with him. The world loved him so much, but there were things about himself that he didn't like so much. Some people call it sin; some people call it conviction. Sometimes you find yourself going away from the things you know you're supposed to do and do not do. I think the combination of all that just took Elvis over the top, over the edge. Plus, Elvis had to sit down and be Elvis.

People ask, what was the most difficult part of Elvis' life. "Being Elvis Presley." He couldn't be a person. Accountability wasn't there. He couldn't communicate his feelings because people expected this superstar to have a super life and super happiness all the time. It just caught up with him. 29 years of being on top, where do you go after you're Elvis?

MW: They say it's tough at the top.

DS: And lonely at the top.

MW: Another point you have made is that Elvis was afraid of not giving his fans what they wanted. Do you think it was this fear, which prevented him from doing all gospel concerts?

DS: No. Elvis did gospel music, but as far as I know, it was never slated. Never got together. I never heard of Elvis doing a gospel show. It would have been great.

He loved gospel, he sat up all night with J D and the Stamps and Imperials. We would go to gospel conventions. If he had lived, he would have done something like that. Elvis always knew where he came from. He was always humble and very grateful for those gifts. He told my brother Ricky, "We all have callings – my calling is to be a gospel singer." He told my brother that, I remember that. Elvis just said, "I very simply missed my calling. The world won't let me be what God called me to be."

MW: That leads on to my next question. Elvis asked the question many times, why had God given him this gift of a wonderful voice and personal magnetism. On reflection do you now have an answer to that question?

DS: Let's talk about his gospel music. Look at the inspiration of the gospel music, look at the Grammy awards. Gospel messages depicted in the structure of that music. Elvis never put a message in a song that was destructive. That's why he didn't like the Beatles. He didn't like anyone talking about drugs, or anti-establishment. Tearing down the family. He was very conservative in his perspectives, and I think that his calling was fulfilled because he did do what he was called to do, those records are still out there and when you talk about Elvis, everyone talks about the gospel, the roots of his life. I think he fulfilled his calling and more.

MW: Did you ever talk about Christian spiritual matters with Elvis? If so, what would you say was he most interested in about the Gospel and what did he have the most questions about?

DS: Elvis read a lot of books. "The Impersonal Life," "The Shroud of Turin," many, but he always went back to the Bible.

During the 26 years after his death, I have been through a lot of journeys myself. Through all the ups and downs of my life, the one thing that stays solid is my faith in God and my love for Christ. No matter whether I am up or down, good boy, bad boy, full of sin, full of grace, I still focus on my relationship with the Lord, and I think that Elvis, although he searched, always went back to the simplicity of God the creator and Christ the Saviour. That was instilled in him. Elvis had adversity after adversity after adversity. I would sit down on his bed and watch him open that Bible and cry his eyes out, "God give me strength!"

One day he's taking a handful of drugs, next he's praying for forgiveness. We're all that way. One thing people need to understand about Elvis is that no one, not even that king was perfect. There was only one perfect king, that was Jesus, and Elvis recognised that. The song *Why Me Lord?* sums it up. 'Why am I this big, huge star? God, I'm no good, I'm capable of self-destruct, rebellion and all kinds of things which don't fall into the structure of what you would want me to do. In spite of all that, why have you picked me?' That was the life of Elvis Presley.

He was a modern-day King Solomon. If Elvis would have lived in Biblical times, there probably would have been a book written about him because he was a modern-day king. Can you imagine living with that? It's almost impossible.

MW: A heavy burden.

241

DS: A very heavy burden. I'm standing here talking to you in Liverpool, 26 years after Elvis died. Tell me about it. The impact this guy had on society, 26 years later, we're talking about him and we're talking about his faith. What he did and how he did it. He was a modern-day king. If anyone says "What killed Elvis?" Being a modern-day king. Forget Elvis, just imagine being that person. That's a tough road!

Look at all the kings, the adversities of King David, King Solomon. Elvis was no different.

MW: It is well known that Elvis had a great sense of humour and that the sullen Elvis often portrayed was far outweighed by the fun-loving Elvis. What is your favourite memory of having fun with Elvis?

DS: The best fun I ever had was when Elvis was playing, whether we were doing firework wars, go-carts, football. People talk about poor miserable rock star Elvis Presley. It wasn't that bad. Elvis had fun. We had fun vacations, we had wonderful Christmases. We had practical jokes. Elvis said, "If it ceases to be fun, quit. If you can't laugh, go home." And Vernon was that way too. Elvis inherited it from his daddy. The best fun I had with Elvis was just being with Elvis when he was in a good mood. Now, when he was in a bad mood, it wasn't fun, but we all get in a bad mood. And when Elvis played, he played hard. He was just a big kid. You would just look at this 39/40-year-old man acting like a 12-year-old kid. My sons look at me and say, "Dad you act like you're a kid." I say, "Thank you." I want to keep that, my youth and my joy and my happiness. At the end of Elvis' life, it wasn't funny anymore. You think of his statement, "When it ceases to be fun, quit." It makes you wonder if he didn't just quit. As a believer, Elvis knew that life is fleeting. It was time to go home. He's having more fun than any of us right now!

MW: You have said that Elvis was both a father figure and a brother to you, but that being a father figure was greater. Was that because you had lost contact with your own father, whereas you still had your other brothers around?

DS: That's a good evaluation. That's exactly right. My father was swept out of my life. Vernon loved us, but his son was Elvis. I had a good relationship with Vernon, my stepfather. He raised me and gave me a roof, took me to school. He did all the father things. Because I had lost my identity, growing up in this fishbowl, surrealistic life with Elvis, the only thing I could grab hold of was Billy and Ricky and Elvis. Billy and Ricky were my age, they were my true brothers, Elvis was that father figure. He was the guy who would pat you on the back and you would know that everything would be OK.

When someone would mess with his family, he was front and centre. He was always up there for you, to protect you. And it was the same with me for him, nobody got to Elvis on my watch. No one was going to hurt him, touch him, beat him up, do anything bad to him when I was around. He wasn't my biological father, but I would call Elvis my dad. It doesn't mean like I'm going to grow sideburns and walk with a cane. He was that influential person in my life that taught me all about life, good and bad. It's taken me many years to soak it all in through my life.

It will always continue to be the dominant force in my life, my father figure, Elvis Presley, and my real father. As Elvis said to me, "Always love your Daddy, be proud of his heritage as a combat veteran, a person who was willing to lay his life down." The greatest compliment Elvis ever gave me was to say, "You're just like your dad." And I am much like my biological father, but Elvis was Pop and I loved him.

MW: It is clear from your writings that you really miss Elvis. Even after all these years you still feel pain. As a Christian do you feel that you will stop grieving and that, as the Bible says, your mourning will turn into dancing, in this life here on earth.

DS: I don't really mourn because I am a believer. I'll see Elvis again. There are times I get sad you know. Probably tonight when I go back to my room and lie down, and all this will start to build. You see people won't let Elvis die. I will never have closure because Elvis will always be. I miss Elvis, but I don't wish he was still around. That would be selfish, and I think Elvis is in heaven, tuning up the choir, whatever he's doing.

MW: Having a ball.

DS: Yeah, whatever the great and wonderful things God promises us.

I get sad. It's like Elvis said, "It's not that I am not liked, I am just misunderstood." No matter how many interviews I give out and how many people I talk to, people never comprehend the simplicity of this very humble God-fearing man. He was just simple. He could do this interview with you – he would find you very disarming and very caring and very qualified in your questions. He would enjoy the process, and you would think this icon, he's above reproach, but he would talk to anybody. And when I think about that and how much he cared about people and the person he was, I miss him, but I miss more about people not getting it – who he really was.

MW: You want to put the record straight, for people to understand him?

DS: Yes exactly. When you think of Elvis, don't be so complex. He was just one of us. He just made a lot more money! And had a tremendous gift.

MW: If you could speak to Elvis now, what would you say to him?

DS: My goodness. If I had one wish in my life, it would be to be able to communicate with Elvis at my age now. All the adversities that I have been through, since he's passed away, and to be able to communicate with him, man to man, not boy to rock star or boy to man, but man to man. I would probably tell Elvis that I love him, that he is loved and how much I appreciate him taking this 4-year-old snotty-nosed kid when he didn't have to. Dee [David's mother] came into his life when his mother had only been gone one and a half to two years. That's tough. He loved my mother and he loved us three boys. When I walked into Graceland, he hugged me and welcomed me and gave me all those years.

People say so many things, "David why didn't you save him, why didn't you do this, do that?" Until you've been there, don't criticise and abuse, until you've walked in David's shoes. My legacy stands for itself. People can say what they like, but Elvis trusted me, and I trusted him. I lost a friend and brother that day. If I could say anything I would probably say, "Thanks." And I am sorry about a lot of things, because it's hard to be the keeper of a legacy. I didn't ask for this position, I got thrown into it. I have done my best along the way. The hardest part about death is the people left behind.

MW: But God gives you the strength.

DS: Right.

MW: And you will see him again.

DS: Yes, that's the good part about it.

I went through rock 'n' roll to evangelism, fell off, crashed, and burned. Never really dealt with the negative ideologies instilled in my life as part of the rock 'n' roll scene. But my life revolves around the grace of God. As long as there is breath in my body, I will always be an instrument of the Lord.

I doubt if I will return to preaching. But I'll say this. I am not ashamed of the gospel of Christ. And anywhere I go as a speaker, a corporate speaker, I always interject my faith. The reason I am breathing is because of my faith. I have survived my years, with and without Elvis, because of my faith. There's a great song by Russ Taff, *I Still Believe.* He says, "I have been caught in a cave for forty nights and nothing but a spark to lead my way. But I still believe, I still believe through the pain."

And through the grief, I'll climb that mountain, on my knees if I have to. I will continue to live and go forward, I still believe. Because of my incredible faith and the grace of God that has sustained me along the way.

Every time I talk about my life and Elvis, I'll be telling you about the Lord.

MW: Thank you very much David for your honest and open answers.

Losing Interest in 1976

In January 1976 Elvis decided to take his family and some friends on a holiday to the ski resort in Vail, Colorado. Several of the group took skiing lessons and were out on the snow most of the day, whereas Elvis seemed subdued and only ventured out on a snowmobile at night.

It was clear by now that Elvis was losing interest in life in general, saying to his friends, "I'm bored, I'm tired of being Elvis Presley." RCA had not been able to persuade him into a studio to record any songs, so they arranged to set up a studio in the Jungle Room at Graceland, hoping that this more relaxed atmosphere would encourage Elvis to deliver.

However, a few days before the session Elvis had attended the funeral, in Denver, of a police officer friend, dressed in his own Denver Police Captain's uniform. It is this uniform which he wore at the first recording session, and he seemed to be distracted, though he did manage to record three songs. After a week of Elvis' erratic behaviour, sometimes not turning up at all to a recording session, RCA's Felton Jarvis was relieved that he had managed to record 12 songs for future release.

Elvis did complete all seven days of his March tour, however many noticed that only a few of the songs were sung with any fervour, and Elvis sometimes appeared confused and often forgot the lyrics to some of the most familiar songs.

Back in Memphis in March, Elvis would surely have been encouraged, oddly enough, by a traffic accident which he came across. He had recently been made a Captain in the Memphis Police Reserve, and after displaying his badge was able to help the victims of the accident.

Although Elvis was suffering and losing interest in his work, even life itself, he still had that charisma that was very attractive. Sonny West's three-year-old son Bryan was not feeling too well and was cranky, not wanting to have anything to do with members of Elvis backing singers who loved him, and he even refused a hug from Linda Thompson. However, when they went to Elvis' dressing room, Elvis was sitting quietly within himself, but when he saw Bryan, he said, "Come here little Bryan," Bryan immediately went into Elvis open arms, and they told each other they loved each other. Sonny remembers that moment as one when he realised that Elvis had a tender heart which children were drawn to. However, after the concert that day, the Long Beach Press Telegram reported "an eerie silence filled the concert hall when he sang 'and now the end is near,' the opening line of *My Way*. It was like witnessing a chilling prophecy."

A few days later, an associate of Elvis, John O'Grady, visited Elvis during his Tahoe gig and was so shocked by Elvis' appearance, that he cried afterwards, as he really thought that Elvis was going to die. He immediately contacted Elvis' Los Angeles attorney, Ed Hookstratten, to discuss trying to get Elvis into a drug treatment programme. Ed, in turn, contacted Priscilla who, in May, flew to Memphis to discuss the idea with Elvis, but Elvis would have nothing to do with it.

After his 22 concerts in April, May and June, Elvis returned to Memphis and spent the next few weeks in his room seeing only his cousin Billy and his wife Jo, as well as Lisa Marie who visited for 10 days.

Trying to Cut Costs?

In July 1976, three members of the Memphis Mafia – Red and Sonny West, and Dave Hebler – were fired by Vernon from their jobs as bodyguards. The official reason was to cut costs, but they felt that they were being punished for trying to save Elvis from his drug habit. They were also worried about his weight gains and mental state, but Elvis rarely took advice and never tolerated criticism of his behaviour from his entourage.

Knowing that Elvis was very good friends with Tom Jones, as they spent a lot of time together in Las Vegas, they turned to Tom to see if he would contact Elvis to try and influence him. They said, "Will you call Elvis? Because he has fired us all and he is destroying himself and we can't help him." Tom has never revealed whether he managed to get through to Elvis at all, although Frank Sinatra confided in him that he, himself, had begged Elvis to change his ways.

Not All Bad

Most of the July and August shows were a critical disaster, describing Elvis as giving desultory performances and Elvis himself being in a sad state of disrepair. The reviewers noted, however, that these performances were greeted by the fans with uncritical adulation and that they were screaming for what he had been and what he symbolised, rather than what he was at that time.

However, the concert in Syracuse on 27th July was one of the better ones, eliciting "a dynamite performance" from one critic. It was also the concert that Pam Heffernan felt changed her life.

Pam was a young mother, with two small children. Her husband had multiple sclerosis. The illness forced him to take a lot of sick time and, consequently, his employer laid him off. The family lived on Pam's income as a nurse. At home, she took care of her ailing husband and their young kids. Everything seemed to be going wrong. Amid all that, she learned Elvis was coming to the Onondaga County War Memorial in Syracuse. She had always wanted to see Elvis perform, but her family had no mooney. However, a group of neighbours, knowing of Pam's dream, had got together, and bought eight tickets. They gave her a ticket and "for that hour or so everything was lifted," Pam recalls. She went home with a quiet confidence that her family would get through its hard times, and for whatever reason, life seemed better after Elvis. To always remember that turnaround, she kept the ticket stub among her precious things in her jewellery box.

Elvis' August/September tour was, again, a mixture of mainly lacklustre performances, when fans noticed that Elvis looked ill, though occasionally they were described as "another knockout show." Certainly, there was still a demand. On several occasions, because of sell-out shows and many more applications for tickets, the Colonel arranged a second concert in the same town.

To rest before his next tour Elvis flew out to LA to join Linda in the apartment that he had bought for her.

Encouragement From Joe Moscheo

Joe Moscheo of the Imperials who had so enjoyed his time being a friend of and singing with Elvis, continued to have occasional contact with him, but he noticed that he was not looking well, and he did not seem happy. Joe began to feel a tug in his heart, a conviction that he needed to do something as Elvis's friend to support him. Joe was always very eager to advise people, "Don't leave Jesus out of your life."

Tyndale publishers had brought out a new Bible, The Living Bible, which is a paraphrase of the Old and New Testaments. Its purpose is to say as exactly as possible what the writers of the Scriptures meant, and to say it simply, expanding where necessary for a clear understanding by the modern reader. Joe knew that Elvis read the Bible, but perhaps only the King James Version, so he thought that it might help Elvis to read this more modern version.

When he saw that Elvis was to perform, on 6th September 1976, in Huntsville, a couple of hours drive from Nashville where he lived, Joe decided to try to get to Elvis and give him the Bible. This he was able to do, and he saw that Elvis did not look good; he appeared puffy and physically worn down and his colour did not seem right. He told Elvis that in all the books he was reading, in all of the people he was talking to, in all of the spiritual and intellectual theories he was now studying, Joe knew that he was looking for stability, for peace. He said: "Elvis, all of the answers you're looking for are right here in this book. Just read it."

He handed the Bible to Elvis, who opened the cover and read the inscription "To Elvis." Joe then experienced something he had not experienced with Elvis before. He says, "Usually, with Elvis, it was always just a handshake. He was not overly physically demonstrative. This time, however, he reached out his arm and cupped the back of my head, then pulled me close to his face. He squeezed our foreheads together in a sort of embrace."

One can see when Joe describes this gesture that he is very moved, as this was the last time he saw Elvis, of whom he said, "He introduced gospel music to a secular world. In a way, he was an evangelist." Also, we have already seen from Dotty Rambo, Elvis did indeed find this version of the Bible, much easier to understand.

Someone else who felt moved to contact Elvis in 1976 was the Rev. Frank Smith, Elvis' pastor at the East Tupelo Assembly of God church. It was one of several compulsions to visit Elvis and encourage him to become a more positive role model, though, he never acted on these compulsions. I wonder if he had, whether he would have been able to see Elvis as, by now, his entourage were very protective and acted as gatekeepers to prevent Elvis being bombarded with requests of various kinds or seeing people whom they were not sure would be beneficial to his wellbeing.

After the tour in October, RCA again set up a studio in the Jungle Room at Graceland. However, they were only able to record four songs. They planned another session in Nashville in January, but Elvis only got as far as his hotel then flew back to Memphis without ever entering the studio. In the end, Felton Jarvis, the producer, and his team went on tour with Elvis in March, April and May and were able to record 26 songs for a new album.

Final Love Interest

On 19th November, George Klein brought Ginger Alden to Graceland to meet Elvis. Ginger, nineteen years old, was the current Miss Mid-South Fair. Elvis was immediately drawn to her and dated her the next night, flying her out to Las Vegas for the night, chaperoned by his cousin Patsy and her husband. Ginger clearly remembers their first meeting and night alone together:

"When he first walked in the room the very first night we met, I just thought he was gorgeous. I was extremely shy, and I blurted out, 'Hi Elvis!' like I'd known him for years. We connected; we shared spiritual interests and musical interests. I didn't even think of the age difference. The only time I thought Elvis seemed a little older was when he was teaching. He loved to teach. He was in a very mellow phase in his life and really searching, on a spiritual quest, on a very serious spiritual quest. We read many nights together.

I wasn't expecting him the first night I was alone with him to read to me. He had this large book with a symbol and said, 'This is an illustration of God.' It was a man with a long flowing beard with symbols of fire, ice and wind to the sides. Elvis started reading it to me, and then he handed me the book and wanted me to read to him. This was the very first night. I was like, 'This is a rock and roll icon reading to me.' It was amazing."

Elvis asked Ginger to join him on his November tour, which she did. He most probably realised that his relationship with Linda was coming to an end, especially as he now had another girl in tow, so he suggested to Linda that she go back to Memphis, where she had a house that he bought her. Linda, who had been gradually detaching herself from Elvis, did leave him and publicly continued a relationship with one of the musicians.

"Elvis You're My Bell Sheep"

Sometimes, words and phrases used in an interest group are not always understood by others, sometimes, even by those within the group. This is the case with Elvis and the term "Bell Sheep."

On 12th December, Rev. Rex Humbard and his wife Maude Aimee were in Las Vegas and wanted to attend an Elvis concert, which J D Sumner arranged for them, with front row seats. Elvis admired Rex's TV ministry shows, and knowing that they were there, he invited them back to his dressing room, as he was eager to meet them. When they appeared, Elvis immediately left the crowd of people and led them into a small room for privacy.

Rex was amazed at Elvis' knowledge of the Bible, both the Old and New Testaments, which he started quoting very soon into the conversation, saying, "The Lord is coming soon, isn't he?" He then talked about his mother's death and his recent illnesses, and he seemed very discouraged. Maude Aimee, then said, "Elvis, I want you to know I've been praying for you for years. You're my bell sheep."

Elvis was puzzled by this terminology and asked for an explanation. She explained to him that shepherds in the Holy Land often tied a bell around the neck of one of the sheep. The rest of the flock would follow wherever they were led by the sound of the bell.

"Elvis," Maude Aimee continued, "I've been praying that you'll have a spiritual experience that will cause you to lead thousands, maybe millions of people to the Lord."

At that point, something happened to Elvis. He began to tremble, and tears began rolling down his cheeks. They all joined hands and prayed. Rex says,

"He [Elvis] rededicated his heart to the Lord. I asked God to bless him and to send His Spirit into his heart and meet his every need." They then tried to leave as they knew that Elvis had another show to do. However, Elvis begged them not to go. Clearly, something had happened that he was hoping to prolong; he had found a place of respite that had apparently long been absent, despite his searching and questioning about various spiritual paths. At this point, Lisa Marie came into the room and asked why her daddy was crying. Elvis reassured her that it was OK, and he would be out soon.

They continued to talk for a while, with Rex telling Elvis that when he went to the Holy Land, he took suitcases of letters from all over the world from people who have unsaved loved ones or people in need. He stood at Calvary and in faith asked the Lord to answer the prayers in the letters. Elvis was amazed by this and, when Rex told him that when he next went to Jerusalem he would pray, "Thank you Lord for what you have done for Elvis," he burst into tears again. Rex and Maude Aimee grasped his hands and prayed some more. At this point the door opened and a voice said, "Almost showtime." Elvis, pulling himself together, said, "You and Maude Aimee coming here today is the most wonderful Christmas present Elvis Presley has ever received. And I want to thank you." He then went out to do his next show.

After their prayer time, Maude Aimee went to the hotel gift shop and bought Elvis a symbolic bell with a little diamond in it. During the evening's second show, Elvis held up the little bell and smiled to as he dedicated *How Great Thou Art* to the couple.

Later Elvis contacted the Humbards to invite them to Graceland, but Rex's schedule wouldn't allow it, so, sadly, that was the last time they saw Elvis.

Cries For Help

During this last engagement of the year in Las Vegas, Elvis wrote a "letter" on the Hilton notepad by his bedside. He then tore off the note and threw it in the waste bin where it was retrieved, reportedly by a maid. It came up for auction several years later and was bought by Wayne Newton, an entertainer friend of Elvis. These are the words on the note:

Help me Lord to get through all of this. I am so tired of it. I think I would like to sleep forever, but rest does not come easy for me. Show me a way out from these problems. I want... and it ends there.

Wayne remembers his last conversation with Elvis in which he talked about his loneliness, his love for his daughter and that he felt that "it was over."

Three other notes were also found by Elvis bedside, on Hilton notepaper, and retrieved by one of Elvis' entourage.

First note: *I don't know who I can talk to anymore. Nor to turn to. I only have myself and the Lord. Help me Lord to know the right thing.*

Second note: *I will be glad when this engagement is over. I need some rest from all of this. But I can't stop. Won't stop. Maybe I will take everyone to Hawaii for a while.*

Third note: *I wish there was someone who I could trust and talk to. Prayer is my only salvation now. I feel lost sometimes – be still and <u>know I am God.</u> Feel me within, before you can know <u>I am there.</u>*

After these shows, Elvis returned to Memphis and spent a quiet Christmas with his family and Ginger Alden.

Some Encouragement

One of Elvis' cooks, Mary Jenkins, so appreciated Elvis that this Christmas she wanted to give him something to express her appreciation, but what could she give to someone "who has everything"?

Mary had started working for Elvis in 1963 as a maid but was promoted to cook when his new bride, Priscilla, arrived three years later. Mary was a lovely Christian lady who said, "If any problem was bothering me. I knew that I could tell Elvis and he would understand. He would always hear me out and then talk to me. He would always bring me up again. Those were the times that he seemed like a father to me. He was younger than I was, but his advice was always beyond his years."

As well as being the cook, Mary was a loyal friend to Elvis and his family and served them for 12 more years after Elvis' death until her retirement. Her unwavering loyalty to Elvis' memory, her ready smile and her gentle grace endeared her to many, including Elvis.

As we know, that feeling was mutual and Mary eventually decided to ask their long-time mutual friend, Janelle McComb, to put her feelings into words for this very personal gift called "A Tribute to My Boss."

There are so many moments in a friendship when one's devotion cannot be measured in words. Friendship is loyalty linked together by the chain of respect. I shall always remain loyal to you because you looked beyond my face and into my heart. You taught me that in judging the worth of any person, I must place the measuring tape around their heart, not around their net worth. Thanks for giving me the courage to believe in myself and the faith to place loyalty and compassion as the prime criteria for service.

From One Who Respects You, Mary

Apparently, this Christmas break, not to mention the youthful company of Ginger, recharged Elvis. When the final tour commenced on 27th December in Wichita, he performed with renewed vigour, surely wanting to impress Ginger. One fan noted that he had much more fire in his voice and a review comment included, "One thing was obvious, Mr Presley's magnetic showmanship can still wrap an audience into a little tight ball - he sings like an angel and moves like a tiger."

In the New Year's Eve show in Pittsburgh, Elvis sat down at the piano and sang, *Unchained Melody* and *Rags To Riches.* As his voice resonated throughout the building, the audience listened in stunned silence. To hear Elvis' voice accompanied only by piano must have been quite amazing. He finished the show by singing *Funny How Time Slips Away* and *Auld Lang Syne*, then saying, "I would like to wish you all a happy and prosperous New Year and health and happiness throughout 1977. He then had the house lights switched on and introduced his father and Lisa Marie to the audience.

A Fan Remembers

One of the people who watched the Las Vegas shows many times is Anne Nixon from the UK who is a well-respected Elvis researcher and writer and a friend of ours at Elvis Gospel. She saw Elvis perform in Las Vegas 40 times during 1972, '73, '74, and '76 and says that Elvis included more gospel songs in his shows as the years went on. She also received two scarves and two kisses from Elvis, as she was one of those who was able to get to the stage front. These are some of her memories of those shows:

"I was lucky enough to see Elvis in Las Vegas in the 1970s and, at many shows, he sang gospel songs. In his secular numbers, he often ad-libbed and joked, but the religious ones were usually sung seriously. An exception was *Why Me Lord?* When he would try to make J D Sumner laugh.

"Songs like *Help Me* and *Bridge Over Troubled Water* were wonderful to hear, but there was one stand out song. No prizes for guessing that it was *How Great Thou Art*. The performances of this dramatic number were the highlight of many shows. It was remarkable to see how the audience in glitzy gambling-mad Las Vegas, known as Sin City, would react positively to this classic.

"Sometimes Elvis would say 'D'you wanna hear it again?' and do a reprise (or two) of the last part of the song. I can see him now caught in the spotlight, pouring his heart and soul into *How Great Thou Art*. Even by 1976 when he looked ill, he still put everything into his performance. Once or twice Elvis spontaneously burst into a few lines of *Further Along* or *Till God Calls Me Home*.[3]

"He enjoyed sharing the talents of his backing singers with us. In 1972, J D Sumner and the Stamps were featured in every show doing *Walk That Lonesome Road*, a song that J D had written, Elvis proudly informed us. But Elvis the practical joker used to throw water over them when Ed Enoch hit a certain high note. He soon learned to wait for that!

"The Stamps were sometimes asked to sing *Sweet, Sweet Spirit* and, in 1976, Kathy Westmoreland was sometimes asked to sing *My Heavenly Father* and Sherrill Neilsen was brought to stage front to sing *Walk with Me,* and how we enjoyed watching Elvis standing at the back with a smile on his face!

"One special memory is of the show when Elvis said he had had a hankering for some time to do something, and with the help of Charlie Hodge and the Stamps, did a short medley of *You Better Run* and *Bosom of Abraham*. How privileged I was to see and hear this. It was like seeing the man behind the image whose first love was gospel music. Elvis must have done many a similar jam session up in his suite.

"When I need a lift or to be comforted, I turn to Elvis' gospel music and often recall the times I saw him sing the gospel on stage, and I find a great deal of strength in the memories and the music."

---

[3] A line in this song is, "I'm goin' to sing till Jesus calls me home" and that's just what Elvis did.

Gallery

Elvis having fun during rehearsal time.

Elvis with the Imperials, signed by Joe Moscheo who has
written "thanks for all you do for Gospel".

Elvis with evangelist Oral Roberts.

David Stanley on the left of Elvis, carrying Elvis' Bible. (Shaun Shaver)

Elvis with Linda, the little blind girl, at his concert in Norfolk, Virginia.

CHAI NECKLACE VERMEIL

As well as owning, and giving away Christian crosses, Elvis wore a chai pendant. Chai is the Hebrew word for Life.

Chapter 8

1977 - A Year Many Will Not Forget

Praise the Lord, my soul; all my inmost being, praise his holy name. Praise the Lord, my soul, and forget not all his benefits.
(Psalm 103:1&2)

A unique concert performance - Elvis accompanying himself on piano in Montgomery, Alabama, singing Where No One Stands Alone on 16th February, exactly seven months before his death.

It is clear by now that Elvis is really struggling. We have seen some of the notes he wrote expressing his feelings. Another note discovered had been folded up and used as a bookmark in a Bible. This is what Elvis wrote:

Here I am sitting alone thinking and watching the moonlight shine. I meditate watching the water flowing in the garden below.

I just started living my life and having some fun. But if I think of all that I've lost, the pain inside me grips me. And it's so slow to leave. Now I'm fully grown and they say I'm a man. But is this really what I am? My heart is so young, it feels like new and the thought that I'm getting old makes me sad. Lord, make me laugh and let me be the clown that I am.

Please give me dignity and grace so that I can have the strength to face these last days that seem to run fast. Give me some more time to do what I can. So that facing death is not a penalty. Please Lord, that's all I'm asking.'

Elvis wrote "Psalm 54" at the bottom of the page, so one assumes he bases this writing on this psalm. It certainly seems so as Psalm 54 says:

"Save me, O God, by your name; vindicate me by your might. Hear my prayer, O God; listen to the words of my mouth.

Strangers are attacking me; ruthless men seek my life – men without regard for God.

Surely God is my help; the Lord is the one who sustains me. Let evil recoil on those who slander me; in your faithfulness destroy them.

I will sacrifice a freewill offering to you; I will praise your name, O LORD, for it is good. For he has delivered me from all my troubles, and my eyes have looked in triumph on my foes."

On 8th January Elvis flew Ginger and her sister out to Palm Springs to celebrate his 42nd birthday.

Later in January, Elvis flew out to Nashville for a recording session, without Ginger. He stayed in his hotel and flew back to Memphis the next day without ever setting foot in the studio.

Most probably wanting to assure Ginger that he was serious about her and perhaps to get her to spend more time with him, Elvis contacted his jeweller, Lowell Hayes, on 26th January to purchase an engagement ring. He proposed to Ginger the same evening.

On 1st February, Elvis and Ginger flew to LA to celebrate Lisa Marie's ninth birthday.

Elvis insisted that Ginger accompany him on the first tour of the year. Because Ginger missed her family, Elvis flew them out for the last few days of the nine-day tour.

A New Experience in Concert

In his 16th February show in Montgomery, Alabama, Elvis announced to the screaming audience that he was going to sing a gospel song that he had never sung on stage before, nor even rehearsed with his singers. He sat down at the piano saying, "I know the chord changes" and called on the Stamps and Sherill Nielson to accompany him. Elvis sang *Where No One Stands Alone* solo until the group accompanied him in the chorus. When Elvis called "repeat fellas" they sang the chorus again with Elvis' personal cry, "Take my hand, LORD, let me stand where no-one stands alone." This must be one of the most poignant on-stage moments, considering it was exactly six months before this death, and one cannot help but notice that this song so passionately sung, does have a hint of laboured breathing.

Where No One Stands Alone lyrics:

Once I stood in the night, with my head bowed low in the darkness as black as could be.

And my heart felt alone, and I cried, "Oh Lord don't hide your face from me."

Like a king, I may live in a palace so tall, with great riches to call my own.

But I don't know a thing in this whole wide world that's worse than being alone.

Take my hand all the way, every hour, every day from here to the great unknown.

Take my hand, let me stand where no-one stands alone.

It seems that Elvis was keen to get closer to Jesus because he knew that it is there, next to Jesus, that a person cannot possibly feel lonely.

These lyrics were written by Mosie Lister and, as with many songs, has a very personal meaning behind it. This is the story as told to Terry Blackwood:

Mosie was going through a tough time and couldn't feel God's presence in his life. He went for a walk and these words flooded his soul "Lord won't you hold my hand all the way, every hour, every day." As he was thinking this, he started raising his hands, trying to feel God. As the words repeated in his mind, he reached higher and higher until his hands were as high as they could go. He felt that God reached down and touched him. He then went on the write the song *Where No One Stands Alone*.

A Concerned Friend

In March, Ann-Margret was recording a TV show in Nashville and half expected to hear from Elvis as they had kept in touch even when they did not see each other for a long time. However, Elvis did not contact her, and Ann-Margret was concerned, having heard that Elvis was not well and had cancelled concerts. She had asked Joe Esposito, but he told her not to worry as everything was fine. There were a few problems, but they were being taken care of. She says that had she known how ill Elvis was, she would have been "there in a second to intervene." When she opened at the Hilton in Las Vegas on August 15th, 1977, for the first time in 10 years there was no guitar-shaped flower arrangement from Elvis. No telegram, no message of any kind. She was concerned that something was wrong and determined to make a phone call the next day, but before she could do that, she received a phone call informing her of Elvis' death.

***

On 3rd March, Vernon insisted that Elvis signed his will, of which Vernon was executor and trustee. He was given total responsibility for the "health, education, comfortable maintenance and welfare" of himself, Grandma Minnie Mae, and Lisa Marie who was the sole heir.

The next day Elvis flew a party of 30 people out to Hawaii for a holiday costing over $100,000. His comment on doing this was "What profit is it to gain the world if you couldn't share your fortune with your friends."

After this holiday, Elvis was feeling much better and ready for the next nine-day tour, however, by all accounts, the concerts were erratic. One concert reviewer said, "His music ran from parody to almost perfect. At times he flashed the old brilliance which put him on top." Also, fans were noticing that he began to tire on stage and Ginger was becoming concerned as Elvis told her that he didn't feel well, and she saw that for the first time he really looked ill. After much discussion with the concert venues, the last four concerts of the tour were cancelled, and they flew back to Memphis with Elvis spending four days in hospital and Priscilla and Lisa Marie flying in to visit. Ginger got on well with Priscilla and she could also see how much Lisa Marie and Elvis loved each other, with Lisa Marie hiding in the garden, not wanting to leave to go back to LA.

A Concerned Fiancée

Elvis' erratic behaviour was beginning to be of concern to Ginger and this was brought to a head one day when she and Elvis were sitting in his bedroom at Graceland talking, and the commode in the bathroom started making a noise. This was clearly annoying Elvis, and he went out of the room and returned with a machine gun. To the amazement of Ginger, he marched right past her into the bathroom and blasted the commode to pieces. Ginger was horrified and angry. How could Elvis think that was acceptable? She knew he would not purposely hurt her, but she decided to leave before Elvis emerged from the bathroom, going to her parent's house where she waited to hear from Elvis, as she did want their relationship to work. They were soon reconciled, and Ginger accompanied him on his April tour of 13 days.

Elvis Shares His Plans

On 22nd April, in Elvis' suite at the Hilton Hotel in Detroit, Larry Geller was having a conversation that took a turn he will always remember. Elvis became very serious and spoke of his nagging health problems: his spastic colon, glaucoma, hypertension, insomnia, sore throats and his fluid retention and bloated condition. He was fully cognisant of all the pills and prescription drugs he was taking, and his unhealthy eating habits. He said that it was a miracle he was still in one piece, and he had definite plans to change his lifestyle and career. He wanted to write a book to put the "record straight," having heard the rumours of his sacked aides planning to write a "tell-all" book. He wanted to tell of his spiritual quest, the vision he had in the Arizona desert, his total belief in God, his struggle to remain healthy, even his medications – then his real story would be known, and he wanted Larry to help him. As we know this never came about, though Larry has written extensively about Elvis' spiritual quest.

More Concern

Another time Larry remembers was a few months before Elvis' death, in Louisville. Elvis was in his bedroom with his doctor when there was a pounding at the front door of the suite. The Colonel entered and went into the bedroom. Larry could see that Elvis was semiconscious and Elvis' doctor was dunking his head into a bucket of ice water while Elvis was moaning.

Larry thought for a moment that a crisis point had come which would force those around Elvis to realise he needed help. He thought to himself, "OK, this is good because the Colonel finally saw the reality. Elvis should be in a hospital; he should not be on tour." However, Larry reports, "About a minute and a half later, Colonel Parker came out and walked up to me and stared coldly into my eyes and said, 'The only thing that's important now is that man is on the stage tonight.' And he walked out. And my heart dropped."

When the doctor left, Elvis called Larry and said "Larry, my life's on the line and I know it. I've been hiding from the truth for too long. There are too many people around me that I've outgrown." He also said that they would go to Hawaii for at least a year and that he was going to get off the pills, read, meditate, and get healthy. He wanted a new life.

Later on, a short time before he died, he also said to Larry, "After I leave this earth, I hope my fans all over the world will begin their own search for God, not with fear, but with joy, knowing that love is the key to the kingdom of God." Then he smiled at Larry with a gleam in his eyes and said, "When that day comes Larry, sing no sad songs for me, I'll be going home."

***

Elvis returned to Memphis and spent most of the next two weeks in his bedroom at Graceland, occasionally taking motorcycle rides around the grounds.

He started his two-week tour in Knoxville, Tennessee on 20th May. Most of the reviews of these shows note that Elvis was still singing well, seemed mostly energetic, though tired easily and sometimes had to leave the stage for up to half an hour. Some critics felt that Elvis was "just going through the motions" but that his fans were as adoring and uncritical as ever. They screamed and shouted, and there was always a rush for the stage when he started handing out scarves.

Elvis returned to Memphis on the 2nd of June and presented Kathy Westmoreland and Larry Geller with a Lincoln Mark V car each as a reward for their continued loyalty.

Elvis Knows That He Will Die Soon

Kathy Westmoreland remembers one of the final conversations she had with Elvis. She says that Elvis revealed his biggest fears about his career, how he would be remembered, as well as his conviction that he would die young, like many in his family.

Kathy says, "He asked me out of the blue, 'How are people going to remember me?' He was worried that they weren't going to remember him much at all. He said, 'I haven't done anything classic.'

"When I first met him, he told me that he knew exactly how much time he had, that he thought he was going to die at the age of 42, close to the age of his mother. It was in her family, her father, grandfather, her whole family – they were born with a heart that was twice the size on one side as it was on the other, and he also told me that he had bone cancer."

***

In a rambling phone call with President Jimmy Carter in June, Elvis tried to help his friend George Klein in a Federal court case.

The June tour, of ten days, began in Springfield, Missouri. Two of the shows were filmed for the CBS TV special, "Elvis in Concert," but it is the one in Rapid City, South Dakota, which was the better show, the highlight of which was Elvis sitting at the piano singing *Unchained Melody*. One reporter, Steve Millburg, mentioned that it was when Elvis sang gospel songs that his voice sounded the most powerful and that his singing of *How Great Thou Art* silenced many of the screaming women. Millburg summed up Elvis' hold over the audience, saying, "He came off as both the supremely confident star and the bashful, disarming country boy, a pretty devastating combination."

More Erratic Behaviour

Elvis had arrived at Madison airport at 1am, on 24th June, still in his stage suit from the previous concert in Des Moines. Driving to the hotel, when stopped at some traffic lights Elvis noticed what appeared to be a fight breaking out between three men at a petrol station. He lowered the window and watched for a moment, then before anyone could stop him, he got out of the car and approached the men. He assumed a karate stance and spoke to them. This could have been a very difficult situation but, within a few moments, they were all smiling and shaking hands. Elvis even posed with them for photos, otherwise who of their friends the next day would believe what happened?

Elvis displayed some more rather erratic behaviour in Cincinnati. The air conditioning at his hotel was not adequate for him and, instead of contacting the hotel manager or getting one of his entourage to find another hotel, he marched off down the street in his jogging suit to find a more suitable hotel. His surprised, if not shocked, entourage rushed after him to witness Elvis trying to get rooms at another hotel, with crowds gradually gathering, as the news that Elvis was on the loose spread. Eventually, he was able to get a room for himself and Ginger and one for some of the guys to share. However, after the show, Elvis returned to Graceland to sleep before setting off for Indianapolis the next day.

Final Concert

No one knew, but this concert on 26th June at Market Square Arena in Indianapolis was not only the last concert of this tour, but also the last concert Elvis would ever perform, and it was one which Todd Slaughter would remember well.

Todd, President of the Official Elvis Presley Fan Club of Great Britain, had been taking fans out to Las Vegas to see Elvis in concert for several years. He is a big fan of Elvis and says, "Elvis has been a strength to me during my life." Todd knew the Colonel, who always treated the Brits as something special. For example, in 1972, the Colonel arranged a private party for the group so that he could entertain and meet the 200 British fans who had come to Las Vegas. He also had arranged for Elvis to greet the British fans from the stage during his concert and for some of the fans, including Todd, to meet Elvis.

This time the Colonel suggested that Todd bring fans to see Elvis on tour, which he did, and that was why they were present at the very last ever Elvis concert. Todd had met Elvis twice before at events and presented him with a trophy from the British Fan Club. That day, the Colonel had arranged for Todd to meet Elvis as he came off the plane in Indianapolis. Todd waited on the tarmac at the bottom of the stairs of the aircraft. Elvis appeared and carefully descended the stairs, had a chat with Todd and said, among other things, "When you come to the States you give me awards. The Colonel and I thought you should have this," and he presented Todd with a trophy for being UK Fan Club President for 10 years. He also stood on Todd's foot as they were asked to get closer for a photo.

Todd reports that Elvis' last concert was "bloody brilliant!" even though Elvis was struggling with his weight and breathing. Many considered it the best of the tour.

Todd says that a lady working with the TV network at the time said to him, "If you get close to Elvis, have a good look at his skin as our makeup artist believes that he is seriously ill and may have only six months to live." As it turned out that six months was only six weeks.

The TV Special was not aired until 3rd October that year. Myrna Smith of the Sweet Inspirations remembers that, on the night of that last show, she told Jerry Schilling that it went really well. Jerry asked, "Well, how did Elvis look?" She replied, "He really looks good, he's lost a little weight." But afterwards, when she watched the TV special, she was shocked, as so many were, and said [of those close to Elvis on stage], "We were all wearing blinders."

Final Words to J D Sumner

For J D Sumner this concert was the last time he saw Elvis. When he walked into his dressing room after the show, Elvis put his arms around his neck and hugged him. He told J D that he wanted him to come to Graceland as he wanted to talk to J D about something he thought he would like. As J D left the room, Elvis said, "J D I love you." Those were the last words he ever heard Elvis say. Over the next few weeks, J D went to Graceland, but the guys told him that Elvis was upstairs in his bedroom not feeling well and that he didn't want to see anyone. J D did not make an issue of it, and one wonders what might have happened if he had. Did Elvis want to make definite arrangements for the all-gospel show they had discussed? It is a question we will not know the answer to this side of heaven.

Lisa Marie Remembers Her Father

Elvis spent most of July in his bedroom rarely seeing anyone from outside. Dr Nick was in attendance and Ginger, although she had not moved into Graceland, stayed with Elvis overnight, going home to see her family and get changes of clothes as well as bringing her niece, Amber, to Graceland to play with Lisa Marie, who had arrived for a two-week holiday. The two girls were of a similar age and had become friends.

So how did nine-year-old Lisa Marie deal with her father's strange lifestyle and failing health? First and foremost, she knew that she was very much loved by him, and she loved him too. She recalls, "He was very protective, very adoring, very watchful. I knew that I was loved, there was no question about that. It's not easy to come by, obviously, but it was very apparent to me. And it was very mutual."

However, she remembers that even at that young age she was aware something was wrong. and she could sense that he was in trouble: "I actually said to him, 'Please, you're not going to die, are you? Don't die.' I didn't know then what was going on. I wish I had. I didn't have any clue what was happening. I just thought, 'He's not happy.'" She also remembers seeing his stomach and being worried to death over that. She would sometimes go and check on him and see him in a bad state. She says, "It was just starting to become too common. He was not too happy. He was in such an ivory tower and so untouchable and so alienated."

"Elvis What Happened?"

The book, "Elvis What Happened?" was published on 4th August. This revealing book, by sacked members of Elvis entourage Red and Sonny West and Dave Hebler, exposes Elvis' dangerous addiction to prescription drugs, which they could see was killing him.

Some believe that they published the book to punish Elvis for firing them, but I am inclined to believe that the overriding motive was one of desperation, hoping that it would shock Elvis into tackling his addiction. The authors were aware of all the good aspects of Elvis, and Red West once chided a reporter: "You should write some of the good things down. Why is it that everyone wants to know the ugly? What about the good? What about the time Elvis read about this coloured lady in North Memphis? She didn't have any legs – only these stumps which she had to drag herself around on. Elvis read that and got so upset that he had a top-of-the-line wheelchair bought and delivered. He sent it over in his limo."

However, as the tone of the book was overall negative about Elvis, he was very distressed, and it did not have the (perhaps) intended positive effect.

More Fun of the Fair

As a special treat for Lisa Marie and her friend Amber, on 8th August, Elvis rented Libertyland Fairgrounds in the early morning hours. Accompanied by Ginger and some other family friends they all had a good time, staying there till 6.30am. Even Elvis appeared to enjoy himself, especially on the Zippin Pippin roller coaster on which they rode in the front car, with Elvis' hands high in the air. In earlier days he would stand up as it hurtled down the steep inclines. (I have been on that roller coaster – how could an old wooden roller coaster be scary? It was – my heart was in my mouth!)

Yet Another Concerned Friend

On 12th August, Linda Thompson, Elvis' live-in girlfriend for four years, who had looked after him so well, had a strong urge to talk to Elvis. She had been thinking about him all week and had a strong sense of foreboding. She called Graceland and told Charlie Hodge that she was concerned about Elvis and just wanted to check on him. Charlie replied that Elvis was fine, he was sleeping. Linda was not satisfied so asked Charlie to go and check on Elvis, which he did and a few minutes later reported back that Elvis was fine, he was alone, he was sleeping, and his breathing was fine. She asked Charlie to give Elvis her love, but she still felt uneasy. She was certain that Elvis was in trouble. Four days later, on 16th August she found out why when Lisa Marie phoned her to tell her that her Daddy was dead. A short time later Elvis' father, Vernon, also phoned her with the news.

Still Searching

Elvis and Ginger went motorcycling on 14th August. Sometime that week, Elvis asked Larry Geller to bring him the new books he had recommended. One was "The Scientific Search For The Face Of Jesus" and, by some reports, it was the book he was reading at the time of his death. This is a book that looks at the scientific evidence for Jesus, by examining the Turin Shroud, which is a linen sheet that carries an imprinted image of the front and the back of a crucified man, including the face. The imprint shows the peculiar characteristics that belong to a photographic negative. If Elvis was looking to science to support his faith in the crucified Christ, then he had slipped a long way from his original simple faith, but he was desperately searching for the spiritual Jesus, who himself exhorted us to ask in prayer, "So I say to you: Ask and it will be given to you; seek and you will find; knock and the door will be opened to you. For everyone who asks receives; the one who seeks finds; and to the one who knocks, the door will be opened." (Luke 11:9-10)

On 15th August, Elvis awoke at his usual time of 4pm and watched TV most of the day before attending his dental appointment with Ginger at 10.30pm.

On his return to Graceland, just after midnight, Elvis had a conversation with Joe Esposito regarding the arrangements for departing that evening for the next concert tour. He also spoke with Sam Thompson, about arrangements for taking Lisa Marie back to LA.

Final Hours

Rick Stanley, one of Elvis' stepbrothers, was on duty that night to deliver Elvis his sleep medications.

Rick had grown up with Elvis as his big brother who was great fun and who cared for him. As a young boy, Rick thought of Elvis as a film star who sang, and he could not really understand why people made such a fuss about him. It was not till the age of 15, when he attended Elvis' opening show in Las Vegas that he finally "got it." Rick says, "I was mesmerised by Elvis' hypnotic ability to single us out and pull us into his song. He was magnificent. He had a power that lifted you up, made you think anything was possible – that gave you hope, consoled your loneliness and inspired you to start again."

Later, when Rick joined Elvis' entourage for the concerts, he started taking uppers and downers, as did almost everybody else in the group. He then started experimenting with cocaine and heroin and soon became addicted, and even ended up in police custody, from which Elvis rescued him. He went into detox for a while, but left against medical advice and returned to Graceland, supposedly to help "take care" of Elvis, but as he said, "I wasn't doing much of a job of taking care of me." So, by August 1977, he was still in quite a state, even though his Christian girlfriend of several years, Robyn, had stuck by him and prayed for him and continued to tell him of his need for Jesus.

At 3am on 16th August, Rick delivered Elvis his first round of sleeping medications. He found Elvis sitting on his bed surrounded by books, one the Bible, one about the Shroud of Turin, and other spiritual books. He told Elvis about a conversation he had just had with Robyn, about his need for Jesus. Elvis said, "She's right, Rick you know that don't you? People who tell you about Jesus really care." Rick was shocked and stared at Elvis who he said looked so tired and so bewildered.

Elvis then waved the "Elvis What Happened?" book at Rick and said, "What am I going to do about this?" Rick tried to make some reassuring comments that the fans loved him and would not take any notice of it.

Elvis then said, "Let's pray" and motioned Rick to sit on his bed. Rick had overheard Elvis pray just one day previously, praying, "God, forgive me for my sins. Let people have compassion and understanding of the things I have done." This time he prayed, "Dear Lord, please show me a way, I am tired and confused and I need your help." He then looked up and softly said something that Rick says he would remember to his dying day. "Rick, we should all begin to live for Christ[4]."

Rick cried inside as he so desperately wanted to help his big brother whom he loved and admired, but who was now a pitiful sight. He remembered how Elvis had been patient with him and even seen his good points and potential, saying that someday Rick would have a big impact on the youth of the country. Here Elvis was being prophetic, as Rick, who gave his life to Christ shortly after Elvis died, became an influential evangelist.

Rick left Elvis to return at around 4am to deliver the second round of sleeping medication. Elvis told him he wouldn't need any more and would call him if he did. After that, being strung out and tired, Rick took several sleeping pills and fell fast asleep in a basement bedroom.

Elvis was still not able to get to sleep, (perhaps because of placebos in his medication, which Dr. Nick did every so often to try to prevent Elvis taking too many drugs). So, he called his cousin Billy and his wife Jo to join Ginger and himself to play racquetball. They played for a while but Elvis soon tired and sat at the piano in the racquetball building and played a few gospel songs before ending with *Blue Eyes Crying in the Rain.*

Elvis and Ginger retired to Elvis bedroom about 6am. At 6.45 Elvis called for his third packet of medication and some painkillers for Ginger who was suffering from menstrual cramps. As they settled into bed, Elvis showed Ginger a couple of the new books he had, including "A Scientific Search for the Face of Jesus." They both soon became drowsy and fell asleep. Around 9am Ginger felt Elvis get out of bed saying he couldn't sleep and was going into the bathroom to read. Ginger soon fell back asleep and didn't wake till around 2pm.

---

[4] In the Bible passage where this theme, that "we should all begin to live for Christ occurs" is 2 Corinthians 5:15. The main emphasis is on reconciliation. Jesus came to reconcile men to God, and those who want to live for Christ are urged to be ambassadors for God, to represent God on earth and have a ministry of reconciliation.

Lisa Marie remembers that morning. She says that around 4am, "I was supposed to be asleep, actually. He found me and told me 'Go to bed.' I said 'OK.' I think he kissed me again and then I ran off. He came in and kissed me good night after that. That was the last time I saw him alive."

So, Elvis had retired to the bathroom to read. Exactly what happened next, we don't know, except one of the maids on the ground floor thought she heard a thump on the bathroom floor above, sometime mid-morning.

When Ginger awoke and found that Elvis was not in bed, after she had dealt with the start of her period, she knocked on Elvis' bathroom door. As there was no answer and the door was partly opened, she slowly opened it more and peered in to see Elvis on the floor in front of the commode looking as if his body had completely frozen in the sitting position when he fell off. His head was slightly turned with his cheek resting on the floor. She bent down calling his name and felt the skin on his back which was cool. His face was blotchy, and gently lifting his closed eyelid she could see that his eye was blood shot and looking straight ahead. She immediately called downstairs for help, and from then on Elvis' entourage took over, trying cardio resuscitation, and calling for an ambulance and Dr Nick.

When the paramedics arrived and tried to revive Elvis, Lisa Marie suddenly appeared in the bedroom doorway asking, "What's wrong with my Daddy?" Ginger gently moved her away towards her own bedroom saying, "Nothing, Lisa." However, Lisa was having none of this and marched back down to her father's room saying, "Something's wrong and I'm going to find out." Ginger shouted to warn those in the bathroom that Lisa was on her way, and they were able to close and lock the door before she got there.

Everyone at Graceland was in a state of shock. However, the practicalities had to be dealt with and Elvis was eventually transferred to the hospital where more resuscitation was attempted, though everyone could see that he had been dead for some time. He was pronounced dead at 3.30pm, saying that early tests indicated the cause of death was a cardiac arrhythmia due to undetermined heartbeat. To those close to Elvis, it came as no surprise that the toxicology report that came out weeks later revealed high levels of pharmaceutical painkillers such as Dilaudid, Quaalude, Percodan, Demerol, and codeine in Elvis's body. The final analysis appears to be that Elvis' death was due to a series of medical conditions (which we have already discovered), not helped by a toxic combination of pharmaceuticals, all of which took a toll on his heart.

Devastation

To those at Graceland, if finding Elvis in such a state was a shock, the news of his death was devastating. Most were crying in disbelief. However, they comforted each other as best they could. Before she left to go to her home, Ginger was able to spend some time with Lisa to tell her that her Daddy loved her, that he was a wonderful father and that he had gone to heaven but would always be watching over her. Lisa received this in silence, at the age of nine, not yet understanding what had happened. She said later, "His body was in the house for three days and there was something oddly comforting about that which made it not necessarily real for me. I stayed in there with it almost the whole time."

I wonder if Lisa later remembered and was comforted by a Bible which she had been given and which Elvis had received from a fan, Mary Harriss. Gladys gave it to Patsy Presley, Uncle Vester Presley's daughter. Patsy later gave it to Lisa Marie and wrote the inscription which says:

Lisa, your dad's mother gave me this little Bible on your dad's birthday in 1957. Many people sent Bibles to Elvis throughout his lifetime. As you can see a fan sent it to him, he always appreciated his Bibles and read them over and over. I hope you will enjoy it and that reading the scriptures will bring you joy and peace. Love, Patsy

She then wrote on another page:

I know in my heart this is the book your daddy had in his hands in the dream I had of him three days after his death. If you have forgotten the story, I will be glad to tell you, once again, all about it. It was a good dream. I love and respect you Lisa and want you to have all the wonderful blessings promised in this little Bible. When you have free time, just enjoy reading this Bible.

Meanwhile, as the news spread around the world, fans began to congregate at Graceland and flowers arrived.

When Eddie Fadal, Elvis' friend from Texas heard the news, he immediately flew out to Memphis to offer any help he could, which included being at the gates helping to deal with the thousands of fans and deliveries of flowers and gifts. Apparently, although the police were out in force, it took some wise decisions and words to prevent the gates being stormed which would have injured, or even killed, many people.

Suzanna's Dream

In the UK, Suzanna Leigh who starred with Elvis in "Paradise Hawaiian Style" and who is very spiritually aware, reports that around eight o'clock on the night of 16th August 1977, she went to bed and fell asleep almost immediately. She had a dream where she woke up in a large room, more a space really, of the most brilliant luminous white – in fact, the white she had seen before when she died after a car crash (She had died in the hospital with serious injuries and loss of blood and had an out of the body experience looking down at the medics working on her "dead" body.)

In this dream, she saw Elvis standing before her dressed in white, the young slim Elvis she first met. He smiled at her and said, with his eyes sparkling, "There is something I have to tell you baby! I have been sick baby, but I'm in no pain now." She replied "Have you been ill? I am so sorry" and went to move towards him but he held his hand up. "It's been in my colon but it's over now, I feel fine. Tell them all I love them." She asked, "Tell who?" He replied, "You will know when the time comes, I have to go now." She called to Elvis, "I love you" and he replied, "I love you too baby, always will." and melted into the whiteness and disappeared. Soon after, she was woken by a telephone call telling her that Elvis was dead.

Funeral Arrangements and Vernon's Care for the Fans

When the hospital had finished the autopsy, Elvis' body was taken to the Memphis Funeral Home where it was embalmed and placed in a copper casket and where Larry Geller and Charlie Hodge fixed Elvis' hair.

At noon on 17th August, a white hearse transported Elvis' body to Graceland where the family had a private viewing.

As well as the private viewing, Vernon, aware of the grief of the fans, wanted as many as possible to be able to view the body and say goodbye. So, at 3pm fans were allowed in to view the body placed in the hallway. Thousands of fans were able to view Elvis' body and pay their last respects over the next three hours. The mourners ranged from pre-teens to middle-aged and older men and women. Several fainted, overwhelmed by emotion and the sweltering heat. One fan, June, remembers that when she came round, she was in the Trophy Room, and someone was washing her face. She was then taken to the racquetball building to recover.

In the evening, those at Graceland had a private wake. Lisa had a silver bracelet that she wanted to put on her daddy's wrist. As she and her mother said goodbye to Elvis, they put the bracelet on his right wrist saying, "We'll miss you."

At 9am the following morning, the thousands of flowers that had been delivered to Graceland were transported to the cemetery. It took 100 vans almost four hours.

Elvis' funeral was held in the music room at Graceland at 2pm. Attending the funeral were Elvis' family and entourage and friends, including some well-known faces. The service was planned by Vernon who asked a friend of the family, Rev C W Bradley, the minister of the Wooddale Church of Christ, to preach. Rev. Rex Humbard preached a guest sermon. Vernon had also asked J D Sumner to choose songs that he felt Elvis would like at his funeral. The songs were sung by members of The Stamps Quartet, the Statesmen, Jake Hess, James Blackwood and Kathy Westmoreland. Songs included *The Lighthouse, I Can Feel the Touch Of His Hand, When It's My Time, Known Only To Him, How Great Thou Art, My Heavenly Father, Sweet, Sweet Spirit, His Hand in Mine* and several others which were not on the quickly-planned, hand-written order of service.

Joe Moscheo remembers that when Jake Hess sang *Known Only to Him* with such feeling, it seemed as if he was singing it straight to Elvis and allowing them to listen.

Elvis' guitar player, James Burton remembers that when they were getting ready to sing *How Great Thou Art*, Joe Guercio, the leader of the orchestra that played at Elvis concerts, said, "I have directed Elvis singing *How Great Thou Art* many times on stage. Would you allow me to direct it just one more time?" Which he did. James said that as he was singing, he looked at Joe and there were big tears rolling down his face.

Although the funeral was scheduled to last only half an hour, it went on for almost two hours.

Rex Humbard spoke to try to comfort those present and talked about the time he and his wife met with Elvis in Las Vegas between shows.

Funeral Sermon

In his funeral sermon C W Bradley said:

"Words do not take away from a man's life and words do not add to a man's life in the sight of God. Though I will make several personal observations concerning Elvis, and from them seek to encourage us, it is not my purpose to try to eulogise him, this is being done by thousands throughout the world.

"We are here to honour the memory of a man loved by millions. Elvis can serve as an inspiring example of the great potential of one human being who has a strong desire and unfailing determination. From total obscurity, Elvis rose to world fame. His name is a household word in every nook and corner of this earth. Though idolized by millions and forced to be protected from the crowds, Elvis never lost his desire to stay in close touch with humanity.

"In a society that has talked so much about the generation gap, the closeness of Elvis and his father and his constant dependence upon Vernon's counsel was heart-warming to observe. Elvis never forgot his family. In a thousand ways he showed his great love for them.

"In a world where so many pressures are brought upon us to lose our identity, to be lost in the masses, Elvis dared to be different. Elvis was different and no one can ever be exactly like him. Wherever and whenever his voice was heard, everybody knew that was Elvis Presley.

"But Elvis was a frail human being. And he would be the first to admit his weakness. Perhaps because of his rapid rise to fame and fortune, he was thrown into temptations that some never experience. Elvis would not want anyone to think that he had no flaws or faults. But now that he's gone, I find it more helpful to remember his good qualities, and I hope you do too.

"We are here to offer comfort and encouragement to Elvis' family. There is much encouragement in all the beautiful flowers sent by loving hands and hearts from around the world. There is so much encouragement in the presence of so many who have crowded into our city in addition to those here, and from knowing that literally millions throughout the earth have their hearts turned in this direction at this hour. There is also much encouragement from the beautiful music. But the greatest comfort and strength comes from knowing there is a God in heaven who looks upon us with love and compassion and who says, 'I will never leave you nor forsake you!'"

He then went on to quote from the hymn by S M T Henry, *I Know My Heavenly Father Knows.*

"We are here to be reminded that soon we too must depart this life. The Bible vividly emphasizes the brevity and uncertainty of life. Once, when King Saul was chasing David across the country, David said, 'There is but a step between me and death' and none of us knows when he shall take that step.

"Elvis died at 42. Some of you may not live to be that old. But it's not how long we live that is really important, but how we live. If we reject the Bible, then personally I find that life has no real meaning. The Bible teaches us that God's plans and purposes for man culminated in the death and resurrection of His son on a cross. Jesus lives today. And because He lives, through Him we too can have hope of a life beyond the grave.

"Thus, today I hold up Jesus Christ to all of us. And challenge each of you to commit your heart and life to Him. May these moments of quiet and thoughtful meditation and reflection of Elvis' life serve to help us to reflect upon our own lives and to re-examine our own lives. And may these moments help us to reset our compass. All of us sometimes get going in the wrong direction."

Afterwards, the coffin was loaded into a white hearse which drove three miles to Forest Hill Cemetery, followed by the mourners in 17 white limousines. There was a short service in the white marble Mausoleum Chapel, then the coffin was placed in a crypt, a few hundred yards from his mother's grave outside.

Vernon had arranged for the flowers and floral arrangements at the cemetery to be given to fans the following morning to take home as a memento and one last gift. More than 50,000 fans came that morning and by noon every single flower was gone.

Grieving in London, UK

Meanwhile, on 18th August 1977 in the UK, a memorial service was held for Elvis in London. Major Joy Webb of the Salvation Army remembers it well. She had a phone call from Rev Donald Churchman, the Anglican priest of Christ Church, Cockfosters saying that he had been asked by the Official Elvis Presley Fan Club of Great Britain to conduct a memorial service for Elvis. He told her that he felt he should do that, as who was he to discourage people from coming to church to pray. The Fan Club had also asked if the "Joystrings," of which Joy was a member, could sing at the service. Although the group no longer sang together, Joy was happy to grab her guitar and a friend to accompany her to the church. She said she had no trouble finding it as there were many people streaming towards it. They were crowding in the graveyard because the church was already packed full. Her uniform acted as a passport to get through the crowd into the church and meet the minister, who decided that they needed to have a second service, to which she readily agreed.

While waiting for the service to begin, Elvis gospel songs were being played, including *You'll Never Walk Alone*. The church was full of flowers and smelt beautiful. Joy said that many of the young men were in their "uniform" – winkle picker shoes, drainpipe trousers, Teddy Boy jackets and ducktail hairstyles. The girls had bouffant skirts and hairstyles. She noted that many of the congregation were tear-stained and disheartened with sincere grief, and she had the opportunity before the service to talk with some and try to comfort them. During the service, Joy sang *It is No Secret What God Can Do*, to the accompaniment of many sobs. The minister spoke lovingly about Elvis, warts, and all, of the loving God whom Elvis knew, who, because of Jesus, accepts everyone as his child. After the service, the congregation filed out to allow the second congregation in. They were not, however, keen to get away and stayed in the churchyard listening to the service again by the open doors or on the recordings they had made.

Fond Remembrances

Many people put their remembrances of Elvis into words, here are just a few of them:

Michelle, Priscilla's sister: "I was five years old when I met Elvis and thirteen when he and Priscilla married. Naturally, I was nervous. Like most kids, I was insecure ... especially around a big star. I remember we watched a movie together – Priscilla, Elvis, and I – and the story got me upset. It was "Chastity," where Cher plays a runaway. Elvis was concerned that the film had affected me so powerfully. He was incredibly sensitive to my reaction. Later he read passages from the Bible. That took me by surprise, but I also found it comforting. He read with beautiful feeling and told Bible stories with great flair and sincerity."

Patsy Gambill, Elvis' double first cousin: "Elvis loved to talk about the Bible and discuss it. One thing about Elvis, he knew his Bible. He also knew he had the gift of making the Bible come alive. That's why he couldn't resist putting on those performances for those of us lucky enough to be living with him. It was always a treat!"

Priscilla: "He'd stand before the roaring fireplace and preach. He'd get up on the table and preach. He'd gather us all around – at Graceland or in Bel Air, in Hawaii or even Las Vegas – and he was Moses with a cane coming down the mountain or John the Baptist greeting the Savior. He was absolutely mesmerizing when he read scripture and acted out the stories. Of course, he'd give them his own twist, but that made it even better. It was the gospel according to Elvis, and you couldn't help but hang on every word."

Patti Parry: Patti was the only female member of the Memphis Mafia. This is how she remembers her times with Elvis:

"I practically lived at his LA homes. He bought me gifts and I ate there every night, going over to the house every day after work. Elvis was like my family because I knew him since I was 17 and so we grew up together. He brought me up. His women knew our relationship was like brother and sister. But with Linda, you know, I got on so well with her. She's such an incredibly nice woman. She was the most fun, so wonderful. You know she looked after him so well. But living with Elvis was really difficult. You really had to be mother, sister and confidant.

"It was very hard to say "no" to Elvis. In fact, Dr Nick was a very nice man, but he got caught up in the, how do I word it, 'The Elvis syndrome.' Nobody could say, "No". In fact, I always managed to be honest with him and told him the truth. I gave him hell when he needed it and he respected that. But Elvis was very crafty, he knew how to work around you!

"When we were at Graceland, we'd all be eating like red-eye gravy and grits together. Those were some of my favourite times when Elvis and the guys would sit around and just sing gospel songs. In fact, the guys commented, when I was singing along, that I was Jewish and shouldn't know all those songs. But I loved that music.

"I last saw him about seven months before he died. He wasn't looking good, and it worried me. When I got the call about him dying, I ran to Linda's house."

Jerry Schilling: When he heard the news of Elvis' death, he was living in LA in a house that Elvis had bought for him. He says that he arrived at the airport in LA early and found that no one had yet boarded the plane [to fly to

Memphis]. He went into familiar surroundings, knowing that Elvis would not be boarding the plane ever again. He walked to the bedroom at the back, already laid out for Elvis to take up residence the next day. Neatly laid out on the bed were a pair of pyjamas, and a few of his favourite books were on the night table, some opened to the page where he had stopped reading. Jerry says, "alone in that bedroom, looking at my friend's empty pyjamas, I found myself wanting to touch something of his. I sat on his bed and grabbed his pyjama top, holding it close. I sat there for just a moment, then went back to the conference room and sat in one of the leather chairs and waited for the others to arrive."

Wanda Hill: "As for Elvis' death, I think that he died as he wanted, at home, with his friends, and everything was all right, just as he said it would be. He was tired, worn out and he was struggling to face the audience looking bloated and being unable to move around as he thought he ought to on stage.

"His health had become a big issue, he couldn't figure out what to do, what he ought to do, but he had hope of getting some time off and getting himself back together. He fully knew what was going on, he knew that things had to change and that he had to do something himself – it wasn't going to be done for him this time. He was in pain, from his colon problems, from his back hurting and his legs and from being given so many pills by his doctors – I don't know how he managed as long as he did!

"He often spoke of his early childhood, had a super memory, and talked about lots of events in his early life, including seeing angels, talking to bright, shiny men, and having memories of talking with Jesus as a young boy. I believed him. And he didn't feel odd or embarrassed telling me."

James Burton, Elvis' guitarist: "What a heart-wrenching three days we had that August in 1977. I'll never forget flying out of LA to Las Vegas that morning of the 16th, then we headed out from Vegas to our first show in Maine when we got word to turn around. None of us knew why. We stopped to refuel in Colorado to head back to Las Vegas when we heard the news that Elvis had passed. My first question was, 'Is this a joke?' Unfortunately, it wasn't."

"My wife Louise and I immediately met up in Memphis to go to Graceland to check on Elvis' Dad, Vernon. As you can imagine, he was just heartbroken." James then described the funeral service. "We could hardly talk to each other; we were in so much shock. So many people that loved him showed up. James Brown spent hours in there with Elvis' body, as did so many others. Louise and I sat there with Vernon and did our best to comfort him. We loved that man."

James and his wife were amazed at all the love people showed and how many had journeyed from all over the world to pay their respects.

James commented; "Elvis constantly gave to those around him and that was such an inspiration. Yes, he was a legend, but Elvis was also my friend. His talent, style, sense of humour and 'in the middle of the night' phone calls just to talk.

"He is dearly missed, and I know he's in Heaven singing and playing with my son, Jeffrey, and I'm looking forward to seeing them both again someday and we'll all jam together."

Wayne Carman: Elvis' friend and karate instructor last saw Elvis alive in late 1974 when he "looked really sharp. His technique was crisp and powerful, and his movements were graceful." Elvis explained to Wayne how karate had helped him, saying, "Wayne, when I'm training, I eat, sleep and even feel better. Sometimes it gets too much though, with the travelling, concerts and business, it becomes a struggle to keep it up."

As well as being a karate instructor, Wayne was a Special Officer in the Memphis Police and helped the security team control the crowds which gathered outside Graceland and get everything ready for the funeral. The news of Elvis' death was "an incredible shock" to Wayne. Elvis had always seemed immortal. "A person so charismatic and larger than life doesn't just 'up and die' at the age of 42." It was startling for him to see his friend, lying in state, however, he takes comfort in knowing that Elvis is in heaven, walking the streets of gold, free of pain and trouble.

George Otis Snr: George pioneered Christian radio and television in the Middle East and influenced millions of Christians around the world. Before that, however, he hosted TV and radio programmes in California where he lived at the time. His energetic enthusiasm for the gospel helped him touch the lives of actors, athletes, and politicians, including Ronald Reagan. He remembers prophesying over Ronald Reagan in late 1960s that "If you walk uprightly before Me, you will reside at 1600 Pennsylvania Avenue" (The White House). Ronald Reagan became President of the USA in 1981.

George remembers interviewing Elvis for one of his TV programmes in the 1970s. He found Elvis to be a very humble, nice person who had a close walk with the Lord. The programme was never aired, as the Colonel felt that Elvis spoke out too much about his faith.

In 1977, George wrote the foreword for the book "Elvis" written by Richard Mann. In his foreword, George acknowledges the battle Elvis had since becoming famous, the battle between Elvis as he was meant to be and the 'Elvis' that was expected of him.

Rev. Jack Hyles: He pastored a church in Texas and only met Elvis once, but it gave him an opportunity which he gladly took. One day, while he was at a radio station waiting for the lift to take him up to the studio to record a programme, the lift door opened, and he saw Elvis and his entourage. The guys tried to stop Jack from entering the lift, but Elvis said it was OK.

As the elevator was going up, Jack, who was always evangelistically inclined, decided to go for it and struck up a conversation with Elvis asking him if he died that evening, did he know for sure that he would go to heaven. Elvis replied that he did. Jack asked him how he knew that. Elvis replied that, when he was young, he had gone down to the altar in a small Pentecostal church and had given his heart to Jesus and asked Him to be his personal Saviour.

Elvis then explained that he was no longer involved with a church as they had too many rules, but that he had always loved gospel music and hoped to do a whole lot more of it. When Jack got to his floor, he shook hands with Elvis and said that he and his church would be praying for him, for which Elvis thanked him.

President Carter: "Elvis Presley's death deprives our country of a part of itself. He was unique and irreplaceable. More than 20 years ago, he burst upon the scene with an impact that was unprecedented and will probably never be equalled. His music and his personality, fusing the styles of White country and Black rhythm and blues, permanently changed the face of American popular culture. His following was immense, and he was a symbol to people the world over of the vitality, rebelliousness, and good humor of his country."

Mick Jagger: He immediately recognised, as many did, that Elvis was unique and special. He first saw him in his first concert in Vegas in 1969. He says that this epic show was nothing like he had ever seen and that is still true today. Mick loved Elvis and the saddest day of his life was when he learned of his death. The Rolling Stones were rehearsing for their next tour when they heard that Elvis was dead. Mick says, "We all stopped what we were doing and none of us said a word, that moment seemed to have lasted forever. There were tears in the room. Keith had his guitar in his hands, and he was shaking, then he started playing the opening riffs of *Can't Help Falling in Love,* and that's what we all sang together. I am proud to say that I love Elvis and that I am an Elvis fan. I can't wait to sing with him when it is time for me to leave this world."

Dr Tony Stone: I did not know Dr Tony Stone at this time. He is an evangelist and former Chaplain of the London Palladium. I met him in 1995, the year I became an Elvis fan, and he is now the Chaplain of our Elvis Gospel Fan Club. He certainly remembers hearing of Elvis' death. He says:

"Together with our children, Shiela and I were on a holiday in Spain when Elvis died. That morning we came out of the hotel in a popular resort invaded annually by the English, and as we walked to the beach there was a newspaper shop with a big headline sheet outside announcing 'The King is dead.' That immediately took my mind back to when George VI died, and someone jumped on our school bus and shouted, 'The King is dead.'

For me as an evangelist, all these things came together, and for many years I would use the events as a simple gospel illustration along the lines of Elvis is dead, but Jesus is alive – using the obvious anagram of Elvis – LIVES. I then shared Elvis's testimony as I got to understand it more. It went down well, particularly with youth. I often used visual aids to get the truth home."

It was in 1978 that Dr Tony Stone virtually "stepped into Elvis' shoes."

"It was Syracuse NY. I had conducted a series of Crusades through Youth for Christ in that city and the local organisers wanted to have a final Crusade during the Easter period the year following Elvis' death. They had tried for the largest indoor arena in the city – only to find it was already booked for an Elvis visit. When the organisers heard the news of Elvis' death, they again applied for a booking at the arena. It was accepted, as the Elvis organisation had cancelled, due to the sad death of Elvis. The arena held thousands, and ultimately, we held our final rally there. There was a large response to the gospel invitation and amongst those coming forward was our young son Julian – what a joy for a parent. He is now an assistant pastor of a large church in the Sherwood Forest and father of four grown-up children!"

So where was Madeleine Wilson, the author of this book about Elvis, on 16th August 1977? At the time of the death of Elvis, I was a wife and mother of two young children very much involved with family matters. Although I listened to Elvis as a teenager in the 50s, I was not a fan and do not even remember hearing about Elvis' death, let alone what I was doing at the time. Although I do remember the street party that we had for Queen Elizabeth's Silver Jubilee in June 1977.

Elvis' and His Mother's Body Reunited at Graceland

Soon after the funeral, on 3rd October there was a failed break-in by graverobbers and, because of fears of another attempt, Elvis' coffin was moved to and buried in the Meditation Garden at Graceland along with Elvis' mother's body. The large statue of Jesus and the footstone from Gladys' grave were moved to Graceland at later dates.

The two memorials to Elvis in the Meditation Garden are the Epitaph and the Eternal Flame Memorial.

The wording of the epitaph on Elvis' tombstone, written by Janelle McComb, commissioned, and directed by Elvis' father is:

ELVIS AARON PRESLEY
January 8, 1935
August 16, 1977
Son of
Vernon Elvis Presley
and Gladys Love Presley
Father of
Lisa Marie Presley.
He was a precious gift from God
We cherished and loved dearly.
He had a God-given talent that he shared
With the world. And without a doubt,
He became most widely acclaimed;
Capturing the hearts of young and old alike.
He was admired not only as an entertainer,
But as the great humanitarian that he was;
For his generosity, and his kind feelings
For his fellow man.
He revolutionized the field of music and
Received its highest awards.
He became a living legend in his own time;
Earning the respect and love of millions.
God saw that he needed some rest and
Called him home to be with Him.
We miss you, Son and Daddy. I thank God
That He gave us you as our son.

A group of Elvis' close associates paid for and placed an eternal flame at the head of Elvis' tombstone. The inscription by Janelle McComb is on its base, followed by their names inscribed on the sides:

TO ELVIS IN MEMORIUM
You gave yourself to each of us in some manner.
You were wrapped in thoughtfulness and tied with love.
May this flame reflect our never-ending respect and love for you.
May it serve as a constant reminder to each of us of your eternal
presence.

Donors to this memorial are: Tommy Henley, Jerry Schilling, Letetia Henley, Dean Nichopoulos, Patsy Gambill, Dr George Nichopoulos, Al Strada, Janelle McComb, Felton Jarvis, Joe Esposito.

Elvis' Take on His Own Life and Death

So, what did Elvis say of his own life and death? Wanda Hill, Elvis' friend in LA, with Elvis' permission, had recorded some telephone interviews she had with him. She has written them in her book, "We Remember, Elvis." These are some things he said about his life and his death:

"I'd like to be remembered when I am gone from this earthly life to bring joy, happiness and a sense of freedom from everyday cares to other human beings. Just think of me as the red bird in the winter-worn bush on a snowy day – a bit of colour in our sometimes dreary world.

"Life isn't something that you're given because it is owed to you. It's given because you need to grow, to learn and to expand your soul and spirit life. Life is often treated as though it is just a time of play and expectation when it ought to be one of service to others. A building often seems empty because people can't picture its potential. And that's how many people's view of life is, empty, because they don't see what it could be. When I get to the point when I can't be helpful for other people in some way, then I don't want to stay here any longer. I'd like to fulfil my purpose in life, but if I can't do everything this time, then I know I'll have another chance. Life is a continuing circle – beginning with birth, ending in death, then beginning again. I believe that – just as I believe in our Heavenly Father and His kingdom everlasting. To me that is the most important thing we have to learn, God is – He always will be. Learn that and everything else comes easy. How can one walk outside and look at the midnight blue heaven, see the magnitude of stars and not know God IS? I find my breath taken away. Chills down my spine and a soaring in my heart every time I view God's heaven, a wonder to behold freely.

"You know, if you look into your own child's eyes and they look back at you, you can easily see what trust really is – and it's scary because they have such perfect love, without question they have faith. And that's what we have to have, that kind of faith when looking into our father's eyes. Perfect trust – as a little child. It must be why God gives children as a teaching tool, right before us, a reminder of what trust ought to be."

Of death, he told June, *"It just means you don't need to have that worn-out body anymore You got a great new spiritual body like Jesus, and you've left this pain-filled world."*

Gallery

Elvis looking relaxed on holiday in Hawaii, March 1977.

Elvis at his last concert on 26th July 1977, with concert ticket. (Paul Lipps Photography)

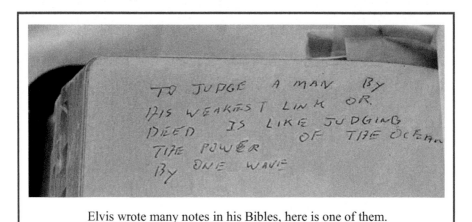

Elvis wrote many notes in his Bibles, here is one of them.

The Mausoleum in Memphis where Elvis' body was originally laid to rest, showing some of the floral tributes which were received on the announcement of his death.

Duncan Terry is comforted by Pat Jones during the Memorial Service for Elvis held in London UK on 18th August 1977 (Alamay)

Chapter 9

Life After Death

Now this is eternal life: that they know you, the only true God, and Jesus Christ, whom you have sent. (John 17:3)

Floral tributes by Elvis grave in the Mediation Garden, Graceland. The Elvis Gospel Fan Club tribute is the red and white Christian cross on the left. (J P Wilson)

In this chapter, we shall be looking not only at how the memory of Elvis is being kept alive, but also more about how the Gospel of Jesus Christ is promoted through the remembrance of Elvis' love of gospel. There is no doubt that his influence was global, anywhere people could listen to his music or watch the films or read about him.

Most probably the person closest to Elvis when he died was his father, Vernon. Elvis' daughter, Lisa Marie, was only nine years old when her father died, though she does remember that dreadful day. When people pass away there is usually an obituary, in Elvis' case there were many. However, perhaps the most personal and poignant is not officially an obituary, but what his father said when he was interviewed by Good Housekeeping magazine in January 1978, five months after Elvis' death.

Vernon Speaks

"First of all, I want to say that telling this story is going to be difficult now that Elvis is gone. Those of you who have lost loved ones, who have suffered what I am suffering now will understand what I mean.

"Yet, even while grieving I've been greatly comforted by the thousands of fans who loved Elvis and who have expressed their sympathy. They know they'll never see him perform again, but they'll always cherish the memory of the pleasure he gave them – as will I. My love for my son began even before he was born on January 8, 1935. At that time there was almost nobody poorer than my wife Gladys and me. But we were thrilled and excited when we learned that we were going to be parents. I was only 18 years old, but, throughout Gladys' pregnancy, it never occurred to me that I wouldn't be able to take care of her and the baby.

"Elvis grew up very close to his mother. He used to call her by a pet name, "Baby". He was also close to me so that we had a wonderful, balanced family relationship. I didn't choose a goal for him and then shove him in that direction. Some fathers want their sons to be football players or lawyers or whatever. I only wanted Elvis to do what made him happy.

"I don't mean that I knew that Elvis was going to be famous because at that time the idea never crossed my mind. A person doesn't have to be a singer or a movie star or a president to fill an important role in the world. He can be a truck driver or a farmer or anything else and make his contribution. I only knew that Elvis had a contribution to make one way or another, that the Lord seemed to have His hand on him.

"Whatever his private life may have been, none of his employees, friends or associates ever went without anything they wanted or needed – be it Cadillacs or diamond rings and furs for their wives. Elvis gave lavishly because it was his nature to be generous. He wanted to share his good fortune with everyone who was close to him. I remember a time not too long ago when I felt that he was carrying too big a crew, so I advised, 'You don't need all of them, especially some who just seem to be out for what they want.' Elvis stopped me cold, answering, 'You see their wants. I look beyond their wants and can see their needs.'

"I spent some of the happiest moments of my life sitting and talking with Elvis.

"A few days before he died, Elvis and I talked at Graceland for five or six hours about all sorts of things until I finally said, 'Son, I have to go home now and get something to eat.'

"'I know, Daddy,' Elvis told me. 'But I want you to know that I've really enjoyed this.' So had I."

***

Now we shall look at how some of the places where Elvis spent much of his time honour his memory.

Tupelo – the place Elvis was born and lived as a child

Elvis Presley Youth Centre – We know that when Elvis returned to Tupelo in 1956, he saw the house he was born in and 15 acres of land for sale. He immediately gave money to purchase the plot "to build a park for the kids of East Tupelo." The Youth Centre, built in 1961 had a pool, playground and picnic area, and school dances were held there. Roy Turner, an Elvis historian and native of Tupelo, attended a Junior High School dance at the Elvis Presley Youth Center when he was a young teenager. The former Youth Center is now the Elvis Presley Birthplace Museum. According to Roy, after it was no longer used as a youth centre it could be rented for events, and they held the Turner Family Reunion there several years in a row until they turned it into a museum.

Birthplace – While fans could see the outside of the two-room cabin, it wasn't until 1971 when the East Heights Garden Club, along with the Tupelo Park and Recreation Department, restored the outside and inside of the home where Elvis was born.

Tupelo Memorial Chapel – After Elvis died, the front porch of his birthplace was covered in flowers from his many fans. The city of Tupelo began receiving contributions from his fans, so they needed to decide on how the funds would be managed. Elvis' friend, Janelle McComb, had spoken to him about building something to honour him. Elvis replied: "Why don't you build a chapel so that my fans will have a place to meditate?"

At the time, only the birthplace cabin and a youth centre were on the park property, so it was decided that the funds should be used to build a chapel. There wasn't enough money to pay for a building, so Janelle travelled to Elvis fan clubs throughout the United States and Europe with a vision of a chapel. Many Fan Clubs contributed and sometimes gave money for specific items, for example, stained glass windows which Laukhuff Studio of Memphis created and installed. On the west side of the chapel are large walls of stained glass. On the east side of the chapel are 18 smaller windows, each paid for by fans and each holding a different meaning.

Meaning of the small stained-glass windows in the chapel:

Lilies – *Which is the Annunciation*; Star – *Nativity;* Loaves and Fishes - *The Miracle;* Bible – *Teaching;* Lamp – Anci*ent Lamp Christians Used to Represent Faith;* Chalice – *Holy Communion;* Dove – *Baptism;* Bag of Silver – *Betrayal*; Scales – *Unjust Trial;* Reed and Sponge – *Suffering on the Cross;* Three Crosses – *Crucifixion*; Tomb – *Resurrection*; Flames – *Seven Gifts of the Holy Spirit at Pentecost*; Torch – *Life Eternal;* Sowing the Seed – *Resurrection;* Crown – *Crown of Life;* Trinity – *Father, Son and Holy Spirit;* Ship – *Church on Earth.*

The chapel, which opened in August 1979, seats about 50 and there have been many weddings held there.

The First Assembly of God Church – The original structure of this church in East Tupelo, where the Presleys worshipped, was, in 2008, moved to the birthplace site and fully restored as it was when Elvis and his family worshipped there. When visiting this church, we are presented with a surround sound/pictures video of the kind of service the Presley's would have experienced, full of joy and praising the Lord. It is very effective, so effective I am told, that a rather cynical journalist watching it was so moved that he stood up with his arms in the air during the virtual service.

Today, the Elvis Presley Birthplace site includes the birthplace home of Elvis Presley, the museum, the Elvis Presley Memorial Chapel, and the Assembly of God Church building where the Presley family worshipped. There is also a huge amount of land surrounding the complex which features the "Reflections" lake, the Overlook Pavilion, and several statues of Elvis.

The Tupelo Festival – This five-day festival held in June celebrates Elvis' life with concerts, performances from ETAs (Elvis Tribute Artists), conversations with people who knew Elvis, and ends on the Sunday with a gospel concert.

In 2002, St Mark's Church, which is opposite Elvis' birthplace, held a gospel concert with The Landmarks group. We were able to help distribute the "Prescripture" tubs, the kind of tubs used for dispensing pills, containing pieces of paper with scriptures written on them, for example, "Hatred stirs up dissention, but love covers all wrongs." The label on the tub says: Your Doctor: THE GREAT PHYSICIAN. Your dosage: Take one daily or as needed for spiritual renewal. Ingredients: FAITH, HOPE and LOVE.

These were given to the fans, hoping that they would be encouraged by what they read and even want to discover more about the Christian faith. Rev. Wally Cason, the then pastor of the church, was very much aware of the advantage of being so close to Elvis' birthplace and therefore, to many fans.

Also in 2002, Tupelo Hardware, where Elvis got his first guitar, were happy to sell my just published booklet, *Prayers of Elvis* and asked me to do a book signing. It was lovely to get to chat to so many fans.

That year we also met Elvis' friend, Janelle McComb, who was chairwoman of the Elvis Presley Memorial Foundation in Tupelo for many years and who knew the Presley family in Tupelo before they moved to Memphis. Janelle said of Elvis, "He was very definitely a Christian, and I know that the Bible we got [for the Birthplace] after he died had a lot of passages marked with a yellow marker. He used to watch different preachers on television on Sunday mornings, and I remember one time asking him – we were talking about talent and people going to Juilliard [Performing Arts Conservatory] and things like that – and I said, 'Well, you know where you got your talent.' He pointed his finger up, and said, 'From the man upstairs.'"

As we move north towards Memphis, Elvis' adopted home, we pass:

The Circle G Ranch in Walls, Mississippi

We know that this ranch not far from Graceland, just over the border in Mississippi, was owned by Elvis for only five years as it proved too expensive to run. Also, Elvis was not able to spend much time there because of his work commitments. Since he sold it in 1972, it has had several owners but was getting into a state of disrepair when Davage "Buddy" Runnels purchased it in 2014.

We were able to visit the ranch in 2015 and met Buddy who outlined the plans for the property which has several historical features including the Honeymoon Cottage, the stable where Elvis kept his horses, a 14-acre lake and the prominent 55-foot cross. The plans for the Ranch include a Welcome Centre, restoration of both the Honeymoon Cottage and the original stables, a Chapel, a restaurant, an amphitheatre and overall, a musically themed "leisure entertainment destination" catering for Elvis fans from around the world.

Lesley Pilling from the UK is the founder of The Circle G Foundation which continues to work hard to achieve the Foundation's mission of working "To preserve and protect the property that was Elvis Presley's Circle G Ranch through discussion dialogue and engagement. To have his presence there recognised and to promote the significance of the ranch in Elvis' story. To be the repository for detailed records and memories of Elvis' tenure. And to commemorate his charitable and humanitarian legacy through our own efforts or by supporting those within the Elvis fan community who wish to do so."

As well as raising funds for charity the Foundation funded a Historic State Marker for the property which was approved by the Mississippi Department of Archives and History and is the first Mississippi State marker to be sponsored internationally.

Now we come to the city where Elvis and his parents moved in 1948.

Memphis

Elvis lived in several houses in Memphis, but the home which was his delight and refuge for the last 20 years of his life was Graceland.

Graceland

After Vernon's death in 1979, Priscilla Presley, as Lisa Marie's legal guardian, began co-managing Elvis' Trust along with the National Bank of Commerce in Memphis and formed Elvis Presley Enterprises (EPE) in 1979. In late 1981, they hired Jack Soden, at the time a Missouri investment counsellor, to plan and execute the opening of Graceland to the public and oversee the total operation. Also, when Graceland Christian Church next door to Graceland, eventually decided to move, the Presley family bought back the land and turned the church into the headquarters of EPE.

Graceland was opened to the public as a museum on 7th June 1982. The site was listed in the National Register of Historic Places on 7th November 1991, becoming the first site related to rock 'n' roll so to be registered. Graceland was declared a National Historic Landmark on 27th March 2006, also a first for such a site. Graceland is the third most visited house in the U.S. after the Biltmore Estate and the White House, with over 500,000 visitors a year, making it the most-visited privately-owned home in America.

The large angel statue which was first at the gravesite site of Gladys Presley at Forest Hill Cemetery was moved to Graceland's Meditation Garden on 1st June 1982. The footstone with the star of David inscribed on it was found in the archives and placed in the Meditation Garden on 14th August 2018, the 50th anniversary of Gladys' death.

Lisa Marie Presley is the sole heir to Elvis Presley's fortune and legacy. After her parent's divorce, she lived mostly with her mother in Los Angeles but also spent time at Graceland with her father, where she was at the time of his death. Elvis is buried there in the Meditation Garden, along with his parents, Vernon Elvis and Gladys Love, and his grandmother Minnie Mae.

In October 2020, Elvis' only grandson, 27-year-old Benjamin Storm Keogh, Lisa Marie's second child with musician Danny Keough, was also laid to rest in the Meditation Garden. Sadly, Benjamin died of a self-inflicted gunshot wound at his mother's home in Calabasas California. Benjamin has a sister, Danielle Riley Keough, and two twin half-sisters, Harper Vivienne Ann and Finley Aaron Love, from Lisa Marie's marriage to Michael Lockwood.

Although Graceland is now a major public monument and hugely popular tourist destination, the upstairs of the house, including Elvis and Lisa Marie's bedrooms, is never opened to the public. On public holidays such as Thanksgiving and Christmas, Lisa Marie and her family and friends still take over the downstairs rooms, including the kitchen and dining room, for meals and celebrations.

There is also a Wedding Chapel in the grounds where many fans choose to tie the knot.

As well as visiting Graceland, there are many other sites one can visit where Elvis spent time. These include Humes High School, Lauderdale Courts housing unit, Sun Recording Studios and the Shell performance area in Overton Park.

Elvis Week

This is the week in August, the month when Elvis died, when a series of events is held in memory of Elvis.

The Candlelight Vigil – It is the constant and main event of Elvis Week. The very first Candlelight Vigil was held in 1978, the year after Elvis' passing. It was a very informal affair with a small group of fans gathered at the gates of Graceland, placing lighted candles on the wall. It has now grown to thousands and is organised by Graceland who shut down Elvis Presley Boulevard for the evening and fans from around the world walk up the driveway to Elvis' gravesite and back down, carrying a candle in quiet remembrance.

My husband Peter and I attended our first Candlelight Vigil in 2002, the 25th Anniversary of Elvis death. Reportedly, there were 70,000 of us present. Being a Fan Club President, I had the privilege of being among the first to pay respect. We said the 23rd Psalm together, Elvis sang *How Great Thou Art* and we all sang *Can't Help Falling in Love*, which I sometimes interpret as a song of praise, (I can't help falling in love with you Jesus, take my hand, take my whole life too.) I did notice that when we go up to the graves in the Meditation Garden and are looking at Elvis' grave, we have our backs to a statue of Jesus, and when we turn away from the grave to walk further along the path, we walk towards the statue of Jesus with his arms outstretched, as though ready to greet us with a great big hug.

As well as being an emotional and spiritual experience, it was also a physical one as there was a powerful thunderstorm with torrential rain, and we literally got soaked to the skin. However, as it was so hot, we just felt that we were having a warm shower. I became concerned that our candles would not stay lit, but by the time we came to light our candles the rain had stopped, and we were soon dry, clothes and all. I like to think that the prayers we prayed with a lady from the Hawaiian Fan Club while we were waiting in line had something to do with it!

Floral Tributes – Many of these arrive at Graceland in August and January (Elvis' birthday). Our Elvis Gospel Fan Club tribute is always a red and white

Christian cross with "love never fails" and "thank you Lord for the life of Elvis Presley" written on the ribbons. We had our first ones made at the Flower Patch, a florist shop that was using the Honeymoon Cottage on the Circle G Ranch as its premises. We were pleased to see that in 2002 our tribute was placed near Elvis' grave. There are so many floral tributes that do not find room in the Meditation Garden but are lined along the paths leading to the garden. I did notice on a visit later in the week that our floral tribute had been moved away from the graveside to the side of the pathway leading up to the Meditation Gardens, though still fully visible. I realise that this is to give all the floral tributes, some time at the graveside. However, a tinge of disappointment passed through my thoughts until I became aware that it could be seen as a sign that we need to move away from focussing on the dead and move into the path of life.

There is usually some more gospel input during the week. These are some from the past which have a gospel theme:

Elvis Presley Memorial Mass – The Mass, fully-named "Mass for the Solemnity of the Assumption of Mary, in Memory of Elvis Presley", was held at St Pauls Catholic Church, Shelby Drive, Memphis for people to come together and pray and remember Elvis. The Mass was always followed by a spaghetti dinner.

Elvis Presley's Sweet, Sweet Spirit Fan Club Gospel Memorial – This featured the Stamps quartet singing some of Elvis' favourite gospel songs. As with most Elvis fan clubs, proceeds from the ticket sales were given to charity, in this case to Presley Place.

A Gospel Brunch at Elvis Presley's Memphis (located in the former Lansky' Clothiers building on Beale Street) – Delicious food was consumed whilst listening to some of the gospel singers who sang with Elvis, delighting us with their harmonies and the joy of the Lord, whom they clearly love.

Marian Cocke's Memorial Dinner at the Peabody Hotel – As we know, from 1975 Marian was Elvis' nurse, friend, and confidante. She started the dinner not only to remember Elvis but also to raise funds for charity. She is a dear lady who, sadly, because of her age (95) is no longer able to organise the event as she is totally homebound. Here is part of her "farewell" Facebook post in 2021:

"Good afternoon, everybody! For 30 years, I hosted The Elvis Presley Memorial Dinner Charity Event. I did it for two reasons: to honour the memory and the legacy of a young man I admired and respected for his goodness and his kindness to others, and whom I grew to love as 'my Kid', also to raise funds for charity.

"Our dinners were of class and held with dignity and a great deal of love, caring and respect for this young man from Tupelo, Elvis Presley.

"I think that all of us who personally played a small part in his life feel very blessed to have been there for and with him; I know that I certainly do, and I ask you to honor him as a man though, and not as a king. There was and will always be only one king and that is Jesus Christ, our Lord and our Saviour and I can honestly tell you too; Elvis Presley would be the first to tell you that!

"Why am I on my soapbox about this?? Because today it became necessary for me to tell someone the difference between two men: Jesus Christ and Elvis Presley. Respectfully, Marian Cocke."

The Fan Club Presidents Lunch – This was held every August to thank Fan Club Presidents for their work encouraging fans and raising funds for charities. There was a different theme each year and we were treated to a sumptuous meal followed by a talk by someone who knew Elvis. I remember one time when Joe Guercio, the conductor of Elvis' orchestra, was speaking about how he especially loved to conduct Elvis singing *How Great Thou Art*, we could see tears streaming down his face. These lunches no longer take place, but there is always a special event for Fan Club Presidents.

A Gospel Concert – Organised by Graceland, this is now a regular event during Elvis Week.

Graceland Christmas Lighting Ceremony – Christmas was Elvis' favourite time of year. The Presleys always put up their Christmas decorations early and, because Elvis so loved the season, decorations stayed up through his birthday on 8th January, a tradition which is kept alive by the Graceland Christmas Lighting Ceremony which takes place in November near to Thanksgiving and the lights stay on through Elvis' birthday.

In 2013, actor, musician, and comedian Charles "Chip" Esten was asked to flip the switch. He stated that this was a dream come true and felt it was necessary

297

to honour Elvis with a special song, *The Lights of Graceland,* which has beautiful lyrics and was greatly appreciated by those there.

When the lights go on at Graceland, and the cool, Memphis night comes aglow,
You could swear that you hear the king singing to the sweet Prince of Peace he loves so.
He'd dream of a white, white Christmas, but sometimes, they'd be blue, blue, blue,
And so, he implored, take my hand, precious Lord, it's no secret what God can do.
He swore he'd be home for Christmas, for it's here that the world went away,
And each silent night, he'd pray that he might, have peace in the valley someday.
So come, won't you come, all ye faithful, as they came all those nights long ago,
Here to sing with the king to the great King of Kings, to the sweet Prince of Peace he loved so.

As part of Christmas celebrations, Elvis purchased a Santa and sleigh garden decoration that reads, "Merry Christmas to All, Elvis" and later he rented a Nativity scene for the front lawn which Graceland eventually purchased and which, with the Santa, continues to be displayed every year.

At midnight on 7th January, fans gather at the gates of Graceland to sing gospel songs. The year that we were able to do that we had the pleasure of singer Colin Paul leading us.

The Birthday Celebrations – On the 8th of January these celebrations start with a proclamation of Elvis Presley Day by Memphis and Shelby County officials and a cake-cutting ceremony on the front lawn of Graceland. On my first visit in 1996, as I was queuing for a piece of birthday cake, I was interviewed by the local Commercial Appeal newspaper. Surprisingly, I became so emotional, that at one point I could hardly speak. I was also surprised to see grown men unashamedly weeping at Elvis' graveside. Being an Elvis fan is full of surprises!

Our Elvis Gospel Fan Club has organised and attended several events in Memphis over the years. It would take a whole other chapter to detail them all, so here are some of the highlights:

I have already mentioned the event which we held in 2001, where we interviewed members of the Imperials. We had hoped that Rev. Rex Dyson who had baptised Elvis and his parents would be able to come and speak to us, but he had a previous engagement. However, we did record a video of him praying for us and telling us some of his memories of Elvis, which we played at the event.

Also, that year there was an open house at Presley Place[5], a 12-unit apartment property in Memphis that consists of two four-bedroom apartments and ten two-bedroom apartments. It was officially opened to its first residents on 10th July 2001 by Lisa Marie Presley, Chairman of the Elvis Presley Charitable Foundation (EPCF)[6].

We were able to visit a couple of the units which were beautifully kept. It was very moving to see neat rows of tiny shoes on the bedroom floor and, in the living room, a Bible. By the state of its cover, it had obviously been rescued from a fire, yet the inside was not damaged at all.

At some later date, the MIFA programme closed and the US Department of Housing and Urban Development (HUD) which administers Federal aid for low-income families to local housing agencies took over the management of the facility.

Gospel Roots – Gospel Fruits – For Elvis week in 2002 our Fan Club had on display in the Center for Southern Folklore an exhibition entitled "Gospel Roots – Gospel Fruits" which traced, in words and pictures, the influence of the Gospel in Elvis' life. On the Saturday, at the same venue, we held our International Fan Club meeting, and international it was! There were fans from the USA, of course, but also Spain, Canada, Wales, England, Holland,

---

[5] Presley Place was a Metropolitan Inter Faith Association (MIFA) housing community funded by EPCF, which has been home to many formerly homeless families. In a comparable way that Lauderdale Courts provided low- income, transitional housing for families like the Presleys, Presley Place sheltered families who were forced from their homes by fire, eviction, or domestic violence. MIFA also provided a comprehensive programme of child day care, career and financial counselling and family management guidance.

[6] The Elvis Presley Charitable Foundation is a non-profit philanthropic organization founded in 1984 by Lisa Marie with Graceland/Elvis Presley Enterprises in the spirit of Elvis' dedication to community service and to honour his legacy. The organization supports a variety of causes, including the Memphis-based counselling centre, Goodwill Homes, and the Elvis Presley Endowed Scholarship Fund at the University of Memphis for students majoring in media and the arts.

Sweden, Belgium, and Australia. We had purposely decided to keep the format very informal. Some people sang for us, some told very moving stories of how Elvis' gospel music had helped them through some very difficult times.

Donnie Sumner, a member of the Stamps Gospel group who sang with Elvis had agreed to come and speak to us at our meeting, however, because of a missed message, he did not get to the event. However, he very kindly sent this message for our Fan Club members:

Hi boys and girls,

Just in case I'm getting too old to be remembered, I was the lead singer for J D Sumner and the Stamps Quartet and the lead singer in Voice. With the Stamps, I sang back up for Elvis three years. With Voice, for an additional three years, I opened all the Elvis shows, lived with Elvis, and sang Gospel Music to him every night and I do mean "every night." Some nights, Voice would sing Gospel Songs to him for three to four hours.

I have a lot of memories. Some I can share and some I will only talk about when I see Elvis again.

I'm often asked, "What was Elvis like?" My usual response is, "He was the best-looking, most talented, most loyal, richest and best friend I ever had."

He truly loved all eighteen of the guys that lived with him. He sometimes put himself in harm's way for us and accepted all of us as brothers.

I am a nobody but when I used the pseudonym "Presley Party" it seemed to get me in places that would otherwise be off-limits to me.

I have never been rich but for three years I carried a folder of Elvis Presley credit cards. I never turned in a receipt nor was I ever questioned about anything I charged.

I have never been handsome but when you're standing on stage beside ELVIS it doesn't matter, no one's looking at YOU anyway.

Yes friends, it was a great life and sometimes it seems like only a dream when I recall my times with Elvis. I resigned from the entourage in September of 1976. I had gotten my life all messed with drugs and was seriously in bad shape.

I experienced a really traumatic religious experience on Saturday morning before Labor Day that year and I hope that when I have the opportunity to talk to you in person, you will allow me to tell you all about it but for right now let me just say: In an effort to get my 'act' together, I left Memphis, came back to Nashville, went into drug rehab and started life all over again under the protection of "Another King"!

In 1980, I entered the ministry full time and, for the last twenty-seven years, I have been trying to help as many people as I can find the peace, joy, satisfaction, and fulfilment that I have come to experience.

I'm still a nobody, in the world's eyes, but really, I'm 'somebody special' because I am now an adopted member in my Heavenly Father's family. I'm still not rich but my Heavenly Father owns it all and has promised to supply all my needs according to all that He has. I'm still not handsome but someday I have the promise of a perfect body for all of eternity.

Yes friends, it is a great life and I look forward to the day 'my dream' comes true. It's a very simple dream and I am assured of it coming to pass. I look forward to the day I can enter my Heavenly Father's "Land of Grace" and see my entire family, along with Elvis and 'all' of you. It's gonna be great!

For at least ten million years we'll all sit down in a golden living room, on golden chairs around a golden piano and sing like there'll be no tomorrows because there won't be.

Without the Heavenly Father's providence, there would never have been a little boy in Tupelo named Elvis. Without fans like you, there would never have been a superstar called ELVIS!

I love you all and thank God that through the person of my friend, ELVIS, our lives have touched.

Your friend, Donnie Sumner

The above letter was written, especially for members of the Elvis Gospel Fan Club. I had also asked Donnie if he knew of any plans Elvis had made to do a full gospel show and this is his reply:

"Hi Madeleine, at least once a night for 6 years Elvis would swear that he was gonna do a gospel concert with the Stamps and Voice and he was gonna do

the bass singing for Voice. Sure wish we could have pulled that off. As far as any real plans, I'm not sure. I left 11 months before Elvis passed away."

Judy Peiser, the manager of the Centre, was delighted with our meetings there. The Centre is designed for people to come together to enjoy the music and other art forms of the South. Our meetings fitted the bill exactly. I think I can confidently say that good times were had by all! We are very grateful to Judy, who gave us so much encouragement and support.

Elvis The Concert – On 16th August 2002, to commemorate the 25th Anniversary of Elvis' passing, Elvis the Concert was held at the Pyramid in Memphis. The idea for this kind of concert developed in the mid-1990s. Elvis Presley Enterprises started experimenting with recordings of Elvis' live concerts and discovered that by using sound mixing they were able to eliminate virtually all the ambient sound from the multitrack recordings, thus leaving only Elvis' voice. After some work, they conceived this special concert. The show featured Elvis' original 1970s backup band and backup singers and was a huge success, gaining worldwide press.

We attended this sell-out concert, and it was wonderful. A real triumph for modern technology. The concert is still taking place and has been all over the world. Today, of course, there are fewer of Elvis' bandmates and singers left to take part, but it is still a wonderful experience. The latest one we attended, in Sheffield UK, was in 2019, with the Royal Philharmonic Orchestra, Ronnie Tutt, Glen D Hardin, and James Burton performing live, hosted by Priscilla Presley and Jerry Schilling. The technology, especially with the sound was greatly improved and Elvis' voice was amazing.

Also, as with all these events we have attended, I note that it is usually the gospel songs that receive the greatest applause.

World-Wide Memorial Events

As well as the events in Memphis and Tupelo, there are many held around the world. Most of the Elvis Festivals honour Elvis' love of gospel music by having a gospel concert and/or a gospel service. Here are some reports of those:

UK - Annual Elvis Party Event at Mablethorpe in 1998 – This was the first Elvis event we attended in the UK. It was here that we met Jerry Sheff and Glen D Hardin and had the opportunity to ask them about Elvis' Christian faith. Glen said that Elvis didn't talk to him directly about his faith but that he could tell that Elvis was a Christian because of his loving, caring personality. He said he thought that Elvis would have made "the best evangelist." Jerry said that had Elvis lived, he believes that he would have become a gospel singer. The Higher Calling Gospel singers from Manchester were wonderful and received a great welcome from the fans. They sang *Amazing Grace, He Touched Me, Swing Down Sweet Chariot, In the Garden, Sweet, Sweet Spirit, Somebody Bigger Than You or I, How Great Thou Art* (for which they did an encore) and two of their own repertoire. This was the first time the party event had ever featured a gospel group.

UK - The Porthcawl Elvis Festival – this was started by Peter Philips in 2003 and we attended our first one in 2005. This little Welsh seaside town of Porthcawl now attracts 35,000 visitors. They say "You can't get away from Elvis here. Every pub, chip shop, café and hotel host its own mini Elvis festival for the weekend. It is wall-to-wall Elvis." That is what some people love, but it is not for everyone. It has developed over the years, but always has a gospel concert, and I have been able to give a "mini preach" to explain the Gospel to the audience.

On one of our visits Rev. Paul Floe of Trinity Church saw the opportunity to reach Elvis fans with the Gospel and held an Elvis Gospel Service. The church was beautifully decorated with a USA and Elvis theme and Paul spoke of three kings, Jesus, David, and Elvis saying that Elvis' life was like the greatest song ever written, full of love. He reminded us that God loves lives of love, and therefore we all need to aspire to be tribute artists imitating Jesus, the King of Kings (JTAs!).

The Sweet Inspirations sang their awesome acapella rendition of *The Lord's Prayer* and ETA Martin Pisani from Malta and his lovely wife renewed their wedding vows. Martin then sang a very rousing and handclapping *Put Your Hand in the Hand* and Kraig Parker from Texas sang *He Touched Me* and *How Great Thou Art,* straight from his heart. The theme of the service was taken from Elvis' favourite Bible Passage (1 Corinthians 13 – The Love chapter).

The Kenfig Hill Male voice choir were excellent, performing songs ranging from Black Spirituals, African songs, Welsh hymns and of course some Elvis songs. The highlight of their performance though, for me, was *When I Survey the Wondrous Cross,* with those amazing voices harmonising and gradually increasing volume to the last verse: "Were the whole realm of nature mine, that were a present far too small; Love so amazing, so divine, demands my soul, my life, my all."

The Sunday evening concert with Kraig Parker and the Sweet Inspirations was wonderful. Kraig is a Christian and is not afraid to show it. He has an excellent voice, well tested by the song *Hurt*, which received rousing applause, but the song which got a standing ovation was *How Great Thou Art*.

The festival has developed over the years and now features Classic Elvis with the Cardiff Philharmonic Orchestra, as well as The Best Festival Elvis Competition, The New Kings, which showcases ETAs making their debut at the Grand Pavilion and, as always, the Elvis Gospel Show.

To date, Trinity Church still hold their gospel service and Gilgal Baptist Church take the opportunity to go into the streets and chat with fans, as well as handing out Gospel information leaflets. Also, in 2019, Ivor Williams sang Elvis gospel songs and Rev. Clive Jones shared the gospel message in a howling gale!

UK, "Ultimate" Tribute Artists Championships and Festival in Bournemouth – In 2011 Bill Blondell started Bulldog Promotions, an Elvis Presley events company aimed at promoting the legacy of Elvis in the United Kingdom. The company uses ETAs and organises several events including the "Ultimate" ETA Championships, in which they have a Gospel Concert.

Australia – At the Parkes Elvis Festival held in Australia in January 2020, the Parkes Ministers Association presented an Elvis Gospel Service, and Rev. Craig Bland who led the service wrote this for us:

Numbers were down slightly due to Bushfires and drought (still 4–5,000), but, in the end, the collection was only down by about $200 with $6800 raised towards ministries in the local Parkes High School and overseas in East Timor where last year's donations helped ship hospital equipment (mostly beds and linen) that benefited around 8 different hospitals and clinics around Dili.

The theme was Frankie and Johnny, [one of Elvis' films] *which is basically about a compulsive gambler who tries to turn his luck around by seeing a fortune teller who tells him that a "red head" will be his good luck charm. Not themes one would normally build a church service around. We had three mini talks throughout the service. The first looked at how we'd all love to know the future and the Bible tells us what the ultimate future holds, not so much for this life but rather for eternity. This also tied into the movie as it has two gospel songs in it, "O When the Saints" and "Down by the Riverside" both of which are about the hope of heaven. The second talk tackled lucky charms and how too many of us are "hoping" to get into heaven when we can actually have a sure bet – Jesus. We followed that talk with "Without Him" which has the lyrics; Jesus, O Jesus, do you know him today? Please don't turn him away. The final talk, focussed in on gambling. and talked about Elvis' time in Vegas while leaving people with the challenge "Don't gamble with your eternity" and how Judgement is not something to fear if you have God's forgiveness, we followed that talk with "Amazing Grace."*

The service was well received and concluded with all performers back on stage and the crowd joining us in singing "Put Your Hand in the Hand" and we had a wonderful reprieve in the weather for the service. It was lovely and cool with no wind."

Europe – Here is a report from Terry Blackwood who, in 2005 with the other Imperials, Joe Moscheo, Sherman Andrus, and Gus Gachus, toured several cities with an Elvis show featuring ETA Oliver Steinhoff. *"That night we sang to a standing room only crowd of raucous Elvis fans with Oliver doing Elvis songs. He was received extremely well, and the people loved his show. He introduced us in the middle of the show, and we sang "Swing Down, Sweet Chariot" and then "Sweet, Sweet Spirit" and you could have heard a pin drop, it was so quiet and respectful. There were positive reviews of the praise songs. All in all, it was a wonderful trip and one that hopefully seeds were sown for future reaping!"*

There have been many similar concerts over the years, performed all over the world and always well received. You can be sure that when Elvis' gospel backing group singers are involved, there will be plenty of gospel input!

Germany – Bad Homburg and Bad Nauheim. Because Elvis was stationed in Germany and spent time in these towns, they are visited by Elvis fans, often with specially organised Elvis tours which are led by folk who have done research and can take people to the places Elvis lived or visited while he was there. Bad Nauheim hosts the European Elvis Festival held in August which has a gospel show on the Sunday.

Ritters Park Hotel in Bad Homburg, now renamed the Steigenberger Bad Homburg, is where Elvis stayed in October 1958. In 2019, they hosted a TCB (Taking Care of Business) Weekend, with music by singer Dennis Jale, Glenn

D Hardin, Paul Leim, The Imperials, and the Holladay Sisters who recorded with Elvis. The special guest was Elvis' cousin, Donna Presley.

We were delighted to be able to attend this event and what a wonderful weekend it was! Most of the people present at the weekend were German or Belgian and others were from Austria, Holland, Switzerland, Slovakia, Spain, and the UK. We had some wonderful conversations with people, of course, starting with Elvis and then leading on to discussion of gospel music, faith, and Jesus. The Holy Spirit was certainly present, especially at the gospel concert presented by The Imperials: Terry Blackwood, Darrell Toney and Will Smith, who interspersed their singing with stories and exhortations to seek the Lord before it is too late. Grown men were weeping and one asked us "What is salvation?" A lady was asking the title of the song about meeting God in the morning, which had clearly moved her.

Other countries where Elvis gospel music is celebrated and in which we have contacts include:

Malaysia – HT Long was one of the first people with a similar vision to reach Elvis fans with the Gospel to contact me. He is known as the Best Elvis Presley of Malaysia, the Man with The Golden Voice of Elvis. In 1968, he became the founding president of the Official Elvis Presley Fan Club of Malaysia.

HT has travelled to many places to sing including Indonesia, Australia, Japan, Hong Kong, Thailand, Singapore, the United Kingdom, and the United States. He has performed to more than a thousand people at the Acacia Hotel in Perth, Australia. He has also performed in many smaller towns in Malaysia.

He says that he has never grown weary of travelling and singing. "Thank God, He has touched my heart and now, it is for me to touch the lives of many people who have lived in the Elvis Golden Era."

Once a self-acclaimed atheist, HT says it was Elvis' death that caused him to turn to God. "In my younger days, I would sing in pubs. I had no time for God," he said. "But, when Elvis, whom I had always thought was the greatest, a demi-god of some kind, died, I was forced to ask the question, 'How can my god, Elvis Presley, die?'" When he finally encountered the true God at a Reinhard Bonnke gospel rally on a November night in 1989, HT said that his life has never been the same. "He touched me. I am changed."

The Netherlands – Rev. Fred Omvlee, an ordained minister in the Dutch Protestant Church says:

"When I was 11 years old in 1977, Elvis died. I only knew Elvis as a chubby old man in a white suit; I loved Abba but, since I got to know the gospel side of Elvis Presley, that really touched me. I must admit that in my study room I felt emotionally and spiritually more fed through his gospels than through the psalms and hymns as they are played and sung in my denomination. Some of Elvis' gospel songs made me feel deeply sad and glad at the same time. Putting the gospel-mindedness of the parish together with my own inspiration, I simply had the idea of using the spirituals of Elvis in a normal church service. The choir leader was enthusiastic immediately."

The first "Elvis Gospel Service" which Rev. Fred organised was held in the Opstandingskerk (Resurrection-Church) in Monnickendam, 10 miles north of Amsterdam on 13th January 2002. 675 people gathered in the church. Only 360 could be seated, so the others stood during the service. Apart from the usual congregation, hundreds of rockers and Elvis fans were present.

Fred reports, "We sang, *Where Could I Go but to the Lord? How Great Thou Art, Mansion over the Hilltop, If the Lord Wasn't Walking by My Side, Peace in the Valley, I Believe, Bye and Bye,* and *You'll Never Walk Alone.*

"After the sermon which was about Elvis, his life, sorrows and pressures and the great promises of God and Jesus for him and for us, we prayed. Then we sang *So High* three times after another, which set the church on fire! Grandmothers who disliked Elvis next to rockers prayed together and now jumped and clapped and cheered! It was a Holy party never seen before in this church. People who hadn't been to church in 30 years, or never in their lives were touched, and the regular churchgoers as well. National TV was present to cover this event, and radio reporters and newspaper journalists as well. Madeleine Wilson from Elvis Gospel Fan Club came and supported us."

Rev. Fred is also an Armed Forces Chaplain and takes Elvis everywhere he goes. He says that every church service, whether it be on board a ship, as in Liberia, or as far away as Afghanistan, Elvis is part of it. He can choose any of the over 80 gospel songs which Elvis recorded to fit into the service. He remembers that on Christmas Eve in 2003 he held a service on a helicopter platform of their ship in Liberia and that the men and the Admiral heard Elvis singing *Peace in the Valley* during that tropical night.

He also remembers the time in Afghanistan where he was with 180 Dutch military men and women who were stabilising and assisting the local government in the Baghlan province. He got to know the local mullah and says, "Even the mullah knows I am an Elvis fan. He even listened to Elvis." The mullah was happy to talk religion with Rev. Fred and told him that to Muslims the Bible is holy, just as the Torah and Quran. They believe that Jesus is the prophet that is closest to God, born from the Virgin Mary, but that he cannot be the son of God because God cannot have children. That is the big difference between Islam and Christianity.

Later a senior mullah was guest in a service on the compound. It was the first Christian service he had attended. Rev. Fred preached and Elvis sang *You'll Never Walk Alone,* after which the senior mullah spoke to the congregation. He said that he had heard nothing that conflicted with his beliefs and was happy to see the people in the service and how important it was to pray and live well.

Japan, Jun Sato – Pastor Jun Sato who leads a church in Tokyo, contacted us through our website and says: "Many thanks to your research on Elvis' Gospel side. Looking forward to working with you for our Lord, and for Elvis, whose dream was to see the peace of Jesus Christ realizing in this world."

We have indeed worked together, sharing ideas, and I was able to help Jun with information for his Japanese translation of Joe Moscheo's book *The Gospel Side of Elvis* published in 2016. Jun is a singing pastor and will often sing Elvis gospel songs during his services. He has also produced information leaflets about Elvis and the Gospel which he hands out at events such as the one in 2016 when he attended The Woman's Christian Temperance Union (WCTU) World Convention in Ottawa, Canada where he sang, among others *Known Only to Him, By and By,* and *Amazing Grace* the latter of which the audience could not resist joining with him in singing.

Brazil, Vanderlei Junior – Another person who contacted me when I first started my research into Elvis, was Vanderlei. He had an Elvis Gospel website in Portuguese, and we were very pleased to find each other. However, over the years I am sorry to say that I have lost touch with him. Though another Brazilian who contacted me is:

Pr. Márcio Sérgio Cassiano de Freitas, a pastor, teacher, and writer. His favourite Bible passage is "The Lord bless you and keep you" (Numbers 6:24 - 26), known as the "Aaronic blessing" as it is the blessing that the Lord told

Aaron to speak over the Israelites. Pr. Marcio is very supportive of what we are doing and has recently translated my booklet *Prayers of Elvis* into Portuguese.

Peru – This information came from one of our Elvis Gospel Fan Club members, Stephen Guschov:

"We are missionaries with Ripe for Harvest Missions of Mesa, Arizona and San Diego, California. I am the Assistant Pastor of a very poor, inner-city evangelical church in Lima where my father-in-law is the Senior Pastor. My ministries include preaching, evangelising, counselling, teaching in our weekly Bible Academy, assisting in the leadership of our weekly prayer service, and writing Spanish-language tracts. My wife directs music and women's ministries in the church. We receive no salary for this work. We rely totally on support from donors in our mission work here in Peru.

"So far over 500 Peruvians have accepted Christ as Savior through our mission work. One day I preached a salvation message to inmates at a dangerous, maximum-security prison in Lima, filled with Marxist terrorists, drug traffickers, and murderers. After the message, 100 prisoners accepted Christ as Savior. Another 400 Peruvians have come to accept Christ as Savior after reading a Spanish-language tract I wrote about the Mel Gibson film, "The Passion."

"Elvis' gospel music also has played a very important role in leading Peruvians to Christ. At times, we have brought the CD "Take My Hand: Elvis Gospel Favorites" to church with us for special worship services. One night we played Elvis' version of *How Great Thou Art* in church. Elvis is very popular here in Peru, and so everyone was excited to hear him singing *How Great Thou Art*. The several hundred Peruvians in church began to sing *How Great Thou Art* in Spanish, so there we were with them (me and a few others singing it in English) and Elvis singing it on the CD! What a wonderful night of blessing. After the Elvis song ended, we preached a salvation message, and about 20 Peruvians came forward that evening to receive Christ as Savior – thanks in a large part to the wonderful, inspirational gospel music of Elvis.

Please pray for our safety here in Peru. Recently a man burst into our church wielding a knife and tried to attack us. Thankfully, I was able to tackle him to the ground before he was able to seriously injure anyone. It was a little bloody, but thankfully no one was seriously hurt by him. God gets the glory for giving me the strength to act in such a dangerous situation. The police, however, only held the man for a few hours before letting him go free, and now he's back, threatening to round up a gang of armed men to get his revenge on us. So, we ask you and all the Elvis Gospel subscribers to please pray for our safety here in Peru, where it's getting increasingly dangerous for us. Many thanks for your prayers and support. Stephen Guschov."

This was several years ago. We did pray and Stephen is now back in the USA.

Israel -The first I heard of The Elvis American Diner at Abu Ghosh near Jerusalem was on meeting evangelist Christine Darg, who at the time made monthly visits to towns and villages in Israel to spread the Gospel of Jesus Christ. When I told her of our mission to reach Elvis fans with the gospel, she invited me to take part in their next visit which would be in the village of Abu Ghosh, where the Elvis Diner is situated. I accepted with alacrity and had a wonderful time meeting Uri Yoeli, the Jewish owner, who was happy for us to chat with his customers and hand out leaflets. He also chose to stock my booklet *Prayers of Elvis.* I remember that as I was explaining the meaning of the song *Life,* which is the gospel in a nutshell, he nodded in agreement with tears in his eyes.

For centuries, both Arabs and Jews have worked and lived together peaceably in Abu Ghosh and both Arabs and Jews work at the Diner.

I have visited several times since and always been made very welcome by both Uri and his son Amir, who took over the management of the Inn.

Known as the "Mountain Inn Truck Stop" when it opened in 1974, it displayed a few of Uri's photos of Elvis. Gradually, it became informally known as the "Elvis Inn." Uri was all too happy to embrace this new identity more officially, renaming the restaurant the Elvis American Diner.

In the grounds are two statues of Elvis, one painted gold and the other made of bronze. Since 1976, the Elvis Inn has been home to a vast collection of Elvis memorabilia, as well as a fully stocked Elvis jukebox. The diner has more than 1,000 Elvis photographs and posters from movies and concerts. There are two statues of Elvis inside, one standing at the bar and another sitting at a table. The diner serves everything from Elvis burgers and tempting ice cream treats to Middle Eastern specialties like baba ganoush and baklava.

Don Sundquist, Governor of Tennessee, visited the Inn on January 8th, 1997 while visiting Israel with a delegation of businessmen and academics to create the Tennessee-Israeli Co-operation Committee, aimed at forging business and cultural links.

After Elvis died, Uri invited ETAs to mark Elvis' birthday and his passing with karaoke and an Elvis party. Here is one story from such an event:

On a visit to the Inn, in 2000, while filming for a documentary, Elvis Schmelvis, a Jewish ETA, with a full beard and dressed in a white jumpsuit, being somewhat of a comedian asked if they served kosher peanut butter and banana sandwiches, (one of Elvis' favourite snacks) which of course they were happy to prepare for him.

He noted that meanwhile, outside, a bus full of Palestinian children arrived on a day trip from the Gaza Strip. The children were very excited when they spotted Schmelvis, and their teacher asked him to sing for them. Schmelvis climbed up on the statue and sang. His cameraman reported:

"The children go nuts swarming around him, banging drums and singing along with him. Their teacher stands beside me and surveys the scene of an Orthodox Jewish Elvis impersonator bonding with Arab school children.

"'Elvis brings peace through the children' says the teacher.

"'Will you say that on camera?' I asked her. 'I can't, I would be in grave danger.'

"Schmelvis boards the bus to say goodbye to the children. 'You've been a wonderful audience. Thank you very much.'"

I love this story and it makes me wonder what Elvis himself might have done about trying to bring peace to the Middle East through his singing, had he lived.

***

Elvis admired the Jews and knew that he had Jewish blood in him, but I wonder how much he considered the Jewish roots of the Christian faith. I certainly did not appreciate the strong connection until much later in my walk with the Lord. Of course, I knew that Jesus was Jewish, but had not realised that Christianity is the ongoing story of the Jewish faith. I learned more about this in Memphis where there is a Messianic Jewish Congregation. These are Jewish people who have accepted Jesus (Yeshua) as their Messiah.

We were in Memphis at Easter time, which, that year, coincided with the Jewish Feast of the Passover. The Passover commemorates the night when the Angel of Death passes over (does not visit) the houses of the Israelites in Egypt, because of the lamb, which they had sacrificed and painted its blood on their doorposts, according to God's instructions. (This can be read in the Bible in Exodus 12.) In the New Covenant, Jesus is the perfect sacrifice (that is why he is called the Lamb of God) and all who use (plead) the blood of the perfect sacrifice are saved from spiritual death. We attended a wonderful meal and drama production by the Messianic Jewish Congregation, held at a lovely Country Club. We learned a lot about the significance of all the various parts of the Passover meal. And of course, the Holy Communion or Lord's Supper celebrated by the Christian church is in fact a remembrance of the Passover meal (Last Supper), which Jesus celebrated with his disciples the night before he was crucified.

During this meal, I looked out of the large picture window at the beautiful clear blue sky and saw a full rainbow. There was no rain nor clouds in sight. Somehow, I was very encouraged by that. Apparently, it is a very rare phenomenon caused by raindrops blown in from miles away, all that is needed is moisture droplets in the air to refract the sunlight, splitting it into its seven colours.

***

There are several organisations in the UK which have a membership and newsletter and organise Elvis conventions and tours to USA and Europe.

The Official Elvis Presley Fan Club of Great Britain began in 1957. In 1967, Todd Slaughter became the President and, as we have seen, developed a special relationship with the Colonel, resulting in Fan Club members receiving privileges such as special parties in the USA, meetings with Elvis and, in the UK, being able to watch Elvis movies before they were screened in the cinemas. The idea behind the 1973 satellite TV show, "Elvis: Aloha from Hawaii" was originally conceived by Todd, who shared the idea with the Colonel. More recently, Todd wrote to President Trump and encouraged fans to do the same, requesting that Elvis posthumously receive the Presidential Medal of Freedom. Our Elvis Gospel Fan Club did this, enclosing a CD of Elvis' gospel songs.

The Elvis Gospel Fan Club was established in August 1999 by my husband, Peter, and myself. As has already been reported, we organised several events in Memphis. We also hosted a conference in Manchester, UK and have held several Elvis Gospel Services and concerts at our local churches. I have been contacted over the years by UK radio and TV stations and have had the opportunity to talk about Elvis' love of gospel music and, of course Jesus! We now mostly operate via our web site www.elvisgospel.com and a monthly newsletter. We also have a Facebook page – Elvis Gospel UK. Our Fan Club is for people who enjoy the gospel music that Elvis sang, and whom we hope to encourage to appreciate more deeply the wonderful Gospel of Jesus Christ.

Strictly Elvis UK was started in 2009 by David Wade when his long-established Elvis Travel Service and the Elvis in Wales Fan Club joined forces to put the "real" Elvis into the Porthcawl Elvis Festival which then featured only Elvis Tribute Artists and it was rare even to hear Elvis' voice. They took this as a challenge and so, during the festival, hosted an all-day free admission Elvis Open House followed by an all-Elvis Video Disco. It was a tremendous success – thus Strictly Elvis was born. They organise many trips to the USA and other Elvis fan get-togethers including an annual week-long event. Unlike many other organisations they don't use ETAs as, of course, they are "strictly" Elvis.

We attended the Strictly Elvis Festival in Great Yarmouth in 2015. They always include a Gospel Service. Rev Derek Aldred, an Elvis fan was the preacher. He is a "natural" at telling us of the love of God in an amusing and challenging way and had us singing gospel songs along with Elvis. The Bible passage he chose, 1 Corinthians 13, was Elvis' favourite Bible passage and Linda Thompson had the last verse engraved on a plaque for Elvis.

Strictly Elvis has organised Elvis Gospel Concerts in Llandaff and Coventry Cathedrals and the Brangwyn Hall in Swansea, which featured Elvis' Imperials and the wonderful Morriston Orpheus Male Voice Choir.

Essential Elvis headed up by Andrew Hearn is another organisation which does not use ETAs. They organise events for the sale of memorabilia and musical events with guests who knew Elvis. One such event we attended was in 2004 where the special guests were the Sweet Inspirations.

The "Sweets" are great fun and gave us an enjoyable time of reminiscences of Elvis. They also spoke warmly of Priscilla and Lisa Marie. Myrna Smith, who was married to Jerry Schilling for a time, was the most talkative and spoke of the fact that it was impossible to capture the wonder of Elvis' voice on a recording. She said that it had a quality that could only be appreciated when heard live. When asked what she thought Elvis would be doing if he were still alive today, her answer was, "singing and have a gospel ministry." She said that Elvis knew that God had put him on earth for a purpose.

The highlight of the event was near the end when Shayne Driscoll, who was interviewing them, asked if they would sing for us. This is how Shayne described that time:

"What followed was a minute or two of sheer heaven. Without any kind of assistance, everyone became stunned when the Sweets performed a chilling version of *The Lord's Prayer* (one of Elvis' favourites), totally unaccompanied. Their powerful voices forced several people to tears and demanded a standing ovation. It really was one of those moments you'll never forget."

Essential Elvis also organises tours to the USA and Germany and are still researching Elvis' time in Europe to add extra sites to their visits.

CDs and DVDs

Since Elvis died there have been many CD compilations and DVD films produced, some of which are specifically gospel. These include:

"He Touched Me: The Gospel Music of Elvis Presley" DVD – This was produced in 2000, and I often wondered why the Bible is open at Psalm 40 in some frames of this video. Admittedly, it is difficult, but not impossible, to read the artfully blurred image and identify it as Psalm 40. I asked Joe Moscheo, one of the Imperials who sang with Elvis and who was involved with the film, about this and he seemed to think that the Bible was randomly opened for the shot. If it was chosen deliberately then it is a good choice, if it was a random choice then it is amazing because I would like to suggest that this psalm (prayer/song) of King David would exactly express Elvis' feelings in those last few months as he approached his death. If you read it for yourself, I believe you will see the parallels in Elvis' life. Here are the first three verses:

1. I waited patiently for the Lord; he turned to me and heard my cry. 2. He lifted me out of the slimy pit, out of the mud and mire; he set my feet on a rock and gave me a firm place to stand. 3. He put a new song in my mouth, a hymn of praise to our God. Many will see and fear the Lord and put their trust in him.

The Royal Philharmonic Orchestra – In 2015, "If I Can Dream: Elvis Presley with The Royal Philharmonic Orchestra" was released. It was recorded at Abbey Road Studios and features new versions of some of Elvis' hits including *Bridge Over Troubled Water, How Great Thou Art* and *If I Can Dream.*

Conceived by producer Don Reedman with the backing of Priscilla Presley, the Royal Philharmonic added "lush new arrangements" to original vocal tracks recorded by Elvis. Elvis' voice has previously been posthumously added to duets on the *Duets and Harmonies* album, featuring Barbra Streisand, his daughter Lisa Marie and Susan Boyle.

The Royal Philharmonic CD was so successful that it was soon followed by the albums *The Wonder of You* and *Christmas with Elvis.*

"Where No One Stands Alone" – This CD containing 16 of Elvis' gospel songs was released in 2018.

Joel Weinshanker, managing partner of EPE, was involved with the productionof this album. In the liner notes, he says, "The idea of this came from the stories told by Lisa Marie and by Elvis' friends, musicians, singers who would talk with such passion about his love of the gospel, how he would sing each song as though it was the first time or last time ever. What I was not prepared for was the raw power and emotion that came, not only from the amazing singers we were so blessed to have been able to bring back to the same studios where they recorded with Elvis more than half a century ago and from Lisa Marie singing with her dad, but also from being in the studio with "his" voice. Many a tear (of joy) was shed making his album. I hope this experience has been as meaningful to you as it has been to me."

Lisa Marie says in her liner notes: "Some of the most vivid memories of my father are of him singing gospel. In fact, there were times where I was woken in the middle of the night, (which I did not mind at all) by the sound of my father's indelible voice coming from his bedroom at Graceland singing this incredible music.

"This was his favorite genre – no question about it, he seemed to be at his most passionate, and at peace while singing gospel. He would truly come alive – whether he was singing just for himself and me at home, or on stage in front of thousands of fans.

"It was very a very powerful and moving experience to sing with my father on *Where No One Stands Alone,* the lyrics speak to me and touch my soul. I'm certain that the lyrics spoke to my father in much the same way."

This album provided a first for Elvis as it entered the Billboard Top Christian album chart at No. 1, It was also No. 1 on the Billboard Physical Albums chart and the Billboard Vinyl Albums chart. The album debuted in the Top 10 in the UK, marking Elvis' 53rd UK Top 10 album.

Posthumous Awards

The Induction into the Gospel Music Hall of Fame – The ceremony for this was held on 27th November 2001 at the First Baptist Church, Franklin, situated a few miles south of Nashville. I flew via New York and had a few hours between flights so was able to visit Madison Square Garden where Elvis had performed in 1972, and then on to the Empire State Building. It was sad to not see the twin towers shown on the diagram at the top, as it was just a couple of months earlier that they had been destroyed by the airplane attack on 11th September (9/11). As a response to this attack, in October that year, RCA released *America the Beautiful*, sung by Elvis, all the proceeds of which went to the American Red Cross Disaster Relief Fund.

The Induction Ceremony was preceded by a wonderful reception. I have attended many events where buffet-style food is provided, tables laden with delightful goodies, a feast for the eyes as well as the stomach. This, however, must be one of the best. There was even a chef cooking fresh chicken and vegetables with which he replenished the serving plates. A delicious mulled cider and fresh strawberries dipped in chocolate provided a final treat. In one way I was sorry that I did not have time to try all the delicious fare, but that was because I was so busy talking with and listening to the other guests. I couldn't miss the opportunity to talk with Gordon Stoker of the Jordanaires and his wife, Ed Enoch, formerly of the Stamps, but now with The Golden Covenant, who told me that Elvis was hoping to perform an all-Gospel concert after his 1977 summer concert tour. Joe Moscheo, a former Imperial, was as ever very kind and helpful. He told me that it had been in (GMA) Gospel Music Association's plans for a while to induct Elvis. Now seemed the right time. Joe was a permanent member of the GMA board so, I am sure, had no little influence in the decision to induct Elvis! I was also able to personally thank Bill Gaither for the release of the "He Touched Me – the Gospel Music of Elvis Presley" videos. It was also good to meet, for the first time, Jack Soden and Todd Morgan of EPE (Elvis Presley Enterprises) and to renew acquaintance with the wonderful Patsy Andersen, Fan Relations Manager of EPE.

After the reception, we then moved to the sanctuary (auditorium) of the first Baptist Church. Forget the hard and sometimes cold pews and surroundings of many of our churches in Britain. This was more like a very modern comfortable theatre with plush seating and a well-appointed stage, lighting, sound etc. I had gone to the event with singer/entertainer, Don Richmond, an enthusiastic Elvis fan. We were given priority seating near the front so Don could video the event. My grateful thanks to Don who did such a good job and was able to produce some stills which I have been able to use in reports and articles and, of course, also in this book.

Each inductee, there were eight altogether, was introduced via a tribute artist or video, and then the inductee was presented with the certificate, having already received the medallion. Joe Moscheo, Gordon Stoker and Ed Enoch introduced Elvis, and Jack Soden accepted on behalf of Elvis. In his acceptance speech, Jack recognised that gospel music was Elvis' favourite music and read out a message from Lisa. Marie.

Some of the other inductees had an Elvis connection. Larry Norman, one of the founding fathers of Jesus music in the sixties was an admirer of Elvis and had even written a song, *Elvis Has Left The Building, But God Is In The House.* DC Talk, a Christian rock group, introduced Larry Norman. One of their members, Toby Mac said that Larry and Elvis were his heroes.

It was a wonderful event, but the most moving and treasured part for me, was that I was able to hold and inspect both the medallion and certificate awarded to Elvis. Call me sentimental, but I felt it was a great privilege. Thanks to Jack Soden for allowing me to do that.

The Presidential Medal of Freedom – This was awarded to Elvis on 16th November 2018 by President Donald Trump.

This award, bestowed by the President, is, along with the Congressional Gold Medal, the highest civilian award in the United States. It recognizes those people who have made "an especially meritorious contribution to the security or national interests of the United States, world peace, cultural or other significant public or private endeavors." The medal was established by President Truman in 1945 to recognize notable service in the war. In 1963, President Kennedy reintroduced it as an honour for distinguished civilian service in peacetime.

According to a statement from the White House: "Elvis Presley defined American culture to billions of adoring fans around the world. Elvis fused gospel, country, and rhythm and blues to create a sound all his own, selling more than a billion records. Elvis also served nearly six years in the United

States Army, two years in active service, with four years in the reserves, humbly accepting the call to serve despite his fame … Elvis Presley remains an enduring American icon four decades after his death."

Jack Soden, CEO of Elvis Presley Enterprises and Graceland accepted the award. He said, "On behalf of the Presley family, Elvis' friends and millions of fans, it will be a great honour to accept this award. Elvis loved his country, served proudly in the US Army and would no doubt consider this one of the great honours of his life. We look forward to displaying it proudly at Graceland so the millions of visitors from around the world will be able to see it up close."

Academia

Although Elvis was not interested in "formal" education, it is certainly interested in him. Several universities include the study of Elvis in their courses or hold conferences. In 1995, The University of Mississippi held their first conference on Elvis Presley, entitled, "In Search of Elvis: Music, Race, Religion, Performance, Art. A later conference was entitled, "Then Sings my Soul: Elvis and the Sacred South."

In 2001, The Christian Brothers University in Memphis held a photographic exhibition featuring Elvis, entitled: "Highway to The King – Faces of the Faithful."

In 2004, the inaugural National Elvis Presley Conference was held in Canberra, Australia, organised by Susan Mc Dougall. Susan asked me to contribute a session, "Stories of the Gospel Songs," which I did, though, at the time, was not able to travel all that way from the UK so Susan presented it for me. There were also two academic papers presented, "Elvis Sightings and Faith: Making Sense of the Seemingly Absurd" by Nigel Patterson and "Elvis Presley: Hero with a Thousand Faces" by Susan McDougall. A street parade, an ETA contest, movie screenings and rock 'n' roll dancing were also part of this celebration of Elvis' life.

"New Perspectives on Elvis" – A One-Day International Conference was held in March 2017 at the Memphis Public Library. Their aim was to offer fresh perspectives on Elvis, not only grounding him in the context of his place and time, but also interpreting him in relation to developments both inside and outside the academy. Papers were invited on a range of topics such as class, race, and gender. The Advisory Committee included representatives from, Tennessee State University, University Paul Valery in France, University of

Liverpool and University of Texas. Dr. Mark Duffett, Reader in Media and Cultural Studies at the University of Chester in the UK was also involved.

Dr. Eric Mazur, an Associate Professor in the Religion Department at Bicknell University in Lewisburg is convinced that Elvis' faith was not only genuine but was also an exploring and growing faith. One of Dr. Mazur's courses was "Graceland, Disneyland, Holy Land: Sacred Space in America."

Professor Christine King is an unashamed Elvis fan. When I met her, she was Vice-Chancellor of Stafford University in the UK and was giving a lecture about Elvis in York. She has authored several papers on Elvis and is also a recognised expert on the Holocaust.

Researcher and author, Wanda Schindley, has written, "Elvis Presley and Mark Twain: Two Centuries' Greatest Entertainers Shared Roots of American Exceptionalism" which is a very interesting study of these two American icons.

As we can see, Elvis certainly has a life after death, in the sense that the memory of him has not faded and, in some ways, is becoming even stronger. I have noticed that in the last three or four years there have been more books written about Elvis by people who knew him and who now want to share their stories.

In the next chapter we shall find out more about the continuing interest in Elvis, and how he is such an inspiration.

Nativity scene on the front lawn of Graceland (JP Wilson)

Statue of Elvis outside the Elvis American Diner, near Jerusalem, Israel. Seated are the Inn Manager Amir Yoeli with Madeleine and Peter Wilson. (JP Wilson)

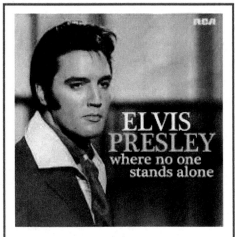

Album released in 2018 on which Lisa Marie sings the title song with her father.

Elvis' GMA Hall of Fame medallion presented in 2001. (Don Richmond)

The Presidential Medal of Freedom awarded to Elvis by President Trump in 2018

This might have been Elvis' reaction at receiving the Presidential Medal of Freedom.

Lisa Marie as she records the song with her father. (elvisinfonet.com)

Chapter 10

The Beat Goes On

There will be no less days to sing God's praise than
when we first began. (From the song – Amazing Grace)

Finalists at the Graceland Ultimate Elvis Tribute Artist Contest. (Graceland)

We have seen that the memory of Elvis is kept alive in many ways, including ETAs. These singers, at least the ones I have met, are sincere fans of Elvis and want to honour him by continuing his legacy. There are around 35,000 ETAs and some were not even born when Elvis died. Some of them have amazing voices and do sound very much like Elvis. I am sure also that they enjoy the admiration they receive, and some have their own Fan Clubs as, to some fans, they are the next best thing to Elvis. It is clear that some people do not like ETAs as they want only the real Elvis. This was the case with EPE as, initially, they were not interested in ETAs and tried to legally prevent people from dressing up and performing as Elvis.

Todd Morgan, EPE's director of media and creative development, had said, "We represent the real thing. The impersonator thing for the public and the press has often been negative. When you think impersonator, you think of parody. We could never find a comfort level in embracing it."

However, in 2006, he said something very different. "Over the past year, we have had a lot of discussion about the Elvis tribute artist phenomenon and what to do about it. We realized it was never going to go away. It has gotten bigger, and the entertainment has gotten better. So, we thought maybe if we get involved in some way, maybe we can bring attention to the most talented tribute artists." Thus, the first Annual Ultimate Elvis Artist Tribute Contest in which they were looking for the "best representation of the legacy of Elvis Presley" was held at Graceland in 2007. It was won by Shawn Klush of Pennsylvania.

As the song *Amazing Grace* says, "When we've been there, ten thousand years, bright shining as the sun, we've no less days to sing God's praise than when we'd first begun." So, when we think of singing, whether it be Elvis, ETAs, opera singers or ourselves, we know that because of Jesus we can be singing God's praise forever! The beat, or the rhythm, of life is eternal as it is not limited to the physical but is spiritual. I am looking forward to having a new body and singing glorious songs, perhaps even with Elvis!

This will also be the hope of the Christian ETAs, some of whom do use their act to promote the Gospel of Jesus Christ. Here are the stories of just three of these very talented people:

Ron Moore – Canadian Ron Moore, has a voice very close to Elvis', and, in fact, it is the closest that I have heard. He first 'met' Elvis in 1956 when he and his brother raced downstairs on Christmas morning to see an Elvis Presley album tucked under their tree. They witnessed Elvis' career unfold and lived it in real time like so many millions of others. Ron says, "We were very fortunate to be alive during the birth of rock 'n' roll. It was a giant era that lived within us. It was a feeling that still lives in me today some 60 years later."

He spent many hours 'with' Elvis, listening to his records and singing with him, trying to sound like Elvis. People who could hear him through his bedroom window would compliment him on how his voice was virtually identical to Elvis'. He would thank them but never gave a second thought to this fact playing a major role in his life. As his skill developed, he started singing in concerts and would always try to promote the Gospel. It has been a great adventure for him, he was even at one time asked to sing for the cast of the TV series, "The West Wing."

Ron has also produced "The Church of Elvis," a three-part documentary that traces Elvis' spiritual journey throughout his life. He has performed many concerts to raise funds for charity, including one where he was backed by the Jordanaires.

Andy Kelso – Andy was born in Yorkshire but has lived in Zimbabwe, South Africa, Ireland, and Switzerland. He survived a near-fatal 75 mph motorcycle accident when he was 19 years old. This caused him to pray for the first time in his life. After training as an actor and running his own theatre company, he felt the call to train for Christian ministry and was a vicar for 25 years, mainly on tough council estates in the UK.

When he retired from parish ministry in 2009, he prayed for 15 months for God's direction. He says, "Out of the blue, I felt God say, 'Take Elvis to the churches.'" He launched his first Elvis concert in 2011 and has been amazed at the positive response. He says, "It's been a thrilling journey to connect with those who normally never go to church!" He finds that the gospel songs "really touch hearts" as he weaves in stories about his own troubled childhood and teenage years. Describing his show, Andy sees it "as a form of reaching out to people, using the king of rock 'n' roll to introduce people to Jesus, hopefully in a way that will be fun."

He has also presented an Elvis Gospel Service on BBC Radio, singing gospel songs and talking about Elvis' own spiritual journey which proved to be very popular, with people phoning in for copies of the broadcast.

I have previously mentioned that had Elvis lived, he might have gone to Israel to help in the peace process in some way. Well, Andy was asked to help with the Irish peace process in Belfast in Northern Ireland. Even though the conflict was officially resolved in 2011, today there is still a wall, like that in Bethlehem or the former Berlin Wall, dividing part of the city and, in 2014, there was still much tension in the air. So, a local church minister in the troubled area of Belfast invited Andy to bring his "Ministry of Elvis" message of peace.

During the day "Elvis" walked the Peace Line and met residents. Andy recalls, "When Saturday morning came lots of people had heard about the walk so there were a lot of tooting horns and "Go for it Elvis" shouted. I had a police escort and a posse of photographers. I walked up to the Falls Road library and sang some songs on the steps there, talking to people. I then walked to the Peace Gate and sang some more songs before walking to the Shankill Road library where I sang even more. It was a humbling experience as I passed so many places where people had been murdered."

In the evening, Andy performed a concert to raise funds for the Northern Ireland Children's Hospice. Although there was a police presence, it was not needed as "Elvis" can indeed bring peace.

Jeff Mew – Jeff, born in the USA, heard Elvis' music from an early age. Growing up as a child, he and his siblings would play their favourite songs, having fun dancing and singing and goofing around. He says, "Now as an adult, and with a heart for Christian music, I admire Elvis for his kindness to others and his love for Christ, which was communicated through his passion for gospel music." He observes that Elvis' award-winning gospel performances touch the lives of many, and often bring joy, hope and peace.

"Inspired by his legacy, I was led to pursue a dream and step out of my comfort zone in a unique way that allows me to honor God and to serve others. Performing as a Tribute Artist allows me a unique way to serve others through music by singing classic hymns and timeless hits. I believe God still uses Elvis' likeness to inspire others for use for His Glory. I regularly perform around the area and entertain at many senior care facilities. My performances are well received, and I am blessed each time.

"I pray that [as you listen to the gospel songs] your spirit is lifted, your heart filled with joy and a smile shines upon your face. Continue to seek the Lord and trust Him with your whole heart and He will open doors in ways you never knew possible.

"I pray God's blessing and continued favour! Live your dream!"

***

Some ETAs have even started their own events, such as:

Walk a Golden Mile in my Shoes. Blackpool, UK – This is the title of the European Elvis Tribute Artist Contest organised by Martin Fox and Michael King, both ETAs. My husband Peter and I attended the event for a second time in 2005 as we were asked to help organise the Wedding Vows Renewal and Gospel Service on the Sunday. Sky TV News was very interested in the Wedding Vows Renewal Service and interviewed us, giving us the opportunity to say something about the Gospel of Jesus Christ.

We were also very honoured to be asked to be judges of the contest semi-finals and finals along with Larry Geller and a music journalist. We felt that this was an awesome responsibility as these men put so much work into their acts: the singing, the moves, the costumes. Over the two nights, we heard over 100 songs performed, some of them several times. We focused carefully on each artist and were amazed at their dedication. It was so difficult to choose as they were all so good, though it was clear who just had the edge on others. There was such a great atmosphere of appreciation of each other. Those who did not win, though some were clearly disappointed, were pleased for the winners and readily congratulated them.

The European Elvis Championships & Convention, Birmingham UK – In 2011, Michael King decided to start a contest in Birmingham. As well as an overall winner there is a separate Gospel Contest, and we have been judges for that. Again, such a very difficult task often with only a few points difference.

Bridlington, East Yorkshire – This is another seaside town in the UK which hosts an Elvis festival. In 2010, Steve Caprice, at the time an ETA, and his wife, Barbara, started working with the Bridlington Spa to host the Elvis Weekender consisting not only of an ETA competition, including a Gospel Contest, but also concerts, films, and informal fun events. A Gospel Service is held at Emmanuel Church featuring ETAs singing gospel songs as well as, of course, a presentation of the Gospel of Jesus Christ. Many people who would not normally attend a church come along and are blessed, saying that they have never heard before what the Gospel is all about. The Bishop of Selby, Martin Wallace, an Elvis fan, was one of the preachers at this service, where everyone received a miniature key to remind them of Jesus being the key to the Kingdom of God. Bishop Martin retired in 2013 and, at his leaving service in York Minster, he had an Elvis gospel section, where Steve Caprice, in his white jumpsuit finery, to the delight of the congregation, sang *Where Can I Go but to the Lord?* and *Working on a Building.*

The English Elvis Experience – This was founded in 2019 by Matt and Monica King. It is a three-day event with tribute acts from Europe and the USA. It also features original Elvis concerts on-screen accompanied by live music from an eight-piece band with backing singers. I am pleased to say that they do have a gospel show on the Sunday. Although there are ETAs involved, it is not a competition, and the main purpose is to have fun enjoying Elvis and his music. Matt King says about Elvis: "Through all my journeys and highs and lows in life, this man and his inspiration have never failed to pull me through."

***

The beat also goes on in many other one-off events such as:

Elvis Artist of the Century Ball Birmingham, UK 1999 – This was a very enjoyable evening organised by the Official Elvis Presley Fan Club of Great Britain. The highlight of the evening was a performance by Shaun Neilson, who sang as part of Elvis' backing singers in the '70s. Shaun sang gospel and other songs of Elvis, but it was the gospel songs which received the most applause.

I had the opportunity to speak with Roger Semon, who worked for RCA compiling the Elvis releases and, at the time, was acting as an advisor to them. He told me that they were working on a new gospel album. I asked him why the song *Life* had never been included in a gospel album, as it was the gospel in a nutshell. He agreed that it was and said he would include the song *Life* in the compilation, just for me. I am pleased to say that he kept his promise!

Another person we met was Ron Harper, an Elvis fan whom we did not know, but who felt that he needed to come and speak to me. Ron told us that he had recently had an urge to sing Elvis gospel songs. We talked about the gospel songs and the importance of getting right with God. A few weeks later, Ron wrote to us to tell us that he had given his life to the Lord.

Ron has more than a passing resemblance to the '68 Comeback Elvis and has a good singing voice. His workmates and friends often say, "Here comes Elvis." Ron and his wife Denise are now wonderful evangelists, wanting to tell everyone about the love of Jesus. They have ushered many souls into the Kingdom of God. I always enjoy phone calls from Ron as they are full of the good news of all the wonderful things the Lord is doing.

Does God Break Guitar Strings? – Terry Mike Jeffrey is a Christian singer, songwriter and actor from Kentucky, USA. He sounds very much like Elvis but does not try to look or act like Elvis. We had previously seen him perform at an Elvis event in Leicester and looked forward to seeing him at the Elvis Monthly Road Show in Birmingham in January 2000. He was due to perform after the interval. During the interval, I asked him if he was going to sing any gospel. He said he might sing one. Due to family illness, he did not have all his backing group with him and the stand-in musicians he was using had not rehearsed the gospel songs. Peter and I prayed that, despite this, he would sing some gospel.

Terry Mike started his show, which was as professional and excellent as ever. He was into about his third Elvis song when an interesting incident took place. His guitar string broke. He looked straight at us and said, "We know why that happened, don't we?" He then had to reorganise his programme and proceeded to sing several gospel songs, accompanying himself on keyboards. He included *How Great Thou Art* and *Swing Down Sweet Chariot*. They were the most appreciated songs of the whole event, bringing tears to many an eye. Todd Slaughter, Chairman of the Official Elvis Presley Fan Club of Great Britain, who was hosting the show, thanked Terry Mike for the "gospel section" and said that it was a side of Elvis which was often neglected. We, of course, know that it is a side which is now gaining recognition, for which we thank God.

"The King" – this ballet by Peter Shaufuss was performed at Sadler's Wells Theatre in London, in April/May 2000. Being a ballet, the movements are open to various interpretations but, for me, the essence of the ballet was that it focussed on Elvis' relationship with God. Out of the nineteen Elvis songs played, seven were gospel songs. It was not only that, but the juxtaposition of the songs which were interesting. The first act finished with Elvis singing *He Touched Me*, which clearly refers to Jesus, and that was followed by Elvis singing *The Wonder of You*. In both cases, the dancer playing the "Elvis" character was reaching up to heaven many times during his performance. This was so poignant for me because I have always thought that *The Wonder of You*, which is a love song – someone praising his or her lover – could also be used as a worship song to Jesus. After all, the Bible says that Jesus is the lover of our soul, so we could show our appreciation of him by singing this song to Him. The second act ended with the *American Trilogy* (Glory, Glory, Hallelujah – "Hallelujah" meaning "Praise the Lord"), followed by *He Is My Everything*. One of the most dramatic dances was near the end, when "Elvis" in his white jumpsuit, dropped to the floor and his cape was snatched off his back. He then crawled to gather up the cape, folded it up then, kneeling, lifted it up to heaven, as though handing his "mantle" back to God. Powerful stuff! I doubt there was a dry eye in the place.

Joseph and his Amazing Technicolour Dream Coat – Many people will have seen this musical, perhaps, like me, several times. It is great fun and life-affirming. It tells the Biblical story of Joseph, one of the 12 sons of Jacob, who is sold into slavery by his brothers, but eventually triumphs. Bill Kenwright who produced the musical is an Elvis fan, and could not resist portraying Pharoah, the king of Egypt, as Elvis. In the film version of this, Pharoah and the dancers are even wearing blue suede shoes!

"Elvis" Saves U2 Concert – In 2015, a technical failure turned into an Elvis opportunity at a U2 concert in California. When a piano failed, Bono engaged in some impromptu banter with the crowd. Noticing an ETA in the crowd, he invited him on stage. He asked him, "What's Elvis doing in the crowd?" Pretending to be awed by the presence of 'Elvis,' Bono bowed down in front of the ETA and said, "Dude, I have everything by you. Everything. This is unbelievable. I always wanted to meet you, dude. Love your early work." The Edge tried to rescue the situation by starting a song, but Bono signalled for him to wait and asked the ETA to sing *Can't Help Falling In Love*, which he did, to rapturous applause. (The ETA was "Dodger Elvis" – Danny Del Toro)

In the past, Bono has noted, "Elvis Presley is like the 'Big Bang' of rock 'n' roll. It all came from there, and what you had in Elvis Presley is a very interesting moment because you had two cultures colliding there. You had a kind of White, European culture and an African culture coming together – the rhythm of Black music and the melody chord progressions of White music. That was the moment. Out of all that came the Beatles and the Stones, but you can't underestimate what happened. It does get back to Elvis."

"Thank You Very Much" – 17th July 2019 was the world premiere, in Manchester, of this theatrical dance event featuring Claire Cunningham and Tanja Erhart, two dancers who can only move around using crutches. They were performing with two able-bodied dancers, Daniel Daw and Vicky Malin, all dressed in jumpsuits. I was privileged to be at that performance.

Claire, born the year that Elvis died, would not call herself an Elvis fan but she was fascinated by the ways he danced, moved, and behaved when he was a young singer. She could see that he disturbed people. She recognised that was how people are inclined to treat disabled people – when they move and speak, people find them disturbing, even troubling. She visited the Porthcawl Elvis festival to see how the ETAs worked and realised that they connected to her own work. She grew to understand their care and dedication as performers, their desire to create respect rather than make fun of Elvis.

In her work, Claire desires to confront the able-bodied expectations of disabled people. She feels that many of us have an idea of how everyone should move, look, be – the unspoken presence of an ideal, to which they are compared and fall short, and that standing out in a crowd can be intimidating or transformative.

This really was a very moving and thought-provoking performance. The Herald review summed it up well, "Astonishing…a life-affirming display of community spirit that would make Elvis quiver with pride."

***

As we have already seen, Christian ministers often use Elvis to help promote the Gospel of Jesus Christ. Rev. Bruce Sheasby of Your Grace Land Ministries in the USA is another of the Christian ministers with whom we are in contact, and who uses Elvis' music to promote the Gospel. Rev. Sheasby, aka "Reverend Elvis" is an ordained minister with over 25 years' experience as a pastor and spiritual leader, who also has a long history of being inspired and influenced by the musical style of Elvis. This has become part of his ministry, which he says, "helps people to connect with Divine Grace, through message, prayer, meditation and music, including weekly half-hour services, radio podcasts and more."

In 1998, he hosted an International Elvis Gospel Festival as a church fundraiser in the small town of Vauxhall in Alberta, Canada. At that time, he was nicknamed "Reverend Elvis" and later added Elvis to his legal name. He has recorded and performed with Elvis' Imperials and raised hundreds of thousands of dollars for charities in his Rev. Elvis and Friends Blue Christmas benefits. He is planning a book, entitled "Your Grace Land – Maybe It's Time."

***

As well as inspiring people to continue the memory of Elvis, sometimes love of or interest in Elvis has been life changing. Here are some more stories:

Elvis Was My Speech Therapist – As an 18-year-old, James Bradley was involved in a horrific car accident that left him unable to speak or walk. Doctors said he would never recover yet, through a combination of attitude, determination and Elvis music playing continuously in his room, James made a full recovery, a recovery his doctors called a miracle.

The Gates of Heaven – Patrick Byrne, an Elvis fan and ETA, remembers a significant event, featuring an Elvis song. He writes:

When I was in intensive care for six days, I was weak but awake, I saw many people come in and they were very ill so I would pray for them and their

330

families. On day three, I was weaker and thought I needed prayers but then thought "no!" it was selfish to pray for oneself, so I did not. So, on day six, I was in so much pain with very little movement. That night I looked at the ceiling listening to *The Impossible Dream* and said, "I need your help," and soon fell to sleep. I had a dream. I was at the bottom of the longest staircase I have ever seen and there were three boxes with a sign saying, "pick one," so I did. Inside, was a golden key so I took it out and then started to climb the stairs. It took me most of the night to get to the top and at the top there were gates. I looked around and there was no one around so I tried the key in the lock. It would not turn so I shook the gates to loosen the lock but still it would not unlock, and, at that point, I see a man walking towards me, so I shouted, "Hello can you help me?" The man drew closer and said to me "Can I help you, my son?" I said, "The key don't work." He said, "I know." I said "Why?" He replied with a soft voice, "It's not your time yet, you have so much more to do for me, I will call you when I need you." At that point, I just turned around and started back down the long stairs. Next day, I woke up and I was so much better. So did my prayer work? Did this Elvis song pull me through? Or was it my faith? Make of this what you want. All I know, something brought me back. So, this song means so much to me. May God bless you all, Yours, Pat (Elvis Tribute Patrick Byrne).

Journey from Fear to Freedom – An inspiring story I came across recently is that of Adrian Keller, who was born in Romania and who, as a young man, suffered deprivation and torture under the Communist regime. However, he was able to escape, though he vividly remembers the gunshots being fired at him as he crossed the border. He eventually found a sponsor in Dallas, Texas, so was able to move to the USA to work. However, his main focus was to get to Memphis and Graceland. He so admired Elvis, born into relative poverty, having persevered, and worked hard to become successful. To this young man, what Elvis had done represented freedom. He had been free to live out his dreams. It gave Adrian a sense of hope, that he could do the same.

Aged 18, he made his way to Memphis in an old car, which he needed to sleep in as he had no job. Impoverished and hardly speaking any English, he was able to get to Graceland at 3am, with the help of a bemused police officer, where he placed a rose on Elvis' grave. As he contemplated Elvis' life at his graveside, he thought of how Elvis showed the world that singlehandedly a man can change the world for better, that there is good in this world, that the human spirit is always free and, above all, there is *hope*.

Adrian eventually found himself working for the owner of Crown Electrics, where Elvis worked as a teenager. The owner, Mr James Tipler, who employed Elvis, gradually opened up and told some interesting stories which give a clear picture of the young Elvis before he became Elvis the icon. Adrian recalls all of this in his book "Elvis Before Graceland."

Adrian Keller's dream has come true. He gained a PhD in Aerospace engineering and is a Mathematics and ACT (American College Testing) Instructor.

He is also following Elvis' example by helping people. In 2017, an Air Force veteran and father of four, Devin Wilson, was shot and killed in a Memphis restaurant trying to break up a fight between a man and woman. Adrian set up a donation fund for the family and offered his tutoring service for all of Devin's children until they finish high school. He said that he would also help prepare them for the ACT.

"Elvis Lives in Me" – Peter Westerveld, a Marine in the Dutch Royal Navy says, "Elvis is not dead, he lives inside of me." When Elvis passed away on 16th August 1977, the day his brother turned eleven years old, and who, like him and his mother, was a big Elvis fan, Peter says, "I was nine years old at that time, and I couldn't understand that my mother was crying that afternoon when I got home from playing with my friends. Maybe she was sad because my father was at sea on this happy occasion. She said to me: 'Peter, sit down, I've got something to tell you: Elvis has died.'

"It felt like a shockwave went through the house and I was blown away by this news. The man who brought so much joy in our household, the man who made my mum sing, was gone. I was brought up with Elvis music and couldn't imagine that there wasn't going to be a new song by the King. Of course, I was wrong about this, Elvis became bigger and bigger after his unfortunate death, and so did my interest in him. I feel like he has never passed away; he just got bigger and bigger inside of me.

"As a result of this, Elvis goes with me wherever I go. For example, when I'm at sea or in foreign parts, like the Caribbean or Afghanistan. The tours would not be complete for me if I didn't have the music of the King. It helps me through all my moods, the happy ones but especially the sad ones. The King is dead, long live the King."

An Overcomer - Julie Anne McBride contacted me by phone from Australia in the late 90s soon after we had established the Elvis Gospel Fan Club. She was very keen to help with what we were doing, and I am sorry I did not take her up on all the help she offered. She very kindly sent us a 25th Anniversary Limited Gold Edition set Elvis the Definitive Collection of 8 DVDs covering Elvis' life and beyond. It had been produced by the newly formed Australian Company, Rayjon Vision. Because Julie found it difficult typing, she preferred phone calls and we had several. She was a lovely enthusiastic lady, and I was sad to hear that she passed away in 2019. I want to honour her as a fellow Christian and Elvis fan who was determined to let people know about the love of Jesus, so here is an overview of her amazing story:

Julie Anne Lambert was born in 1951, suffering from cerebral palsy. When she was five years old her parents reluctantly decided to put her into institutional care. Although her parents drove the four hours twice a week to bring her home for the weekend, her time at the institution was not happy and Julie Anne did not progress very much. Eventually, during her teens her intelligence and gifting were recognised, and she had teachers who helped her Matriculate. Her first job was in a sheltered workshop which she was loved and enjoyed working and learning new skills. She knew also that when her parents could no longer care for her, her brother, her only sibling would continue her care. There was little to fear. That was until 1975 when her brother was killed by an exploding drum of weedkiller on the family farm. This was a great shock to Julie Anne, and she started to ask, "Where is God?", "What is there for me?" "Who will look after me?" She said to God "If you are real help me to understand why you took my brother."

The next day she came across a youth pastor of a church she had once attended and he introduced her to Jacob's Ladder, a Christian community ministering to Adelaide's poor and marginalised. It was through the care of this community that Julie Anne moved from being a nominal Christian to a living relationship with Jesus. She said, "I have never had any trouble believing in the cross or the virgin birth, but I was 24 before I was born again." With the support of the community Julie gained confidence and independence and she began caring for others, eventually setting up a community house for people with disabilities and for the able. This was a new concept, but Julie Anne was given a grant from the government for her Koinonia ministry. What she had learned at Jacob's Ladder, cooking, washing, interdependence, and a meaningful existence she passed onto others. Because of this she has something in common with Elvis. In 1985 she was presented with the Jaycees Award.

Soon after this she married Neville McBride with whom she had become friends and the relationship had developed. They believed that the Lord had drawn them together because of the work they were doing. They both continued helping the disabled by setting up the Koinonia Trust. Part of that work is raising community awareness of the worth and talents of all people, especially those with disabilities.

Julie Anne's (JA) husband Neville, tells us:

"JA's interest in Elvis started when she was very young and was probably taken by his charisma and love and respect that he portrayed to people. I'm told she had a large poster of Elvis on her bedroom ceiling where she was staying in the support accommodation in Adelaide.

"In the days of LPs, JA had records of Elvis that could not be bought in Australia. On becoming a Christian at the age of 24 (when her brother was killed), where she had Elvis as KING, she swapped the King title to Jesus her Lord and Saviour.

"JA always wanted to go to America but unfortunately didn't make it. The advent of computers and the internet opened a whole new and wide world for someone with a disability. JA would research and investigate; she had the endurance and tenaciousness to push through with drive and determination."

Julie Anne surely was an overcomer, who found Elvis a source of inspiration and encouragement and who, like Elvis, wanted to be a blessing by helping others.

"What Elvis Meant to Me" – James Thompson had a life-changing experience while standing by Elvis' graveside. He so wanted to share his story that he wrote a letter to be published far and wide. I have edited it for length.

Dear Friend of Elvis,

I would like to share with you "What Elvis Meant to Me." I became an Elvis fan when I was about 11 or 12 years old. It started when my mother got the record The Wonder of You. There was something special about that record. Shortly after that, I started going out and buying Elvis records, it got to the stage where I was buying anything that had Elvis' name on it. I also joined several Fan Clubs and attended film shows and discos.

On the 13th of August 1980, I was on the Elvis Memorial Tour in Memphis. On the 16th, I was up at Graceland with thousands of other fans.

I was standing at the side of Elvis' grave when I heard a voice asking me, "James, where would you be if you were to die tonight?" I looked round to see who it was but there was no one near me. Then the Bible verse John 14 verse 6 came to me "Jesus saith, I am the way…" Another verse came to me, Genesis 6 verse 3, "My spirit shall not always strive with man…" That night I went back to my apartment and got down at the side of my bed and asked the Lord Jesus Christ into my life.

For me to tell all of what the Lord has done for me would take until next week. I have seen the Lord answer prayer and heal a young lad before my eyes. There have been other times when he has answered prayer. "He sticketh closer than a brother." When my father was called home to be with his Saviour, the Lord was really close to my family and me. My friend, if you don't know the Lord Jesus Christ as your own personal Saviour you don't know what you are missing. You know the Lord doesn't promise us next month, next week or tomorrow. He doesn't even promise us our next breath. Some people I talk to say they are too young to become Christians, they say "I'll leave it until five minutes before I die." WILL YOU HAVE 5 MINUTES?

I would like to ask you the same question the Lord asked me, "Where would you be if you died tonight?" Must close for now. Yours, James Thompson

Does God Visit Shopping Malls? – When I first met Patsy Anderson, it was in her office at the EPE headquarters, sited next to Graceland in the building that used to be the home of the Graceland Christian Church. Patsy is a wonderful Christian lady, very warm and friendly. She did an excellent job as the Fan Relation's Manager and has now retired from that. She is very interested in our Gospel Fan Club and very supportive.

Whilst I was with her, she told me a wonderful story of a letter she had received, in about 1989, from a lady who had written to her because she thought "people need to know." This lady was a single mum with two children, but she was in the depths of despair. She had found no other alternative but to commit suicide. She had bought the gun and chosen the date. She had bought her children new clothes and made all the preparations. Last minute, however, she decided to go out and buy some more things she thought the children would need. As she was passing by a record store in the shopping mall, they were playing Elvis, singing a gospel song. She then felt some hands on her shoulders, holding her, so that she could not move, but had to stop and listen to the song (there was no visible person behind her). After hearing the song, she realised that she must not kill herself, but must go on with God's help. At the time of writing the letter, she was happily settled into her new life and was an active member of a church. Patsy later shared this story at one of the Porthcawl Elvis Festivals.

Elvis Gospel Fan Club – Some of our members told us of their favourite gospel songs and shared their stories of being inspired or helped by Elvis' singing:

John – "I heard his songs *How Great Thou Art*, and *Amazing Grace*. These two songs have touched my life. When I hear his voice with these songs, I really feel within myself some sort of strength."

John – "*We Call on Him*, the words are so true to life, 'we call on him in times of trouble, why is it that only when were lonely.' I used to be like that but now I speak to God every day, thanking him for all that he has given me in life. I also love *Mama Liked the Roses*, again lovely words describing how much Elvis loved his mum, it also made me appreciate how much my mum means to me."

Celia – "Elvis has always impacted my life especially since my husband died. Every time I listen to my Elvis gospel CDs, I remember my husband's funeral where I played *Amazing Grace*, it comforts me so."

Don – "I would say that when I accepted Christ in 1978, not knowing anything about Contemporary Christian music yet, the only Christian music I really knew at the time was the five gospel albums from Elvis."

Brenda – "At the end of the day, I read my emails and do computer work and listen to Elvis singing *Take My Hand, Precious Lord*. This takes all the day's troubles and cares away and refreshes me, just singing about the Lord taking my hand and leading me and hearing it done so magnificently by Elvis. Also, I don't think anyone can hold a candle to his rendition of *Amazing Grace* and *How Great Thou Art*."

Fay – All his songs have a meaning throughout my lifetime, mainly because I suffer from clinical depression and have tried to kill myself several times and only by listening to Elvis, did I find some peace of mind. I found that parts of our lives have run parallel but in different ways. His songs have been of some help to getting me back to a living life!"

Jan – "Elvis' songs do have a very positive effect on me in general. But I remember one song, it was the first time I heard it and I got tears in my eyes. It was the song *Don't Cry Daddy*. The lyrics are so sad, and Elvis managed to tell the story with passion and feeling and it touched me so. I could feel the pain the family was suffering which made me cry. It made me see that every day is a gift and I enjoy every day with my wife and two girls. And we all enjoy Elvis and his songs."

Kyle – "When my parents divorced, I was already an adult. My little sister called me in tears to tell me my dad had left, and as I talked to her, I remained as calm and steady as I could, for her benefit. Likewise, when I talked to my mom that night, I was as strong as I could make myself be. But later, when I was alone, I broke down and cried it out for a good hour or more before going to bed. The next morning, as I was preparing for my day, I put on an Elvis gospel album, as I often do. The second song that played was *You'll Never Walk Alone* which I had heard hundreds of times before. As I listened this time, though, the emotion in Elvis' voice and the power of the words and music struck a chord somewhere within me. I had to stop and cry again for my parents. But, in my time since then, whenever I begin to get depressed about the things the devil throws at me, I remember that song, and I take courage in the assurance that I never walk alone – the Lord is with me, and He will guide me through whatever trials I face."

Anne – "It is hard to pick one particular song by Elvis because his music affected me in many ways. My younger brother was diagnosed with a rare cancer in early 1976 and we thought we were going to lose him. I prayed to God that if he would let me see Elvis in concert and get a scarf from him, I would give it to my brother because he loved Elvis. The Lord answered my prayer and I saw Elvis in concert in 1977 and got one of his white scarfs. I gave it to my brother. My brother was healed in 1977 from this rare form of cancer and left the hospital a couple of days before Elvis died. It was like one life was given for another taken. Elvis was very special, and it didn't matter what song he sang it always touched someone. I don't think anyone could have been closer to God than Elvis whenever he thought of others before himself and he gave with a loving and humble heart."

Annette – "My favourite is *How Great Thou Art*. When my grandparents passed away my thoughts turned to the day when Elvis passed away and my grandfather saying that Elvis could not sing that song with such conviction if he hadn't been saved!! It made it a little easier to get through the grief!"

337

Lady Oaks – "Until I became an Elvis fan back in the early 60's, I'd never ever heard of gospel music. Raised as Catholic which I didn't understand, it was Elvis' gospel music that introduced me and my family to Jesus and my Christian faith. I am blessed for this!"

Rosemary – "There's something about him that made me turn to GOD. Most people would say I was mad, and I thought I was but every time I thought of Elvis, GOD was on my mind too. It was not Elvis' gospel music that made me think of GOD, I never played gospel in my life. It's so strange what's happened, I have loved Elvis for forty years and then, out of the blue, I see Elvis in a different way. It was because of him I love the Lord. Do you know of anyone else going though such a strange but moving experience? Thank you."

Annek – "Elvis is my 'bell sheep,' his music fills me with the Holy Spirit and my faith has deepened listening to him praise God with his songs."

Alex – "The gospel music of Elvis has always been a great comfort in my life. When the world seems dark, I go into my studio and, there, I embrace the humble music and words that Elvis tells. It humbles me and I go back to the world, alive and with confidence. The gospel music of Elvis and J D Sumner have been and still are, a great comfort. I sing with them, and through them, I kneel to God and praise His awesome wonder!"

Madeleine – "Of course, Elvis has been a great inspiration to me, to start the Elvis Gospel Fan Club and to write this book! As I discovered more about his Christian roots and his love of the Gospel, I felt that I was getting to understand a side of Elvis that is often neglected. A side which I hope you, dear reader, will appreciate and perhaps even want to discover more about the incomprehensible but not unknowable God to whom Elvis loved to sing."

For God is the King over all the earth. Praise Him with a song! (Psalm 47:7)

Gallery

Pharaoh/ 'Elvis' in the Musical "Joseph and his Amazing Technicolor Dreamcoat".

Rev. Fred Omvlee in Afghanistan welcoming an Islamic Mullah to one of his Christian services. Rev. Fred often played Elvis gospel songs during his services and discussed Elvis with the Mullah.

Japanese Prime Minister Junichiro Koizumi who is an avid Elvis fan, having fun with Priscilla, Lisa Marie and President George Bush when his "dream came true" and he visited Graceland in 2006.

No, Elvis is not consulting his mobile phone by his front door at Graceland, but it is fun to think that he could be if they were available then. He would certainly have owned one, or several.

"Thank You Very Much" musical. (Hugo Glendinning)

Photo used for the cover of the America the Beautiful CD (2001) with the inscription "All record company and artist net proceeds will be donated to the American Red Cross Liberty Disaster Relief".

Epilogue
Why?

As the years go by, this is a question that is increasingly being asked. It is a question which Elvis himself asked many times. Why did God give him such a wonderful voice and so much success? Why was he loved and admired by so many people? Others are now asking why is Elvis still so successful and, one may say, even more popular today, with many more people becoming fans and being deeply moved by his music? Why is Elvis known worldwide? Someone once said that there are three names which are recognised all over the world. They are Jesus, Elvis, and Coca Cola.

There were two comments I read in a well-known Elvis magazine which, I feel, reflect the thoughts of many people. One was from Bill Burk, the editor of the magazine and a friend of Elvis. "How deeply Elvis touched so many millions of lives during his lifetime and continues to do so has never ceased to amaze me. And it crosses political, financial and social boundaries." The other is in the form of a question from Kathy Braquet, a fan from Texas, who wrote: "What is it about this one man that keeps thousands of fans coming back [to Memphis] year after year from all over the world. It's obviously his God-given talent/voice, his sensuous, gorgeous looks, his deep spirituality, and his kindness to others. But it goes *much* further than all of that. It's something that blows my mind, and I can't seem to put my finger on."

Since I became an Elvis fan in 1995, I have also been amazed, and continue to be, by the phenomenon that is Elvis. After researching into his life, particularly the influence of the Gospel in his life, I have discovered many things and have come to the following conclusion, which you may like to consider.

Elvis' upbringing in the "Bible Belt" in the 1930s and '40s, where attending church two or three times a week was normal, ensured that he had a great love for God, a good knowledge of the Scriptures and that he knew how to pray. When they moved to Memphis, his parents made sure that they had a good church to belong to and, having got to know their pastor, Rev. Rex Dyson, I am convinced that his passionate preaching had a great effect on the young teenage Elvis.

341

When they moved to the First Assemblies of God Church, Elvis would continue to get good teaching. After Elvis started travelling and became famous, he no longer had time to attend church regularly and, in any case, was concerned that his presence caused a stir and took the focus away from God. He got his preaching from the television evangelists and, as we have seen, his praise took the form of many hours of singing gospel songs, before, after and in between the shows, with his backing singers such as The Imperials and J D Sumner and the Stamps. At one stage in the '70s, he even had his own gospel group, Voice, whom he employed to sing gospel whenever he required, which often was late at night and into the early hours of the morning.

It is clear that Elvis had many Godly characteristics: beauty, kindness, a sweet nature, a sense of humour, generosity, and an interest in and a desire to help people. His lifestyle, however, did not always reflect the holiness of the awesome God whom he served. There were many forces in his life attempting to lead him away from God, and I am amazed that he kept his sweet nature till the end, even in the face of the most vicious attacks. It certainly is a case of "Amazing Grace."

Having been brought up as a Christian, Elvis knew that he was on earth not only to live a good life and to help people, but that the Lord had a specific purpose for his life. He endeavoured throughout his life to discover that purpose.

It was his desire to be a full-time gospel singer. I believe that, at the time of his death, a full gospel concert was being planned. I believe also that he was called to be an evangelist, that is, not only to sing of God's goodness and love and to give hope but, also, to bring people to a point of recognition of the need for redemption which comes only through Jesus Christ.

So, if this was God's plan for Elvis' life, what went wrong? I would maintain that nothing went wrong, in the sense that God's purposes for Elvis' life are still being worked out. It is true that if Elvis had made a strong and determined effort to break free, he could still be alive, travelling the world, singing, preaching, and leading many people into the Kingdom of God. As it was, Elvis was caught in a trap, from which he could not escape. He was clearly very ill and unhappy in the last few months of his life, and the sickness brought about by his inherited diseases and misuse of prescription drugs caused his demise. However, I believe that as he had accepted the Lordship of Jesus and what he did for him on the cross, he was received into heaven – a place where he now sees Jesus face to face and is having a ball singing gospel forever. As the song says, "we've no less days to sing God's praise than when we first began."

Perhaps Elvis was a type of Samson. Samson was an anointed man of God, who served God well by destroying God's enemies with his exceptional strength but, because of his moral weakness, he lost his strength, was captured, and reduced to being mocked in front of his enemies. Through his death, however, he destroyed more of God's enemies (did more for God) than when he was alive.

Samson's story can be found in the Old Testament of the Bible in Judges:13–16. Of course, we need to keep in mind that since Jesus chose to give up his life and rose again, God's and our enemies, Satan, and his demons, have been defeated. We do not serve God by physically killing his enemies, but by proclaiming the victory over evil that we now have because of Jesus. "Our struggle is not against flesh and blood, but against the rulers, against the authorities, against the powers of this dark world and against the spiritual forces of evil in the heavenly realms." (Ephesians 6:12 in the New Testament of the Bible.)

Perhaps it will be that through his tragic death, which has captured the imaginations of millions and helped to continue the "mystery" of Elvis, Elvis will have reached more people with the gospel than when he was alive. There are many stories of people who came to accept the gospel of Jesus Christ when Elvis was alive, because of attending a concert or listening to recordings of him singing gospel songs. Since Elvis' death, many more people have become Christians from listening to the gospel songs, or even while standing by the graveside at Graceland.

So, that is why I have concluded that what it is about this man, Elvis, is the Holy Spirit. Elvis' lifestyle was not always exemplary in holiness, but Elvis was given a gift to communicate the Gospel, and the gifts of God cannot be revoked, therefore, the charisma of that gift was very attractive, whether or not he used it fully. People are still attracted to, and hungry for, the anointing of the Holy Spirit and the presence of love, which was so evident in Elvis' life.

Why Elvis was and is still so famous and loved is, I believe, because God's plan for Elvis is that hundreds of thousands of people would hear the Gospel through him and be saved. Although Elvis is dead, God is not and, by his Holy Spirit, still reaches out to us to let us know that he loves us passionately and does not desire for any of us to perish.

343

Most fans are horrified by the people who "worship" Elvis in an open physical way. These "worshippers" bow down and kneel before statues of him and look to him to answer their prayers. Elvis consumes almost every aspect of their lives. Most people inherently know that this is wrong and yet one wonders how many "ordinary" fans do in fact worship Elvis without really realising it. During a conversation I had with an "ordinary" Elvis fan who was very happily married and living a very normal life, I asked, "How would you feel if, for some reason, you would never be able to listen to Elvis singing again, for example, if you went deaf, or all of Elvis' recordings disappeared from the face of the earth?" His reply was, "It would be the end of the world. There would be no more reason to live without Elvis. Elvis is everything to me."

Could it be that many fans in their attitude to Elvis are worshipping, not Elvis, but an "unknown God"? They see in Elvis something desirable but cannot quite define what it is. Perhaps it is similar to the situation that the Athenians were in when the apostle Paul found their altar inscribed "TO AN UNKNOWN GOD."

Paul said to them, "Now what you worship as something unknown I am going to proclaim to you. The God who made the world and everything in it is the Lord of heaven and earth and does not live in temples built by hands. And he is not served by human hands, as if he needed anything, because he himself gives all men life and breath and everything else. From one man he made every nation of men, that they should inhabit the whole earth; and he determined the times set for them and the exact places where they should live. God did this so that men would seek him and perhaps reach out for him and find him, though he is not far from each one of us. 'For in him we live and move and have our being.' As some of your own poets have said, 'We are his offspring.' Therefore, since we are God's offspring, we should not think that the divine being is like gold or silver or stone – an image made by man's design and skill. In the past, God overlooked such ignorance, but now he commands all people everywhere to repent. For he has set a day when he will judge the world with justice by the man he has appointed [Jesus]. He has given proof of this to all men by raising him from the dead." (Acts 27:23-31)

These words are as true and relevant today as they were when they were first written.

So next time you listen to Elvis singing gospel, remember that he was a servant of God bringing a message of love and hope to you. And it does indeed "go further than that." God is still alive, only a prayer away, waiting for our response to his ultimate gift. For he so loved everyone in the world, that he gave his only son Jesus that all who believe in him may not perish but have eternal life. It is, as Kathy Braquet says, "something that blows our minds" and may perhaps elicit that trembling question, "What must I do to be saved?"

Perhaps if he were still alive, Elvis would say something like this to us:

"You can just say about all that Gospel stuff *Return to Sender* because *I've Got a Lot of Livin'* to do. You can also say that religion is just a kind of *Good Luck Charm* – only a bit of superstition to make you feel better when you get *All Shook Up* once in a while, or regret paying the heavy price for *One Night of Sin.* Some however are afraid that they're too bad and that it is too late for *A Fool Such as I* and that they have missed their chance of finding God. Some fear they've *Lost That Lovin' Feeling* for the things of God they once had, and that's that.

But *I Believe* that God gives us another chance. You may feel deep down about God, that *You're Always on My Mind* and when the chips are down and I'm left to my thoughts, *I Just Can't Help Believin'*, but beware, *It's Funny How Time Slips Away...* I tell you *Doncha Think it's Time* to *Reconsider Baby.*

Are You Lonesome Tonight? Is there an emptiness in your heart? If you feel stirred and moved and would really like to know the Lord for real, perhaps for you *It's Now or Never.* When you think of Jesus dying on the cross you may not understand all about it, but *If That Isn't Love*, nothing is. Many before you have said *Where Could I Go but to the Lord?*

It is easy to begin that relationship with Jesus, even a simple prayer sincerely said is how you can *Put Your Hand in The Hand (Of the Man from Galilee).* All I can say is that when anyone is willing to *Reach Out to Jesus,* they will know in their heart *He Touched Me*, and then they will want to sing for all to hear *How Great Thou Art. Only Believe* and there will be everlasting *Life* and *Peace in The Valley* for you."

(Thank you to the pastor in Wales who wrote this imaginative encouragement above using the titles of some of Elvis' songs.)

We can have a living, personal relationship with Jesus, through the Holy Spirit. Jesus is only a prayer away. That is a unique phenomenon, true of no other human being who has died. Jesus was fully human and fully divine. Jesus' presence can be felt all over the world, always. He is not restricted by space nor time.

There are four main books written about the life of Jesus. The Gospels of Matthew, Mark, Luke and John. These men were in the company of Jesus, daily for approximately two years. They knew and loved him. Each gospel is a personal account and so each one is different, though many of the events are mentioned in more than one account. In his Gospel, John says that Jesus did many other things as well, and if every one of them were written down he supposed that even the whole world would not have enough room for the books that would be written. I fully recommend these accounts to you and pray that, as you read them, you will understand who Jesus really is, and that like so many others you will come to love and trust him.

The truth is that although Elvis displayed many Godly attributes and brought love, hope and peace to many, he is now dead and can no longer be personally accessed. If all the recordings and films, writings and memories of Elvis were removed from the earth, there could be no more Elvis fans. If all the books and writings and memories about Jesus were removed from the earth, God could still show us directly by his Holy Spirit that the way back to him is through Jesus who is accessible to all humanity.

Elvis is dead, but Jesus is very much alive, by his Spirit. He is the perfect partner in life. However good or reliable a human partner or friend is, they cannot avoid "letting us down" if they die. That is why the grieving process includes anger. We are angry that people die and leave us. Jesus is the perfect partner in life and needs to be our first choice, as He never leaves us nor forsakes us.

Finally, a message for you from Ed Hill, a member of the Stamps Quartet, who sang with Elvis. Just under seven months after writing this for us, Ed went to Glory so will be joining in the heavenly chorus with Elvis.

First of all, I was NOT a Christian when I worked with ELVIS...Just like ELVIS, I was raised in a Christian home. My Dad pastored for 60 years. I knew how to act like a Christian, talk like a Christian. I never asked the LORD to forgive me and come into my heart as Savior.

ELVIS and I was taught the right way to live. All of the people on this earth have sin, and until they ask for the LORD to forgive and come into their heart, they won't go to HEAVEN. I'm glad that, in November 1979, when I asked the

346

LORD to become my Savior he didn't say "I'll let you know" or "Let me think about it," he came into my heart that very minute. I'm so thankful for my earlier teaching just like ELVIS. 'Train up a child in the way he should go and when he is old, he will not depart from it.' PROVERBS 22-6

I pray all your readers, if they don't know the LORD, will make their decision to ask the LORD for forgiveness and come into their heart as their Savior. Ed Hill

Appendix 1

Living the Good Life

In this book, we have seen that some of Elvis' final words, a few hours before he passed away, were to his stepbrother, Rick Stanley, when he said, "Rick, we should all begin to live for Christ." This phrase occurs in the Bible where it says: *And he died for all, that those who live should no longer live for themselves, but for him [Jesus] who died for them and was raised again.* (2 Corinthians 5:15)

Elvis would be aware that, because of some choices he made, he was not always living the good life which the Lord promised him. When we accept that our inherited, broken relationship with God is restored because of Jesus and that we are now reconciled and have a good relationship with God, we automatically want to please him and live for Him. However, because we are not perfect, we still make mistakes, even when we become a Christian, but Jesus is eager to forgive us – all we need to do is ask and we are free from shame.

The most important relationship for every one of us is our relationship with Jesus Christ. Choosing to believe that he is who he claimed to be – the Son of God and the only way to restoring this intentionally good relationship (aka salvation) – and receiving him by faith as our Lord and Saviour is the most vital thing anyone will ever do.

The Bible promises, *"If you declare with your mouth, 'Jesus is Lord,' and believe in your heart that God raised him from the dead, you will be saved. For it is with your heart that you believe and are justified, and it is with your mouth that you profess your faith and are saved."* (Romans 10:9-10) For *"Everyone who calls on the name of the Lord will be saved."* (Romans 10:13)

Living the good life simply means that once we are saved, we are free to love and forgive much more than humanly possible and this leads to peace and contentment. God didn't put us here and leave us stranded without any guidance. He sends His Holy Spirit to teach and guide us on this sometimes-perilous path known as life on earth.

Another very important aspect of living the good life is prayer. This is conversation with God. Sometimes we don't know how to pray, so Jesus taught his disciples how to pray, now called The Lord's Prayer. There are several translations/versions. This is the one which Elvis sang. It is the King James translation (KJV):

Our Father which art in heaven, Hallowed be thy name. Thy kingdom come, Thy will be done in earth, as it is in heaven. Give us this day our daily bread and forgive us our debts, as we forgive our debtors. Lead us not into temptation but deliver us from evil: For thine is the kingdom, and the power, and the glory, forever. Amen.

When praying, we need to be honest with God, (he knows our thoughts anyway) and just pour out our heart to him. He will always listen and respond. When you read some of the Psalms you will see how David, as well as praising God, poured out his heart in times of trouble.

Also, when we don't know how to pray, sometimes speaking in tongues, a heavenly language, is very useful. (This can also be a human language, as on the day of Pentecost everyone heard the Gospel spoken in their own language by the disciples even though the disciples hadn't learned those languages.)

If you have not yet committed your life to Jesus, please make sure that you ask the Lord to come into your life by saying, aloud, this simple prayer:

Dear God, I believe that you love me and that you sent your son, Jesus, to die for me and rise again, so that I can have a good relationship with you. Please forgive me for all the wrong things I have said, thought or done. I ask you, Jesus, by the power of your Holy Spirit to come into my life right now. From now on I want to live the joyful, peaceful life you have promised me. Amen.

The very moment you commit your life to Jesus Christ, you are "born again" and God's Holy Spirit comes to dwell in you, and you can enjoy living your new victorious life.

To grow in faith and enhance your life you will need to have access to a Bible of which there are many good versions. Some people prefer the "old fashioned" King James Version (KJV), which has some very beautiful language. Others prefer the more modern language of the New International Version (NIV), which is the one that I have used mainly in this book. We at Elvis Gospel have several different translations and paraphrases and we use them all. It is good sometimes to compare different versions to get the full meaning of the passage you are studying.

349

If you are not already a member of a church fellowship, do pray and ask the Lord which of your local churches you should join. There are many diverse kinds of Christian churches, all believing in the same Lord Jesus, but preferring different ways of worshipping and/or focussing on different ministries.

If you know a Christian who is a member of a Christian fellowship, then you can ask them for advice and/or information. They will most probably be very happy to pray with you and help you.

I would also recommend the book "The Fusion of Humanity and Divinity – God's Design to Partner with Us" by Victoria Cooper. It shows us how we can grow in grace and live more fully the loving, peaceful, victorious life the Lord desires for us. Interestingly, Elvis gets a mention in the book as being "a classic mix of broken humanity and beautiful Divinity, colliding in a person's soul."

If you need any further information or help, please do not hesitate to contact us at Elvis Gospel: info@elvisgospel.co.uk

We will be very pleased to help you as best we can. That is why we are here!

NOTES:

1. In addition to joining a church, there are several Christian radio and TV stations you can tunc in to so that you can receive positive and encouraging music and speech.
2. In the UK there are radio stations Premier Christian Radio/Premier Praise (www.premierchristianradio.com) and UCB1/UCB2 (www.ucb.co.uk) broadcasting nationally on DAB (Digital Audio Broadcasting) and online.
3. USA Christian local radio stations include the Salem (https://salemmedia.com/radio-stations/) and K-LOVE (www.klove.com) networks.
4. Other countries have Christian radio stations such as Spirit Radio (www.spiritradio.ie) in Ireland and Radio Christian Voice (https://rcvoice.co.zm) in Zambia.
5. Christian TV channels such as God TV & TBN are easily available via their own websites or streaming using Roku Streamers (www.roku.com), offering over 250 Christian channels, or on broadcast linear TV.

Appendix 2

More about the Christian Faith

By J Peter Wilson – Retired Broadcasting Regulation Consultant

Bible-believing Christians know that our Lord Jesus Christ died on the cross and rose again, after three days, in order to overcome death so that the Followers of Jesus can have eternal life after our physical body has died. The Apostle Paul's words are recorded in 1 Corinthians 15:51-53 (CEV): *I will explain a mystery to you. Not every one of us will die, but we will all be changed. It will happen suddenly, quicker than the blink of an eye. At the sound of the last trumpet, the dead will be raised. We will all be changed so that we will never die again. Our dead and decaying bodies will be changed into bodies that won't die or decay.*

Today, and ever since Jesus ascended into heaven, all Followers of Jesus have lived under the New Covenant where God's Word says He does not judge or punish us on this earth – it is the Satan or the devil who seeks any opportunity given to him, by us, through our negative thoughts, words, and actions, to steal, kill and destroy our lives. At the end of our lives, we will stand before God to be judged. In Hebrews 4:13 in The Living Bible (TLB), which is the version of the Bible given to Elvis by Joe Moscheo, we read: *He knows about everyone, everywhere. Everything about us is bare and wide open to the all-seeing eyes of our living God; nothing can be hidden from him to whom we must explain all that we have done.* However, Christians are blessed as we will have Jesus as our advocate at the time of judgement.

The Bible presents salvation as a life-transforming experience. Change is one of the distinguishing characteristics of a true believer of Jesus. Yet, failure to understand that this change takes place in the spirit first, and then is reflected in our outward appearance through our thoughts and actions in direct proportion to the way we renew our minds, causes much confusion. This especially applies to people, who think that they are Christians because they were born into a "Christian home" but have not received Bible-inspired teaching at a local church or through another Christian ministry.

The Christian faith is not a leap in the dark. It rests upon the Word of God. The Apostle Paul emphasises faith when he says at the beginning of Hebrews 10:38

(KJV): *Now the just shall live by faith* and then again in Romans 2:6-7 (NIV) he says: *God "will give to each person according to what he has done." To those who by persistence in doing good seek glory, honour, and immortality, he will give eternal life.*

This change in Christians takes place in our born-again spirit first. Why is that? If you were fat before you got saved, you will be fat after you get saved, unless you go on a weight loss diet regime. Your body doesn't instantly change and neither does your soul or mind.

It is the Christian's spirit that is instantly changed at salvation:

- It is perfect, as it says in 1 Corinthians 15:49 (NIV): *And just as we have borne the image of the earthly man, so shall we bear the image of the heavenly man.*

- It cannot sin, as we read in 1 John 3:9 (B4E): *Everyone who is fathered by God does not go on sinning, because God's offspring remain in him; they cannot go on sinning, because they have been fathered by God.*

- So, everything that is true of Jesus is true of a Christian's born-again spirit. The spiritual salvation is complete. At salvation, the Christian receives the same spirit that he or she will have throughout all eternity. It will not have to be changed or cleansed again.

- It is sealed with the Holy Spirit as it says in Ephesians 1:13 (CSB): *In him, you also were sealed with the promised Holy Spirit when you heard the word of truth, the gospel of your salvation, and when you believed.*

- And therefore, it is sanctified and perfected forever as it says in Hebrews 10:10 (TLB): *Under this new plan we have been forgiven and made clean by Christ's dying for us once and for all.*

For the remainder of the Christian life, a born-again Christian doesn't need to try to obtain faith, joy or love from God, but can release what they already have in their spirits into their soul and body.

In Galatians 5:22-23 (NKJV) we read: *But the fruit of the Spirit is love, joy, peace, longsuffering, kindness, goodness, faithfulness, gentleness, self-control. Against such, there is no law.* Failure to understand this has caused some people to despair when they don't see sufficient change in their life after coming to the Lord for salvation. It must be understood that the change is internal in the Christian's spirit and the outward change will take place as he or she renews their minds through God's Word.

There are three passages in the New Testament of the Bible (each one a long sentence in the original Greek text) that contain the most important theology, that is the study of the nature of God:

- The first on the incarnation (or as the Oxford English Dictionary definition says, "a person who embodies in the flesh a deity, spirit, or quality") is found in John 1:14 (NIV): *The Word became flesh and made his dwelling among us. We have seen his glory, the glory of the one and only Son, who came from the Father, full of grace and truth.*

- The second about the triune, or the three-in-one purpose and glory of God, is fully found in Ephesians 1:3-14 and specifically in Ephesians 1:3 (TPT). We read: *Every spiritual blessing in the heavenly realm has already been lavished upon us as a love gift from our wonderful heavenly Father, the Father of our Lord Jesus – all because he sees us wrapped into Christ. This is why we celebrate him with all our hearts!*

- And the third on justification (the action of showing something to be right or reasonable), redemption (the action of saving or being saved from sin, error, or evil), and propitiation (the action of appeasing a god, spirit, or person) is fully found in Romans 3:21-26 and in Romans 3:22 (MSG). It says: *The God-setting-things-right that we read about has become Jesus-setting-things-right for us. And not only for us but for everyone who believes in him. For there is no difference between us and them in this.*

If a Christian understands these three then they have a solid foundation for their faith. For God looks for diffidence in the way people walk with him, as it says in 2 Thessalonians 3:13 (NIV): *And as for you, brothers and sisters, never tire of doing what is good.*

In the Old Testament Book of Micah 6:8 (MSG) we read: *But he's already made it plain how to live, what to do, what GOD is looking for in men and women. It's quite simple: Do what is fair and just to your neighbour, be compassionate and loyal in your love, and don't take yourself too seriously – take God seriously.*

Yes, we must take God seriously and remember that the Bible presents salvation as a life-transforming experience. Change is one of the distinguishing characteristics of a true believer. This change takes place firstly in the spirit, and then is reflected in our outward appearance through our thoughts and actions in direct proportion to the way we renew our minds.

A prayer that Elvis knew well, is known as the Lord's Prayer, and Madeleine used the King James Version (KJV) that Elvis would have known in Appendix 1– Living the Good Life. However, one of the Bible versions that we use is The Passion Translation (TPT) and the words of the Lord's Prayer said by Jesus in Matthew 6: 9-13, in this version, are as follows: *Pray like this: 'Our Father, dwelling in the heavenly realms, may the glory of your name be the centre on which our lives turn. Manifest your kingdom realm and cause your every purpose to be fulfilled on earth, just as it is fulfilled in heaven. We acknowledge you as our Provider of all we need each day. Forgive us the wrongs we have done as we ourselves release forgiveness to those who have wronged us. Rescue us every time we face tribulation and set us free from evil. For you are the King who rules with power and glory forever. Amen.'*

So that is why the final words from me are found in Colossians 2:6-7 (HCSB): *Therefore, as you have received Christ Jesus the Lord, walk in Him, rooted, and built up in Him and established in the faith, just as you were taught, overflowing with gratitude.*

NOTES:

1. Bible versions referred to in the appendices of this book are:

   - Bible for Everyone (B4E) – John Goldingay & N T Wright (SPCK)

   - Christian Standard Bible (CSB) – Holman Bible Publishers (B&H Publishing Group)

   - Contemporary English Version (CEV) – American Bible Society (Thomas Nelson)

   - Holman Christian Standard Bible (HCSB) – Holman Bible Publishers (B&H Publishing Group)

   - King James Version (KJV) – Public Domain

   - Living Bible (TLB) – Kenneth N Taylor (Tyndale House Publishing)

   - Message Bible (MSG) – Eugene H Peterson (NavPress)

   - New International Version (NIV 1984 & 2011 Anglicised Editions) – Biblica (Hodder & Stoughton)

- New King James Version (NKJV) – Arthur L. Farstad, NKJV Executive Editor (Thomas Nelson)

- The Passion Translation (TPT) – Passion & Fire Ministries (BroadStreet Publishing)

2. Over the years Peter, the author of this appendix, has read many Bible commentaries, listened to excellent teaching in many churches and attended Christian conferences, all of which have helped his understanding of the Christian Faith.

Appendix 3

How radio was, and still is, vital to Elvis' success

By J Peter Wilson – Retired Broadcasting Regulation Consultant.

Throughout this book, written by my wife Madeleine, you will have read how Elvis was promoted by local DJs, firstly in Memphis TN, West Memphis AR, and Tupelo MS, playing Elvis records and how that helped in getting his music known in the mid-south via stations such as KWEM, WELO & WHBQ and then throughout the USA and around the world.

In 1950s America most parts of the country had local commercial radio stations which played popular music. These stations mainly played music by either White or Black artists for their respective audiences, plus most of these US radio stations would often broadcast Christian programmes sponsored by a local church as well as the music. Churches in the 1950s had either White or Black congregations, so when Elvis would go and listen to the gospel music in Centenary African Methodist Episcopal Church and East Trigg Baptist Church in Memphis he was almost certainly one of the few white faces in the congregation. I had a similar experience while I worked in Zambia in the 1990s, programming Radio Christian Voice, and when I attended some church services in Lusaka, I was often in a minority of two or three White people.

American radio was founded on a commercial basis in the 1920s and all the radio stations were local stations broadcasting from the large towns or cities in the state concerned. The radio stations situated east of the Mississippi have their identification letter as a W, as in WHBQ, while those west of the river start with K, as in KWEM. You can now hear KWEM outside West Memphis and around the world at www.kwemradio.com playing 1950s/60s/70s Elvis, blues, country and rock 'n' roll music. Nearly all the artists who appeared on KWEM ended up at Sam Phillips' Memphis Recording Service, which later became Sun Records.

Today, US radio stations broadcast using AM/MW, FM, or HD Radio, which is the American system of Digital Radio used for extra channels within FM or AM bands and requires a special radio receiver. Also, US Satellite Radio is operated by SiriusXM, and special radio receivers are required and a subscription to receive the service including Elvis Radio, which is broadcast from Graceland. A feature of American radio, as it is mainly commercial radio, is that stations have been allowed to change their format such as from pop music to talk, often overnight. Stations on which Elvis broadcast back in the 1950s can have a very different output today as compared with Elvis' day, as an AM/MW station broadcasting popular music would often change to say a talk format when a new FM music station, with clearer reception for music, started on-air. Shortly after her booklet "Prayers of Elvis" was published in 2002 Madeleine was interviewed on the Talk station, WREC, "live" in their Memphis studio.

In the UK, radio was set up in a different way from in the USA. In 1922, the BBC (British Broadcasting Company becoming British Broadcasting Corporation) was given a radio broadcasting monopoly. Other public service broadcasters started in New Zealand and Denmark in 1925 followed by Australia's ABC in 1932 and Norway's NRK in 1933. While in Canada CBC (Canadian Broadcasting Corporation) was set up in 1936 to operate alongside the existing commercial radio stations which, like those in the US, had started in the 1920s.

By the 1950s the BBC operated three national stations – Home Service, Light Programme and Third Programme – of which, only for a few hours each week on the Light Programme, was any popular music of the style sung by Elvis, Tommy Steele, and Cliff Richard broadcast. This meant that anyone interested in pop music had to listen to Radio Luxembourg's English service of pop music in the evenings on 1440 kHz/208 metres. The English service started at dusk to allow maximum benefit to be gained from skywave propagation at night that covered the whole of the British Isles. Most programmes were live shows by the Luxembourg-based DJ team and included songs by Elvis and other artists of the 1950s and 1960s.

Up to March 1964, Radio Luxembourg enjoyed a monopoly of English commercial radio programming in the UK until Radio Caroline's broadcasts started during the daytime to the south of England from a ship anchored outside the 3-mile limit, thus avoiding the law governing the BBC's radio broadcasting monopoly. Following the success of Radio Caroline, others including Radio London, Radio Scotland and Radio 270 started broadcasting from ships moored off the coasts of Essex, Yorkshire, and the Isle of Man plus near to the Clyde Estuary. They were soon broadcasting 18 to 24 hours per day.

Then, in August 1967, the Marine Broadcasting Offences Act passed into British law and forced all but Radio Caroline off the air by making it illegal to sell advertising in the UK. Following the closure of offshore commercial radio known as "pirate radio" the BBC created a non-commercial national pop station, Radio 1, in September 1967 on 1215 kHz/247 metres. Today it broadcasts on DAB (Digital Audio Broadcasting), FM and online.

It is interesting to note that 60 years after off-shore radio was made illegal in the UK, Radio Caroline was finally given a land-based licence in 2017 to broadcast on 648 kHz to Essex, Kent and Suffolk from an ex-BBC transmitter site! They also broadcast on DAB in parts of the UK and online. Caroline Flashback broadcasts, weekly, Todd Slaughter's "Elvis Hour."

It was in 1972 that the UK Government passed into law the Sound Broadcasting Act and so, in 1974, Independent Local Radio (ILR) started, thus breaking the BBC's radio monopoly. These new stations played pop songs by the Beatles, Elvis, The Rolling Stones and other artists.

Changes to UK radio started in the 1990s when extra stations were licensed to broadcast jazz music – Jazz FM, Christian music and speech – Premier Christian Radio and classical music – Classic FM. DAB started in 1995, increasing choice, so most places in Britain today can receive 60–100 stations compared to just three BBC stations and off-shore radio in the 1960s.

The other thing that started to happen is that audiences preferred to listen to specific types of music and so the wide variety of music offered by the radio stations owned by the two major radio groups, Bauer and Global, started to dominate listenership, thus Elvis songs are now mainly heard on the BBC's stations as well as on Boom Radio, Gold, Greatest Hits Radio and other "oldies" stations while his gospel music can be heard on Premier's radio stations.

There are also Elvis Internet-Only Stations such as Always Elvis Presley Radio, Crooner Radio Elvis Presley, Exclusively Elvis, and Pure Elvis Radio which can be heard via their own websites and also via various software including My Tuner (https://mytuner-radio.com) on computers, Smart TVs, Fire and Roku TV streamers and on radios with internet access.

So, wherever you live in the world, radio, in its many forms, will continue to be the most important way in which we can hear the repertoire of Elvis Presley whether it be on radio sets at home, at work or in the car, via tablets/computers, on mobile/cell phone apps, via digital TV and streaming devices or by asking our Alexa, Google or Siri smart-speakers to play the music of Elvis Presley.

NOTES ABOUT PETER

He was born in Yorkshire in 1945 and has been happily married to Madeleine since 1969. They have three children and five grandchildren. They have lived in Yorkshire (Harrogate and Bridlington) and in Wolverhampton. He read textiles at Leeds University (1963-66) before working in the wool textile, publishing, and radio industries. His interest in radio started in the 1960s listening to offshore radio and then, while working in textiles, he broadcast on BBC Radio Leeds. He lobbied Parliament on various broadcasting related matters from 1988 to 1990 while working for a London-based publishing company. During visits to Memphis with Madeleine, they both attended Gospel Music Association and National Religious Broadcasters conferences in Nashville. He was one of the founders of Harrogate's Stray FM, including being the first station manager, before programming Zambia's Radio Christian Voice. He again lobbied Parliament this time for faith-based stations to have access to DAB prior to the 2003 Communications Act, including giving evidence to a Joint Parliamentary committee. He then ran a West Midlands trial DAB Christian music station, Day One Radio, before both Premier Radio and UCB (United Christian Broadcasters) started to broadcast nationally on DAB. He is now "officially" retired but still has an interest in both Christian radio and local radio.

Peter and Madeleine Wilson in front of Graceland on
a cold and frosty morning. (J P Wilson)

Appendix 4

SOUTH & MID-SOUTH RADIO STATIONS

Below you will find details of the American radio stations mentioned in this book.

Station/Town	Frequency 1950s	Frequency 2020s
Elvis Radio – Memphis TN	----------------------	SiriusXM Channel 75
KRLD – Dallas TX	1080 kHz (50 kw)	1080 kHz (50 kw)
		105.3-HD2 MHz (250 w)
KWEM – West Memphis AR	990 kHz (1 kw)	93.3 MHz (FM-LP 100 w)
		www.kwemradio.com
WDIA – Memphis TN	740 kHz (250 w)	1070 kHz (50 kw/5 kw*)
WELO – Tupelo MS	1490 kHz (250 w)	580 kHz (770 w/95 w*)
		104.3 MHz (250 w)
WHBQ – Memphis TN	560 kHz (5 kw/1 kw*)	560 kHz (5 kw/1 kw*)
		98.5 MHz (250 w)
WLOX – Biloxi MS (1950s)	1490 kHz (1 kw)	1490 kHz (1 kw)
		106.3 MHz (250 w)
WANG – Biloxi MS (2020s)		
WMC – Memphis TN	790 kHz (5 kw)	790 kHz (5 kw)
WMC-FM – Memphis TN		99.7 MHz (300 kw)
WMPS – Bartlett TN	680 kHz (250 w)	1210 kHz (10 kw/250 w*)
		103.1 MHz (250 w)
WREC – Memphis TN	600 kHz (5 kw)	600 kHz (5 kw)
		92.1 MHz (250 w)
WSM – Nashville TN	650 kHz (50 kw)	650 kHz (50 kw)
		www.wsmradio.com

NOTES: 1. Radio station power is given in watts (w) or kilowatts (kw). **2.** US radio stations that are clear-channel, the only station on a frequency in the entire USA, like WSM show just one figure for their power output, whereas most other AM/MW (Medium Wave) stations reduce power at night, shown with a *, such as WELO. **3.** WDIA in June 1954 was licensed to increase its power from 250 to 50,000 watts, which meant moving from 740 kHz to 1070 kHz. **4.** WLOX changed call letters to WANG. **5.** KWEM has been operated by the Arkansas State University Mid-South since 2014 as an Internet Radio Station and as a low-powered FM-LP station. **6.** HD Radio stands for High Definition radio, which is the US form of Digital Radio used to broadcast extra services within the AM/MW or FM frequencies allocated to a radio station and is different to DAB (Digital Audio Broadcasting) which is used in Australia, Norway, UK, and most countries in Europe.

Bibliography

Author	Title	Publisher	Year
Adams, Nick	The Rebel & The King	Water Dancer Press	2012
Alden, Ginger	Elvis & Ginger	Berkley Books	2014
Ann-Margret	Ann-Margret My Story	Orion/Putnam Berkley	1994
Bayles, Martha	Hole in our Soul	University of Chicago Press	1996
Bell, Rob	Velvet Elvis	Zondervan	2001
Bertrand, Michael T	Race, Rock And Elvis	University of Illinois Press	2000
Böhm, W & Eiermann, R	Atomschlag in der Oberpflaz (Winter Shield I & II)	Tankograd Publishing	2013
Bradley, James Lee	Elvis was my Speech Therapist	Trafford Publishing	2002
Brogan, Hugh	Longman History of United States of America	BCA/Longman	1987
Bull, Andy	Strange Angels	Black Swan	1995
Burk, Bill E	Early Elvis – The Humes Years	Red Oak Press	1990

Burk, Bill E	Early Elvis – The Tupelo Years	Propwash Publishing	1994
Burk, Bill E	Elvis Through My Eyes	Burk Enterprises	1987
Burrows, Kurt	"Just Pretending" – Guide to being an ETA	Memphis Mansion	2009
Cales, William J	The 1953 Senior Herald: Humes High School	Walk A Mile	2003
Canada, Lena	To Elvis With Love	Everest House	1978
Carman, Wayne	Elvis's Karate Legacy	Legacy Entertainment	1998
Chartock, Roselle Kline	The Jewish World of Elvis Presley	McKinstry Place	2020
Clayson, Alan & Leigh, Spencer	Aspects of Elvis: Tryin' To Get To You	Sidgwick & Jackson	1994
Cocke, Marian J	I Called Him Babe	Memphis State U P	1979
Cooper, Victoria	A Fusion of Humanity & Divinity	Deep Blue Publishing	2019
Cotton, Lee	Did Elvis Sing in Your Hometown?	High Sierra Books	1995
Cotton, Lee	Did Elvis Sing in Your	High Sierra Books	1997

	Hometown Too?		
Coulter, Cricket-Marie	Elvis' Real Gold: The Spirit of His Fans	Self-published	2002
Crouch, Kevin & Tanja	The Gospel according to Elvis	Bobcat Books	2007
Curtin, Jim	Christmas with Elvis	Celebrity Books	1999
Curtin, Jim	Elvis – Unknown stories behind the legend	Celebrity Books	1998
Duffett, Mark	Counting Down Elvis: His 100 Finest Songs	Rowman & Littlefield	2018
Dundy, Elaine	Elvis and Gladys	St Martin's Press	1985
Early, Donna Presley	Precious Family Memories of Elvis	D P Early & Edie Hand	1997
Erwin, Sara	Over The Fence	The King's Press	1997
Finstad, Suzanne	Child Bride	Berkley Boulevard Books	1997
Fadel, Eddie & Fadel, Janice	Elvis Days	Self-published	2018
"Friendfromyesteryear"	The Final Curtain…a Love Story Untold	Friendfromyesteryear	2015
Geller, Larry	Leaves Of Elvis' Garden	Bell Rock Publishing	2007

Geller, Larry	If I Can Dream, Elvis' Own Story	Simon & Schuster	1989
Guralnick, Peter	Careless Love	Little Brown	1999
Guralnick, Peter	Elvis Day By Day	Ballantine Books	1999
Guralnick, Peter & others	Elvis Then & Now – 25th Collector's Edition	Gruner Jahr Publishing	2002
Guralnick, Peter	Last Train to Memphis	Little Brown	1994
Harrison, Ted	Elvis People – The Cult of the King	Fount/HarperCollins	1992
Harrison, Ted	The Death and Resurrection of Elvis Presley	Reaktion Books	2016
Hart, Mother Dolores	The Ear of the Heart	Ignatius Press	2013
Hazen, Cindy	The Best of Elvis	Memphis Explorations	1992
Hazen, Cindy & Freeman, Mike	Memphis Elvis-Style	John F Blair Publishers	1997
Henderson, William McCranor	I, Elvis	Boulevard Books	1997
Hill, Ed with Hill, Dr Don	Where is Elvis?	Cross Roads Books	1979
Hill, Wanda June	We Remember, Elvis	Wanda J Hill/Book Surge	2006
Hopkins, Jerry	Elvis	Macmillan/Abacus	1972

Humbard, Rex	The Soul-Winning Century	Clarion Call Marketing	2006
Jenkins, Mary	Memories Beyond Graceland Gates	West Coast Publishing	1989
Jorgensen, Ernst	Elvis Presley: A Life In Music	St Martin's Press	1998
Juanico, June	Elvis in the Twilight of Memory	Little Brown & Co	1997
Keenan, Frances	Elvis You're Unforgettable	Axelrod Publishing	1997
Keller, Adrian	Elvis Before Graceland	Self-published	2018
Klein, George	Elvis My Best Man	Virgin Books	2010
Krogh, Egil "Bud"	The Day Elvis Met Nixon	Pejama Press	1994
Leigh, Suzanna	Paradise, Suzanna Style	Pen Press Publishers	2000
Littlesugar, A & Cooper, F	Shake Rag from the life of Elvis Presley	Philomel Books	1998
Long, Rev Marvin R	God's Works Through Elvis	Exposition Press	1979
Loyd, Harold	Elvis Presley's Graceland Gates	Jimmy Velvet Publishing	1987
McLafferty, Gerry	Elvis Presley – The Power & the Persecution	New Millennium	2000

Mann, Richard	Elvis	Bible Voice	1977
Mansfield, Rex	Living The Moments	Xulton Press Elite	2017
Mansfield, Rex & Elisabeth	Sergeant Presley	ECW Press	2002
Marcus, Greil	Double Trouble – Bill Clinton & Elvis Presley…	Henry Holt and Company	2000
Matthew-Walker, Robert	Heartbreak Hotel: Life & Music of Elvis Presley	Castle Communications	1995
Morgan, Todd	Graceland – The Living Legacy of Elvis Presley	Ted Smart	1993
Moscheo, Joe	The Gospel Side of Elvis	Center Street/Hachette	2007
Neale, David	Roots Of Elvis	iUniverse, Inc.	2003
Nixon, Anne E	King of the Hilton	A & R Publication	2014
Parker, Ed	Inside Elvis	Rampart House	1978
Presley, Dee & Stanley, B,R & D	Elvis: We Love You Tender	New English Library	1980
Presley, Priscilla & Lisa Marie	Elvis By The Presleys	Century/Random House	2005
Presley, Priscilla Beaulieu	Elvis And Me	Berkley Books	1986
Presley, Vester	A Presley Speaks	Wimmer Books	1978
Pritchett, Nash Lorene	One Flower While I live	Shelby House	1987

Roy, Samuel	Elvis Prophet of Power	Branden Publishing	1985
Roy, Samuel & Aspell, Tom	The Essential Elvis	Rutledge Hill Press	1998
Schilling, Jerry	Me and a Guy Named Elvis	Gotham Books	2006
Schröer, Andreas	Private Presley	Boxtree Limited	1993
Segev, Tom	Elvis in Jerusalem	Metropolitan Books	2001
Shapre, Heart Lanier	Elvis Through My Eyes	Author House	2005
Simpson, Trevor	Elvis – His Songs of Praise Vol 1	Pål Granlund	2016
Simpson, Trevor	Elvis – His Songs of Praise Vol 2	Pål Granlund	2017
Slaughter, Todd	Elvis And More – The Spoils Of War	Todd Slaughter	2020
Smith, Gene	Elvis's Man Friday	Light of Day Publishing	1994
Stanley, David	Life With Elvis	Fleming H Revell/MARC	1986
Stanley, David	Raised On Rock – Growing Up at Graceland	Mainstream Publishing	1996
Stanley, Rick	Caught In A Trap	Word Publishing	1992
Stanley, Rick	The Touch of Two Kings	T2K	1986

Stearn, Jess	Elvis' Search For God	Greenleaf Publications	1998
Sumner, Donnie	In The Shadow Of Kings	Life Line Books	2012
Sumner, Donnie & Hill, Ed	"Elvis" Special Memories	Mike L Moon	2015
Sumner, Donnie & Hill, Ed	The Elvis You Didn't Know	Mike L Moon	2015
Sumner, J D	Elvis His Love for Gospel Music	Gospel Quartet Music	1991
Taylor, William J Jnr	Elvis in the Army	Presidio Press	1997
Tharpe, Jae L	Elvis: Images and Fancies	University Press Mississippi	1979
Thompson, Linda	A Little Thing Called Life	Harper Collins	2016
Tillery, Gary	The Seeker King	Quest Books	2013
Torrance, Lori	Elvis In Texas	Republic of Texas Press	2002
Tunzi, Joseph A	Elvis Sessions	JAT Publishing	1996
Turner, Steve	Hungry for Heaven	Virgin Books	1988
Wertheimer, Alfred	Elvis '56 In the Beginning	Macmillan/Pimlico	1979
West, Red & others	Elvis: What Happened?	Ballantine Books	1977
West, Sonny	Elvis Still Taking Care of Business	Triumph Books	2007
Westmoreland, Kathy	Elvis and Kathy	Glendale House	1987

Whatley, Bruce	Elvis Presley's The First Noel	HarperCollins	1999
Wiegert, Sue	Elvis For the Good Times	Blue Hawaiians for Elvis	1978
Wiegert, Sue	Elvis Precious Memories Vol 1	Blue Hawaiians for Elvis	1987
Wiegert, Sue	Elvis Precious Memories Vol 2	Blue Hawaiians for Elvis	1989
Wilson, Charles Reagan	Judgment & Grace in Dixie	University of Georgia Press	1995
Wilson, Madeleine	Prayers of Elvis	Shalom Publishing	2002
Yancey, Becky	My Life with Elvis	St Martin's Press	1977

There are also two web sites which I have used for information and which I can fully recommend:

Elvis Information Network: https://www.elvisinfonet.com
Elvis Australia: https://www.elvis.com.au

Printed in Great Britain
by Amazon

10136406R00210